S0-CDY-063

CONTRIBUTORS

*Ian Fletcher*

*A. J. L. Busst*

*David Howard*

*R. A. Forsyth*

*A. G. Lehmann*

*Michael Hamburger*

*Annette Lavers*

*W. J. Lucas*

# ROMANTIC MYTHOLOGIES

EDITED BY

*Ian Fletcher*

NEW YORK : BARNES & NOBLE INC.

*Published in the United States of America* 1967
*by Barnes & Noble, Inc., New York, N.Y.*



*Printed in Great Britain*

# CONTENTS

# ILLUSTRATIONS

# FOREWORD

SOME years ago, the late Professor Willey discovered the hopelessness of any attempt to talk of a nineteenth-century 'background,' background being, indeed, a word at most times suspect. To impose a tradition on that century, to impose a great chain of seeing, is to suppress much that for us ought to remain still vivid and cogent. It is to corrupt literary history by simplifying what at bottom amounts to a set of complex inter-connections of ideas and actual movements. Indeed, so specialized and so rich is the field that perhaps we may properly hope to recover inter-connections only, never coherences.

There is a sense in which it can be said that everything is central to the century, nothing tangential. Our images of the past and of the figures who inhabit that past are always in motion, and nineteenth-century figures, in spite of their chronological neighbourhood, seem to change as radically as most. And since the end of the century, the period from 1870 on, represents a transition to our own moment—whether in England with new Unionism and the onset of a series of depressing trade-cycles which retain too melancholy a topicality; or the end of the gilded Second Empire in France and the beginnings of a 'new' Germany—we are the more unfortunately placed to stabilize a history that we are still acting out.

The approach in these essays is, in broad terms, through imagery; and less historical than literary. Much admirable work in the English literary field has consisted in re-interpretation of major figures; some essays in the crucial area of the periodical, microcosms of contemporary culture, have been written; others have treated of decades, which barely aspired to the coherence which has been thrust upon them: the sceptical 60s; the idealist 70s; the aesthetic 80s, the naughty and yellow 90s.

Problems become central in so far as they are discussed by major figures. Major figures realize potentials existing in the age. Literary historians often (always perhaps) concern themselves with discriminating between these potentialities. And such occur variously, fuse (perhaps unpredictably—though literary historians attempt to lay bare the area of predictability) to produce a realized matrix. For that reason, the imposition of schematic traditions becomes vicious. It can take no account of the variety of potentialities, of cross-fertilizations; of historical accidents, perhaps, where one potentiality flares into life at the expense of another. And literary history is, in essence, much concerned with the recovery of failed (or metamorphosed) potentialities.

This is not to consign to futility all attempts to make sense of the century; it is to argue merely that sense will hardly survive the insensitive pruning-away which will treat the work of Pater, say, as an aberration of the Arnoldian stress on Hellenism, or confine it in a fish-net stocking of Aestheticism. If we think of the relatively serious status accorded to Pater by historians of art and the jocose contempt in which he is held by so many literary critics, that will make the point that 'the nineteenth century' is hardly held in common. And if, though this perhaps is to have things both ways, it is argued that Arnold is, after all, more central, we may ask more central to what? Not certainly to the actual current of creation to which some of the major figures of our century belong, a Yeats, a Pound, a Joyce, a Hart Crane.

If we take the nineteenth century as a dark flow, we might see ourselves too blushingly perhaps in the role of surveyors on a moving raft trying with different instruments, at random places, to guage the rate of the current, the depth of the water. To disembark from the metaphor, the main theme of this collection may seem difficult to establish, and although some kind of iconographical approach unites the contributors, differences in stress may still seem puzzling. The range is from the relentless detail of Dr Busst's study of the nineteenth-century image of the Hermaphrodite to John Lucas's essay on Wagner and Forster where the axis is towards literary criticism. What in fact is offered is less a coherence, or even a sequence of encounters and crises at different moments in the century; it is rather a distinctly modest sequence of inter-connections or recovered potentialities with certainly the familiar theme of the isolation and alienation of the artist, and the consequent necessity for images of reconciliation, a continuing motive.

Such a sequence must surely begin with France, for French influences after 1870, however timidly received, were in England paramount. The sequence could, indeed, have begun farther back with Germany, with, say, some consideration of scholarship, historical or theological; or, to choose another field, with the imagery of the Nazarenes. Or, again, with the various versions of primitivism which persist from the eighteenth century and which do, in some sense, emerge in three of these essays, those on Barnes, on Hawthorne, and on Bedford Park, all of them concerned with versions of pastoral.

The essay on the image of the Hermaphrodite, a microcosm of inter-connections, records the failure of a reconciling image: the shift from seeing the Hermaphrodite as resolving religious and social antinomies to its appearance as an emblem of desperate psychology.

In the dating of a building, scholars of architecture tell us that we must add thirty or more years if it lies in the provinces. So the reader is invited to apply the curve of Dr Busst's majestically detailed essay to the English scene at a slightly later date. After Ann Lee, there was that female Messiah of the proletarians, Joanna Southcott, but interest in the 'displaced' Feminine was channelled into more practical educational activities. We can distinguish the transition from pleased or mere frivolous connivance with the image in Swinburne's *Hermaphroditus* of 1863, his *Fragoletta* and Roden Noel's *Ganymede* of the same decade. The dubious limbs and faces in Simeon Solomon's *œuvre* raise some mild problems of source—are there suggestions there of Jewish mysticism? At one point in its trajectory, the image can be related to that neo-Grec cult of the Aesthetes (Albert Moore, say) whose rather fuddled aesthetician was Grant Allen in his *Physiological Aesthetics* (1877), with Gautier as ancestor: the presentment of bodies which by their strong serenity seem to subdue all sexual conflict. (How different from those provocative male nudes in Baron Corvo's photographs in the early *Studio*!) Oxford Platonism, and the cult of 'Uranian Love' in John Addington Symonds, say, and in Edward Carpenter, mark another stage and we can trace the androgyne finally as it answers anxious narcissism with glittering sterility. The image becomes associated with whiteness, and with adolescence among the poems and paintings of the 1890s, in, for example, some of the last paintings of Whistler. The image's centrality in the English scene can be disputed; but it is valid enough for the literary historian to pursue it in a period of the 'new woman' and homosexual dandyism.

In the essay on *The Marble Faun* and the ambiguous attitude towards the corrupt European paradise, we are offered an example of one of the century's most fascinating inter-connections, that of past and present, isolated in a more purified form, given a unique tension by being presented through American eyes; through figures emblematic of a nation coming to vast identity and radically requiring articulateness. The line here is familiar from Fenimore Cooper, through Hawthorne, Melville and Mark Twain to Henry James. Adam and corruption: Adam in prelapsarian innocence in a pastoral America; an Eden with its free virgin spaces, the image which corrects a Europe choked with its own past, its now dry usages and infinitely ruined monuments.

Such an inter-communication of past and present offers itself for evocation through Barnes and the poetry of a special loss that springs from the paradox of a predominantly agricultural country, which is yet the most advanced, revolutionized indeed, industrially in Europe. From such potentialities flow different realizations: the novels and short stories of Richard Jefferies, the work of Hardy, evoking the ensuing moment, when the balance between town and country irremediably fails, and when industrial decline, paradoxically, begins; and, in our own century, Lawrence.

What are required are new metaphors of existence. The tenor of a post-Romantic world must go with the vehicle of individual resolutions. Again, the hermetic inclusiveness of so many different metaphors suggests the difficulties that attend such attempts to establish priorities. Metaphor is quick to drop tenor. Hence myth. Hence, too, a re-ordering of the quotidian of existence.

The Pre-Raphaelites and their successors, the Aesthetes, had arrived at a point of historical self-awareness where the myth of a cultural 'fall' could be overcome by a species of time-travelling. This can be related to, among other things, the battle of architectural styles—programmatic buildings, in an unambitious sense. That battle of styles is in kind quite other from an earlier conflict when an image of Rome in severity and virtue provided the common impetus for both Vanbrugh and Hawksmoor on the one hand and Pope and Lord Burlington on the other; different, also, from the relatively uncomplex conflict between 'Pagan' neo-classical architects and their Gothic 'Christian' opponents which, at its most intense between the 1830s and 1850s, echoes on until the early 1870s. The fining down of the historical unit from eighteenth-century era, to century, to decade, to an unstable passing *now*, issues in the progressively feverish fashions in middle and later nineteenth-century architectural style, once Gothic in all its varieties has been exhausted, although the era of 'free' neo-Gothic is still to come. Simultaneously, we have the beginnings of the consciously a-historical *art nouveau*, though architecturally that style was hardly to be consummated in England. Before that, and after the neo-Gothic movement has exhausted itself, we have the Aesthetic movement, more felt perhaps in architecture and the applied arts than in painting and literature. The stress still falls on the English past, if only secondarily on the medieval. The Aesthetes represent the point where a myth contrived by individual producers can be enjoyed by connoisseur consumers. That daily lives could be conducted in an imaginary museum of taste and time-travelling was one of their amenities. In the London suburb of Bedford Park, they attempted a *mélange* of periods, medieval, Carolean, seventeenth and eighteenth century, that apparently frozen medieval society, the Japanese, along with an attempt, timid admittedly, to create an inclusively autonomous world of art, excluding the Philistine from their sunset-coloured suburb. Bedford Park was certainly programmatic and provoked images both hostile and aggrandizing.

In that autonomous world, the imaginary museum, lives Pierrot: the figure who made most articulate the notion of the artist as society's dupe. Another mythic embodiment, and one now of a figure in entire isolation, whose history is a breviary of the later nineteenth-century artist's conception of his own rôle. Only by becoming aware of what Pierrot *was*, can we recognize the force of what he became at that historical moment when history itself became unstable to the point of returning on itself, or having a stop. Again, it is possible to pursue this image, at a slightly later date, in England. From that 'Aesthetic Pierrot' who first makes his self-mocking appearance in volumes devoted to Fancy Dress about 1881 to his captivation in lunar melancholy by poets like

Dowson and Symons, though never arriving, indeed, at the nihilism of his French cousin.

A more, in fact the most expressive, because impersonal mask for the artist was only discovered towards the century's end; that of the dancer (followed in wider contexts by Frank Kermode) and, secondarily, that of the actor. A related interest in the dancer goes back to Gautier in France, but the recognition of origins once more defines the new, disparate identity of the *fin de siècle* artist. It defines also the application of that remark by one of Wilde's 'masks' in *Intentions*: in an ugly and sensible age, the arts do not imitate nature, they imitate one another. That same inter-relation of the arts is found also in the figure of Beardsley, wavering between the literary and the visual experience and searching always for a mythic embodiment of the self; trying to invent himself.

These three essays I have touched on are concerned with individuals (or with movements) who attempt to construct their own mythic universe: a world without God (the agnosticism of so many Bedford Park inhabitants). Even Beardsley's Roman Catholicism is, I myself believe, in spite of Dr Lavers's comments on the rejection of the *Lysistrata* drawings, an attempt to find a place for God in the artist's dream; if God will not take his place, either he or art itself must be abolished.

For the need of a Religion, not personal merely, but social, generally valid, reverberates to the end of the century, and beyond. It is long since the confident Romantic Socialism of the earlier part of the century, revived in part by the change of current in Anglo-Catholicism from the 1870s, from ritualism to Christian Socialism. There would have been scope here for tracing the connections between the Christian Socialist and the Guild Movement and Total Art. Total art as such was the supreme means of recovering a universe in its meaningful integrity; or reconciling the rift between classes, religions, nations. Yet Symbolism, in spite of its sophisticated practitioners and in spite of magnificent if isolated triumphs, remained too primitive a solution with its anti-rationalist, anti-scientific bias—the imagination almost unequivocally as God. The individual's sense of the universe was now, indeed, so fragmented that the pursuit of private religion became as much the scientist's as the artist's obsession. A consequence of myth—evolution included—is solipsism, and total art, after all, is only more solipsism.

Of the total artists who attempted to discover a faith which was inclusive essentially, Wagner was the most prominent. The last two essays have been forced to make mention of him. The next deals more centrally with this artist-god, with his sanctuary at Bayreuth. At that life-giving source the neophyte could enter a newly constructed Universe, an Eden twice lost, twice regained. As a reaction, however, to the deification of art—poor Oscar had hardly risen after his *sparagmos*—the Edwardian period found a new divinity 'life', but preserved the vocabulary and unction of religion. As Richard Ellmann has pointed out, novelists as diverse as E. M. Forster, Wells and Joyce invest in images that are distinctly sacramental in flavour: 'chalice,' 'epiphany,' and so forth: their work being partly realized in thematic images whose potentialities had been released by the work of Pater. The last essay in this collection deals with Forster's use of the Parsifal myth, secularized now entirely, yet lent religious overtones, innocence re-born.

Although I have tried to suggest some points of connexion between the English and the French scene and some chronological definition, I should like to stress once more that interconnection rather than coherence is necessarily what unites these essays. No attempt has been made to simplify; to be diagrammatic; even to vulgarize, however luminously. Inter-connections persist, not the same ones necessarily from essay to essay: some essays share one link, others other links. The solitariness of Pierrot looks back to the conclusion of Dr Busst's essay as the carnival of Hawthorne's *Marble Faun* flickers out into a *Fête Galante* where one solitary Pierrot, patter, mask and costume gone, disrupts into air.

I.F.

# THE IMAGE OF THE ANDROGYNE IN THE NINETEENTH CENTURY

*A. J. L. Busst*

The distinctions established from time to time between the terms 'androgyne' and 'hermaphrodite' have always been purely arbitrary and consequently often contradictory. Hirschfeld, for example, uses hermaphroditism to designate *hermaphroditismus genitalis* and androgyny for *hermaphroditismus somaticus*;[1] while according to Franz von Baader the hermaphrodite is bisexual and the androgyne asexual.[2] Rather than attempt to choose from or add to the already excessively long list of extremely doubtful distinctions, it is preferable to consider the two terms exactly synonymous[3] by accepting their broadest possible meaning: a person who unites certain of the essential characteristics of both sexes and who, consequently, may be considered as both a man and a woman or as neither a man nor a woman, as bisexual or asexual.

Throughout the nineteenth century, as during every other age, artists and writers were engrossed with the image and the conception of such a person; and, as usual, this interest owed practically nothing to any biological or scientific observations. Perfect human bisexuality is, of course, virtually non-existent, and what was long taken for true hermaphroditism was in fact hypospadias, in which the external organs alone are abnormal, and in which sexual indetermination is usually resolved at puberty. However, it is undeniable that there do in fact exist teratologic cases which fit the definition of androgyny proposed above—a definition which had to be sufficiently wide to include the diverse manifestations of the image during the nineteenth century. Nevertheless, during the preparation of the present essay, not a single instance was found where the conception or image of the androgyne depends in any way on the observation of teratologic cases. And this experience agrees with that of other scholars who have been interested in the same theme. Marie Delcourt considers the hermaphrodite an 'exemple privilégié de *mythe pur*';[4] and, in the opinion of Halley des Fontaines, the observation of teratologic cases could at the very most have enriched and confirmed an already existing notion.[5] Moreover, it has been sufficiently demonstrated that everywhere the notion of the androgyne precedes its pictorial or plastic representation;[6] and that where there are such concrete representations, the originals are still the product of the mind, for they are not copied from anything that exists in reality.[7] Indeed, as Marie Delcourt has underlined, in Classical Greece, at a time when the pure concept, the spiritual vision of androgyny was endowed with the highest value, the horror and fear of divine wrath inspired by any malformation of the genitalia were such that an infant thus afflicted was considered a monster and abandoned forthwith.[8] Moreover, it is difficult to understand how the absolute perfection of classical statues of Hermaphrodite could possibly have been modelled on such an obvious imperfection as eunuchism. Even if, as Winckelmann maintained,[9] eunuchs did serve as models for these statues, they were models which were ideally developed and completely transformed by the human mind in order to aid the realization of a dream—to such an extent that in the final work of art nothing remained to suggest the nature of the model.

It is true that the notion of human androgyny has sometimes been presented as an objective induction from purely biological and scientific observations; but usually in such cases both the observations and the conclusions drawn from them are so absurd as to make it apparent that the notion itself preceded a desire to find a factual foundation. According to Jean Baptiste René Robinet, for example, before attempting the creation of man, Nature tried out her skill on stones, as is shown by the existence of fossils resembling human brains, skulls, jaws, feet, ears, and so on.[10] However man has not yet reached his final state of perfection —a clue to the nature of which is afforded by the Histerolithos:

> *L'Histerolithos*, ou *Diphys*, est une pierre selon quelques-uns, et selon d'autres une coquille bivalve fossile, qui représente d'un côté le [*sic*] partie naturelle de la femme avec les grandes levres fort

étendues et élevées, et de l'autre côté les parties de l'homme. Les unes et les autres sont si bien imitées, dit Pline, qu'on les croiroit propres à l'acte de la génération, si elles n'étoient pas de pierre: *ut concubitui venereo aptum dixeris, nisi lapis esset.*[11]

This fossil, considered in conjunction with 'un hermaphrodisme assez parfait dans certaines espèces animales',[12] shows that Nature will soon have learned enough to create human hermaphrodites. In spite, however, of the attention paid to such 'facts' as 'un moine qui s'engrossa lui-même',[13] Robinet lets us glimpse an aesthetic dream, far removed from reality, as a more probable source of his idea:

[. . .] quand la Nature sera parvenue au point d'allier dans un même individu les organes parfaits des deux sexes, ces nouveaux Etres réuniront avec avantage la beauté de Venus à celle d'Apollon: ce qui est peut-être le plus haut degré de la beauté humaine.[14]

It was also as an 'induction objective', arrived at by the observation of purely physical facts, that Auguste Comte presented his notion of the future androgyny of woman.[15] The impending realization of his positivist utopia, which would be, among other things, 'l'utopie de la Vierge-Mère',[16] 'l'utopie du moyen âge, où la maternité se concilie avec la virginité',[17] he found indicated by the present extremely limited participation of the male in procreation:

La rationalité du problème est fondée sur la détermination du véritable office de l'appareil masculin, destiné surtout à fournir au sang un fluide excitateur, capable de fortifier toutes les opérations vitales, tant animales qu'organiques. Comparativement à ce service général, la stimulation fécondante devient un cas particulier, de plus en plus secondaire à mesure que l'organisme s'élève. On conçoit ainsi que, chez la plus noble espèce, ce liquide cesse d'être indispensable à l'éveil du germe, qui pourrait artificiellement résulter de plusieurs autres sources, même matérielles, et surtout d'une meilleure réaction du système nerveux sur le système vasculaire [. . .] cette indication se développe surtout chez la femme, vu le concours continu de trois symptômes spéciaux: la minime participation de ce liquide à la fécondation; l'établissement du flux mensuel; et l'influence de la mère sur le fœtus.[18]

The notion of hermaphroditism is, however, frequently present in Comte's work independently of the *Vierge-Mère*. The *Grand-Etre* of Comte's religion: Humanity considered as an individual, is of course androgynous like the individual Adam of the occultists, who was later divided into myriads of men and women. Moreover, in Comte's system, as in so many of the contemporary philosophies which will be examined below, woman often represents: love, feeling and matter, and man: intelligence and spirit. Since positivism represents the synthesis of the spiritual and the material, of theology and science, the hermaphrodite resumes Comte's philosophy; and, precisely, Comte points out that woman's ability to fecundate herself would depend on the marriage within her of mind and body, spirit and matter.[19] Therefore, the facts which Comte advances in support of his notion of the future androgyny of woman being so obviously imagined and not observed, this notion, rather than the result of any objective induction, was quite definitely inspired by excessive zeal for a system in which the conception of androgyny already occupied a central position.

The continuous and widespread interest focussed on the hermaphrodite during the nineteenth century owes therefore almost nothing to observation of the natural world. Numerous, nevertheless, were the sources of the image and the conception, for the hermaphrodite was constantly and conspicuously present throughout the century in many different places and guises.

Von Römer, Halley des Fontaines and Marie Delcourt[20] have amply demonstrated that the conception and representation of androgynous men and gods figure prominently in almost every religion and mythology of practically every country and age. During the nineteenth century, the most important religious source of this conception was undoubtedly the androgynous Adam of the occult and mystical philosophies associated with the Judaeo-Christian tradition, such as for example the Kabbala, gnosticism, freemasonry, rosicrucianism and the philosophy of Boehme. A. Viatte has shown how widespread such philosophies were at the beginning of the nineteenth century and what a tremendous impact they had on Romanticism.[21] They maintained their popularity so well throughout the century that in 1896 Jules Bois could speak of: 'La Kabbale, la Gnose, presque de mode à notre époque'.[22] However, the prevalence during the Romantic era of religious syncretism,[23] accompanying the 'Oriental Renaissance' so admirably analysed by the late Raymond Schwab,[24] assured widespread knowledge throughout the century of an infinite variety of religions, and of course of the androgynes they frequently contained.

The wide dissemination of the conception and image of the androgyne during the nineteenth century also owed much to alchemy, for in this pseudo-science the androgyne played a very important rôle, symbolizing above all the Great Work. Alchemy exercised a strange fascination on many people throughout the century, from early German Romantics to *fin de siècle* symbolists and Decadents. Among the papers of Novalis, for example, there was a *Chemisches Heft* giving details of alchemical works studied by the German philosopher-poet.[25] Towards the end of the century, the eminent chemist Berthelot's objective study: *Les Origines de l'alchimie* (1885) only contributed to the appeal of this mysterious science by making it better known. As August Strindberg observed, Berthelot thereby did mysticism a service he had not suspected[26]—so much so indeed that in the first volume of his *Essais de sciences maudites* (1890), which contains a long analysis by Papus of the alchemical meaning of Henry Khunrath's androgyne,[27] Stanislas de Guaita quotes Berthelot in defence of alchemy against its detractors;[28] and the year following the publication of Berthelot's work, we find J.-K. Huysmans studying alchemy.[29] A fair idea of the multiplicity of alchemical studies after 1800 is afforded by the lengthy bibliography of nineteenth-century works on alchemy contained at the end of Albert Poisson's *Théories et symboles des alchimistes. Le grand-œuvre* (1891).

Another extremely important source of the nineteenth-century image of the hermaphrodite may be found in the profusion of statues and paintings representing androgynous persons—not only such standard works of art as the sleeping Hermaphrodites, which could be seen in so many museums in Europe, but also rarer works, widely known nevertheless through reproductions: for example, engravings of the Colonna Palace bas-relief of Dionysos published in Montfaucon's *Supplément au livre de l'antiquité expliquée et représentée en figures* (1724)[30] and in Gerhard's *Antike Bildwerke* (1830),[31] or the Pompeian painting representing an androgynous Adonis magnificently lithographed for Raoul-Rochette's *Choix de peintures de Pompéi* (1844) under the title *Toilette de l'Hermaphrodite.*[32]

For visual representations of the hermaphrodite, however, the nineteenth century naturally did not depend only on such works of art proper. All the sources of the conception of androgyny mentioned above frequently contained illustrations of hermaphrodites: in the occult and mystical tradition, for example, among representations of androgynes widely known in the nineteenth century were illustrations of androgynous primitive man in rosicrucian and masonic works, and, of course, Boehme's *Adam*;[33] pictures of androgynous gods—Indian, for example—could be found in Creuzer's *Symbolik und Mythologie der alten Völker* (1810–23); and many of the numerous drawings of alchemical hermaphrodites were reproduced in nineteenth-century works of vulgarization—for example, several different figures of Rebis by Poisson and *Le Grand Androgyne alchimique* by Stanislas de Guaita.[34]

The prevalence during the nineteenth century of the sources so far mentioned undoubtedly stimulated interest in the conception and image of the androgyne. However, such sources, which existed outside and independently of the individual, do not alone account for the presence of the conception during this period. Indeed, the very continuity of such exterior sources throughout the ages reflects the permanence of the notion of androgyny within the human mind itself.

C. G. Jung, particularly in his magnificent study *Psychology and Alchemy*, has shown that the androgyne is an archetype of the collective unconscious, that the human psyche is itself androgynous. As Gaston Bachelard pointed out:

> Qui parle d'androgénéité, frôle, avec une double antenne, les profondeurs de son propre inconscient.[35]

For Jung, of course, the unconscious is a first nature and not merely a repressed consciousness or the sum of forgotten memories. However, there are forgotten memories of childhood, existing in the subconscious of every adult human being as universally as the collective unconscious itself, which contain the notion of androgyny. Freud, for example, has demonstrated the relationship between the conception of androgyny and childhood confusion about the part played by the two sexes in generation and birth.[36]

The constant association of interior and exterior sources in the inspiration and elaboration of the conception and image of the androgyne is underlined by the uncertainties which bedevil any investigation of the precise origin of a particular androgynous image. In his Freudian analysis of the life and work of the German pietist Ludwig von Zinzendorf, for example, Dr Oskar Pfister[37] attempted to explain Zinzendorf's notion of androgyny by psychological factors. He maintained in particular that Zinzendorf's portrayal of the androgyny of Christ, apparent in his depiction of the wound in Christ's side as an equivalent of the female genitalia,[38] originated principally in a revival of memories of childhood speculations about the nature of the vulva. According to Freud, the external female organs are often considered in childhood as a wound; and Pfister asserts that such childish fantasies would be encouraged in Zinzendorf's day by the presence in almost every nursery of a picture depicting parturition through a wound, namely the representation of the creation of Eve from Adam's rib, in which the man's open side appears as an organ of birth.[39] In Pfister's view, the mature Zinzendorf's sexual repression occasioned a revival of these childhood notions of Adam's androgyny, which became closely associated with the androgyny of the 'second Adam', Christ; for, Pfister explains, Zinzendorf's repressed sexual desires were sublimated and projected towards Christ, who was thereby endowed with the essential female characteristics, thanks to the wound in his side, similar to the opening in Adam's.[40]

Psychological factors may possibly have contributed to stimulate Zinzendorf's interest in Christ's androgyny, but the ingenuity which Pfister displays in adducing such factors to explain the origin of the conception in Zinzendorf's work is quite excessive. Zinzendorf did not have to look to his childhood for conceptions of Christ's androgyny, or even for the idea that the wound in Christ's side is an organ of birth: such ideas surrounded him in profusion at every moment of his life. Throughout the ages, the mystical tradition has considered Christ an androgyne, from gnosticism[41] through Jacob Boehme[42] to Mme. Blavatsky.[43] As for the comparison of the wound in Christ's side with the external organ of birth, the image of Christ producing his bride, the holy Mother Church, through the wound in his side in the same way as the first Adam produced Eve, is to be found in the most orthodox Christian theology and liturgy, and in St. Augustine himself.[44] In the *Biblia Pauperum* of the Lyceum library in Constance, there is an illustration comparing Eve's birth from

Adam with Christ's productive wound. And in the St. Florian *Biblia Pauperum* we find a triple illustration showing, in the centre, Christ on the cross, his side being opened; on the left, the separation of Adam and Eve; and, on the right, Moses striking the rock, a prefiguration of Christ's wound.[45]

Nine years after Pfister's study of Zinzendorf, A. Kielholz, writing a similar treatise on Boehme, encountered in the work of the 'philosophus teutonicus' the notion of Adam's hermaphroditism.[46] Already acquainted with Pfister's theory that Zinzendorf owed his conception of Adam's androgyny to childish fantasies, Kielholz, finding this conception occurring long before Zinzendorf in the work of Boehme, might have been expected to beware of over-insistence on psychological factors as the source of such a conception and to consider the possibility that an even older religious tradition was Boehme's principal source. Instead, he asserts categorically that Jacob Boehme's notion of Adam's bisexuality can be explained according to Freudian principles by a revival of childhood uncertainty about sexual differentiation.[47] He then reproaches Pfister for overlooking the fact that: 'the theory of Adam's original androgyny comes from Boehme'[48]—that is to say, that Zinzendorf's conception of androgyny is derived, not from his own childhood memories, but from those of the Silesian shoemaker!

More recently, David Bakan has tried to restore to the mystical tradition the position it lost to psychological factors as the source of the notion of androgyny: he has suggested that Freud's own theories of psychological androgyny were themselves inspired by Kabbalistic doctrines.[49] Truly, it is the question of the hen and the egg!

The impossibility of distinguishing with any degree of certainty between the influence of exterior and that of interior sources of the image of the androgyne indicates that none of these sources plays a decisive rôle in determining the meaning or value of the image they engender. The meaning of the hermaphrodite of the exterior sources created by the human mind must be relative to a particular individual living in a certain civilization and environment, and consequently will probably not be valid for a different person living in a different place at a different time. In the Greek civilization, for example, where pederasty was extremely widespread, highly esteemed and morally acceptable—it constituted, in fact, for the intellectual élite the *noblest* form of love—the androgyne frequently represented a homosexual dream.[50] In the class strife of post-Revolutionary France, on the other hand, the androgyne often signified, as will be seen in the following pages, absolute social equality.

The interior sources of the image of the androgyne are no more responsible than the exterior sources for the meaning of the creation they inspire. The androgynous unconscious can be manifested only by the individual, and therefore in function of a certain education and experience of life. Consequently, the androgyny of the psyche no more accounts for the value or meaning of any individual realization of the image or conception of the androgyne than other constant psychological or physical characteristics of man. Sexuality, for example, must influence the elaboration of the image of the androgyne, not only on account of its direct implication in notions of the asexuality or bisexuality of hermaphrodites, but also quite simply because it is a constant human characteristic. Consequently, to say that an androgyne is a sexual image is to pay just as little attention to its individual meaning as to say that it is a human image. The hermaphrodite has often symbolized the ideal sexual union, but the particular form of union represented varies according to the artist or author's education and experience of life. According to the mystic Boehme, for example, the hermaphrodite represents the objective of the union in love of a man and a woman; for by joining with woman man hopes to recover his former androgyny and immortality; in woman he hopes to find the divine virgin, his lost half, the divine image which has become effaced in him:

> [. . .] it is the divine inclination, and continually seeketh the virgin, (which is) its playfellow; the masculine seeketh her in the feminine, and the feminine in the masculine [. . .] from whence cometh the great desire of the masculine and feminine sex, so that they always desire to copulate [. . .].[51]

In a society where pederasty was widely practised, however, the hermaphrodite, as it has been seen, often represents homosexuality; and, consequently, according to Plato's *Banquet*, the reintegration of an androgyne may be accomplished not only by heterosexual but also by homosexual unions. According to the Dutch moralist Jacob Cats, better known as 'Vader Cats', the hermaphrodite represents the permanence and sanctity of the marriage union, for he states that it is by marriage that men and women seek reintegration with their lost half. His woodcut entitled *Quod perdidit optat*, which depicts the separation and reunion of Adam and Eve, serves to illustrate a charming little poem translated into many languages, the French version of which runs:

> Veus tu sçavoir, Amy, pourquoy la douce rage
> Nous pousse par amour au port du mariage?
> Escoute la raison, l'amant qui est blessé
> Se veut unir au corps, dont il est desmembré.[52]

For the dissipated *fin de siècle* religious leader, the abbé Boullan, on the other hand, the hermaphrodite represented the wildest promiscuity. His so-called 'Unions of Life', by which man's primitive androgyny would be restored, consisted of adultery, incest, bestiality, incubism and onanism.[53]

We must therefore come to the conclusion that both exterior and interior sources of the image of the androgyne play little part in determining its meaning or value in any particular work: these depend uniquely on the preoccupations and convictions, ideals and aspirations of the individual artist or author which, if not always those of his whole generation and civilization, are at least largely conditioned by his upbringing and environment.

This conclusion alone explains how the two images or conceptions of the androgyne which dominated the nineteenth century, while both being the product of the same sources, were not only different, but even diametrically opposed. While the one image is clearly optimistic and healthy, the other is pessimistic, unhealthy and decadent. Each of these two contradictory images occurs in the work of a great number of authors and artists during the century; but how far the individual's preoccupations and aspirations are conditioned by the attitude of mind of his particular generation and environment is indicated by the fact that at different times, different images clearly predominate. In France, for example, where, of all European countries during the nineteenth century, the image of the hermaphrodite is most frequent, it may be said in a very general way that at the beginning of the century, in an age of optimism, the hermaphrodite was a symbol of optimism, and at the end of the century, in an age of pessimism and despair, the hermaphrodite was a symbol of pessimism. Since, however, the two distinct attitudes, optimistic and pessimistic, which condition the images, both persist, whether feebly or triumphantly, throughout the century, a certain degree of overlapping is necessarily inevitable in the development of the two images.

Since, in nineteenth-century France, the early images of the hermaphrodite are mostly optimistic and the later ones mostly pessimistic, and since by far the greater part of this essay will be devoted to the study of the hermaphrodite in that country precisely—where it most frequently appears—this study will follow a roughly chronological order, treating first of the optimistic image and then of the pessimistic image.

No study of the androgyne in the nineteenth century, however, could omit an examination of at least one of the numerous androgynes of German Romanticism. In this instance, however, it will be necessary to sacrifice chronology to clarity. Many characteristics of the pessimistic and decadent hermaphrodite are also characteristics of the Decadence; and yet the Decadence itself is no more than what Mario Praz has called *The Romantic Agony*—that is to say, the exaggeration and often the direct outcome of certain tendencies and philosophies which characterized early Romanticism. If, for the sake of convenience, one referred to these characteristics as 'decadent', it could be said that early German Romanticism was generally far more decadent than early French; so that, although in France, during the first part of the century, the symbol of the hermaphrodite is predominantly optimistic, in Germany, at the same time and earlier, it is predominantly, but not exclusively, pessimistic and decadent. Consequently, certain aspects of the image of the androgyne in German Romanticism will be examined in that part of this essay which is devoted to the French Decadence.

Before any generalizations are made about either of these two distinct images of the androgyne, one alone will first of all be examined in its various manifestations during the nineteenth century, and then an attempt will be made to arrive at a synthesis of these manifestations and also at a generalization about the other image, which is the exact antithesis of the former in all respects. And so, firstly, the optimistic image will be studied, and secondly the pessimistic image. Consideration will then be given to some nineteenth-century androgynes which, for one reason or another, cannot satisfactorily be placed in either category.

Finally, it should be mentioned that, limitations of space having imposed a choice between a superficial catalogue of all the manifestations of the image and conception of the androgyne in the nineteenth century and a detailed examination of several representative images and systems, the latter alternative seemed more desirable.

## I

The image of the androgyne in early nineteenth-century France was characterized above all by its important historical, social and even political associations. The androgynous Adam of the occultists, divided into myriads of individual men and women, gradually recomposing itself throughout all ages and civilizations, became a symbol of the whole of mankind considered as an individual, endowed with a single mind, pursuing its single destiny throughout all the events of universal history. Contemporary preoccupation with the question of man's unity in time and space assured this symbol of immense popularity among not only erudite mystics and historian-philosophers but also poets and novelists. Thus, the occult orientalist Fabre d'Olivet was obsessed with 'l'homme collectif, l'Homme formé abstraitement par l'assemblage de tous les hommes',[54] 'l'Homme en général, l'Homme universel'.[55] The gentle mystic of Lyon, the historian-philosopher and social reformer Pierre-Simon Ballanche declared the fundamental conception of his *Palingénésie sociale* to be: 'l'homme universel [. . .] l'homme général, c'est-à-dire l'homme pris dans l'ensemble des générations [. . .] l'homme cosmogonique';[56] and the Christian democrat Lamennais echoed: 'L'homme seul n'est donc qu'un fragment d'être: l'être véritable est l'être collectif, l'Humanité'.[57] Victor Hugo's *Légende des siècles*, according to the *Préface* dated 12th August 1859, was inspired by meditation on 'cette grande figure une et multiple, lugubre et rayonnante, fatale et sacrée: l'Homme'. And Balzac could marvel at 'ce grand être appelé humanité', 'l'humanité tout entière, s'animant comme un seul être, raisonnant comme un seul esprit, et procédant, comme un seul bras, à l'accomplissement de ses actes'.[58]

The prevalence of this conception of mankind as an individual owed much to the numerous philosophies of history which were elaborated during the Romantic era and were preoccupied with the task of proving, in a variety of ways, that the whole of mankind has been since the creation steadily progressing towards a definite goal.

The affirmation of the continuity of human progress throughout the ages, of the unity of mankind, was an easy task for the early historian-philosophers. Not only did this period witness an immense and rapid accumulation of new facts about man, resulting from the discovery of hitherto unknown civilizations, languages and literatures, but above all these discoveries were made at a time when a scientific evaluation of the new facts was impossible, for the disciplines of archaeology, of comparative linguistics, mythology and religion did not yet exist, or were at least in a very rudimentary state. Free of all restraint, the lively minds of Romanticism could give full rein to their imagination when using these new facts to construct their systems. That facts could be found to uphold any philosophy is shown by the multiplicity and the diversity of the systems elaborated.

One of the most widespread ideals of the Romantic era, closely associated with the symbol of androgynous universal man, was a work tracing the progress of mankind from a single individual through universal history to the four corners of the modern world, and discussing the general significance of each nation and civilization.[59] This ideal could of course never be achieved with any degree of completeness in works of scholarship, but it provided a constant source of epic inspiration for poets and thinkers like Lamartine, Ballanche, Vigny, Quinet, and above all Hugo. For, if the epic needs great exploits and heroes capable of representing a race, a nation and a whole civilization, what more epic subject could be conceived than the history and exploits of Man himself, the development of mankind considered as a single individual—a subject which would resume and complete all epics?

The primitive androgyne was not, however, merely the perfect symbol of the continuity of human progress; it was a dogma, and one to which the special circumstances of the beginning of the nineteenth century lent peculiar force. The hermaphroditism of Adam had always been a current belief among mystics from long before the Kabbalists down to Martinès de Pasqually and after, but not until the beginning of the nineteenth century had this notion ever appeared scientifically demonstrable. It was indeed characteristic of early Romanticism that religious and mystical theories—subjects for infinite speculation—could draw on the vast accumulation of new facts for seemingly scientific proofs.

The discovery of India, as R. Schwab has shown, was mainly instrumental in bringing about, at the turn of the century in Europe, a juxtaposition of civilizations, a dialogue of creeds, such as had followed the conquests of Alexander the Great or the taking of Constantinople. In 1816, for example, Fabre d'Olivet describes Paris as a city:

> [. . .] où se concentrent, en ce moment, les rayons de gloire échappés à cent villes célèbres, où refleurissent, après de longues ténèbres, les sciences des Egyptiens, des Assyriens et des Grecs [. . .].[60]

Under such circumstances, the combing of other cults for proofs and elucidations of religious convictions seems inevitable—witness the religious syncretism of Philo Judaeus, Plotinus, Steuchus, Ficino, Pico della Mirandola. But the diversity of creeds brought to light by Alexander's wars also convinced many people of the relativity of all beliefs, as is shown by the sceptical philosophies of Greece; and the Renaissance produced Montaigne. At the end of the eighteenth and beginning of the nineteenth centuries, however, few voices are heard proclaiming the relativity of truth. Indeed, it would appear that the criterion of truth has never been for more people *quod semper*, *quod ubique*, *quod ab omnibus* than during this era which needed so much to believe in the unity of mankind.

The similarities discovered between different religions and mythologies tended to prove the original unity of humanity by confirming the age-old notion of a primitive revelation, given by God to Adam and transmitted from generation to generation, from civilization to civilization. Lamennais, among many others, believed that this revelation had been preserved more or less intact by the Judaeo-Christian tradition, and he sought in other cults superficial similarities which would confirm the content of this tradition.[61] More interesting were the efforts of Schelling and Schlegel, who wanted to reconstruct the pure religion whose fragmentation had been underlined by Creuzer. The notion that religious truth could be arrived at by a synthesis of all cults and religions is particularly important in as far as the image of the hermaphrodite is concerned, for it gave priority to number, and necessitated the reconciliation of *Genesis* with other cosmogonies, so many of which relate the existence of a primitive androgynous man. A comparison of Moses' account of the creation of man with similar accounts in, for example, Plato's *Banquet*, the *Poymandres*, the Phoenician cosmogony of Sanchuniathon and the Babylonian cosmogony of Berossus—all of which speak of androgynous primitive men—would thus prove in favour of the Kabbalistic interpretation of *Genesis*. And so, Ballanche, who wanted to compose in *La Vision d'Hébal* (1831):

> une cosmogonie composée de toutes les cosmogonies, car toutes sont des transformations les unes des autres,[62]

relates the division of androgynous universal man into two sexes.[63] And Fabre d'Olivet, proving that Adam was in fact universal man, is anxious to point out that the first man of the Chinese, Hindous and Parsees, *Pan-Kou*, *Pourou*, or *Kai-Omordz*, should be similarly 'universalized'.[64] The social mystic Pierre Leroux, who wished to discover the 'eternal and successive Revelation' contained in all religions, ancient and modern,[65] and who accepted the tradition of the androgyny of Adam,[66] found this dogma proved by the agreement of Plato and Moses, who both derived their learning from the Egyptians and Hindous.[67] And the 'Indo-Christian' pseudo-baron Eckstein, after describing how, in *Genesis*, man and woman appear united in a single body and a single mind, compares Eve's birth from Adam's side with Minerva's birth from Jupiter's head.[68]

The dogma of primitive androgynous man, which completed the history of humanity, associated the image of the hermaphrodite with one of the most constant preoccupations of the nineteenth century: the problem of evil. The Judaeo-Christian mystical tradition had always considered the androgynous Adam Kadmon a glorious image of purity and innocence, and had looked on the rupture of the primitive unity as a result of the Fall. Moreover, Plato, in the *Banquet*, presents the splitting into two of the dual primitive men as a punishment for their revolt against the gods. Thus, an explanation of the circumstances of man's division into sexes would provide at the same time an elucidation of the problem of evil. It is therefore understandable that, in early nineteenth-century France, many philosophies of history concerned with the demonstration of man's unity and of the continuity of his progress—symbolized by the image of the hermaphrodite—should be preoccupied with the effects of the Fall and of the division of the primitive androgyne on the course of universal history.

Many, indeed, of the historical, social and political philosophies of early nineteenth-century France are based to a large extent on the conception of androgynous universal man. They are distinguished by the amazing variety of theories about the causes and effects of the division of the primitive androgyne and about the manner of his recomposition.

Fabre d'Olivet, for example, explains the whole course of universal history by the conflict of the three forces separated by the tripartite division of the primitive androgyne: Destiny, Providence and Will; and he bases his political theory on the reconstruction of this triple unity.

According to Fabre d'Olivet's so-called 'restitution' of *Genesis*, the independent will or 'volitive faculty' which individualized man emanated from man himself: it was *Isha*, the woman of *Genesis*, II, 23.[69] For the 'deep sleep' which God caused to come over Adam was, in fact, a magnetic sleep;[70] and Fabre d'Olivet's experiments had taught him that the effect of animal magnetism was precisely to awaken the will.[71] Thus, for Fabre d'Olivet, the man and woman of *Genesis* together form universal man and constitute a single androgynous individual.

Since Fabre d'Olivet himself provided no illustration, it is to Stanislas de Guaita that the curious are indebted for their knowledge of the probable appearance of this primitive androgyne. In his *Essais de sciences maudites* (1890), Guaita analyses Henry Khunrath's androgyne in terms of Fabre d'Olivet's philosophy, so that his reproduction of this image serves also to illustrate Fabre d'Olivet's universal man.[72]

The Fall was brought about when man's will was seduced by a desire to take possession of the very principle of his existence, in order to exist in an absolute manner and rival God.[73] Hereupon, thanks to divine mercy, Adam was taken out of eternity where he would have remained in eternal anguish and suffering, and placed in time. His nature was divided among his three sons, who gave birth to humanity. The object of this division was to alleviate the ills Adam would have suffered together and eternally, by disseminating them throughout space and time, so that each individual member of humanity would have to bear only an incalculable subdivision of them. These ills cannot be eternal since they are now enclosed in time, and their intensity must gradually diminish as mankind expands in time and space, until they become infinitely small and finally disappear completely. When this division of man and of evil is infinite—that is to say, complete—time will stop, space will cease to exist, and universal man will return to his former state of 'indivisible and immortal unity'.[74]

The mode of Adam's division, which was a consequence of his nature and also of God's, had an immense impact on universal history. God, the sacred tetrad, embraces in his unity the universal triad: Providence, Will and Destiny.[75] Universal Man constitutes one of these three powers: Will, which, in *L'état social*, Fabre d'Olivet generally considers as a mediator between the other two, whereas in his *Vers Dorés de Pythagore* (1813) it is Providence which holds the balance. Man himself represents an image of the universe, just as the universe represents an image of God;[76] consequently, man's unity too consists of a triad, for he unites the three elements: body, soul and mind, to which correspond respectively his instinct, understanding and intelligence. Moreover, the same forces which rule the universe, operate also within man, for instinct represents Destiny, understanding Will, and intelligence Providence.[77] These three forces should have operated harmoniously in man, as they do in God; but, on account of the Fall and man's subsequent division, they were separated and each was represented by one of Adam's sons: Will by Cain, Providence by Abel, and Destiny by Seth.[78] After being temporarily reunited in Ram's universal empire (!), the three powers separated once more: Destiny reigned in Asia and Africa through despotism, and Will in Europe by democracy, while the intellectual government of Providence prevailed in a few strongholds in the Middle East.[79]. Since 2100 B.C., the conflict of these forces has shaped universal history, which Fabre d'Olivet analyses in great detail and with unlimited imagination in *L'etat social de l'homme* (1822), republished two years later under the more arresting title: *Histoire philosophique du genre humain*. This continuous conflict was sometimes momentarily suspended by the temporary victory of one force: by the triumph of Will over Destiny at Thermopylae,[80] for example, or during the Punic Wars;[81] or by Christ's Providential mission or Charlemagne's re-establishment of the rule of Destiny.[82] Joan of Arc's victory over the English represented a temporary rout of Destiny by Providence,[83] and Destiny lost again, this time to Will, during the Reformation.[84] Destiny regained some ground thanks to the Society of Jesus,[85] only to surrender it again to Will when royalty was sacrificed to popular sovereignty with the execution of Charles I.[86] And so it goes on right up to the Restoration.

The political lesson Fabre d'Olivet wishes to teach us by his survey of universal history is this: any form of government in which a single force dominates is bad, for it conflicts with the triple nature of man and prevents the re-establishment of the harmony and unity of the primitive androgyne. There are in fact three forms of government corresponding to each of the three spheres of man: theocratic, which is Providential and intellectual; republican, which represents the rule of Will and soul; and monarchial, which is Fatalistic and instinctive.[87] Vain attempts have been made in modern times to overcome the pernicious effects of the predominance of a single force, by creating forms of government in which one force is counterbalanced by another—the monarchial and Fatalistic by the republican and Volitive in the constitutional monarchy of Louis XVIII, or the exact reverse in the English 'emporocracy'. However, these two antagonistic forces can be reconciled only with the aid of a third, mediatory power: Providence.[88] But since the only form of government into which Providence can be incorporated is a theocracy, it is this which must be universally established—not, however, the pure theocracy of Moses, but a true, unitary theocracy which, representing equally all three forces, would reflect 'l'harmonie des trois sphères de la vie hominale',[89] and bring about the unity of cosmogonical man.

Since the conception of androgynous universal man thus plays such an important part in Fabre d'Olivet's philosophy, why does the bisexual or even asexual nature of the androgyne usually tend to be overlooked? The reason is that, following his philosophical system, Fabre d'Olivet sees everything not double but triple.

The peculiarly compulsive logicality which the image of the

hermaphrodite assumes in the vast and extremely erudite—if faintly ridiculous—historical, social and religious system of Ballanche springs precisely from the reduction of Fabre d'Olivet's triad to a duality, each element of which is represented by one of the sexes. Ballanche borrowed a great deal from Fabre d'Olivet, particularly in matters of detail, but his influence on later thought was incomparably greater than Fabre d'Olivet's, for the latter, although aware of political questions, never managed to perceive what was to be the real problem of the nineteenth century: the social problem. In the work of Ballanche, the image of the hermaphrodite appears for the first time—but by no means the last—as a vast social symbol.[90]

The social problem was of course intimately connected with questions of the continuity of human progress and the unity of mankind, and consequently with the conception of the hermaphrodite. After the Revolution, it was extremely difficult for Catholic liberals to know what to think about theories of social equality which, while apparently in agreement with Christian ethics, nevertheless seemed contrary to tradition and authority, and even threatened to destroy the society and religion established by God. While Maistre and Bonald denounced the decadence, while Lamennais was still above all occupied with his common-sense philosophy, Ballanche's originality allowed him to reconcile tradition with progress, to show that social equality was a necessary stage in the development of universal man. The whole of this vast system rests on the image of the androgyne, divided into sexes and recomposing itself through social equality.

Ballanche borrowed from Fabre d'Olivet the notion that *Isha* is man's will; but, whereas for Fabre d'Olivet the creation of woman represents the addition of will to universal man, for Ballanche it represents the removal of this will and the division of the primitive androgyne into two sexes. Since man's will was responsible for the Fall, Ballanche considers that if only this part of man were 'initiated', the whole of man would be rehabilitated. However, God cannot act directly on man's will without reabsorbing it into his own will, and depriving man of his individuality, and therefore of the opportunity of proving his worth. The 'initiation' of man's will, upon which the rehabilitation depends, must consequently be the task of man himself. God made this task possible by dividing the androgyne into two parts, by separating his will from the rest of his being. Since then, there have always been two principles in humanity: the volitive or passive principle must be 'initiated' by the active principle.

This division occurs throughout humanity, at every level and on every scale. After the parting of the sexes, the female, representing will, is 'initiated' by the male. But sexual duality is merely one aspect and an emblem of the total division of cosmogonical man; for, irrespectively of sex, the whole of mankind is divided into Sethites and Cainites, and this universal distinction still persists in the division between East and West. The Sethites and Orientals represent the active, initiatory, male principle, whereas in the Cainites and Westerners the volitive, passive, 'initiable', female principle is incarnate. The same distinction is to be found, on a lesser scale, in the division between peoples: for example, Ballanche considers as initiators the European nations who inherited the Pelasgian and Oriental tradition, whereas the Hellenes represent for him the 'initiable' principle.

It is, however, by establishing this same division within each country and each society that Ballanche brought his philosophy to bear on the contemporary social question—or, rather, reflection on this question probably represented the starting-point of his whole system. For, in the conflict between castes and classes, Ballanche saw the same process of 'initiation': will is incarnate in the plebeian, who must therefore be 'initiated' by the patrician. Although originally divinely ordained for the rehabilitation of universal man, the class system is no more permanent than any of the institutions which divide humanity; for progress consists in the gradual recomposition, reintegration of the hermaphrodite, and consequently in the reunification of the male and female, active and passive principles. This reunification will be brought about when human will has been fully 'initiated' in all its manifestations—that is to say, when it has successfully completed its period of corrective detention.

Ballanche, in fact, considers the effects of the Fall on man's will as a sort of imprisonment: this will has committed a crime which must be expiated through punishment by imprisonment. This incarceration is, however, not only punitive but also preventive: the freedom of man's will, which in the beginning threatened to disturb the harmony of the universe, must henceforward be restricted. Of the several forms which this imprisonment takes in Ballanche's system, we are here concerned only with the one which results from the bipartition of universal man: the detention of human will in the custody of the other part of the primitive androgyne. The male, active principle is thus the gaoler of the female, passive principle, man of woman, the patrician of the plebeian. The male principle thus appears to the female as Destiny; and indeed, Ballanche often designates these two principles by Fabre d'Olivet's terms: Will and Destiny.

What has happened to Fabre d'Olivet's third power: Providence? The fact that Ballanche identifies Providence sometimes with Will and sometimes with Destiny has caused him to be accused of shallow thinking both by his friend Claude-Julien Bredin and, recently, by Fabre d'Olivet's historian, L. Cellier.[91] Both these critics, however, were so preoccupied with Fabre d'Olivet's ideas that they failed to understand the originality of Ballanche's system. It is fitting that a philosopher who theorized so much about prisons should consider that this particular form of incarceration must not only punish the criminal and prevent him from committing further crimes, but also, and above all, rehabilitate him. The male, patrician principle will rehabilitate the female, plebeian principle by gradually initiating it into the knowledge of the religious, moral and civil laws which God gave man to prevent him from misusing his liberty, and which the patricians handed down from generation to generation. This whole initiatory system depends on conflict, for the plebeian would rather be emancipated immediately than slowly initiated, whereas the patrician prefers to slow down the initiation and prolong the imprisonment. In this theory of class conflict, Ballanche follows very closely Vico's *Scienza nuova*—undoubtedly the greatest single influence on his philosophy; but to the Vichean conception of the plebeian's struggle for civil and religious rights Ballanche adds the notion of 'initiation'. Providence looks down on this struggle between Will and Destiny and watches over the harmonious working of the two principles. Although Providence cannot really be identified with either principle, it can in turn side with each; for, if one principle so completely dominates the other that the initiatory system is brought to a halt, God must intervene in favour of the weaker principle and strengthen it in order to restore the balance. Thus, God, who had helped Will and the plebeians to bring about the French Revolution, sided a few years later with the patricians in their efforts to restore the monarchy.

The initiatory system will continue until human will in all its manifestations has been fully re-educated. When the plebeian has been initiated to the same degree as the patrician, the class structure will disappear—partly because it will not be necessary any more to restrain human will, which, thanks to its initiation, will no longer misuse its liberty; and partly because, the degree of initiation being equal on both sides, the class distinction will in fact have ceased to exist. As for sexual duality, although recognizing that physiological differences between the sexes will persist until the end of this cosmogonical cycle, Ballanche yet foresees the time when woman, this incarnation of man's will, ceasing to be the slave of the male, will become his equal, thereby showing that human will has reached the necessary degree of perfection to warrant its reunion with the male principle in the androgyne. Thus, when social equality is truly established, the two principles will become confused and reunite, and man will be rehabilitated. The image of the androgyne, symbol of man's rehabilitation, is also therefore the symbol of social equality and of the emancipation of woman.

If man's rehabilitation must be his own work, what part can Christianity play in Ballanche's system? Ballanche's thought is again resumed by his conception of the androgyne. For Ballanche, the Redemption is to a large extent the result of the active co-operation of man's will with God. It was, according to *Genesis*, the seed of woman which would bruise the serpent's head, and the Gospel informs us that the Virgin accepted her mission. When alluding to these passages of the Scriptures in his *Vision d'Hébal*,[92] Ballanche is anxious to point out that the Redeemer had to be born of man's 'faculté volitive'. The mission of the Redeemer was above all to prepare for the rehabilitation, for the recomposition of the androgyne, by reconciling the two principles. First of all, for the old 'solidarity' which united the members of the same caste, Christ substituted 'charity', the love of all mankind, which knows no social bounds, which attests the unity of cosmogonical man and prefigures the reintegration. More important still, by preaching his doctrine in public, Christ placed at the disposal of all human beings the moral and religious knowledge which had been reserved for the patricians alone in the initiations of antiquity, and thus removed the foundations of the whole caste system. According to Ballanche, social evolution since Christ has consisted merely in the progressive recognition by law of the abolition of castes and classes which Christ had brought about by taking away their religious foundation; and the mission of the French Revolution itself was limited to this: 'faire passer l'émancipation chrétienne de la sphère religieuse dans la sphère civile'.[93]

Thus, the conception of the androgyne, divided into sexes and classes, recomposing itself through social equality, is the pivot of Ballanche's philosophy, religious as well as social. It also provides the key to his interpretation of history. Ballanche, like so many of his contemporaries, is not content with abstract reasoning; he is anxious to avail himself of the vast accumulation of new facts about man in order to demonstrate his philosophy. The panorama of universal history which he presents in his humanitarian epic *La Vision d'Hébal* shows human progress, from the earliest times right up to 1831, in terms of the initiation of human will and the gradual removal of the barriers which separate the two halves of the divided androgyne. Ballanche looks forward to the time when the whole of mankind will act as a single being, when the return to unity will be complete, the androgyne reconstituted and man rehabilitated.

Ballanche's androgyne leads us to two others which his philosophy undoubtedly influenced: that of the painter Paul Chenavard and that of the Saint-Simonians.

It is to what Baudelaire aptly called the 'hieroglyphic' art of Ballanche's fellow Lyonnais Chenavard[94] that we must turn for the finest pictorial expression of the optimistic image of the androgyne in nineteenth-century France. Indeed, the conception of universal man underlies all the vast pictorial epic of humanity which Chenavard was commissioned to create, in a gigantic series of murals, for the adornment of the Panthéon in Paris. The whole spirit of an age is represented by this immense panorama of universal history, mythology and religion, this legend and apotheosis of humanity, which now lies rolled up in the cellar of the museum in Lyon. In the words of Théophile Gautier, who has provided nearly a hundred pages of admirably detailed analyses of this colossal work, Chenavard therein depicted the 'synthetic' history of:

> ce grand être collectif, multiple, ondoyant, ubiquiste, éternel, composé de tous les hommes de tous les temps, dont l'âme générale est Dieu, et qui, en marche depuis Adam, s'avance d'un pas ferme et sûr vers le but connu de lui seul.[95]

One of the murals significantly depicts two colossal figures of Adam and Eve: 'les principes actif et passif, les deux portions séparées de l'androgyne primordial'.[96] The primitive androgyne is not itself represented here pictorially, although as a conception it permeates the whole of this enormous composition. This absence is, however, amply compensated by the prominent position allotted to the figure of the androgyne in Chenavard's painting *Divina Tragedia*, exhibited at the Paris Salon of 1869. Although the official catalogue described the work as representing the triumph of the Christian Trinity over the gods of paganism[97] —an interpretation difficult to reconcile with Chenavard's avowed anticlericalism—the painting in fact portrays, as Paul Casimir Perier pointed out,[98] the victory of human reason over all religions. That the *Divina Tragedia* is dominated by the figure which the catalogue describes as: 'l'éternelle Androgyne, symbole de l'harmonie des deux natures ou principes contraires, coiffée du bonnet phrygien, et assise sur sa chimère', is indicated not only by its prominent position in the top left-hand corner, but also by the fact that, among all the gods and goddesses of the world, this person alone is given a sort of halo. This figure represents not only the starting point of human history, but also its goal: the rehabilitation, the reintegration of man, the recomposition, by the destruction of false religions, of the primitive hermaphrodite, now wearing the Phrygian cap—the Republican symbol of liberty. Incidentally, Chenavard's painting could also serve equally well as an illustration of Auguste Comte's *Grand Etre*, of 'la statue de l'humanité divinisée sur l'ancien autel de Dieu'.[99]

The powerful religious influence which Ballanche exercised around 1828 on the as yet materialistic school of Saint-Simon is attested by Sainte-Beuve;[100] but any search for precise debts would remain largely hypothetical since Ballanche's philosophy itself is a synthesis of so many contemporary systems. It could, however, be conjectured with some degree of probability that Ballanche played a not unimportant rôle in the introduction of the image of the hermaphrodite as a social symbol into Saint-Simonism, where it became intimately connected, not only with the question of the emancipation of women, but also with the campaign for universal industrialization, which was to bring about the material prosperity of mankind.

Before labour, industry and production could be accepted as worthy aims for modern society, the material world must be shown to be in no way inferior to the intellectual or moral world, the activity of the body to the activity of the mind, manual labour to philosophy. This so-called 'rehabilitation of matter' was the purpose of Saint-Simon's monistic philosophy, later developed by Enfantin, which postulated that thought and matter are not two distinct entities but just two aspects of existence, two abstractions which help us to analyse life and divide its unity in order to understand it. Since God is everything that exists, the goal of all intellectual activity, of all learning, is knowledge of the Divinity; and the object of all physical activity, of all industry, is to serve God. By exploiting and consequently modifying the globe, man participates in the successive transformations of the divinity and thus continues the work of Creation. Industry, therefore, becomes the true form of worship.[101] Bazard extended this conception of the divine essence to include the material part of man himself which industry was to satisfy; and in Enfantin's doctrine, the rehabilitation of matter became definitely associated with the rehabilitation of the flesh. It was at this point that the fundamental religious and philosophical principles of Saint-Simonism became involved with the question of the emancipation of woman and the image of the hermaphrodite.

Woman had been considered in Christianity to be a material being dominated by material instincts, the personification of the flesh, the diabolical instrument which caused men to fall into sin. Around 1830, however, Enfantin began to feel that physical love was legitimate as part of the natural activity of the body, itself a manifestation of God. To raise woman up from her inferior position, to make her mistress of her own destiny and free to choose her own mate, was then not only to legitimize sexual pleasure but also to rehabilitate matter. And so, Enfantin could lump together in a single category: 'l'industrie, la femme, les appétits physiques'.[102]

Before the great schism, during the stormy discussions of 1831–2, Bazard accused Enfantin of perverting the doctrine of the rehabilitation of matter by using it to justify feminism and to legalize promiscuity. In the face of increasing criticism of his feminism, Enfantin defended himself by adopting the doctrine, supposedly borrowed from Charles Fourier, that the social individual is a couple, composed of a man and a woman—in other words, that the individual citizen is an androgyne. The female would thus have an equally important position as the male in this joint performance of the citizen's social functions.

Although, as Mme Marguerite Thibert pointed out as early as 1926,[103] this conception of the citizen-couple positively does not exist in Fourier, it is surprising how many people have been deceived, and still are, by the Saint-Simonians' proclamation of this fictitious debt.[104] The Fourierist Victor Considérant, however, was not taken in: in a letter to Fourier, written in January 1832, ridiculing the Saint-Simonian interpretation of Fourierism, he urged Fourier to marry if he wanted to be complete, and not an $\frac{\text{‘\textit{individu social}’}^{105}}{2}$.

This conception of the androgynous citizen, of the citizen-couple, which, while demanding the equality of women, made a single person seem incomplete and sterile as a social being, was an attack on celibacy. By giving to the activity of the body the same importance as to the activity of the mind, and consequently attesting the fundamental unity of matter and spirit, it represented the restoration of the harmony of life destroyed by Christianity, and the justification of industry. But matter and spirit are united also in a slightly different way in the androgynous citizen: woman, the personification of matter, of the flesh, is here joined equally with man, the personification of the spirit, of intelligence. Love, which thus alone joins these two manifestations of God, appears therefore as life itself—or God himself—in its unity. And so God, considered in his unity, is not only spirit and matter, but also the Divine Androgyne, male and female. Enfantin is reputed to have said during his trial:

> Notre Dieu n'est pas le vôtre; *Il* n'est pas seulement bon comme un père, *Elle* est aussi tendre comme une mère, car *Il* est et *Elle* est la mère de tous et de toutes.[106]

And before receiving the symbolic necklace, the Saint-Simonian disciple had to make this profession of faith:

> Je crois en Dieu, le Père et Mère de tous et de toutes éternellement bon et bonne. . . .[107]

The constitution of the individual from a couple raised, however, certain moral problems: how would marriage, legitimacy, paternity and divorce be affected by the emancipation of woman, by her absolute right, as man's equal, to dispose of herself as she wished in her dealings with men? Enfantin said that only woman could formulate the definitive moral code; and, henceforth, The Woman, who would represent her whole sex, was anxiously awaited. Man had cured the ills of the city by proclaiming the civil law; Woman would cure the ills of the family by proclaiming the moral law. The true Redemption would thus be operated in two moments, and the Messiah, like the citizen and like God, must be androgynous. As Barrault put it in his appeal *Aux Femmes juives*: 'le Messie n'est pas un homme, c'est un homme et une femme. . . .' This Messiah, comprising the Father and the Mother, would also be the pope, the 'couple-pape' of the Saint-Simonian religion. Enfantin, the Father, was therefore incomplete: he was only half a Pope and half a Messiah. Accordingly, d'Eichtal, in a moment of illumination, awoke Enfantin early one morning with these words:

> 'TU ES LA FUTURE MOITIÉ DU COUPLE RÉVÉLATEUR, et JÉSUS VIT EN TOI.
> 'COUPLE MESSIE, l'humanité t'aimera, t'adorera, te divinisera plus qu'elle n'a fait de JÉSUS [. . .] j'appelle la FILLE de DIEU qui doit s'asseoir à tes côtés, pour fléchir le genou devant votre dualité sainte'.[108]

Enfantin, indeed, at a meeting of the Family on 21st November 1831 had appeared with an empty chair beside him—the symbol of his incompleteness. Who the Woman Messiah was, and where she might be found was a matter for much speculation among the Saint-Simonians. Their quest for her in the East, and their hope of uniting East and West in the person of an androgynous Messiah bears some similarity to Ballanche's theory of the reconstruction of the primitive androgyne by the reunion of East and West.

What Enfantin does not seem to have known is that the female Messiah had already been and gone. She was Ann Lee, head of the Shaker sect, transported from England to America in 1774. The figure of the hermaphrodite played a prominent part in this religion, which taught that man's original androgyny could be restored only through total sexual abstinence. Moreover, according to the Shakers, the male part of the Messiah had appeared in Jesus; the incarnation of the female part in Mother Ann was the occasion of the 'second coming of Christ'.[109]

Although Pierre Leroux broke with the Saint-Simonians in 1831, his philosophy, a curious blend of transcendental idealism and social mysticism, remained similar in many respects to that formulated by Enfantin in his *Lettre à Duveyrier sur la vie éternelle*, written in June 1830, published in 1834, and reproduced in his *Science de l'homme* (1858) and in his later work *La vie éternelle* (1861). However, the hermaphrodite which appears in Leroux's work, and which completely resumes his philosophy, represents something rather different from what is symbolized by the Saint-Simonian androgyne already analysed.

According to Leroux,[110] each individual human being is manifested only through his fellow men and the universe. Without this objective life, his subjective life would remain latent and undeveloped. The life of humanity in general and of each individual depends therefore on unceasing communication. Thus, the life of the individual does not belong to himself alone; nor does it exist in himself alone; it exists also outside him, in his fellows and in the world. Consequently, all barriers which divide mankind in time or space and prevent mutual communication and improvement detract from the life of the individual. And in all cases of oppression, the tyrant is hurt just as much as the victim:

> vous ne pouvez pas faire le mal sans vous faire du mal à vous-même. Puisque je suis votre objet comme vous êtes le mien [. . .] je vous défie de me rendre malheureux sans vous nuire à vous-même.[111]

Thus, the religion preached by Leroux rests on a special kind of charity, on the blending of the Christian love of the neighbour with the natural love of the self. This true charity is: 'la loi d'identité et par conséquent d'identification du *moi* et du *non-moi* [. . .]'.[112]

This notion of the unity, solidarity and fraternity of mankind, both in time and in space, which plays such an important rôle in Romantic literature and thought, appears then as essential to Leroux's philosophical system. It is the 'DOGME MÊME DE L'HUMANITÉ, considérée comme formant un seul être collectif'[113] and it finds its clearest expression in the 'myth' of the androgyne Adam.

Leroux accepts the traditional mystical interpretation of the Bible that Adam was androgynous, that a consequence of the Fall was Adam's division into sexes, and that mankind will eventually be restored to its former androgynous state. However, for Leroux, this 'myth' is true only symbolically and psychologically. Certainly, Leroux follows Fabre d'Olivet's interpretation of the *Sépher* in maintaining that Adam is mankind in general; but this universal man is not the same as the physically androgynous or asexual Adam of Fabre d'Olivet and Ballanche. For the latter, the original Adam was individual, whole, undivided humanity, a single entity, a single force, and did not comprise an infinite number of individuals. According to Leroux, Adam is universal man in that he is an abstract symbol of the whole of humanity, which has its own life. But he is also universal man in as far as he is an individual. For humanity has always existed and will always exist only in individuals. Adam is an *homme-humanité*. From the moment he first appeared on earth, man has always been exactly the same physically, and always will be—that is to say, that he has always belonged to a human race composed of both men and women. The immense changes that have taken place in man have been psychological; and these psychological changes are symbolized by the tradition of the primitive androgyne, his Fall and separation into sexes, and his rehabilitation and reintegration.

The androgyny of Adam expresses:

> le *moi* et le *non-moi*, dans leur plus grand attrait, et dans leur plus complète communion [. . .] dans une indécomposable unité.[114]

The union of self and non-self in this psychological androgyne was such that Adam, quite unconscious of his existence and completely absorbed in universal life, was like a plant or an animal; but, because he had been created in God's image and likeness, his destiny was to pass 'de l'état d'animalité à l'état de connaissance ou de réflexion'.[115] However, since consciousness and knowledge necessarily entail distinction and individualization, how could Adam acquire consciousness without giving in exchange something infinitely more important—that is to say, without sacrificing his androgyny which, uniting his subjective and objective lives, was and remains the condition of his existence? The answer is that Adam, in his quest for consciousness and individualization, should continually have been prompted not by selfishness and pride which entail separation and disunion, but by charity which, as has been seen, unites the self and the non-self and consequently maintains androgyny. *Genesis* itself, as interpreted by Leroux, shows that it would have been possible and, indeed, in accordance with the will of God, for Adam to remain an androgyne after his acquisition of consciousness. Asserting that, in St. Jerome's translation: *tulit unam ex costis ei* (*Genesis*, II, 21), *unam* refers literally to the female principle existing in Adam, Leroux maintains that by this action, which constituted the first stage in Adam's progress towards knowledge, God separated the male and female principles, the subject and object, without destroying the fundamental unity of the androgyne. Adam, indeed, was becoming individualized without being disunited, for this woman was bone of his bones and flesh of his flesh:

> Lorsqu'il voit Eve, qui est lui et qui a été tirée de lui, qui est son *moi* et son *non-moi* par un inconcevable mystère, il sent commencer pour lui une existence nouvelle; car l'identité et la distinction lui sont révélées à la fois.[116]

Like most contemporary social mystics, Leroux allows his fanatical belief in the symbolic wisdom of the Bible to lead him to discover the confirmation of his whole philosophical system in the very words used by *Genesis*. Thus, after this first separation of the male and female principles, the name given to woman still contains the idea of unity. She is not yet called Eve, but *Isha*, because she has been taken from *Ish*: 'l'être est encore un, bien que partagé dans la dualité des sexes'.[117]

At this point, however, the androgyne was seduced by the serpent which Leroux, following Fabre d'Olivet, considers as a symbol of selfishness: 'l'egoïsme', 'l'ardeur cupide', 'l'intérêt', 'l'envie'.[118] The resulting division of self and non-self and the destruction of the unity of the androgyne are indicated by the fact that hereupon Adam changed *Isha*'s name to Eve. This selfish distinction between self and non-self, between the two halves of the androgyne, is for Leroux the origin of all social ills, and particularly of inequality. As regards the relationship between the sexes, men and women were equally selfish, with the result that the weaker woman became a slave to man, in accordance with

*Genesis*, III, 16. Outside the family, *mine* and *yours*, dividing the earth, gave rise to misery and toil. Since the division of the androgyne, everywhere we find:

> cette dualité qui a divisé et rendu si malheureuse l'espèce humaine, sous les formes diverses de *riche* et de *pauvre*, de *fort* et de *faible*, de *tyran* et de *sujet*, de *maître* et d'*esclave*, de *noble* et de *roturier*, d'*aîné* et de *puîné*, etc.[119]

For Leroux, as for so many social mystics, Redemption means the reintegration of these two principles, the recomposition of the androgyne. Like Ballanche, Leroux believes that the hermaphrodite will be recomposed by the progressive abolition of the barriers which divide mankind, and which for Leroux prevent the complete communion of subject and object, self and non-self. But there will be no physical change in man, and his Redemption will take place on earth. Like Adam, rehabilitated man will be androgynous only psychologically, in that in him subject and object, self and non-self, will be united. A first stage in the recomposition of this universal man was God's making of Abraham '*l'homme-peuple*, destiné à devenir *l'homme-humanité*'.[120] But it is Christianity which will bring about the complete recomposition of the androgyne. According to Leroux's definitions, Christ himself is androgynous, since in him God and man, subject and object are united.[121] And the Christian 'new man' who will gain eternal life is none other than the androgyne in whom the two principles, self and non-self, are united by charity,[122] and who, although suffering death as an individual, must live for ever as part of mankind. Charity is indeed the essential characteristic of Leroux's androgyny: it is the doctrine of the *retour à l'unité par la connaissance*.

The androgynous Pope of the Saint-Simonians was to have been a composite being. A few years later, the sculptor and religious leader Ganneau became an androgyne all on his own—if only in name. It was as the Mapah, a name composed of the first syllables of *ma*ter and *pa*ter that Ganneau, after a chequered career, announced his advent in his first manifesto dated 15th August 1838, the first day of the Evadian Era. A hatter's son, after squandering a fortune on revelry and dissipation, Ganneau had managed to earn a living as a phrenologist. The death of his mistress, who had been won by adroit phrenological caresses, was such a grievous blow that Ganneau became seriously ill. His life and mentality were so changed that henceforth he wished to be known as *celui qui fut Ganneau.*[123]

What Champfleury calls 'la flamme des anciens souvenirs', which consumed the Mapah during his last illness,[124] undoubtedly helped to determine some of the more important symbols of his new religion: the phallus, for example, and the androgyne. Sexual preoccupation, as a general trait of human psychology, is of course never very far away from the image of the hermaphrodite. However, Ganneau's use of this image as a symbol of both the emancipation of woman and Revolutionary ideals bears the stamp of his age.

The Mapah's religion, like his title, was founded on the principle of androgyny. Recognizing the union of the male and female principles everywhere in Nature, he was indignant that in modern society woman should be so completely absorbed by man as to be obliged to sacrifice her name to her husband's. In Ganneau's system, man and woman would equally contribute the first syllable of their names to the unitary name of the couple:

> afin que de ces deux génériques soit constituée l'unité dans la dualité; ainsi Evadam de Eve, Adam. [125]

And so, the Mapah called his religion Evadism, after the Great Androgyne Evadam.

The Evadist, however, observed Ganneau's disciple L.-Ch. Caillaux (*celui qui fut Caillaux!*), believes not only in the emancipation of women, but in all social equality:

> C'est un homme qui proteste intégralement contre la forme religieuse, politique, sociale, comme n'étant que l'expression monstrueuse de l'absorption de la femme par l'homme, du pauvre par le riche, du faible par le fort.[126]

Indeed, in the works of Ganneau and Caillaux, the hermaphrodite becomes a symbol of the glorious ideals of the French Revolution. It was the Revolution which completed the Redemption. According to Caillaux, since androgyny is the universal principle, not only of man but also of God, Christ, the incarnation of the male principle alone, was imperfect as a Saviour. Just as God completed the creation by giving Adam a companion made of his own flesh and blood, so the Redemption will be complete only when Christ, the new Adam, has been joined with his Eve.

And as it was Eve who introduced man into the realm of progress, it is fitting that this progress should not be completed until she is reunited with Adam. However, the new Eve has already appeared as the virgin Liberty, incarnate in the Revolutionary French people. In a hymn, Caillaux evokes France-Liberté as a young virgin, as the Redemptress, the new Eve who will crush the serpent's head.[127] Jesus, said Ganneau, was a man who proclaimed the brotherhood of men; France was a people who proclaimed the brotherhood of peoples. Both were crucified. And so:

> Waterloo est le Golgotha-Peuple.
> Waterloo est le vendredi-saint du grand Christ-peuple.[128]

Thus the Redemption is achieved:

> En Christ,
> Et en liberté.
> Dernier terme de l'évocation génésiaque; dernier symbole de l'unité divine,
> De l'unité dans la dualité!
> Ainsi soit-il!
> *Hosanna!*[129]

Much of the interest of the Mapah's portrait by Traviès, the Swiss satirist and caricaturist and probably a member of the Evadian sect, lies in the enigmatic emblem in the background. Indeed, in spite of the portrait's seriousness, befitting a religious leader, this emblem is, Champfleury observes, all that distinguishes the cloaked, bearded and turbaned Oriental-looking gentleman from a seraglio pastille-seller.[130] The ex-abbé Constant informs us that the sculptor Ganneau excelled in the execution of learned and beautiful representations of his religion,[131] and the emblem in Traviès's picture is undoubtedly an extremely simplified reproduction of the image which served as the Mapah's coat of arms and which figured prominently on the manifestos with which he flooded Paris between 1844 and 1846. The original work sculptured by Ganneau was very similar in content and scope to Chenavard's *Divina Tragedia*: it provided an interpretation of successive religions conceived in terms of the progress of the hermaphrodite towards its apotheosis through liberty. We owe to the ex-abbé Constant this detailed account of the original work:

> sous la forme hiératique d'un ostensoir, il avait sculpté la synthèse religieuse la plus complète et la plus absolue. Le pied de l'ostensoir,

> c'était le monde, et le premier couple humain le couvrait de ses bras étendus; des deux têtes humaines sortait une création symbolique analogue à celle des six jours, et le génie peuplait à son tour le ciel comme le principe créateur avait déjà peuplé la terre. Dieu avait créé progressivement l'homme, et l'homme à son tour créait progressivement l'idée et le culte de Dieu. Toujours le couple primitif reparaissait transfiguré dans les synthèses successives, Isis et Osiris, Jupiter et Junon, Jésus et Marie. Puis à Marie, succédait la liberté affranchie par les douleurs rédemptrices de la mère, et la dernière synthèse unissait, dans le ciel de l'intelligence, le Dieu fait homme et la liberté devenue mère. Il fallait entendre Ganneau expliquer tout cela![132]

The ex-abbé Alphonse-Louis Constant, who, under the name of Eliphas Lévi, was to become one of the great masters and historians of occultism, had not always felt this immense enthusiasm for Ganneau's doctrine. In his *Histoire de la magie* (1860), he tells how, in the company of Esquiros, he went to ridicule the Mapah, and came away from this meeting—converted. Constant, indeed, learned much of his social mysticism from the Mapah; and it is a fair tribute to the latter's eloquence that Constant's work, like his, should be dominated by the symbol of the hermaphrodite, representing the emancipation of woman and 'apocalyptic liberalism'.

Perhaps also the Mapah inflamed Constant as much as himself with his burning memories; for, considering God as an extremely active hermaphrodite, perpetually engaged in an ecstatic communion with himself, the ex-abbé was wont to confuse godliness and sexuality.[133] Evil, then, is what prevents the true union of man and woman, particularly in the form of the materialistic preoccupations of society. After the division of the primitive androgyne, Adam closed up his side and hardened it with gold and silver to prevent Eve from returning to her birthplace,[134] and since then man has never been truly united with woman. Marriage, dominated by financial considerations is really no better than prostitution: in both cases, love, the redeeming force in the world, is corrupted. Indeed, according to Constant, original sin is precisely this profanation of man's birth, prostitution in marriage, and the corruption of love.[135] It is money which prevents the recomposition of the hermaphrodite, for it is money which divides the sexes by corrupting love, by prostituting marriage and, consequently, by keeping woman in a position of inferiority. True, reciprocal love cannot exist until woman becomes man's equal; and this cannot be until society ceases to be founded on greed.

The question of woman's emancipation, of the division of the sexes, is thus seen to be intimately connected with the larger problems of society: the uneven distribution of wealth and the distinction between rich and poor. Eternal happiness will not come until love, which is good, has been substituted for individualism, which is evil;[136] until rich and poor, man and woman, have been absorbed into the unity of the androgyne. When woman is recognized as man's equal:

> Les deux sexes n'en feront plus qu'un, selon la parole du Christ; le grand androgyne sera créé, l'humanité sera femme et homme ....[137]

It is to this time that Constant looks forward, particularly in his work *L'Assomption de la femme* (1841), which takes the form of a commentary on the *Song of Songs*, considered by Constant to be the epithalamium for the 'grande noce humanitaire': the union of the two halves of the divided androgyne.[138]

How much of Flora Tristan's posthumous work *L'Emancipation de la femme* (1845)[139] should be attributed to Constant is uncertain. As has been conjectured,[140] he may have written it entirely himself, but certainly at least some of the ideas expressed were held by Flora.[141] Indeed, from Constant to Flora Tristan the distance is considerable: the former believed passionately in the emancipation of woman; the latter seems rather to have desired absolute domination for her sex. The image of the androgyne remains; but while for so many it represented absolute social equality, in her system it becomes the symbol and the justification of gyneocracy.

Flora Tristan did not merely denounce, particularly in *Méphis* (1838), the slavery of woman in modern society; she did not merely vindicate the right of woman to dispose freely of her affections, the re-establishment of divorce, the education of woman and equal pay for equal work; in short, she did not confine her aims to securing emancipation, equality and justice for woman: the ultimate ambition of this female Messiah was, as Constant himself perceived: 'la souveraineté et l'autocratie de la femme'.[142]

Her feminism was supported by her mysticism. In Flora Tristan's system, the unity of the Divine Androgyne comprises three elements: for God is not only male and female; he is also the world, the wonderful embryo of this eternal generation, constantly developing within his breast.[143] In order to show God's triple unity, Flora always refers to him as *Dieux*, but uses this plural grammatically as a singular. Her androgynous religion was symbolized by the sign which appeared on her writing-paper and on her seal: a triangle, representing God, with one word at each side: 'père', 'mère', 'embryon'; and 'Dieux' in the middle.[144] Flora's analysis of the working of the three divine elements serves to defend her gynecratic notions. Whereas, for Enfantin, the mind and spirit were incarnate in the male principle, and body and matter in the female, Flora sees the reverse. However, although in her system the intelligence becomes the female principle, it nevertheless retains the traditional male characteristic: activity. For her, it is the active female principle, representing intelligence and love, which animates the as yet passive male principle, representing force, which is then stirred to fecundate the loving intelligence. Humanity, which is the manifestation of God, has his triple nature: father, mother, child. Intelligent love, the active, creative, animating principle is woman, whereas man is merely force. And so, in society as in God, the male should be subordinate to the female, since for all his activity he depends on an initial impulse from woman. He is even denied the right of paternity:

> La femme, maîtresse de ses faveurs, anime qui il lui plaît du feu sacré de l'amour, et celui qu'elle a choisi, elle le fait participer un instant à son privilège de mère.[145]

1845, the year of *L'émancipation de la femme*, also saw the dawn of the 'Fusionist' era. Among the many systems and conceptions fused together in this strangely coherent social philosophy—there are traces of Fabre d'Olivet, Herder, Ballanche, Hegel, Leroux . . . — were first and foremost the androgyne of the Mapah's Evadism and that of Leroux's social idealism.

The Fusionist Louis-Jean-Baptiste de Tourreil designates his androgynous deity by the monogram MAP, pronounced 'Map' and composed of the initials of God's real name: MèrAmour-Père.[146] The MAP is the 'Unity-Trinity'; he is everything that exists, the 'omnisubstance', matter and spirit, male and female, the eternal father and mother of all being, eternally creating by eternal love. The sacred progeny of God, eternally engendered, has both sexes, like God himself in whose image it is created; it is the universal androgyne Evadam which, manifested with its two sexes throughout nature and the universe, finds its highest expression in this world in man and woman.[147]

Man's task is to perfect himself until, by bringing about the unity of the androgyne Evadam, he becomes the object, the true manifestation of God, his faithful reproduction and complete realization. The unity of the universal androgyne will be realized by the awakening of the 'collective conscience', which will embrace the multiplicity and diversity of individual beings, past, present and future, without any limit in time or space. Universal man is, indeed: 'l'univers vivant et conscient de lui-même'.[148] The individual, 'universalized' by his participation in the collective conscience, will be freed from time and space and live for ever; but, although having attained eternal perfection, he must yet perfect that part of him which is still imprisoned in time and space.[149]

Fusionism, insisting on the fundamental unity existing between man and the universe, man and man, and man and God, is essentially a religion of universal equality, solidarity, fraternity and love which, excluding eternal damnation for any person, makes individual salvation, happiness, perfection and wisdom conditional on the state of mankind as a whole. During the interview granted to Erdan in 1854, Tourreil exclaimed:

> 'Oh! Monsieur, si vous saviez come cela est vrai, qu'il faut que nous nous aimions les uns les autres! si vous le saviez! si vous le saviez! Le sentez-vous? Sentez-vous que tous les cœurs humains doivent se fondre un jour, et que tout cela doit palpiter à l'unisson du cœur de Dieu, ce cœur divin dont les batemens sont la vie du monde?'[150]

And Auguste Guyard who saw in Fusionism the absolute reign of fraternity, and whom Erdan calls 'un des plus nobles cœurs de ce tems-ci',[151] wrote in 1848:

> Ainsi, avec la solidarité intime et indissoluble qui fait de l'humanité entière un seul corps, NUL NE PEUT ÊTRE HEUREUX QU'AUTANT QUE TOUS SERONT HEUREUX.[152]

Although, after about 1850, the image of the androgyne generally becomes more dissociated from social thought in order to symbolize something completely different, the relationship between the two does not abruptly end; indeed, although far less common, it persists right up to the end of the century. In *L'Eternel Messie féminin*, for example, the fifth chapter of his article 'La femme nouvelle' inserted in an 1896 number of the *Revue encyclopédique* devoted to feminists and feminism, Jules Bois, after declaring: 'J'ai été conduit au féminisme par le mysticisme', mentions among the mystical inspirations for his feminism the Kabbala which proclaims as the supreme objective: 'le couple ne formant plus qu'un seul être', and according to which: 'l'Adam-Kadmon, le Verbe, le Logos est androgyne, féminin et masculin'.[153] According to *L'Eve Nouvelle* (1896), the emancipation of woman is brought about by true love, and a man and woman who love each other truly become a single, androgynous individual. True marriage creates a third being—not the child, who will soon exist independently:

> mais une véritable troisième personne formée des deux que nous voyons, un être supérieur complet qui existe au-dessus d'eux, d'une vie divine.[154]

Although the image of the androgyne may thus be found as a social symbol long after 1850, there is no doubt that after that date it occurs as such far less frequently. Indeed, even for a while before then, this optimistic symbol of the androgyne tended to be eclipsed by a completely different symbol.

From the foregoing examination of a considerable number of the manifestations of the optimistic image of the androgyne, it may be concluded that this image symbolized confidence in the future, if discontent with the present, and continuous progress towards ideal, absolute perfection. It symbolized above all human solidarity, the brotherhood of man, the unity and continuity of generations and civilizations; and consequently charity, the sense of social justice, sympathy for the downtrodden, for all those who are oppressed, whether women or men. It represented too the original and fundamental goodness and purity of mankind, the transitoriness of sin and of all forms of evil, individual or social; and if not always sufficiently religious, in the accepted sense of the term, to symbolize the future restoration of a transfigured mankind to the presence of God, it nevertheless constantly represented man's arrival in some sort of Paradise, sometimes even the Paradise of universal industrialization or absolute social equality. At the same time, it was the symbol of human dignity, and of the immense significance of any and every human life.

That it symbolized all these things was not, however, due to any permanent, intrinsic quality of the image or the conception of the androgyne itself, which did no more than reflect the mentality of those who looked at it. However, the beliefs which characterized this mentality were for the most part mere myths, devoid of any solid foundation—myths such as universal and eternal human solidarity, the primitive revelation, and endless progress. These myths were never universally accepted, and those who rejected them could be equally fascinated by the image of the androgyne; but, of course, they too would see in it the reflection of their own attitude of mind. The image of the androgyne could then assume one of two distinct meanings or values according as these particular myths were accepted or rejected. As long as the latter were generally acceptable, the optimistic image of the androgyne dwarfed its rival; but as soon as they began to crumble, the tables were decidedly turned.

## II

The image of the androgyne which predominated during the latter part of the nineteenth century, since it represented an attitude of mind which rejected the myths symbolized by the earlier image, was quite naturally its exact opposite in almost every respect. Just as the earlier image was optimistic because it symbolized solidarity, fraternity, communion, continuity of progress, trust in the future, in God and in the fundamental goodness of man, so the later image was pessimistic because it symbolized lack of belief in all those things, and consequently: isolation, loneliness, self-sufficiency, independence, and despair in the future, in God and in man. And whereas the earlier image was above all a symbol of virtue—of the three cardinal virtues, in fact—the later image is above all a symbol of vice, particularly of cerebral lechery, demoniality, onanism, homosexuality, sadism and masochism.

Throughout the nineteenth century runs a current of disillusionment, of dissatisfaction with reality, with normal, everyday life, together with the despair of any possibility of improvement and the need to transcend this disappointing reality, or to escape into ivory towers, where one could stand aloof, immersed in one's own mind, preserving it from contamination by the inferior external world. This conviction of the worthlessness of normal, everyday existence was accompanied by a rejection of generally accepted moral values and standards.

Already among the German Romantics, disillusionment and scepticism often occasioned withdrawal from reality into the mind, which became invaded by diseased imaginings. This is how Henri Lichtenberger, in his excellent study of Novalis, describes these early German Romantics:

> Des décadents: car ces contempteurs de la société et de la culture du temps sont en même temps des blasés rongés par le spleen, sceptiques jusqu'au complet nihilisme moral, déprimés par l'abus de l'analyse dissolvante d'eux-mêmes et de l'ironie corrosive, destitués de toute énergie pour l'action virile; ce sont des acteurs qui jonglent avec les mots et les sentiments, qui se composent des attitudes théâtrales, qui sont devenus incapables, finalement, de discerner au juste où finit chez eux la sincérité et où commence le cabotinage.[155]

In France, this dissatisfaction with reality goes right back to the *mal du siècle* and characterized the work of the earliest Romantics, of Chateaubriand, for example, Musset and Nodier; it was reflected later in the theories of *l'art pour l'art*, according to which the artist, divorced from practical life, recognized no other value than art. As the century wore on and the earlier optimistic myths proved erroneous, there seemed to be more grounds for despair. Industrialization, which Saint-Simon thought would bring about universal material prosperity, was enriching only certain sections of the community, behind whose apparent respectability lurked the disturbing things seen, for example, by Beardsley. The underlying belief of most early socialist doctrines, that material prosperity would end moral degradation, proved unfounded. Moreover, the realists' depiction of the uglier aspects of everyday life could only increase disillusionment. Finally, symbolism, joining with certain nineteenth-century idealisms, asserted the necessity of transcending the mediocre appearances of immediate reality if any true values were to be found.

One of the earliest and most important examples—and certainly the most influential—of the image of the androgyne conditioned by this second attitude was provided by Théophile Gautier. Gautier often expressed his admiration for the artistic excellence of the classic statue of the sleeping Hermaphrodite, not only in the famous poem *Contralto* of *Emaux et Camées*, but also in *Mademoiselle de Maupin* (1835–36), this novel which, like Latouche's *Fragoletta* and Balzac's *Séraphîta*, tells the story of a person who appears sometimes male and sometimes female, and is loved by both a man and a woman. Speaking of the 'délicieuse figure délicatement couchée sur un matelas de marbre', he said that in *Mademoiselle de Maupin* he had 'caressé avec un amour de statuaire cette gracieuse chimère, rêve de l'Antiquité'.[156] In this novel, indeed, d'Albert enthuses over the 'charming monster':

> Il ne se peut rien imaginer de plus ravissant au monde que ces deux corps tous deux parfaits, harmonieusement fondus ensemble, que ces deux beautés si égales et si différentes qui n'en forment plus qu'une supérieure à toutes deux, parce qu'elles se tempèrent et se font valoir réciproquement [. . .].[157]

He goes on to say that Mademoiselle de Maupin herself would be an excellent model of this type of beauty. Indeed, Gautier is at pains to show that she is not merely a Lesbian, that in fact she is to a certain extent androgynous. Nor is it simply a question of a male mentality in a female body: her mind and body alike possess something of both sexes so that she feels she belongs to a third sex:

> En vérité, ni l'un ni l'autre de ces deux sexes n'est le mien [. . .] je suis d'un troisième sexe à part qui n'a pas encore de nom [. . .] j'ai le corps et l'âme d'une femme, l'esprit et la force d'un homme, et j'ai trop ou pas assez de l'un et de l'autre pour me pouvoir accoupler avec l'un d'eux.[158]

However, Maupin is not and cannot be perfectly androgynous, for the true hermaphrodite is too far removed from reality to be represented otherwise than imperfectly by a living character in a novel which aspires to any degree of realism. And it is precisely because it does not truly exist in reality that the hermaphrodite, this 'chimère ardente',[159] 'une des chimères les plus ardemment caressées',[160] is so beautiful. 'Rêve de poète et d'artiste',[161] it is the product of pure art, the 'effort suprême de l'art',[162] and consequently far superior to anything that mediocre reality has to offer. In the 1890s, the Sâr Joséphin Péladan expresses the same notion when he says that, for beauty, a woman's body, the product of nature, is completely eclipsed by the androgyne, the creation of art:

> l'art a créé un être surnaturel, l'androgyne, auprès duquel Vénus disparaît.[163]

It must not be thought, however, that because it is the product of the mind, it is removed from sexuality or from lasciviousness. On the contrary. For the lechery which is associated with the pessimistic symbol of the androgyne is above all cerebral; indeed, cerebral lechery is the *vice suprême* which best characterizes the attitude of disillusionment and withdrawal from practical life which conditions the symbol. The desire of those disillusioned with exterior reality can be contented only by the mind, and consequently the fact that the hermaphrodite does not truly exist in reality otherwise than as the creation of the mind, of pure art, accounts not only for its beauty, but also for its voluptuousness. For Péladan, desire is satisfied only by art, this 'miroir magique où notre désir se satisfait'.[164] And according to Gautier's *Contralto*, the hermaphrodite, the supreme effort of art, is also the 'effort suprême [. . .] de la volupté'.

D'Albert and Maupin have in common with Chateaubriand, Musset and so many other contemporaries, a weariness of the world and of reality, which is accompanied by a vague longing for what is not and cannot be, for some exquisite emotion, some refined, intense passion. D'Albert confesses: 'J'attends,—quoi? Je ne sais, mais j'attends';[165] and Maupin writes: 'quelque chose d'inassouvi gronde toujours en moi'. This yearning, finding no suitable object and consequently no possible fulfilment in reality, can only become more intense. And the gulf between the ideal and the real can no longer be bridged once all the possibilities of pleasure offered by reality have been exhausted in the imagination by a desire still unsatisfied but with ever loftier aims. D'Albert discovers that to desire something too intensely is to kill desire for that particular thing, for when the objective is finally attained, it no longer matches an intensified desire. The moment must come when such a highly imaginative person is completely *blasé* on reality without ever having tasted of its pleasures. No sexual pleasure offered by reality could possibly satisfy the desire of such a *débauché*. And so, the ideal of sexual gratification rises high above reality. What vistas d'Albert's statement opens to the imagination:

> nous ne sommes plus au temps des métamorphoses;—Adonis et Hermaphrodite sont morts.[166]

The figure of the hermaphrodite, refused by reality, represents the sexual ideal of those two cerebral perverts d'Albert and Maupin—the one who, confessing to being possessed by the late Roman emperors' thirst for the impossible, exclaims: 'j'ai souhaité d'être femme pour connaître de nouvelles voluptés',[167] and the other: 'ma chimère serait d'avoir tour à tour les deux sexes [. . .] homme aujourd'hui, femme demain'. [168]

This particular perversion, cerebral lechery, is by no means incompatible with total sexual abstinence. Indeed, since 'l'abstinence use plus que l'excès',[169] it is the virgin who is capable of the greatest excesses in this respect. Maupin, for example, who is 'vierge,—vierge comme la neige de l'Himalaya'[170] exclaims:

> je suis possédée des plus violents désirs,—je languis et je meurs de volupté [. . .] une idée de plaisir qui ne se réalise jamais flotte vaguement dans ma tête [. . .] je reste chaste et vierge [. . .] au sein de la dissipation la plus éparpillée et entourée des plus grands débauchés du siècle.—Cette ignorance du corps que n'accompagne pas l'ignorance de l'esprit est la plus misérable chose qui soit.[171]

In *Mademoiselle de Maupin*, hermaphroditism is thus closely associated with virginity, not merely because the apparently androgynous Maupin remains a virgin until the last few pages of the novel, but also because if the hermaphrodite is the supreme object of cerebral lechery, the virgin is the supreme cerebral lecher. Indeed, as the century advances, in as far as both represent this special form of asexuality which consists in purely intellectual depravity, the hermaphrodite and the virgin become more and more confused in a single image.

This Decadent association of androgyny with asexuality and virginity seems to have completely escaped the attention of

Mircea Eliade, whose sweeping generalization about the image of the androgyne during the Decadence is quite unacceptable:

> Chez les écrivains décadents, l'androgyne est compris uniquement comme un hermaphrodite dans lequel les deux sexes coexistent anatomiquement et physiologiquement.[172]

Disillusionment with the realities of practical life and with human relationships, foreknowledge of the impossibility of finding satisfaction in the exterior world, withdrawal into the mind and consequent loneliness and frustration—all this is expressed by the tremendous vogue of cerebral lechery which constantly increased after *Mademoiselle de Maupin* until the end of the century and which found its most perfect symbol in the hermaphrodite, which was to dominate the 1890s.

In particular, it dominated the work of the Sâr Joséphin Péladan, which is not surprising since this work—and this consideration alone justifies the space devoted to it in this essay—represents the caricature of so many Decadent tendencies. As Anatole France observed, Péladan is 'hanté par l'idée de l'hermaphrodite qui inspire tous ses livres'.[173] One of the most important functions of Péladan's hermaphrodite is precisely to symbolize cerebral lechery. And this the hermaphrodite represents in Péladan's work in much the same way as it did in *Maupin*: that is to say, it appears as both the object and the subject of cerebral desire.

In the writings of Péladan, the hermaphrodite becomes the object of desire for those who can find no satisfaction in reality and yet whose desires only increase for not being satisfied. For them, the only satisfaction possible is to be found within their own minds, in lecherous fantasies; and among these fantasies the androgyne takes pride of place.

In order to measure fully the disillusionment of the Decadence symbolized by the androgyne, one can do no better than compare the attitude of a Balzac and a Péladan to physical love. In Balzac's *Béatrix* (1838), Claude Vignon explains to Camille Maupin that love is:

> un royaume idéal, plein de sentiments nobles, de grandes petitesses, de poésie, de sensations spirituelles, de dévouements, de fleurs morales, d'harmonies enchanteresses, et situé bien au-dessus de grossièretés vulgaires [. . .].[174]

And elsewhere, Balzac can speak of: 'l'infini rendu palpable et transporté dans les plus excessives jouissances de la créature'.[175] Such an attitude, of course, is not constant in Balzac, and one may doubt his sincerity. Nevertheless, he expresses the extremely widespread early nineteenth-century thirst for the infinite in love, and the current elevation of absolute communion, of devotion to the beloved, to the status of sacrament. Nearly a half century later, however, Péladan's intellectual *débauché* Guy de Quéant replies:

> A tout chercheur d'impossible, la déception est due [. . .] nous demandons à la même femme vice et vertu, lasciveté et pudeur; nous cherchons en elle l'infini, et elle ne peut donner qu'un spasme.[176]

And, in the same novel, Mérodack scoffs: 'Chercher l'infini entre les deux draps d'un lit, est-ce pas risée?'[177]

This dissatisfaction and disillusionment with the exterior world is accompanied by refusal of contact with it, by physical sexual abstinence. The Princess d'Este, a 'vivante allégorie de la décadence latine',[178] is completely ignorant of the sin of the flesh:

> Il est encore un inconnu pour elle, la sensation sexuelle. Mariée, courtisée, elle ne sait pas le plaisir du péché.[179]

Indeed she is: 'satisfaite, dans le soin de sa gloire, d'être indemne des ivresses animales de la sexualité'. Since all that reality offers is so mediocre, the principal consideration is to preserve one's mind and one's dreams from contamination, by refusing contact with the exterior world. After defining his art of visual possession, De Quéant says:

> Jamais satisfait, oui, mais jamais dégoûté. Rien de la possession ne vient ternir mon beau rêve érotique.[180]

And, according to Léonora d'Este:

> L'amour doit être un rêve voluptueux, une parole troublante, un désir aigu, une sensation commencée, pas plus.[181]

Moreover, Mérodack's disillusionment with past sexual experiences and his awareness that his imagination is so intense that it will never be matched by reality, inspire him with this comment on the impossibility of happiness in love:

> Mon rêve dépassera toute réalité, toujours [. . .] J'ai le cœur à la tête, je suis le fiancé des idées [. . .].[182]

Since, for the refined, reality offers so little gratification, true satisfaction can be enjoyed only in one's own mind, in the imagination. Therefore, the ideal love-affair is that of the 'androgyne' Samas and the 'gynandre' Stelle in Péladan's novel *L'Androgyne* (1891). Stelle exhibits herself naked morning and night at her window in the most indecent postures, while, across the street:

> Samas dyspeptisé par ses tisanes, son bromure et ses infusions de nénufar est fier: il reçoit l'initiation sexuelle sans un contact.[183]

Indeed, Samas has understood:

> *que la volupté saine est celle de l'esprit, et qu'au delà du rêve le dégoût seul existe.*[184]

However, although fully aware that reality cannot satisfy his craving, the cerebral pervert does not cease to desire. On the contrary; continually unsatisfied and continually solicited, his desires only become stronger, fix on to ever loftier ideals. Aubrey Beardsley's characters want, in the words of Arthur Symons:[185] 'more pleasure than there is in the world, fiercer and more exquisite pains, a more intolerable suspense'. Léonora d'Este rejects all men without ever having experienced pleasure; she spurns reality without tasting it, convinced of its inferiority to her ideal pleasure. Her mind alone is active: 'La tête remplissait les emplois de tout l'être [. . .]'.[186] And so, in spite of her physical chastity, she has: 'son âme pleine de passion, son corps pétri de désirs'.[187] Indeed, she is racked with passion:

> Le baiser du bouc se donne aussi avec la pensée [. . .]
>
> Elle a ce cauchemar: l'obscénité des choses. Des boucs, louchant de lubricité, brisent leurs cornes en des caresses furieuses: une phallophorie enfiévrée défile; et se déroulent les frises intérieures d'un temple de Priape [. . .]

And, after this nightmare of desire:

> Fébrile, énervée, haletante, le regard troublé, elle laisse pendre ses bras dans une dépression épuisée.[188]

Divorced from reality, her desires, like those of Maupin and d'Albert, are so intensified that they fasten on to the dream of the androgyne, the supreme object of the mental erethist:

> Oh! Etre deux! deux cœurs et le même battement, deux esprits et la même pensée, deux corps et le même désir.

> Ces deux cœurs fondus en une adoration, ces deux esprits unis en une admiration, ces deux corps enlacés en une délectation.
>
> Deux! la voix et l'écho. Deux! l'existence double! un être ajouté à son être; en soi deux, à côté du désir la satisfaction; le rêve saint de l'androgyne réalisé selon les lois, la création initiale retrouvée.[189]

The androgyne thus appears as the supreme object of cerebral desire and consequently may be considered as a symbol of mental erethism. However, mental erethism is symbolized in yet another way by the figure of the androgyne: for the subject, the cerebral lecher himself, is regarded during the Decadence as androgynous.

In appearance, Princess d'Este possesses some of the characteristics of the male: Péladan insists on her flat chest and narrow hips.[190] However, her androgyny is not so much to be attributed to this partial bisexuality as to a basic asexuality. Her possession of male characteristics may also be regarded as a lack of the corresponding female characteristics: the Princess d'Este thus appears to be without certain attributes of the sex to which she should belong, and consequently, considered from this point of view, she is to a considerable extent sexless. Nor does her asexuality derive from this cause alone; in a more general way, she is sexless because her lecherous fantasies cause her to spurn the realities of sex, because with regard to the exterior world, her life is completely asexual. Thus, the cerebral lecher, in as far as his mental erethism renders him physically continent, may be considered without sex.

Asexuality, however, has always been synonymous with androgyny in the long tradition, followed by Ballanche for example, which regarded the primitive Adam as sexless and sex as the result of the Fall. And so, during the Decadence, the cerebral lecher, because of his apparent asexuality, was regarded as an androgyne. In the work of Gustave Moreau, for example, sexlessness and lasciviousness are often characteristically fused in androgynous-looking figures.

The asexuality associated with mental erethism may also be seen in the androgynous faces drawn by Pre-Raphaelites such as Burne-Jones and Simeon Solomon, in whose works, as in those of Moreau, it is often impossible to distinguish a man from a woman. Here, asexuality and consequently androgyny are to a large extent the result of the mental exhaustion of the cerebral lecher. A. Symons observes of Solomon's drawings:

> These faces are without sex; they have brooded among ghosts of passions till they have become the ghosts of themselves; the energy of virtue or of sin has gone out of them, and they hang in space, dry, rattling, the husks of desire.[191]

The Decadent association of lasciviousness and continence found its extreme expression in the cult of the virgin as the logically pre-eminent lecher. Thanks to her absolute continence, which she would thus owe to superlative mental erethism, the virgin appeared supremely asexual and consequently supremely androgynous. In Rachilde's novel *Monsieur Vénus* (1884), for example, the physically chaste and mentally perverted Raoule de Vénérande is tormented by desire for a love as asexual as herself, an 'amour étrange n'ayant pas de sexe et procurant toutes les voluptés'. And during the Decadence, Rachilde herself—or, to call her by her real name, Marguerite Eymery—was considered equally lascivious, virginal and androgynous as the characters she created. In his preface to the 1889 edition of *Monsieur Vénus*, Barrès marvels at: 'Ce vice savant éclatant dans le rêve d'une vierge';[192] and Jean Lorrain, also dwelling on her combination of mental erethism and virginity ('Couche-t-elle?—Non, chaste, mais elle a dans son cerveau une alcôve . . .'), stresses her androgynous appearance: 'Une pensionnaire [. . .] au profil grave d'éphèbe grec ou de jeune Français amoureux'.[193] Moreover, if Gustave Moreau's Salomés—who provide, according to Huysmans, the best representation of the Decadent 'femme vierge et lubrique'[194]—do not exhibit their androgyny physically, its presence in their world is at least hinted at by the figure of the hermaphrodite who appears in both the water-colour *L'Apparition* (1876) and the oil-painting *Salomé* (1870). Huysmans himself, in his famous description of *Salomé*, did not omit to mention:

> l'hermaphrodite ou l'eunuque qui se tient, le sabre au poing, en bas du trône, une terrible figure, voilée jusqu'aux joues, et dont la mamelle de châtré pend, de même qu'une gourde, sous sa tunique bariolée d'orange.[195]

Of all Decadents, however, Péladan was the most systematic in his identification of virginity and androgyny—an identification which, as will be shown below, forms the foundation of his peculiarly perverse idealism. According to his novel *L'Androgyne*:

> l'androgyne n'existe qu'à l'état vierge: à la première affirmation du sexe, il se résout au mâle ou au féminin.[196]

But androgyny is quite compatible with cerebral sexuality: it ceases only with the loss of virginity. Samas, androgynous as long as he was content with purely cerebral sexual relations, becomes a man as his desire for physical contact increases: 'O l'horreur, androgyne, de se sentir devenir homme'.[197] And when on the point of having intercourse with Yvette, he is overcome with grief: 'de sentir l'androgyne mourir, de devenir l'homme horrible et sexuel'.[198]

The cerebral lecher and the virgin, then, are considered as hermaphrodites because of their continence, which is regarded as asexuality; but they are androgynous also on account of their solitary self-sufficiency. For cerebral lechery can be and indeed was considered as a kind of onanism; and onanism naturally implies the notion of self-sufficiency which has so frequently been one of the dominant elements in the conception of the androgyne.[199] Huysmans, indeed, in his description of the exhibition of the Moreau water-colours identifies cerebral lechery with 'spiritual' onanism:

> Une impression identique surgissait de ces scènes diverses, l'impression de l'onanisme spirituel, répété dans une chair chaste; l'impression d'une vierge, pourvue dans un corps d'une solennelle grâce, d'une âme épuisée par des idées solitaires, par des pensées secrètes, d'une femme, assise en elle-même, et se radotant, dans de sacramentelles formules de prières obscures, d'insidieux appels aux sacrilèges et aux stupres, aux tortures et aux meurtres.[200]

And in Péladan's *Vice suprême*, Mérodack denounces cerebral lechery as a form of masturbation:

> 'toutes ces imaginations se polluent. Oh! l'onanisme immonde de la pensée [. . .] l'âme titillant le corps! L'ivrognerie des sens est hideuse; l'emportement organique, honteux; mais cela! cela! c'est le *vice suprême*'.[201]

The mentally lascivious virgin may then well be, in the words of Gustave Moreau: 'dégoûtee de toute satisfaction de ses désirs',[202] for her desires are in themselves their own satisfaction; like Narcissus, she has the self-sufficiency of the androgyne and needs no sort of communication with the exterior world, with this disappointing, inferior reality. Mary, in Rachilde's novel *La Marquise de Sade* (1887), says:

> j'ai horreur de l'homme en général [. . .] De plus, *je suis assez*, EN ÉTANT [. . .]'.[203]

The cerebral lecher's solitary self-sufficiency was indicated not only by this special kind of onanism, but also, on occasion, by the practice of demoniality. Consequently, the androgyne, as a symbol of this self-sufficiency, represented the demonialist just as much as the onanist. Demoniality, indeed, provides an extreme example of the cerebral lecher's perpetual and ecstatic communion with himself, represented so well by the ideal of the androgyne; it is, Péladan explains in *Le Vice suprême*:

> le péché lettré, patricien et décadent par excellence [. . .] c'est la copulation des hommes avec les démons succubes, des femmes avec des démons incubes [. . .] la démonialité est une œuvre de chair qui consiste à s'exalter l'imagination, en fixant son désir sur un être mort, absent ou inexistant.[204]

During the Decadence, demoniality was fairly widely publicized by word and image, and frequently associated with androgyny. Henriette Maillat, for example, who, together with Berthe Courrière, instructed Huysmans in the occult, and who served as a model for Péladan's androgynous Princess d'Este, managed at first to resist Huysmans' advances by claiming that her initiation into the mysteries of incubus and succubus rendered his physical presence, and that of any other man, quite unnecessary.[205] And the abbé Boullan, founder of a religion centred on the principle of androgyny, used to exorcise nuns visited by devils by expounding obscure rites which would enable them to be possessed instead by saints, or even by himself.[206]

Towards the end of the nineteenth century, the mentally lascivious woman frequently appeared as an *allumeuse*. Madame Livitinof, for example, in Jean Lorrain's *Très russe* (1886), who represents, as Mario Praz has observed,[207] 'the type of the *allumeuse*', considers that: 'la chasteté est l'extrême désir'. Naturally, the *allumeuse*, as a cerebral lecher, is sometimes presented as an androgyne—as, for example, in the ambiguous form of Princess d'Este, of whom Barbey d'Aurevilly says: 'Elle n'avait soif que des désirs qu'elle allumait [. . .]'.[208]

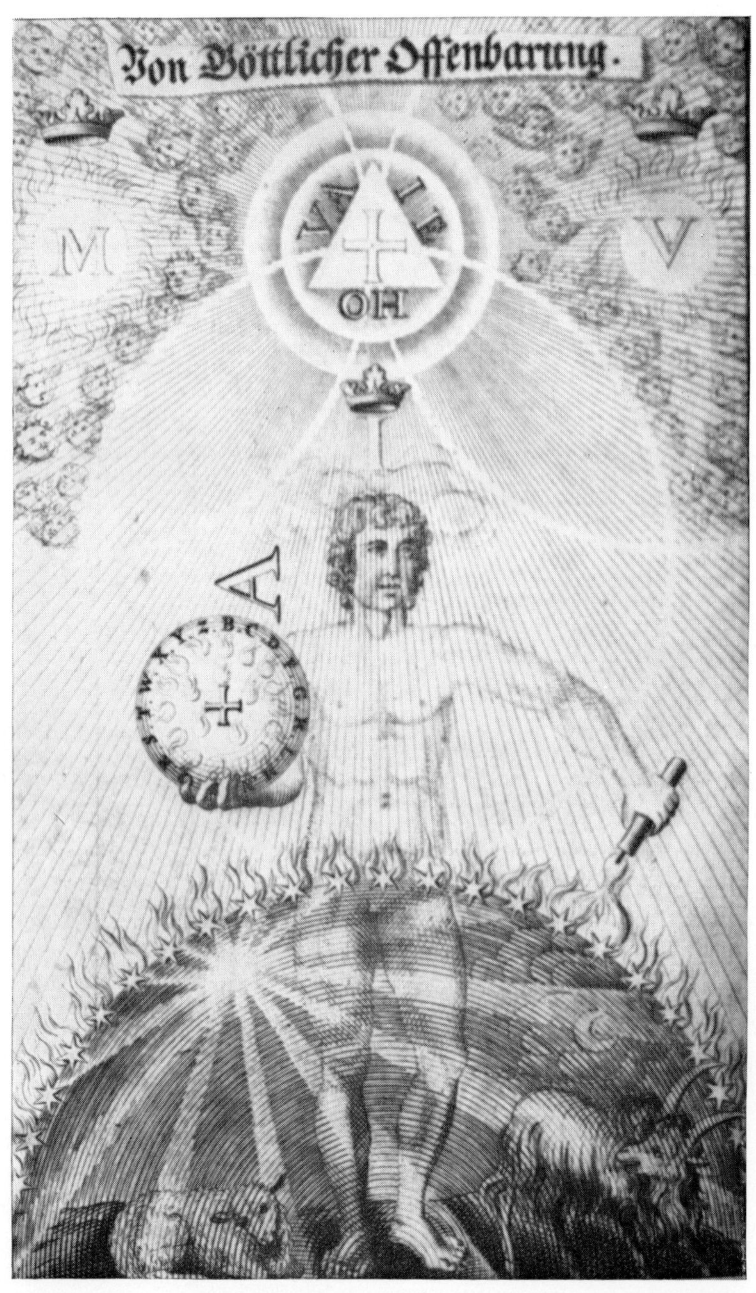


Boehme's *Adam:* from *Titul-Figur von Göttlicher Offenbahrung in 177. Theosophischen Fragen*, Amsterdam, 1682

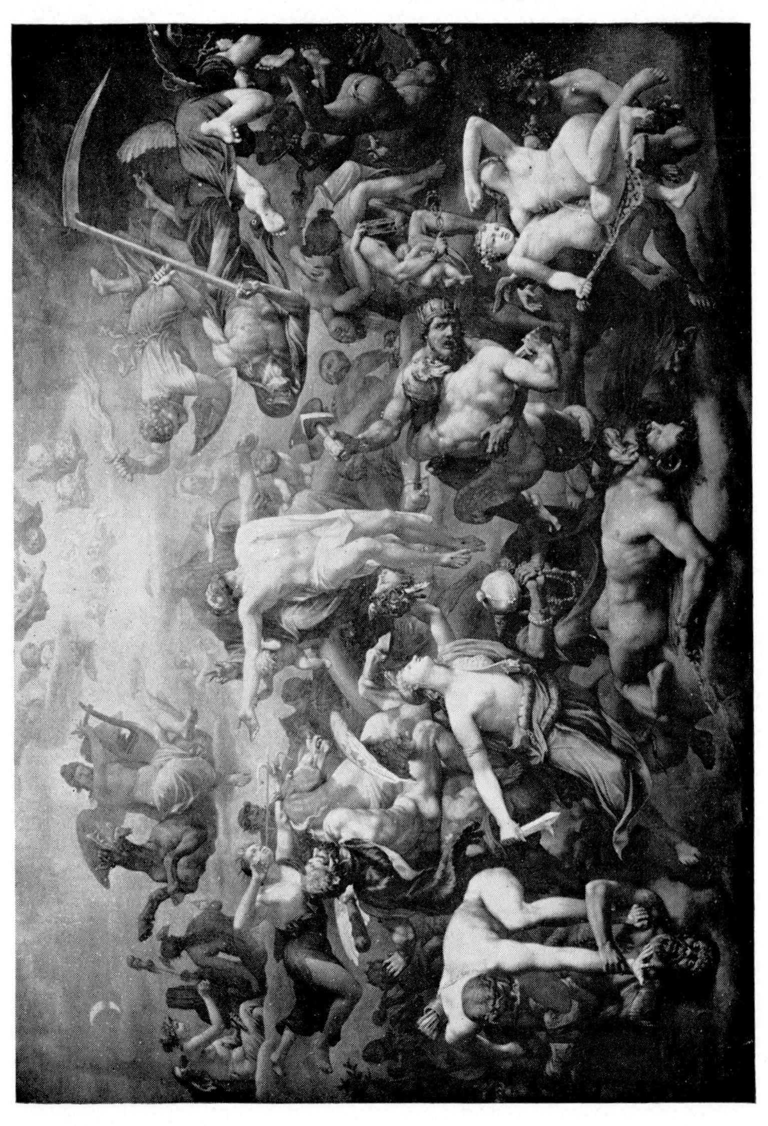

Paul Chenavard: *Divina Tragédia*. Musée du Luxembourg

*Le Mapah. D'après Traviès (vers 1834) :* from Champfleury, *Les Vignettes romantiques*, Paris, 1883, p. 239

*Overleaf* Simeon Solomon: *The Singing of Love* (1870). Museum and Art Gallery, Birmingham

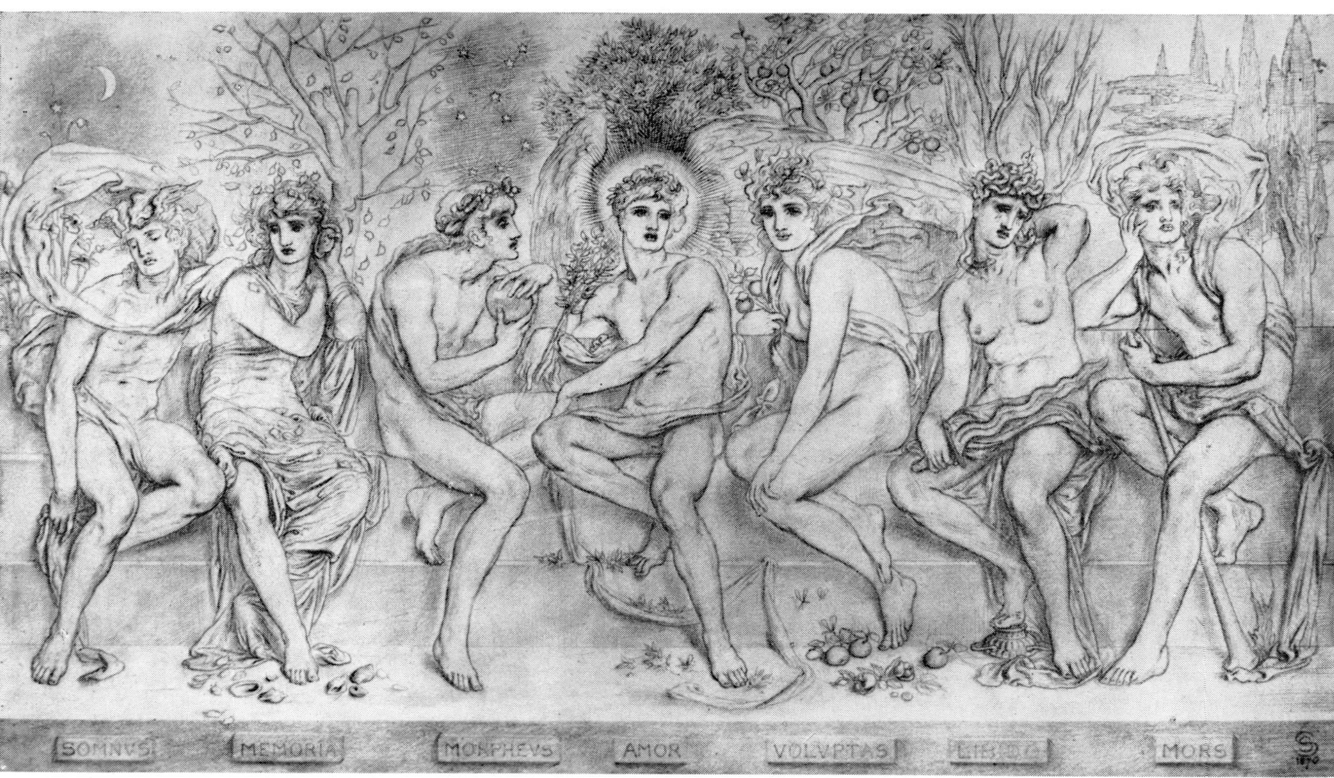
SOMNVS
MEMORIA
MORPHEVS
AMOR
VOLVPTAS
LIBIDO
MORS
SS
1870

Simeon Solomon: *Night and Sleep* (1888). Museum and Art Gallery, Birmingham

Leonardo da Vinci: *Saint John the Baptist.* Louvre

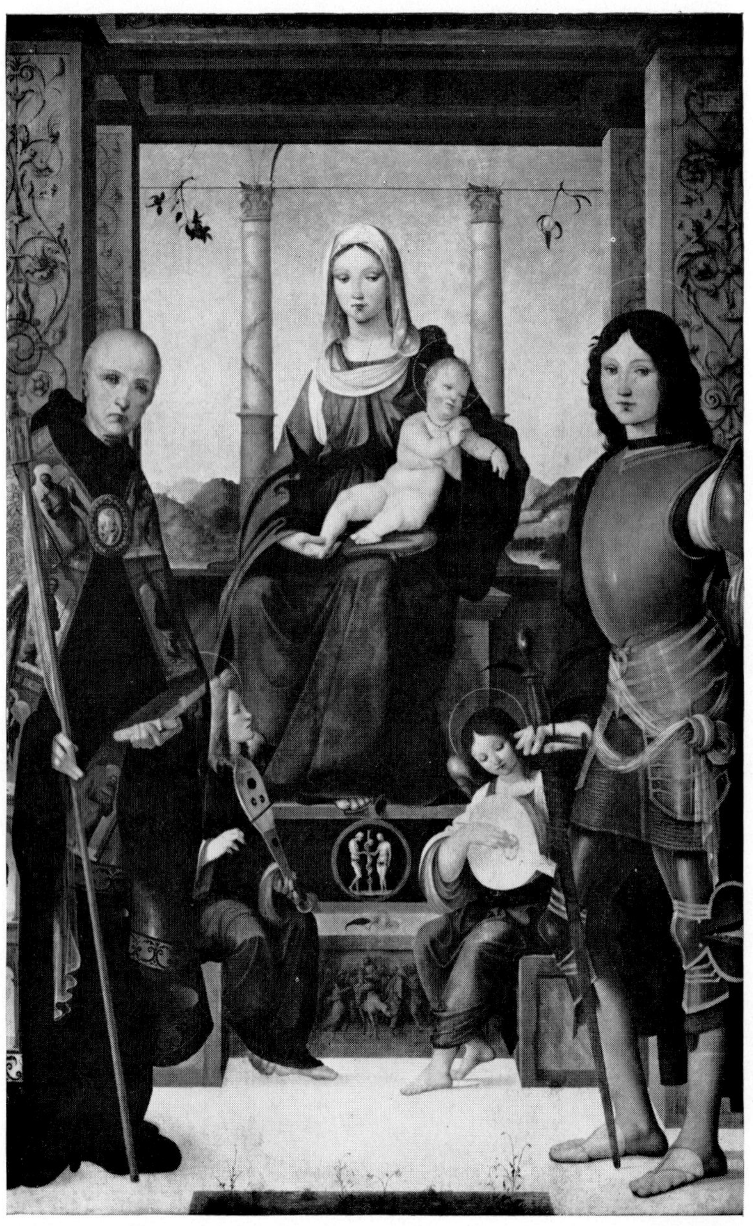

Alessandro Araldi: *Virgin and Saints*. Louvre

The cerebral lecher thus combines lasciviousness with continence, and this sinful purity or virtuous depravity,[209] like the *allumeuse*'s 'murderous chastity',[210] is symptomatic of an age without convictions or values, and consequently often incapable of distinguishing between right and wrong. Thanks to its link with cerebral lechery, and also because its constant connection with such vices as demoniality, onanism, homosexuality and sadism did not always obscure its celestial nature,[211] the androgyne which earlier had symbolized the triumph of good over evil, now often represented the ambivalence of good and evil. During the Decadence, indeed, in both art and literature, sexual ambiguity and moral ambiguity were frequently associated. The androgynous characters of Gustave Moreau and Simeon Solomon, for example, seem, as has already been noted, too weary to distinguish any longer between good and evil; and such people, who might be either men or women, were seen to be potentially both saints and sinners. Péladan's Princess d'Este, because of her androgynous appearance, could serve as a model both for Perversity and for Saint Michael;[212] and in the drawings of Simeon Solomon, as Arthur Symons observes:

> The same face, varied a little in mood, scarcely in feature, serves for Christ and the two Marys, for Sleep and for Lust. The lips are scarcely roughened to indicate a man, the throats scarcely lengthened to indicate a woman.[213]

The Decadent association of hermaphroditism with the ambivalence of good and evil is perhaps most pronounced in perverse interpretations of Primitive and Renaissance paintings depicting apparently androgynous saints. Since Walter Pater's *Studies in the Renaissance* (1873), Leonardo da Vinci's *Saint John the Baptist* was particularly subject to such perverse criticism. In his essay on Leonardo, insisting on the apparent contradiction between subject and mood in his paintings, which made it 'that though he handles sacred subjects continually, he is the most profane of painters', Pater said that very often the purpose or expression of an original Leonardo was brought out more clearly in the variations produced by his pupils.

> It is so with the so-called Saint John the Baptist of the Louvre—one of the few naked figures Lionardo painted—whose delicate brown flesh and woman's hair no one would go out into the wilder-

> ness to seek, and whose treacherous smile would have us understand something far beyond the outward gesture or circumstance. But the long, reedlike cross in the hand, which suggests Saint John the Baptist, becomes faint in a copy at the Ambrosian Library, and disappears altogether in another in the Palazzo Rosso at Genoa. Returning from the last to the original, we are no longer surprised by Saint John's strange likeness to the Bacchus which hangs near it [. . .].[214]

The sexual and moral ambiguity of Leonardo's *Saint John*, underlined by Pater, became almost a commonplace in *fin de siècle* literature. Péladan, for example, after maintaining that on account of its harmonizing of female grace with male strength the androgyne was the supremely artistic sex, went on:

> Dans le *Saint-Jean* la mixture des formes est telle, que le sexe devient une énigme. . . .[215]

in his *Hymne à l'Androgyne*, he made the following invocations: 'Anges de Signorelli, S. Jean de Léonard';[216] and, in the same novel, *l'Androgyne*, he associated Saint John's sexual ambiguity with perversity:

> Le sourire qui vibre aux lèvres du saint Jean glissa sur la bouche de Samas [. . .] l'androgyne avait vaincu.[217]

Two years later, Pauline Tarn (alias Renée Vivien) wrote in her poem *Donna m'apparve* in *La Vénus des aveugles* (1903):

> Vois! l'ambiguité des ténèbres évoque
> Le sourire pervers d'un saint Jean équivoque.

Huysmans also, in his art criticism, frequently underlines a relationship between the sexual ambiguity and the moral ambiguity of the androgyne. In his essay on Bianchi, for example, published in *Certains* (1889), Huysmans enthuses over the ambiguous figure of Saint Quintin in a *Virgin and Saints* which he attributes to Bianchi but which in reality is by Alessandro Araldi:

> Et l'aspect entier du saint fait rêver. Ces formes de garçonne, aux hanches un peu développées, ce col de fille, aux chairs blanches ainsi qu'une moelle de sureau, cette bouche aux lèvres spoliatrices, cette taille élancée, ces doigts fureteurs égarés sur une arme, ce renflement de la cuirasse qui bombe à la place des seins et protège la chute divulguée du buste, ce linge qui s'aperçoit sous l'aisselle

> demeurée libre entre l'épaulière et le gorgerin, même ce ruban bleu de petite fille, attaché sous le menton, obsèdent. Toutes les assimilations éperdues de Sodome paraissent avoir été consenties par cet androgyne dont l'insinuante beauté, maintenant endolorie, se révèle purifiée déjà, comme transfigurée par la lente approche d'un Dieu [. . .] un hermaphrodite cuirassé de fer, un chevalier qui, après avoir été affamé de tracas luxurieux, agonise sous le poids de ses peines.[218]

The image of the androgyne thus represents the frequent confusion of good and evil characteristic of this age deprived of values and convictions. However, this mingling of all contraries in a vague, confused unity, which shows just how vain must be any hope of choosing the correct course of action, found expression in yet another theme also symbolized by the androgyne and extremely widespread during the Decadence: incest. In the paintings of Moreau and Simeon Solomon, for example, since the same face is so little varied when used to show a different sex, it is often difficult to distinguish between a man and a woman; for the same reason, it is possible that a pair of lovers could be brother and sister, or even two brothers or two sisters. Moreover, Huysmans, in his study of the *Virgin and Saints* just mentioned, imagines the androgynous Saint Quintin implicated in incest:

> Et alors l'on s'aperçoit que toutes [ces hautes figures] se ressemblent. On dirait du saint Benoît, le père, de Marie et du saint Quentin, la sœur et le frère, et du petit ange vêtu de rose jouant de la viole d'amour, l'enfant issu du diabolique accouplement de ces Saints. Le vieillard est un père qui a résisté aux aguets d'épouvantables stupres, et dont le fils et la fille ont cédé aux tentations de l'inceste et jugent la vie trop brève pour expier les terrifiantes délices de leur crime; l'enfant implore le pardon de son origine, et chante de dolentes litanies pour détourner la souveraine colère du Très-Haut.[219]

The association of androgyny and incest was by no means new. Marie Delcourt has pointed out the connection between the androgyne image and brother-sister incest in Greek and Roman mythology, in primitive societies, and in alchemy;[220] and C. G. Jung derives the theme of incest from the androgyne archetype. However, the perverse Decadent presentation of the incest associated with the androgyne could scarcely differ more from these early myths and primitive practice, in which the principal considerations were the preservation of the purity of the race, and the recomposition of the original unity by imitation of the initial incest of Heaven and Earth.[221] Like the image of the androgyne with which it is so frequently connected, incest may vary in significance from one age to another.

That the image of the hermaphrodite should symbolize the confusion of good and evil is, of course, to a certain extent a reflection of the artistic climate: if art has no other end than itself, and if, artistically, good and evil are meaningless words, then the hermaphrodite, as a product of pure art, must be beyond and above good and evil. However, if *l'art pour l'art* ignored any distinction between good and evil, after Baudelaire the more decadent poets frequently tended towards a positive identification of evil and beauty. Accordingly, the supremely beautiful hermaphrodite could well appear supremely evil. But the hermaphrodite was a symbol of evil not just for those impressed by its grace; in a more general way, it represented evil for those who looked for evil in everything, and usually found it. Widespread conviction of the absence of values was accompanied by impatience with those who still believed in the existence of values. This impatience was manifested on the one hand by the desire to expose the hollowness of conventional morality and to dwell on the prevalence of vice, often in works of realism; on the other hand, it found expression in an attitude of revolt which, springing not only from the desire to shock bourgeois complacency, but also very often from dissatisfaction and despair, called for total immersion in evil and vice.

The religion founded by the abbé Joseph-Antoine Boullan, which flourished in Lyon during the '80s, was a sign of the times; in it, the hermaphrodite became the symbol of and excuse for the wildest promiscuity. Embroidering on the age-old tradition which regarded marriage as reconstructing the primitive androgyny of man and as restoring him thereby to his former perfection, Boullan taught that promiscuous sexual intercourse presented the only road to salvation, and that consequently it was the '*Sacrement des sacrements*'. In the second volume of his *Essais de sciences maudites* (1891), Stanislas de Guaita resumed in this way the religion of Boullan (to whom he gave the pseudonym of 'Dr Baptiste'):

> L'union des sexes, restitutive de l'androgynat (qui fut l'état édénal) a pour éternel symbole l'arbre même de la Science du Bien et du Mal [. . .]
>
> Hors des *unions*, point de salut. Tous les hommes, dans la secte, possèdent toutes les femmes, et réciproquement. Ce communisme de l'amour fait partie intégrante de la religion: l'autel est un lit; l'hymne sainte, un chant d'universel épithalame; le baiser est un acte sacerdotal et qui s'étend à tous les êtres [. . .]

In short, Boullan's temple was 'un lupanar sacré'.[222]

As a symbol of evil and vice, however, the hermaphrodite represented not only promiscuity, but indeed all sorts of perversions: besides cerebral lechery, onanism, demoniality and incest, which have already been mentioned, it symbolized homosexuality, sadism and masochism.

The tremendous vogue of homosexuality and of Lesbianism in particular during the nineteenth century is well known:[223] celebrated from Gautier through Baudelaire, Swinburne and Verlaine to Conder and Péladan, it seemed to be constantly extending its appeal. This extremely widespread vice found an apt symbol in the image of the androgyne, with which it had a very ancient connection. In Plato's *Banquet*, as we saw above, both male and female homosexuality was associated by Aristophanes with the myth of the androgyne; and the later Greek representations of Hermaphrodite unite those characteristics of both sexes which were the erogenous zones *par excellence* for a civilization whose libido was centred on pederasty.[224] Moreover, among both male and female homosexuals, certain ones may be considered androgynous in so far as they combine the nature and function of different sexes, or the physical characteristics of one sex with the psychological characteristics of the other. This androgyny of homosexuals is particularly evident during the nineteenth century in the numerous novels—such as Gautier's *Mademoiselle de Maupin* or Balzac's *La Fille aux yeux d'or*—which present one person in relationships with members of both sexes. However, homosexuals appeared as hermaphrodites in many other places as well: Huysmans, for example, in the quotation reproduced above, found Sodom expressed in the androgynous Saint Quintin; and Péladan's *Vice suprême* introduced the flat-chested, narrow-hipped Lesbian Lady Astor, *née* Claire Pitau and labelled Nino-Nina (after Balzac's Séraphîtüs-Séraphîta), 'l'androgyne pâle, vampire suprême des civilisations vieillies, dernier monstre avant le feu du ciel'.[225] It should be mentioned in passing that here, as often in his works, Péladan does not observe the distinction he established in *La Gynandre* between the terms *androgyne* and *gynandre*, according to which the former designates: 'l'adolescent vierge et encore féminin', and the latter: 'la femme prétendant à la mâleté, l'usurpatrice sexuelle: le féminin singeant le viril'—not only the Lesbian, but 'toute tendance de femme à faire l'homme: et cela s'entend d'une mademoiselle de Maupin comme d'un bas-bleu'.[226]

In addition to homosexuality, the hermaphrodite symbolized two more vices which flourished during the nineteenth century and were intimately connected with the general decay of ideals: sadism and masochism. There is obviously nothing androgynous about a male sadist or a female masochist; but a sadistic woman, in as far as she dominates her male victim, may be considered virile, since she exhibits strength, a male characteristic; and her ability to indulge in her vice depends to a large extent on the male's abdication of his own virility, his masochistic willingness to be ruled—even tormented—by the female showing a weakness of character generally associated with effeminacy. His refusal to assert himself often indicates awareness of the vanity of all action, which must accompany loss of convictions in a world without values, where good is often indistinguishable from evil. It is therefore not surprising that male masochism and its necessary counterpart, female sadism, should be associated so frequently with the attitude of despair and disillusionment reflected in the pessimistic symbol of the androgyne. Halley des Fontaines has shown that already in German Romanticism, male masochism was associated with androgyny: Wilhelm von Humboldt's desire to be dominated by his wife was related to a purely psychological bisexuality which helps to explain his aesthetics centred on the androgyne ideal.[227] On the other hand, the androgyny of the female sadist is above all evident in the Fatal Woman theme, which, as Mario Praz has shown in his *Romantic Agony*, flourished so extensively in the latter part of the nineteenth century. Cleopatra, who became the type of the *femme fatale*, is often endowed with male characteristics: Louis Bouilhet, for example, in his poem *Méloenis* (1851), presents her as the 'type éternel de grâce et de virilité'. Moreover, Ivan Gilkin, in his poem *Amour d'Hôpital*, published in the collection *La Nuit* (1897), portrays a sadist with a 'mâle cœur' who, Praz observes, is 'a sort of *non plus ultra* of the Fatal Woman type'.[228] Salome too, whose hermaphroditism has already been remarked upon in this essay in other connections, seems the perfect example of the woman executioner, the 'bourreau de marbre' which Barbey d'Aurevilly finds in the androgynous Princess d'Este.[229]

Numerous are the works of the *fin de siècle* which present a couple of lovers whose sex has become so ambiguous that they may be considered a pair of androgynes. In his treatise *La Science de l'amour* (1911), Péladan observes that a 'troisième sexe', the category of the androgyne, is made up by those whose souls are of a different sex from their bodies. Finding an example of this androgyny in Wagner's treatment of the Tristan and Isolde legend, where: 'Yseult est l'homme et Tristan la femme', he wonders if Wagner knew that he was portraying 'le mythe très secret de l'androgyne'.[230] Péladan's own works, of course, provide many examples of such pairs of androgynes. In the strange affair between the effeminate painter Nebo and the masculine Princess Paule Riazan described in *A cœur perdu* (1888), the rôles of the sexes are completely reversed—as they are also in the purely cerebral relationship between the androgyne Samas and the gynander Stelle related in *L'Androgyne* (1891):

> *Gynandre, tu osas, agressive, saisir le rôle militant, tu fus le séducteur et non pas la maîtresse, tu fus l'amant.*[231]

Huysmans' *A Rebours* (1884) also, this 'breviary of the Decadence', tells of the infatuation of des Esseintes for the American Miss Urania, 'au corps bien découplé, aux jambes nerveuses, aux muscles d'acier, aux bras de fonte'. Des Esseintes could not understand the strange allurement she had for him, until he realized that as he watched her night after night at the circus, she gradually changed in his mind from a woman, first to an indistinct androgyne, and finally to a complete man.

> Alors, de même qu'un robuste gaillard s'éprend d'une fille grêle, cette clownesse doit aimer, par tendance, une créature faible, ployée, pareille à moi, sans souffle, se dit des Esseintes; à se regarder, à laisser agir l'esprit de comparaison, il en vint à éprouver, de son côté, l'impression que lui-même se féminisait, et il envia décidément la possession de cette femme, aspirant ainsi qu'une fillette

> chlorotique, après le grossier hercule dont les bras la peuvent broyer dans une étreinte. [232]

In the same year as *A Rebours*, Rachilde published her notorious *Monsieur Vénus*, which relates how a chubby, dimpled young man with his 'corps équivoque' is completely desexed by the virile Raoule de Vénérande. Barrès, in his analysis of the work written for the 1889 edition, observes that *Monsieur Vénus* is symptomatic of the 'maladie du siècle': for, underlying this denial of the characteristics of the sexes is the dream of an 'être insexué'.[233]

Cerebral lechery, onanism, demoniality, ambivalence of good and evil, incest, promiscuity, homosexuality, sadism and masochism—these elements of the pessimistic symbol of the androgyne, isolated above in order to facilitate rational analysis, rarely occur in isolation during the nineteenth century. In fact, on account of the intimate connection they all have with the attitude of disillusionment and despair which determines this particular image, several of these elements are almost always combined in the *fin de siècle* androgyne, either simultaneously or at different phases of the work in which it appears—as, for example, in the androgynous Princess d'Este, who is a cerebral lecher, a Narcissist virgin, a sadist, an *allumeuse*, a Fatal Woman and a Lesbian.

Thus far, the pessimistic symbol of the androgyne has shown itself to be concerned above all with sex and, unlike the optimistic symbol, perfectly comprehensible without reference to more or less complicated philosophical systems closely connected, on account of their three phases, with the esoteric Biblical tradition of Adam Kadmon. It would, however, be just as wrong to suppose that this later image of the androgyne owes its pessimism to its connection with sex and dissociation from complex philosophies and esoteric traditions, as to conclude that the earlier image was optimistic merely because it possessed such philosophical and Biblical connections. In the first place, since in certain images of the androgyne—those of Enfantin, the Mapah and the ex-abbé Constant, for example—sexual preoccupations were compatible with and even subordinate to social optimism, it is obviously not such preoccupations alone which stamp the later symbol as the product of an attitude of despair or as an indication of the decay of ideals, but on the one hand, the acceptance of sexual pleasure, real or imaginary, as a supreme value, and on the other hand, the cerebralization and perversion of sex. In the second place, what could be called, for the sake of convenience, 'pessimistic' androgynes are often associated with philosophies just as complex and equally influenced by Biblical traditions as those connected with 'optimistic' androgynes. If, for example, Leroux's optimistic androgyne reflects his version of transcendental idealism, the androgyne of Novalis, representing a different and rather more complex version of the same philosophy, must be considered, as will be shown below, fundamentally Decadent and pessimistic. And Péladan's interpretation of *Genesis*, which will be examined afterwards, provides the very foundation for his Decadent philosophy centred on the androgyne.

The philosophical system associated with the pessimistic symbol of the androgyne in the work of Novalis is indeed so complex that, for considerations of space, its detailed study must preclude examination of the many other and equally important manifestations of the image and conception of the androgyne during German Romanticism—for example, in the philosophies of Franz von Baader, Wilhelm von Humboldt and J. W. Ritter.

The philosophy of Novalis, which is dominated by the image of the androgyne, is a curious blend of transcendental idealism, Plotinism, magnetism, Herrnhut pietism, alchemy, and physics à la A. G. Werner. It follows the three phases of the mystical Christian tradition: unity, fall or rupture of unity and reintegration, which underlie most of the philosophical systems in which the androgyne appears.

Primitive man before the Fall—*der himmlische Urmensch*, as Novalis calls him[234]—was doubtless for the young poet an androgyne. But this androgyne united in his person not only the two sexes but also soul and body, self and non-self, spirit and nature, subject and object. According to Novalis's cosmogony, the period of the primitive, amorphous, unconscious chaos was in fact the Golden Age when there was no distinction between spirit and matter, no separation between individuals, when love and poetry reigned supreme and man, close to the natural sources of life, heard directly the voice of nature in his heart and possessed the gifts of magic and prophecy. This age of innocence did not last. A cataclysm took place which was for the whole universe what the Fall was for man: it represented the rupture of the primitive unity. The human soul became divided from nature; man was isolated in his own conscience, sacrificing spontaneity and joy to abstract science, with which he constructed an artificial universe to replace primitive, poetic nature. Nature also showed its isolation from man by becoming inhuman. The primitive unity of the universe was split into two antagonistic poles: subject and object, mind and body, spirit and matter. This antagonism is not permanent. The unity between man and nature will be re-established as soon as man has progressed sufficiently to discover his true place in nature, and when nature, in turn, thanks to art, has become more human. The synthesis of the two contradictory principles man and nature, spirit and matter, is represented in Novalis's work by the image of the hermaphrodite, by the union of a couple in a single androgynous body:

> Einst ist alles Leib,
> Ein Leib,
> In himmlischem Blute
> Schwimmt das selige Paar.[235]*

However, if the hermaphrodite thus symbolizes what is most important in Novalis's philosophy, it does so only ultimately and indirectly. More immediately, the hermaphrodite represents the union of the sexes, which occupies not only symbolically but also in its own right a central position in Novalis's system. Constantly, Novalis presents the image of the hermaphrodite as a symbol of eternal, ecstatic sexual union. The hermaphrodite of the *Geistliches Lied* just quoted, who symbolizes the reintegration, is consequently by no means asexual, but very actively bisexual, engaged in perpetual communion with himself:

> Nie sättigt die Liebe sich [. . .]
> Und so währet der Liebe Genuß
> Von Ewigkeit zu Ewigkeit.[236]†

Moreover, the union which Novalis's lovers demand is always so perfect, so eternal and so absolute as to necessitate their complete

* 'One day all will be *one* body; in heavenly blood the blissful couple will float.'

† 'Love will never be sated [. . .] and so the pleasure of love will last to all eternity.'

fusion into a single, androgynous body. In *Heinrich von Ofterdingen*, for example, Heinrich says to Mathilde:

> Mein ganzes Wesen soll sich mit dem deinigen vermischen. Nur die grenzenloseste Hingebung kann meiner Liebe genügen. In ihr besteht sie ja. Sie ist ja ein geheimnißvolles Zusammenfließen unsers geheimsten und eigenthümlichsten Daseyns. [237]*

A poem which was to have been placed in the second part of *Heinrich von Ofterdingen* suggests that the putrefaction of the body after death will make possible this longed-for blending of two people into a single, self-sufficient substance. In the grave:

> Immer wächst und blüht Verlangen
> Am Geliebten festzuhangen,
> Ihn im Innern zu empfangen,
> Eins mit ihm zu sein.
> Seinem Durste nicht zu wehren,
> Sich im Wechsel zu verzehren,
> Von einander sich zu nähren,
> Von einander nur allein.[238]†

During life, the realization of the hermaphrodite, the complete and permanent assimilation of the beloved into one's own body is made possible, in idea at least, by a highly imaginative interpretation of love in which the Biblical definition of marriage: *duo in carne uno* receives an unexpectedly literal application. Love, or at least sexual desire, Novalis says in a Fragment written about 1800, is really the appetite for human flesh:

> Ueber die Geschlechtslust, die Sehnsucht nach fleischlicher Berührung, das Wohlgefallen an nackenden Menschenleibern. Sollt es ein versteckter Appetit nach Menschenfleisch seyn?[239]‡

The beloved is thus ideally an object to be devoured and completely assimilated into one's own body in the satisfaction of

* 'My whole being shall mingle with yours. Only the most boundless abandonment can satisfy my love. For in that my love consists. It is a mysterious fusion of our most secret and most personal existences.'

† 'The desire ever increases and flourishes to cleave firmly to the beloved, to receive him in one's innermost being, and be one with him. Not to resist his thirst, to consume each other in the exchange, to feed on each other, on each other alone.'

‡ 'About sexual desire, the longing for carnal contact, the pleasure in naked human bodies. Can it be a concealed appetite for human flesh?'

sexual hunger. Conversely, all eating and drinking appear to Novalis as similar to the sexual act, as in the infantile 'cloacal' theory of birth described by Freud.[240] In such perspectives, the Last Supper assumes a special significance. Eating, drinking, sexual intercourse, the sacrament of communion—all these are connected with the *synthesizing* of man and woman into the androgyne:

> Synthesis von Mann und Weib. (Grund der Gastfreundschaft der Alten—Abendmahl; gemeinschaftliches Essen und Trinken ist eine Art Vereinigung, ein Generationsact.)[241]*

The sexual union symbolized by the hermaphrodite lies at the very heart of Novalis's system for love is the magical link which joins the self with the world; it is the reintegrating force which reduces spirit and matter, soul and nature, to unity. Love abolishes the distinction between spirit and matter in that, by magnifying the flesh, it spiritualizes it, and at the same time tends to materialize the spirit by inclining it towards the body. Above all, love alone can give man that knowledge of nature which will restore his unity with nature—and this is the lesson of the *Märchen* contained in *Die Lehrlinge zu Sais*. In this story, Novalis tells how, one fine day, Hyacinth is smitten with the love of science and leaves his beloved Rosenblüte in order to look for the temple of Isis and learn the secret of the mother of nature. When, after many wanderings, he finally reaches the temple and, in a dream, raises the veil of Isis—Rosenblüte falls into his arms.[242] The union of lovers, symbolized in its absolute, eternal state by the androgyne, thus appears as the means by which the primitive unity of spirit and nature will be restored.

However, at the same time as the hermaphrodite symbolizes the union of the sexes, it represents in addition the self-sufficient narcissist union with the self with which Novalis's philosophy is so preoccupied. For, through their relationship with the beloved, Novalis's lovers seek communion with themselves; and by possessing the beloved, they possess themselves. Like the union of the sexes which it underlies, this narcissism symbolized by the androgyne has itself in Novalis's work a philosophical founda-

* 'Synthesis of man and woman. (Foundation of the hospitality of the ancients —communion; communal eating and drinking is a sort of union, an act of generation.)'

tion. If a beloved person alone can give that knowledge of nature necessary for the restoration of the primitive unity, it is because he or she alone reflects the self. It is only within itself that the soul can find the true image of nature; it is consequently only by knowing itself that the soul can know nature:

> Nach innen geht der geheimnisreiche Weg. In uns oder nirgends ist die Ewigkeit mit ihren Welten, die Vergangenheit und Zukunft.*

Indeed:

> Selbstheit ist der Grund aller Erkenntniß.[243]†

However, since the soul can perceive itself only if it is reflected in nature, and since nature can be known only through love and sympathy, a beloved person alone effectively sends back the image of the self, which can then be adored and cherished. One of Novalis's fragments reads:

> Veredlung der Leidenschaft—durch Anwendung derselben als Mittel, durch freywillige Beybehaltung derselben als Vehikels einer schönen Idee, z.B. eines innigen Verhältnisses mit einem geliebten Ich.[244]‡

Nevertheless, the androgyne, in so far as it represents the joining of the couple, does not symbolize merely the means of communion with the self, but actually this very communion; for since, according to Novalis, the exterior world is exactly identical to the interior world, and the barrier separating individuals just as illusory as the dualism of spirit and nature, then the beloved not only reflects the self, but in fact *is* the self. The union of a couple, then, is not the fusion of two distinct entities, but the revelation of an underlying unity: and the androgyne which symbolizes this union merely reveals a pre-existent androgyny.

This philosophy is evident in many parts of Novalis's work and constantly associated with the conception of androgyny. It is clear, for example, from a *distique* which Novalis composed in 1798 and which provides an alternative ending to the Hyacinth and Rosenblüte *Märchen*, that the beloved and the self are

* 'The mysterious path leads within. In us or nowhere is eternity with its worlds, the past and future.'

† 'Selfhood is the basis of all perception.'

‡ 'Refinement of passion—through its use as a means, through its retention as the vehicle of a fine idea, e.g. of an intimate relationship with a beloved self.'

fundamentally identical and that, consequently, the reunion of the lovers represents the reintegration of Hyacinth's androgynous self:

> Einem gelang es—er hob den Schleier der Göttin zu Sais.
> Aber was sah er? Er sah—Wunder des Wunders—sich selbst.[237]*

And the same ideas are to be found in Novalis's speculations on alchemy. The alchemical couple whose total union in a single androgynous being symbolizes the philosopher's stone often appears in Novalis's work—for example as Heinrich and Mathilde in *Heinrich von Ofterdingen*, as Eros and Freya in Klingsohr's *Märchen* in the same novel, and as Hyacinth and Rosenblüte.[245] Now, according to Novalis's poem *Kenne dich selbst*, the philosopher's stone itself, the *Stein der Weisen*, is also the *Stein ewiger Weisheit*; and eternal wisdom is the Delphic 'Know thyself'. Thus the alchemical androgyne ultimately represents for Novalis that union with the self, that special form of hermaphroditism on which depends the return of the Golden Age.

As a symbol of the unity of self and non-self, Novalis's androgyne, like those of so many ancient cosmogonies, appears as a demiurge. For the whole universe must be the product of the creative imagination of this symbolically androgynous self—a fact which finally the self, dividing into subject and object, discovers by 'intellectual intuition'.[246]

Reminiscent of the identity of the Logos and Christ, Novalis's androgyne is not only the demiurge but also the Saviour. For if, as Novalis believes, the Redemption consists in the restoration of the unity of self and non-self, then the Redeemer, in Novalis's perspectives, is the beloved—just as in the ancient mystical Christian tradition which represented the union of the soul with Christ as a marriage. Depending on the sex of the possessor of this fortunate soul, Christ may be a man or a woman: the Messiah is both the Bride and the Bridegroom, in other words an androgyne. And he is androgynous for Novalis not only before the Redemption, when he is about to save both men and women, but also afterwards, as a consequence of this very Redemption which, as has been seen, consists precisely in the 'hermaphroditization' of each part of the couple. Thanks to Novalis's confusion of Sophie

* 'One succeeded—he raised the veil of the goddess of Sais. But what did he see? He saw—wonder of wonders—himself.'

von Kühn and Christ, the Messiah is so much a hermaphrodite that he appears as both a man and a woman in the same sentence:

Hinunter zu der süßen Braut,
Zu Jesus, dem Geliebten.[247]*

Wirst du nur das ganze Herz ihm zeigen,
Bleibt er, wie ein treues Weib, dir eigen.[248]†

Since Redemption is equivalent to the restoration of the primitive androgyny, the person united with the hermaphrodite Christ himself becomes an hermaphrodite. But the union of the human hermaphrodite and the hermaphrodite Christ produces a single entity itself androgynous—or rather the removal of the illusory barrier between the human hermaphrodite and the hermaphrodite Christ reveals the existence of a single entity which is at once the human hermaphrodite, the hermaphrodite Christ and the Redeemer of Nature.

Novalis owes much to medieval German mysticism which appears, as represented by Meister Eckart for example, as a sort of pantheistic monism, very similar to neo-Platonism. For Plotinus, Dionysius the Areopagite and medieval mystics, God is the pure unity admitting of no distinction, a sort of non-being, a nothingness or abyss into which the mystic's soul falls, losing its personality, its individuality.[249] On the other hand, the world is the image of God; and all creation contains the Spirit. Deep down at the bottom of the soul is an uncreated spark which is God. The Spirit lives in every soul, unites all humanity into a single being, a single soul which is God. Contemplate yourself, your own soul, and you not only live in God, you are God.[250]

For Novalis, Christ is thus the Whole, the Universal Soul, 'the Spirit of the Earth';[251] he is the Christ-community, the 'christliche Gemeinde', as Hiebel says.[252] But as the Universal Soul, he is also the self; so that union with Christ is in reality union with the self. Moreover, by this union, the soul becomes Christ. The hermaphrodite thus symbolizes this passage of the soul to Christ with which Novalis's *Hymnen an die Nacht* are concerned.

The Messiah, however, redeems not only individuals, but also the universe. For nature has suffered the same fate as man,

* 'Down to the darling bride, to Jesus, the beloved.'

† 'If you will only show him all your heart, like a faithful wife he will remain your own.'

having lost its primitive unity and been divided into spirit and matter. Its unity can be restored only when it again becomes conscious of itself; but it is in its own image alone, in man, that nature can manifest and see itself. And so the hermaphrodite, as a symbol of the union of the self and the non-self, represents also the *Messias der Natur*. In the work of Novalis, the androgyne is in fact a symbol of the total reintegration of all things.

Situated at the very heart of his philosophy, the androgyne thus represents the object of all Novalis's aspirations. It is therefore to be expected that what has always been regarded as the symbol of Novalis's yearnings, and by extension of the yearnings of the Romantics in general—the famous 'blue flower' of *Heinrich von Ofterdingen*—should itself be associated with the androgyne image. We learn of the exact shade of this enigmatic bloom when Heinrich compares Mathilde, who is identified with it,[253] to a priceless sapphire.[254] Precisely, in works of alchemy one finds the image of the 'sapphire blue flower of the hermaphrodite'.[255]

What characterizes Novalis's androgyne as a Decadent image? Above all the rejection of life and the withdrawal into the mind which it represents. In the work of Novalis, the androgyne reflects the conviction of the worthlessness of what is generally accepted as the real world, and retreat from this inferior reality into a dream world, into the marvellous past of the Middle Ages, into the world of the fairy tale—above all into the self. Love is as essential to the magic idealism of Novalis as it is to the social idealism of certain French Romantic philosophers; but the distance which separates these two forms of love is as great as that which divides the androgyne of the Decadence from the 'optimistic' androgyne. For Leroux, Tourreil and Guyard, love requires involvement in the world of reality, the practice of charity, and true communication with other people. For Novalis, however, love exists quite independently of any exterior manifestation or any true communication with the outside world; its objective is a sterile awareness and contemplation of the self; and it is particularly significant in this respect that Novalis, as one critic has already pointed out, loved Sophie von Kühn far better dead than he could have done alive.[256] It is understandable therefore that Novalis's religion of love should not lead to involvement in reality but, on the contrary, to the longing for night and death. Moreover, in Novalis's cerebralization of his desire for

Sophie lurks the mental erethism characteristic of the Decadent symbol of the androgyne; and as so often among Decadent authors, Novalis's solitary imaginings, his ecstatic dreams of impossible unions, are frequently tainted by sadism. Novalis's unshakeable conviction of the transcendent power of poetry must surely have contributed to his poetic achievement; yet, as I shall show below when dealing with the work of Péladan and Mallarmé, this conviction is itself a characteristic of the Decadent symbol of the androgyne. Even Novalis's religious beliefs, expressed with unmistakeable sincerity in many of the later poems, reflect, as we saw above, the fundamental egocentrism of the Decadent androgyne.

The association in Novalis's work of the pessimistic symbol of the androgyne with complex philosophical systems and ancient mystical traditions demonstrates that the latter were in no way responsible in themselves for the optimism of the first androgyne examined. Indeed, the mystical tradition of Adam Kadmon in particular contributed so little to this optimism that, in the work of Péladan, as will be shown in the following pages, the perverse characteristics of the Decadent image of the androgyne, which spring above all from the identification of the androgyne with the virgin, are actually founded on his interpretation of *Genesis*. It would thus appear that such mystical traditions are just as subject as the image of the androgyne itself to varying interpretations determined by changing attitudes.

Péladan's novels contain for the most part merely the application of his philosophy of the androgyne, which is set forth principally in two volumes of the *Amphithéâtre des sciences mortes: Comment on devient fée. Erotique* (1893), and *La Science de l'amour* (1911). Although the best will in the world could not completely remove all the inconsistencies of this system, it yet remains extremely interesting, not only as an example of the mystical tradition of the androgyne reinterpreted by an attitude of despair, but also for the light it sheds on other works of the period—particularly, as will be seen later, Mallarmé's *Hérodiade*.

According to Péladan's interpretation of *Genesis*, Adam, in his original androgynous state, was complete and happy; yet, just like a colossal cat among the other beasts, he had no possibility of evolution.[257] Being bisexual, he contained his own reflex, and therefore could never reach consciousness of himself, for there was no transition between the conscious and the unconscious, no intermediary between nature and Adam. On account of his androgyny, therefore, Adam, incapable of evolving between instinct and understanding, was condemned to eternal stagnation.[258] In order to remedy this situation, God divided the androgyne. Adam's reflex was taken out of him to become Eve—as is shown by the exclamation which, in Péladan's very original 'translation' of *Genesis*, II, 23, Adam uttered on first seeing Eve: "*Voilà le réflexe de ma sensibilité et la forme qui correspond à ma forme*".[259]

Adam's destiny is to progress from an unconscious unity to a conscious unity through division; and this he will do by means of the desire inspired by woman. This desire is first of all sexual, but ultimately it is more than that: Péladan observes that desire is situated above sex, as musical genius is situated above the pianist.[260] For Eve was seduced by the idea of knowledge presented by the devil, who let her glimpse 'le monde supérieur de l'esprit et de la causalité';[261] and in arousing Adam's desire, Eve passes on to him her own thirst for knowledge, which will bring about his evolution to consciousness.

This separation of the two parts of the androgyne is however for Péladan, as it was for Leroux, purely psychological:

> Cette opération de chirurgie qui semble couper le premier être dans le sens vertical, mérite qu'on la prenne pour l'image forcément lourde et brutale d'un fait mental.[262]

Consequently, Adam before he desired was exactly the same as adolescents today—that is to say, that virginity and initial androgyny are one and the same thing:

> l'androgyne n'existe qu'à l'état vierge: à la première affirmation du sexe, il se résout au mâle ou au féminin.[263]

Thus, Adam's adventure is that of every individual. The appearance of the opposite sex before a virgin or *puceau* is exactly equivalent to the appearance of Eve before Adam and the splitting of the androgyne: in both cases, the male must become conscious of himself through woman.

> Dès que la femme se révèle, comme une nouvelle personne, Adam la reconnaît pour sa moitié, il précise sa mission de réflexe et de complémentaire. Il sait qu'elle sort de lui; il exulte d'être ainsi

dédoublé. Il vit, car il désire; il vit, car il aime. Qui? Lui-même encore, puisqu'Eve est une moitié de lui-même.

Le puceau, à la vue de la jeune fille, s'écrie aussi: 'Voilà le réflexe de ma sensibilité et la forme qui correspond à ma forme', et plus moderne il dirait: 'voilà le moyen de mon évolution, et le thème initial de ma conscience'.[264]

The desire for woman, necessary for man's progress towards consciousness, will also assure his return to unity. Love indeed is: 'l'effort du Moi pour se compléter et se confirmer'.[265] However, since physical union with woman results only in a momentary and artificial restoration of androgyny, reunification in consciousness of man and woman will be complete only when sexual desire has been transmuted by the intellect into consciousness. Man must progress from voluptuous desire, to moral desire and finally to spiritual possession; he must sentimentalize his instinct and spiritualize his sentiment;[266] in short, his excited sensibility must be elevated to idea and art.[267] When their love has been thus spiritualized, the lovers will discover that they are no longer two, but three, for:

> ils auront vraiment engendré de leur chair, de leur cœur et de leur esprit un enfant, à la fois fils et fille, le véritable androgyne [. . .].[268]

And the repetition in art throughout the ages of the secret of the androgyne shows that art and love are essentially identical, for both engender the androgyne. But art creates visibly, eternally and for all, whereas love creates invisibly, potentially and for two.[269]

The division of the androgyne, however, was twofold, for it resulted not only in the distinction between man and woman, but also in the separation of spirit and matter. Indeed, sexuality seems to be identified by Péladan with matter [270] and androgyny with the unity of the spirit; so that if the hermaphrodite is an angel[271] in whom spirit and matter are harmoniously synthesized, a sexual man or woman is a dual being in whom the body, the beast,[272] constantly triumphs over the spirit. The duality of spirit and matter will, however, be abolished by exactly the same means as the duality of man and woman; for, if sex is identified with matter, then the intellectualization, cerebralization of sex is a spiritualization of matter—as it was discovered in *Le Vice suprême* by Mérodack, who had in this way 'détruit la dualité de son être'.[273] The cerebralization of sex, therefore, by uniting man with woman, and spirit with matter, doubly operates the androgyne's return to a conscious unity.

It would be difficult to discover any worth in the hollow-sounding 'conscience' which represents for Péladan the supreme value in existence. Péladan's Decadent idealism is, of course, in agreement with his despair and discontent with reality: life exists only to be transformed into consciousness and art; human relationships are consequently valueless in themselves; and love does not have as its objective communication with another, but awareness of the self.

The dominant characteristic of the Decadent androgyne appears, then, as we have seen earlier, to be its identification with the virgin. In Péladan, this identification is backed up by an idealism which, varying considerably in its details but rarely in its general purport, is so often associated with *fin de siècle* symbolism. The identity of the virgin and the hermaphrodite, and the relation between this identity and symbolist philosophy, throw an unexpected light on the virgin in Mallarmé's *Hérodiade*. The fact that in this poem Mallarmé presented an androgyne has always escaped the attention of critics, precisely because this androgyne appears as a virgin. Hérodiade is, however, as typical of the pessimistic image of the androgyne as certain aspects of Mallarmé and his work are typical of the attitude that produced it.

Mallarmé's virgin, like that of Péladan, has this in common with the androgynous Adam of so many systems that she must pass from unconsciousness to consciousness through division. Moreover, like Adam, her awakening to passion coincides with a double division, a double loss of identity with herself. In the first place, passion coincides with the origin of sexual duality, which is the division of Adam and Eve for mankind, and the feeling of incompleteness, of being only half, for the virgin. This sexual division of the androgyne is represented in Mallarmé by the severing of the virgin's hymen. Secondly, passion, the greatest manifestation of life, now predominates over spirit and disrupts the unity of intelligence and sensation, which in certain philosophies, as it has been seen, is as much a characteristic of the state of androgyny as sexual unity. Sexual love, the cause of the double loss of unity and its consequent evils is original sin in the individual virgin's destiny, just as, according to a long mystical tradition, it was for Adam himself. The double restoration of the virgin's unity is similar to the twofold reintegration of the androgyne in certain of the systems examined above: gaining consciousness by spiritualizing her passion, rejecting life and transforming it into pure thought, she synthesizes anew her intellect and sensation, and recovers her sexual unity by her spiritual union with her beloved.

Such is the fate of Hérodiade. At the beginning of the poem, the virgin represents the harmonious synthesis of intelligence and sensation, and the symbolism of winter, ice, cold and loneliness suggests the purity of this original unconscious state. Hérodiade, however, is 'attentive au mystère éclairé de son être';[274] she is, in the words of Jean-Pierre Richard: 'une héroïne de la réflexion'.[275] Before she can reach reflexive consciousness, however, her unity must be divided by passion. In the *Scène*, she appears to want to remain alone and virginal, but is tormented by the need for love. Her unfurling hair, as often in Mallarmé, symbolizes the imminence of passion. The Nurse, symbol of life and love, goes to touch the falling tress and Hérodiade rebukes this attempted 'crime'—a word which in Mallarmé is reminiscent of original sin and the division of the primitive androgyne, for it always represents the loss of serenity or identity with oneself caused by passion.[276]

With the approach of love, the virgin, like the divided androgyne, becomes aware of sexual duality. Now another division takes place in Hérodiade: at the end of the *Scène*,[277] her 'froides pierreries', symbols of pure thought, begin to draw away as she becomes immersed in life and passion.[278] As G. Davies has shown, for the princess to realize herself completely, her virginal beauty had to become fully conscious of itself by passing through this revolt of the flesh.[279] But she manages to dominate her flesh: 'chair encore sanglotante d'avoir été niée'.[280] By ordering the death of John the Baptist, she succeeds in spiritualizing her passion; consequently, she becomes eternally and absolutely joined with John the Baptist and realizes again the synthesis of love and thought, thereby doubly recovering her unity. To use the symbolism of the poem, she is able to become a virgin again—a virgin who has reached full consciousness of herself, who has realized herself completely, and a virgin also who resembles certain reintegrated androgynes, since she has not only abolished in herself the dualism of thought and sensation, but has also recovered her sexual unity.

This spiritualization of love, which permits the new synthesis, is shown by Hérodiade's mystic marriage with the dead John the Baptist and by her purely symbolic defloration and division. *Les Noces* refer to Hérodiade's 'nubilité [originally *virginité*] disjointe'.[281] Indeed, the beheading of John corresponds with the symbolic division of Hérodiade and her loss of virginity. When she says:

> Le glaive qui trancha ta tête a déchiré mon voile,[282]

she is referring not only to her denudation, symbolic of virginity lost, but to the actual severing of her hymen—an interpretation confirmed by the line:

> C'est toi cruel qui m'a blessée en dessous par la tête [. . .] par le bond de la pensée.[283]

The blood which runs from John the Baptist's head on to Hérodiade's white thighs again symbolizes her mystic marriage and defloration: 'idée saigne—sang sur ses cuisses'.[284] However, it is precisely this blood which gives the virginal thighs their royalty: 'pourpre des cuisses et leur royauté'.[285] Since this symbolic defloration represents a spiritualization of passion, an idealization of sexual union, it allows Hérodiade to recover her unity by realizing the synthesis of thought and passion, mind and body, and to be truly a virgin by becoming fully conscious of herself, of her virginal 'royalty'. And so, she accedes to a second virginity, a 'virginité mûre'[286]—just as Péladan's divided androgyne or that of Novalis attains to a mature or 'conscious' unity by idealizing *his* passion. Contemplating John the Baptist's head, reflecting herself in his dying eyes, she realizes herself completely:

> Comme soufflant le lustre absent pour le ballet
> Abstraite intrusion en ma vie, il fallait
> La hantise soudain quelconque d'une face
> Pour que je m'entr'ouvrisse et reine triomphasse.[287]

Like the reintegrated androgyne, as Hérodiade reaches a conscious unity of thought and sensation, she also recovers her sexual unity, for within herself man is now joined with woman. By his death, John the Baptist is truly united with Hérodiade: as A. R. Chisholm puts it: 'Animus lives on in Anima'.[288] In fact they are just as much one as was Mallarmé with the dead Harriet Smyth; for if, as A. R. Chisholm believes, the 'sœur' of *Prose pour des Esseintes* is Harriet, then the line: 'Nous fûmes deux, je le maintiens' [289] refers to Anima living on in Animus,[290] to the creation of another androgyne by the spiritualization of passion through the death of a lover. Hérodiade and John the Baptist, Mallarmé and Harriet Smyth, thus realize the androgynous synthesis the lovers of *Tristesse d'été* despair of ever attaining:

> Nous ne serons jamais une seule momie
> Sous l'antique désert et les palmiers heureux—[291]

that is to say, as J.-P. Richard has observed,[292] we will always be separate, always two, far from the original, ancient state where nature, represented by the 'palmiers heureux', covered so well the unity of souls, this absolute state of identity. The word 'momie' here—like the 'sépulcre à deux' which will be the pride of the couple in *Sonnet*[293]—shows that the twofold return to unity is effected by a spiritual union of man and woman, which is death for the senses. Indeed, this 'momie' is a symbol of complete androgyny: for, besides representing the absolute union of man and woman, it symbolizes the spiritualization of sensual passion, and consequently the synthesis of sensation and intellect.[294]

In the virgin Hérodiade are to be found almost all the perverse characteristics of the androgyne of the Decadence: rejection of reality, withdrawal from life, refuge in solitude, confusion of good and evil, narcissism, mental erethism and cerebral lechery, accompanied by sterility and sadistic and masochistic imaginings.

A. Thibaudet[295] has compared Hérodiade with Villiers de l'Isle-Adam's *Axël*: 'attitude pareille de l'esprit qui dit non à la Vie, parce que son rêve l'a épuisée toute'. Like Maupin and d'Albert also, Hérodiade derives infinitely more pleasure from imaginings than from actions. She shrinks from physical contact with a man and her ideal marriage is consummated in a purely intellectual manner. Indeed, she succeeds in imagining life so well that she has completely exhausted it, so that her still unsatisfied desires could now be contented only in the imagination. With her Narcissist self-sufficiency, she is a typical 'femme fatale':

> Oui, c'est pour moi, pour moi, que je fleuris, déserte![296]

And who could better be called a 'femme-bourreau' in the strict sense of the term? Her sadism, however, is mingled with masochism: as J.-P. Richard has observed,[297] she is obsessed with rape, pursued by images of virginity ending violently in blood. Constantly referring to her mystic marriage as if it were a mutual feast,[298] she appears haunted by the sadistic-masochistic dream of absolute fusion with the beloved by an actual assimilation of flesh, which, as was seen above, was for Novalis one way of reconstructing the androgyne. Moreover, in Hérodiade, who provides a striking example of the *chasteté homicide* underlined in Barbey d'Aurevilly's study of the androgynous Princess d'Este, we find that sinful purity, that mixture of physical chastity and intellectual perversity, characteristic of the Decadent confusion of good and evil. These perverse characteristics of Hérodiade were doubtless appreciated by Huysmans' des Esseintes, who regarded Moreau's Salomé (whose Decadent traits were noted above) and Mallarmé's Hérodiade as one and the same person—so much so that he would sip Mallarmé's lines whilst gazing at Moreau's *l'Apparition.*[299]

The traits of Hérodiade's character are recurrent themes in Mallarmé's life and work. Frequently, Mallarmé expresses contempt for life, and above all for love, deemed incapable of satisfying his vague longings, and delight in solitary imaginings, in purely intellectual pleasure. Huysmans says of Mallarmé that he:

> se complaisait, loin du monde, aux surprises de l'intellect, aux visions de sa cervelle, raffinant sur des pensées déjà spécieuses, les greffant de finesses byzantines [. . .].[300]

In a letter to Cazalis (3rd June 1863), Mallarmé classes himself among the 'malheureux que la terre dégoûte et qui n'avons que le Rêve pour refuge'.[301] His contempt for love and praise of sterility have been underlined by Paul Delior, who rebukes: 'cette impuissance d'aimer, une impuissance dédaigneuse et préméditée'.[302] To what extent this attitude is to be attributed to an apparent guilty feeling about sex or to a self-proclaimed youthful 'priapisme' is difficult to assess.[303] However, as in the case of so many Decadent androgynes and their creators, it is only physical chastity which is valued. When shunning the realities of sex, Mallarmé often finds within his own mind the lecherous fantasies which so often accompany the dream of the androgyne. J.-P. Richard has stressed Mallarmé's 'érotisme oculaire', which affords ideal possession of a woman.[304] Physical contact with woman in Mallarmé's poetry usually stops short of the sexual act, for love-making, like everything else, is better completed by dreams than by actions. Charles Chassé, after showing that Mallarmé's aversion to the sexual act by no means excludes eroticism, observes:

> Ce qu'il s'interdit [. . .] c'est la possession. Mais, à part cela, toutes les privautés sont autorisées.[305]

Before leaving the Decadent image of the androgyne, we should perhaps state that, considered out of context, the main characteristic of this image—the identification of the androgyne with the virgin—is no more novel than the association of androgyny with incest. Quite apart from the tradition of the asexuality of the virginal Adam, the androgynous virgin is a conception frequently encountered among primitive peoples, as is shown by Mircea Eliade's explanation of ritual androgynization in primitive puberty initiations. From the fact that among many primitive peoples the uninitiated are considered asexual, and that for them attainment of sexuality is one of the consequences of initiation, Mircea Eliade concludes that the fundamental significance of the androgynization rite is as follows:

> on ne peut devenir un mâle sexuellement adulte avant d'avoir connu la coexistence des sexes, l'androgynie; autrement dit, on ne peut pas accéder à un mode d'être particulier et bien déterminé avant d'avoir connu un mode d'être total.[306]

Of course, the intellectual depravity which above all characterizes the *fin de siècle* virgin androgyne is completely absent from the primitive conception. Consequently, it appears that the virgin androgyne changes its significance completely from one age to another, just as much as the incestuous androgyne examined above. In both, each era sees the reflection of its own mentality.

## III

Although several of the androgynes examined in each of the two preceding categories occasionally contain an element belonging to the androgyne of the other category, nowhere has there been the slightest doubt about the basic optimism or pessimism of the image. For example, the fact that, long before Enfantin, Novalis should have considered the true social individual to be composed of a couple and consequently androgynous[307] does little to alleviate the general despondency underlying Novalis's conception of the androgyne. Likewise, the erotic dreams which participated in the elaboration of Evadism do not really detract from the fundamental optimism and confidence of the Mapah's social thought centred on the androgyne.

There are, however, in the nineteenth century, a few androgynes which, for one reason or another, have no precise, unequivocal meaning, and which consequently cannot satisfactorily be placed in either category. Such are, for example, Latouche's Fragoletta and Balzac's Séraphîta. Latouche's hermaphrodite might in fact symbolize the tormented Romantic hero and belong to the category of pessimistic androgynes; but Latouche treats Fragoletta's adventures so lightly that one is inclined to think that all he saw in the hermaphrodite was a character for a melodramatic novel. As for Balzac, in his androgyne superficial optimism contrasts so markedly with deep-seated pessimism that his sincerity must at times be placed in doubt.

Fragoletta, hero-heroine of the novel of the same name published in 1829 by Hyacinthe de Latouche, and certainly one of the most famous French hermaphrodites during the nineteenth century, not only is loved by both a man and a woman; she herself also loves passionately but ineffectually members of both sexes. In the person of Fragoletta, who physically can be neither a man nor a woman, but who mentally is both, the hermaphrodite becomes in many ways a symbol of the Romantic hero. An unrealizable love convinces this androgynous René of the vanity of his tormented existence:

> 'Otez-moi, comme un fardeau, cette vie qui m'a tourmenté sans but; aidez-moi à sortir d'un monde où je ne puis être aimé!'[308]

Aware of his difference:

> 'Qu'y a-t-il de commun entre moi et les créatures humaines? Je ne suis pas de leur espèce',[309]

he cries out against the capriciousness,[310] the injustice,[311] and even the malice[312] of God.

However, Fragoletta is not really a philosophical symbol. Not that Latouche is completely unaware of philosophical sources of the conception of the androgyne, some of which—Socrates, Plato, *Genesis*—are briefly enumerated in a discussion of the merits of a statue of Hermaphrodite. But he was above all a popular novelist, and consequently it is principally as a hero typical of the contemporary popular novel and specially apt to provoke the situations of this 'genre', that Fragoletta appears. This story of an hermaphrodite loved by, and in love with, both a man and a woman, provides Latouche with what he is really looking for: melodramatic situations, quiproquos and antitheses. In order to show his love for Marius, who loves Fragoletta-Philippe but is also devoted to his sister Eugénie, Philippe-Fragoletta, who also loves and is loved by Eugénie, must go away for ever to avoid marrying her. The stupidity of this situation scarcely matches the ridiculousness of the episode where Philippe-Fragoletta, Marius and Eugénie are travelling together in a coach. Marius, instinctively feeling for Philippe a little more than brotherly love, bestows upon him some 'affectueuses caresses' which Philippe even more tenderly passes on to Eugénie. A chase across France and Italy in which Philippe throws off his pursuer by changing sex was an opportunity not to be missed. And for cheap melodrama, nothing could equal the finale. Philippe, dying, is taken to a monastery to be tended by a medical monk. When the monk begins to undress the unconscious Philippe, he starts back blushing with embarrassment. And the last words of the novel are:

> 'Mes frères [. . .], il faut porter ce cadavre chez les sœurs de la Miséricorde'!

The constant association of Balzac and Latouche at the time when the one was composing *Fragoletta* and the other *Les Chouans*, the lively interest they took in each other's work, Balzac's two reviews of *Fragoletta*, and his comparison of Séraphîta with Fragoletta in his first description of his projected novel,[313] make it likely that it was to his familiarity with Latouche's novel that Balzac was indebted for the basic plot of *Séraphîta*—the story of an hermaphrodite loved by both a man and a woman. The influence of Latouche, however, combined with other influences, and the hermaphrodite does not remain for Balzac merely an amusing character for a novel. Like all writers who dallied with the image of the hermaphrodite, Balzac, both as a philosopher and as a novelist, saw in it the reflection of his own most profound preoccupations.

As in Balzac's work generally, in *Séraphîta*, this curious hotch-potch of mystical notions included in *Le Livre mystique* of 1835, the androgyne appears as an angel, 'un ange arrivé à sa dernière transformation'.[314] *Séraphîta* purports to contain an exposition of Swedenborg's doctrines on angels, and it was indeed to the Swedish mystic that Balzac owed the notion of angelic androgyny. *Conjugal Love* and *Heaven and Hell* contain descriptions of the ecstatic marriages of angels, of the fusion of two people into a single soul. In heaven, according to Swedenborg, a married pair forms not two, but one angel,[315] and a marriage partner is not there known as a husband or wife, but as a mutual or second self (*suum mutuum*).[316] Swedenborg thought he actually saw a man and woman combined in the form of a single androgynous angel: for, as the chariot containing the married pair sent down for his inspection left the highest heaven, it appeared to contain only one angel; but a man and woman were seen in it as it approached the earth. Even on earth, these two were still so united that the words uttered by one seemed to issue from both their mouths.[317]

In accordance with Swedenborg's doctrines, Séraphîtüs-Séraphîta represents the androgynous synthesis of a man and woman—witness this exclamation proffered over his parents' corpses: 'Morts? dit-elle. Non, ils sont en moi pour toujours'.[318] This androgyny coincides with angelization, for the inner man has triumphed over the outer man, the spirit over the flesh. Soon after birth, he appears to his father to be without external senses and 'tout intérieur';[319] and the parson says of him later in life: 'ses facultés, ses sensations, tout est intérieur'.[320]

Balzac's androgyne, then, in so far as it represents an angel, appears at first sight to be a symbol of the triumph of soul over flesh, of spirit over matter. Closer investigation, however, reveals a deeper and rather different meaning. The androgyne which constitutes the angel is itself formed, as was seen above, by the marriage of man and woman, by their union in love. If the angel represents the triumph of the spirit over the flesh, this love might reasonably be expected to be spiritual as opposed to sensual or sexual. In fact, however, in Swedenborg himself, spiritual and sensual love seem far from incompatible. Although Swedenborg says that true 'conjugal' love is of divine origin[321] and exists between Christ and the Church,[322] yet it is often evident that what is disparaged as 'sexual' love differs from 'conjugal' love principally in that it is not directed to one person alone.[323] Moreover, Swedenborg maintains that sexual love in marriage is the effect of unity of soul, and a necessary first stage in angelization;[324] and that 'conjugal' love is intended for the propagation of the human race and of angels.[325]

In Balzac's novel, Séraphîtüs-Séraphîta urges Minna and Wilfrid to love each other and join together in marriage and, in anticipation of this event, he addresses them collectively as if they constituted a single angel.[326] Since, however, *Séraphîta* itself does not state clearly how far the love and marriage which bring about androgyny and angelization are spiritual or sensual, recourse must be had to others of Balzac's works.

In fact, the contemporary philosophical and literary commonplace that the road to eternity passes through erotic love—how far this notion is Platonic is a very debatable and much debated point[327]—influenced Balzac deeply and is expressed throughout the *Comédie humaine*. In the transcendental idealism of Frédéric Ancillon, Balzac read[328] of the doctrine of love as an aspiration towards the infinite, as an emanation from God constantly returning to God, as a tendency to become united with an object, of woman as the incarnation of the infinite, as 'l'infini qui se révèle à nous sous des formes finies'.[329] Lovers, says Ancillon:

> sentent [...] le besoin de se pénétrer réciproquement d'enthousiasme, et de réunir leur forces et leurs efforts pour prendre leur essor vers les sommités de la vie, d'où l'on embrasse un horizon immense.[330]

Like Ancillon's lovers, as also those so often portrayed in contemporary literature—in Nodier's *Adèle*, for example, or George Sand's *Lélia*—Balzac's lovers are frequently in search of the infinite in sensual love. In *Un Prince de la Bohème*, Balzac presents love as 'une combinaison du sentiment de l'infini qui est en nous et du beau idéal, qui se révèle sous une forme visible';[331] and he speaks even more strikingly of 'l'infini rendu palpable et transporté dans les plus excessives jouissances de la créature.[332]

The fulfilment of this quest for the infinite, for eternity, in erotic love, is often represented in Balzac by the image of the lovers' union in the androgyne, and their consequent angelization. The description of the mutual caresses of Etienne and Gabrielle ends with this comment:

> Certes, ils ne pouvaient alors être comparés qu'à un ange qui, les pieds posés sur le monde, attend l'heure de revoler vers le ciel. Ils avaient accompli ce beau rêve du génie mystique de Platon et de tous ceux qui cherchent un sens à l'humanité; ils ne faisaient qu'une seule âme [. . .].[333]

And for Claude Vignon love is:

> un royaume idéal [. . .] où vont deux créatures réunies en un ange, enlevées par les ailes du plaisir.[334]

Carnal love thus paradoxically leads to angelization, the body to the soul, matter to spirit; and consequently the androgyne, in whom this junction takes place, unites in himself both matter and spirit. Thus, according to *La Cousine Bette*, a person capable of satisfying both the needs of the body and those of the soul would be 'ce mystérieux androgyne'.[335]

The union of spirit and matter symbolized by the androgyne is, however, in addition a unity and an identity. It is indeed difficult to imagine how immersion in sensuality can lead to anything that is not also greater sensuality; and if the soul can be found in the flesh, spirit in matter, then the two terms are not contradictory at all, but fundamentally identical. Moreover, by saying that carnal love spiritualizes the flesh—and this is clearly the meaning of 'deux créatures réunies en un ange, enlevées par les ailes du plaisir'—Balzac implies the basic unity of spirit and matter just as much as if he had maintained that spiritual love materializes the spirit. Not only may spirit be found in matter, but also matter, according to Balzac, exists in the spirit, in the angel. Séraphîtüs-Séraphîta says to Wilfrid that the complete love which exists in the angel means the conquest of the flesh and the deprivation of senses: 'l'amour sera si complet en toi que tu n'auras plus de sens';[336] and yet, according to *Un Prince de la Bohème*, 'l'amour complet' is 'idéal et physique',[337] and in *La Cousine Bette* Balzac underlines the fundamental identity of spiritual love of soul and sensual pleasure, 'deux faces différentes d'un même fait'.[338] The inclusion of matter in the pure spirit of the angel, which indicates the fundamental unity of spirit and matter, is of course in accordance with the doctrine expounded in *Séraphîta* itself. For as man and woman join to form the angel:

> son âme est FEMME, et son corps est HOMME, dernière expression humaine où l'esprit l'emporte sur la forme, où la forme se débat encore contre l'esprit divin; car la forme, la chair, ignore, se révolte, et veut rester grossière.[339]

And both these elements—purified, to be sure—enter into the composition of the angel:

> Après la mort, le premier ciel s'ouvre à cette *double* nature humaine purifiée.[340]

The androgyne, which thus symbolizes the unity and fundamental identity of spirit and matter, lies at the heart of Balzac's basically monistic philosophy. Although in Balzac's work man often appears to be composed of two distinct natures: body and soul, and life is presented as the antagonism of *action* (by which term Balzac designates the inner life of the mind, the will and thought) and *reaction* (which signifies the exterior life of the senses), nevertheless, according to *Louis Lambert*, spirit and matter are but different aspects of the same reality, for everything that exists is the product of a single *substance éthérée*, the mysterious fluid revered by partisans of animal magnetism. Moreover, the correspondence of the spiritual and the material, assured by the existence of this fluid which permeates the whole creation, forms the basis for Balzac's psycho-physiological and deterministic theories, which occupy such an important place in his thought.

Although Balzac the philosopher is appreciated less than Balzac the novelist, the image of the androgyne, which occupies a central position in his thought, is not of merely peripheral interest as regards the total Balzac; for, such as it is, his philosophy is in fact closely connected with his literary production and betrays his most profound preoccupations as a novelist. In the philosophical sections of his work, Balzac seems largely preoccupied with providing a guarantee for the truth of his vision of the world, with demonstrating that the image of reality presented in the *Comédie humaine*, although evidently the product of vision or imagination just as much as of observation, is nevertheless as scientifically objective as it was claimed to be in this famous statement of the *Avant-propos*: 'La société française allait être l'historien, je ne devais être que le secrétaire'. Although, for example, Balzac's psycho-physiological and deterministic theories tend to demonstrate that the moral world, just like the world of nature, operates in accordance with certain fixed laws, yet, according to these same theories, scientific observation alone is not sufficient for the understanding of these laws: in addition, one must possess magnetic, intuitive vision. This notion of the rôle of vision in the comprehension of reality naturally owed much to contemporary works on magnetism, which imagined the magnetic fluid permeating the whole creation, making the sap in the trees and the human soul, and forming a thread on which the somnambulist could travel throughout the universe, gathering exact knowledge of all reality.

The scientific, objective nature of Balzac's personal, subjective vision would ultimately depend on the fundamental identity of the knowledge acquired by science and that gained by intuition. This identity is in fact implied by Balzac's monistic theory of the identity of spirit and matter, for Balzac assimilates vision or intuition with the spirit, and science with matter—and the androgyne, which represents the unity and identity of spirit and matter, appears also as the symbol *par excellence* of the unity and identity of science and intuition.

That the androgyne should thus symbolize this latter identity is really a development of Swedenborg's doctrine on angels. According to Swedenborg, although both men and woman each contain the two elements intellect or understanding and will, in each a different one predominates, so that harmony is achieved by the union of husband and wife in one angel:

> Marriage in heaven is the conjunction of two in unity of mind [. . .] The mind consists of two parts, one of which is called the Intellect or Understanding, and the other the Will; and where both these co-operate or act in union, they form one mind. Now the Husband there represents and exercises the intellectual part, and the Wife the province of the will [. . .] where two are so united in Spiritual Marriage, they are not called two, but one angel.[341]

Like Swedenborg, Balzac assimilates the female will with love and asserts that woman has immediate knowledge by intuition, in contrast to the male, who, representing intelligence, can know only by learning, reason and science. And so, in Balzac's story, the androgyne unites both the rational, intellectual, scientific principle Séraphîtüs and the loving, intuitive principle Séraphîta.

It was mentioned above that Balzac considers woman as representing spirit and man matter, so that their attributes intuition or love and science or intelligence could also be considered respectively as spiritual and material. This is of course understandable since in the first case knowledge is immediate and, in the second, depends on perception by the senses. Thus, according to *Séraphîta*: 'La science est le langage du monde temporel, l'amour est celui du monde spirituel'.[342] Like spirit and matter, however, science or intelligence and love or intuition are fundamentally identical. In the androgynous angel, devoid of senses, complete love, as Séraphîta tells Wilfrid, is not only wholly love but also wholly intelligence: 'l'amour sera si complet en toi que tu n'auras plus de sens, que tu seras tout intelligence et tout amour'.[343] The knowledge gained by reason, intelligence or learning must therefore be identical to that acquired by intuition; and Séraphîta, speaking as a woman, defends female instinct as compared to male science by underlining this very identity:

> 'Ce que vous apprenez, vous autres, nous le sentons, nous'.[344]

And so, the unity of science and intuition symbolized by the androgyne is also an identity.

There is therefore a contradiction between the superficial and deeper meanings of Balzac's image of the androgyne. Considered as a symbol of human angelization, this androgyne is undoubtedly an optimistic image; and yet the belief in the fundamental identity of spirit and matter which underlies the image, as it does the whole of Balzac's work, appears rather to imply that man cannot transcend the material part of his being. Such an implication is not, of course, pessimistic in itself; but it is pessimistic when considered in conjunction with the picture painted in the *Comédie humaine* of this part of human nature.

A monistic philosophy which sees two antagonistic forces proceeding from the same source undoubtedly partly accounts for this contradiction; but the probability of Balzac's insincerity should not be overlooked as a contributory factor. How firmly, for example, did Balzac believe what he preached in *Séraphîta*:

that the union of lovers would lead to God? It has been conjectured, not unconvincingly, that Balzac wanted rather to persuade the mystically inclined Mme Hanska (to whom *Séraphîta* is dedicated) that this was so, in order to be better able to seduce her.[345] And elsewhere in his work, Balzac appears extremely cynical about the possible angelization of lovers. In *La Cousine Bette*, for example, he ridicules the *nouvel art d'aimer* which, he says: 'consomme énormément de paroles évangéliques à l'œuvre du diable', and he goes on:

> On aspire à l'idéal, à l'infini, de part et d'autre on veut devenir meilleurs par l'amour. Toutes ces belles phrases sont un prétexte à mettre encore plus d'ardeur dans la pratique, plus de rage dans les chutes [. . .] On est deux anges, et l'on se comporte comme deux démons, si l'on peut.[346]

The possibility of Balzac's insincerity perhaps best explains how the androgyne could appear as an angel in a novel of a series so full of themes characteristic of the Decadent image of the hermaphrodite. Balzac's magnetic theories, for example, closely associated with the monistic philosophy symbolized by the androgyne, often appear as the very foundation of certain Decadent practices related to the pessimistic symbol of the androgyne, and of cerebral lechery in particular. The intellectual possession of women, for example, is undoubtedly in accordance with the magnetic philosophy expounded in *La Peau de Chagrin* (1831) by the antique dealer who, anxious to economize the vital fluid, prizes *savoir* above *vouloir* and *pouvoir*:

> J'ai un sérail imaginaire où je possède toutes les femmes que je n'ai pas eues [. . .]

This antique dealer, indeed, bears a striking and by no means fortuitous similarity to Péladan's cerebral lecher Guy de Quéant, who enthusiastically exclaims:

> 'nulle femme n'est à l'abri de mon désir [. . .] Dans mon sérail, chaque salon de Paris est un harem [. . .]'.[347]

The tension of will necessary for this sinful purity also enters into Balzac's philosophy: the 'monstrously continent' Mérodack,[348] who considers Will the primordial dogma, recognizes himself the disciple of Balzac's Louis Lambert:

> Enfin, comme un arc-en-ciel, dans son anxiété, lui apparut le

> dogme primordial: LA VOLONTÉ. Il composa cette fameuse *Théorie* que Balzac le Grand avait conçue intuitivement [. . .].[349]

Apart from such specific factors as the rôle of erotic love, the apologia of cerebral lechery, and the already mentioned treatment of Lesbianism in *La Fille aux yeux d'or*,[350] there was much in Balzac's work to sustain the attitude of despair which conditioned the pessimistic symbol of the androgyne. Indeed, the general picture of life presented in the *Comédie humaine* was not of the sort to inspire anything but pessimism and despair.

Balzac's androgyne thus appears extremely enigmatic. The most striking attestation of its ambiguity is, however, provided by the constant comparison by Decadent authors of the angelic Séraphîtüs-Séraphîta with Péladan's *fin de siècle* hermaphrodite —for example, by Strindberg,[351] by Stanislas de Guaita,[352] and by Barbey d'Aurevilly.[353]

Among the general conclusions which can be drawn from this survey of the image of the androgyne in the nineteenth century, it must be stated first and foremost that the androgyne is a myth; and that, like all myths, it is constantly reinterpreted, since its meaning or value must agree with the widely varying preoccupations and experience of different eras and individuals. Myths have indeed this in common with history that they reflect like mirrors the attitudes of mind of those who contemplate them.

As such a mirror, however, the myth of the androgyne appears quite unique. For the reflection of mental attitudes may be just as faint in a complex myth as an image in a cloudy mirror. Just as the greater number of tumblers in a lock reduces the number of variations possible in the shape of the key, so the greater the number of essential elements composing a myth, the fewer the interpretations to which that myth can lend itself. The multiplicity of details may indeed make the purely literal and superficial meaning of the myth so precise that some generations can discover in it no profound significance whatsoever; and thus it happens that certain complex myths, just like certain periods of history, can be completely neglected for generations, until a new interpretation is evolved which combines the different elements. Since, therefore, the simpler myth is the better mirror, what myth could reflect mental attitudes more easily than one which can be perfectly resumed in a single word or a single image?

However, if the ability of the myth of the androgyne to reflect so faithfully the preoccupations and experience of widely differing epochs and individuals is due to its extreme simplicity, the fact that it does indeed reflect those things is explained by its universal presence. For no specialized knowledge is necessary for acquaintance with the myth of the androgyne—indeed knowledge of the myth presupposes no education whatsoever, for the androgyne is not only present on all sides in the exterior world, but it also exists in the depths of the human unconscious.

For these reasons, the myth of the androgyne is constantly in evidence, recording by its metamorphoses not only variations occurring in mental attitudes from civilization to civilization, but even the changes in human preoccupations and experience which take place between different generations and different environments during a single century.

## NOTES

[1] F. Giese, *Der romantische Character. Erster Band: Die Entwicklung des Androgynenproblems in der Frühromantik*, Langensalza, 1919, p. 406; cf. pp. 404f.

[2] E. Susini, *Franz von Baader et le romantisme mystique*, t. 3, Paris, 1942, p. 574; J.-C.-L. Halley des Fontaines, *Contribution à l'étude de l'androgynie. La notion d'androgynie dans quelques mythes et quelques rites*, Paris, 1938, pp. 143f.

[3] Except, of course, when 'Hermaphrodite' with a capital letter is used as a proper name.

[4] Marie Delcourt, *Hermaphrodite. Mythes et rites de la Bisexualité dans l'Antiquité classique*, Paris, 1958, p. 1.

[5] Halley des Fontaines, op. cit., pp. 189–203.

[6] Halley des Fontaines, op. cit., p. 203; Marie Delcourt, op. cit., p. 1.

[7] Marie Delcourt, op. cit., p. 2.

[8] ibid., pp. 65f., 68f.

[9] For a lucid explanation of Winckelmann's views on this subject, v. Fritz Giese, op. cit., pp. 41f.

[10] Robinet, *Considérations philosophiques de la gradation naturelle des formes de l'être ou les essais de la nature qui apprend à faire l'homme*, Paris, 1768, p. 18.

[11] ibid., pp. 33f. Robinet quotes Pliny, *Hist.*, Liv. XXXVII, Ch. x.

[12] Robinet, p. 220.

[13] ibid., p. 223.

[14] ibid., p. 223.

[15] A. Comte, *Système de politique positive, ou traité de sociologie, Instituant la Religion de l'Humanité*, t. 4, Paris, 1851–4, p. 276.

[16] ibid., pp. 241, 276.

[17] ibid., p. 278.

[18] ibid., p. 276; cf. p. 67.

[19] ibid., p. 241: 'Le succès devant surtout dépendre du développement général des relations entre l'âme et le corps (. . .)'

[20] L.S.A.M. von Römer, 'Ueber die androgynische Idee des Lebens', in

*Jahrbuch für sexuelle Zwischenstufen mit besonderer Berücksichtigung der Homosexualität*, V. Jahrgang, II. Band, Leipzig, 1903, pp. 707–939; Halley des Fontaines, op. cit.; Marie Delcourt, op. cit.

[21] A. Viatte, *Les Sources occultes du romantisme*, Paris, 1928.

[22] Jules Bois, 'La femme nouvelle', *Revue encyclopédique*, Paris, 1896, no. 169, p. 839; reproduced in *L'Eve nouvelle*, Paris, 1896, p. 314.

[23] A glance at the relevant sections of H. Pinard de la Boullaye, *L'Etude comparée des religions. Essai critique*, Paris, 1922–31, and J. Réville, *Les phases successives de l'histoire des religions*, Paris, 1909, affords an idea of how widespread religious syncretism was during Romanticism.

[24] R. Schwab, *La Renaissance orientale*, Paris, 1950.

[25] Novalis, *Schriften. Kritische Neuausgabe auf Grund des handschriftlichen Nachlasses, von Ernst Heilborn*, Berlin, 1901, II, 685f.

[26] A. Strindberg, *Die Gotischen Zimmer*, München u. Leipzig, 1908, p. 119.

[27] S. de Guaita, *Essais de sciences maudites*, I, Paris, 1890, pp. 126ff.

[28] ibid., pp. 20f.

[29] R. Baldick, *The Life of J.-K. Huysmans*, Oxford, 1955, p. 142.

[30] Bernard de Montfaucon, op. cit., t. I, Paris, 1724, pl. 88.

[31] Eduard Gerhard, *Antike Bildwerke zum ersten Male bekannt gemacht*, Erster Centurie, Drittes Heft, Stuttgart und Tübingen, 1830, Taf. xlii, 1.

[32] Raoul-Rochette, op. cit., Planche 10.

[33] Illustrated, for example, in the *Titul-Figur von Göttlicher Offenbahrung in 177. Theosophischen Fragen*, Amsterdam, 1682.

[34] S. de Guaita, *Essais de sciences maudites*, t. 2, II, Paris, 1897, p. 702.

[35] G. Bachelard, *La Poétique de la rêverie*, Paris, 1960, p. 50

[36] Freud, *On the Sexual Theories of children* (*Über infantile Sexualtheorien*), in *Standard Edition of the Complete Psychological Works of Sigmund Freud*, Vol. IX, London, 1959, p. 216.

[37] O. Pfister, *Die Frömmigkeit des Grafen Ludwig von Zinzendorf. Schriften zur angewandten Seelenkunde*, VIII. Heft, Leipzig, 1910. I quote from the *zweite, verbesserte Auflage*, Leipzig und Wien, 1925.

[38] Pfister, op. cit., p. 58.

[39] ibid., p. 105.

[40] ibid., pp. 106f.

[41] V. von Römer, op. cit., pp. 764f.

[42] V. *Von der Menschwerdung J.C.*, IX, 23, 24; XI, 6.

[43] Blavatsky, *The Secret Doctrine*, 2nd ed., London, New York, Madras, 1888, II, 134.

[44] St. Augustine, Tract. 120 in Joann.; cf. von Römer, op. cit., pp. 785–91.

[45] Both these illustrations are reproduced in von Römer, op. cit., pp. 786, 788.

[46] A. Kielholz, *Jakob Boehme, ein pathographischer Beitrag zur Psychologie der Mystik, Schriften zur angewandten Seelenkunde*, 17. Heft, Leipzig und Wien, 1919.

[47] Kielholz, op. cit., pp. 61, 82.

[48] ibid., p. 64.

[49] D. Bakan, *Sigmund Freud and the Jewish Mystical Tradition*, Princeton, Toronto, London, New York, 1958, pp. 282–5.

[50] Cf. Halley des Fontaines, op. cit., p. 190 and n. 1; Marie Delcourt, op. cit., pp. 102f.

[51] J. Boehme, *Concerning The Three Principles of The Divine Essence*, 13, 39, Trans. by John Sparrow, London, 1910, p. 243.

[52] J. Cats, *Alle de Wercken, So ouden als nieuwe*, Amsterdam, 1655, I, 2: *Sinne- en Minne-Beelden: Quod perdidit optat.*

[53] S. de Guaita, *Essais de sciences maudites*, II, Paris, 1891, pp. 451–4.

[54] Fabre d'Olivet, *La Langue hébraïque restituée, et le véritable sens des mots hébreux rétabli et prouvé par leur analyse radicale*, Paris, 1815–16, II, 58.

[55] Fabre d'Olivet, *De l'état social de l'homme; ou vues philosophiques sur l'histoire du genre humain*, I, Paris, 1822, p. 22.

[56] P.-S. Ballanche, *Œuvres*, III, Paris, 1830, p. 315.

[57] Lamennais, *De la société première et de ses lois ou de la religion*, 4e. éd., Paris, 1850, p. 9.

[58] Quoted by E. R. Curtius, *Balzac*, Paris, 1933, p. 176.

[59] The encyclopaedic minds of Romantic scholars and poets were by no means daunted by such a prospect: cf. Fabre d'Olivet, *Etat social*, I, 1f.; Victor Hugo, *Fragment historique* (*Revue de Paris*, 1827), *Œuvres complètes, Philosophie I, 1819–1834*, Paris, Ollendorf, 1927, p. 293.

[60] Fabre d'Olivet, *Langue hébraïque*, II, p. 191.

[61] Lamennais, *Essai sur l'indifférence en matière de religion*, Paris, 1817–1823, particularly vols. III and IV.

[62] Ballanche, *La Ville des Expiations, publié avec une introduction et des notes par Amand Rastoul*, Paris, 1926, p. 97.

[63] Ballanche, *La Vision d'Hébal*, Paris, 1831, pp. 35f., 40f.

[64] Fabre d'Olivet, *Etat social*, I, 22.

[65] P. Leroux, *De l'humanité*, Paris 1840, viii.

[66] But only as a psychological symbol, see below, p. 29.

[67] *De l'humanité*, pp. 48, 316, 468, 524–6.

[68] *Le Catholique*, I, Paris, février 1826, p. 186.

[69] Fabre d'Olivet, *Langue hébraïque*, II, 106.

[70] ibid., p. 88.

[71] L. Cellier, *Fabre d'Olivet*, Paris, 1953, pp. 177ff.

[72] S. de Guaita, *Essais de sciences maudites*, I, Paris, 1890, pp. 133ff., and the last plate in the volume.

[73] *Langue hébraïque*, II, 94.

[74] Fabre d'Olivet, *Caïn, mystère dramatique en trois actes de Lord Byron, traduit en vers français, et réfuté dans une suite de remarques philosophiques et critiques, etc.*, Paris, 1823, *Remarques*, pp. 196f.

[75] Fabre d'Olivet, *Etat social*, II, 461.

[76] ibid., II, 410.

[77] ibid., I, 62.

[78] *Caïn*, p. 246.

[79] *Etat social*, I, 333f.

[80] ibid., II, 11.

[81] ibid., II, 25–7.

[82] ibid., II, 87–9.

[83] ibid., II, 160–4.

[84] ibid., II, 214.

[85] ibid., II, 238.

[86] ibid., II, 252.

[87] ibid., II, 411.

[88] V., e.g., ibid., II, 332.

[89] ibid., II, 413.

[90] The following examination of the conception of the androgyne in Ballanche's work is based on an exhaustive analysis of all Ballanche's writings, including his unpublished MSS. kept in the *Bibliothèque publique* at Lyons. It resumes the conclusions of certain sections of my study of Ballanche and critical edition of *La Vision d'Hébal*, both of which will be published shortly.

[91] L. Cellier, *Fabre d'Olivet*, p. 345.

[92] *Vision d'Hébal*, pp. 41, 65.

[93] Ballanche, *Œuvres*, III, 262.

[94] Baudelaire, *L'Art romantique*, Paris, 1885, p. 132.

[95] Th. Gautier, *L'Art moderne*, Paris, 1856, p. 5.

[96] ibid., p. 7.

[97] *Salon de 1869. Explication des ouvrages*, Paris, 1869, pp. 65, 472—*Divina Tragedia*.

[98] *Propos d'art à l'occasion du Salon de 1869. Revue du Salon*, Paris, 1869, p. 47; cf. ibid., p. 57. Cf. J. C. Sloane, *French Painting between the past and the present. Artists, critics, and traditions, from 1848* to *1870*, Princeton Univ., 1951, pp. 139f.

[99] Quoted by J. Lacroix, *La Sociologie d'Auguste Comte*, Paris, 1956, p. 8.

[100] Sainte-Beuve, *Portraits contemporains*, II, 'Ballanche', Paris, 1882, p. 43.

[101] *Doctrine saint-simonienne*, ed. de 1854, Paris, p. 434.

[102] Undated letter to Encely, *Archives saint-simoniennes*, II, 110.

[103] M. Thibert, *Le Féminisme dans le socialisme français de 1830 à 1850*, Paris, 1926, pp. 35f.

[104] For example: S. Charléty, *Histoire du saint-simonisme*, Paris, 1931, p. 125; L. Cellier, *Fabre d'Olivet*, p. 354.

[105] Quoted by M. Thibert, op. cit., p. 36.

[106] Quoted by L. Abensour, *Le Féminisme sous le règne de Louis-Philippe et en 1848*, 2e. éd., Paris, 1913, p. 8.

[107] Quoted by S. Charléty, op. cit., p. 202.

[108] *Œuvres de Saint-Simon et d'Enfantin*, VI, Paris, 1865ff., pp. 191–4.

[109] See H. L. Eads, *A short treatise on the second appearing of Christ in and through the order of the female*, Boston, 1853; S. Hutin, *Les Disciples anglais de Jacob Bœhme aux XVIIe et XVIIIe siècles*, Paris, 1960, pp. 121–3.

[110] P. Leroux, *De l'égalité*, Boussac, 1848.

[111] Leroux, *De l'humanité*, 1840, p. 183.

[112] ibid., p. 217.

[113] ibid., p. 504.

[114] ibid., p. 530.

[115] ibid., p. 535.

[116] ibid., p. 534.

[117] ibid., pp. 561f., n. 1.

[118] ibid., p. 545; cf. *Langue hébraïque restituée*.

[119] ibid., p. 566.

[120] ibid., p. 660.

[121] ibid., pp. 874ff.

[122] ibid., p. 744.

[123] Charles Yriarte, *Paris grotesque. Les Célébrités de la rue, Paris (1815 à 1863)*, Paris, 1864, p. 93.

[124] Champfleury, *Les Vignettes romantiques*, Paris, 1883, p. 237.

[125] Manifesto of 15th August 1838, p. 3.

[126] Caillaux, *Arche de la nouvelle alliance*, 1840, p. 117.

[127] Yriarte, op. cit., pp. 103ff.

[128] Ganneau, *Waterloo*, Paris, 1843, p. 12

[129] Letter from Caillaux to Yriarte. Yriarte, op. cit., p. 124.

[130] Champfleury, op. cit., p. 243.

[131] Letter from Constant to Erdan, dated 17th Jan. 1855; quoted by Erdan, *La France mistique. Tableau des excentricités religieuses de ce tems*. Paris, 1855, p. 623.

[132] ibid.

[133] Constant, *L'Assomption de la femme ou le livre de l'amour*, Paris, 1841, pp. 49f.

[134] ibid., p. 32.

[135] ibid., p. 113.

[136] ibid., p. 65.

[137] ibid., p. 78

[138] ibid., pp. 7f., 123.

[139] F. Tristan, *L'Emancipation de la femme ou le testament de la Paria, ouvrage posthume de Mme Flora Tristan, complété d'après ses notes et publié par A. Constant*, Paris 1845.

[140] Quérard, *Les Supercheries littéraires dévoilées*, III, Paris, 1870, p. 855; J.-L. Puech, *Le Socialisme français avant 1848. La Vie et l'Œuvre de Flora Tristan, 1803–1844*, Paris, 1925, pp. 121, n. 1 and 491.

[141] Cf. *L'Emancipation*, pp. 118f.; Puech, op. cit., pp. 390, n. 2 and 414.

[142] *L'Emancipation*, p. 119.

[143] ibid, pp. 118f.

[144] Puech, op. cit., p. 391, n.

[145] *L'Emancipation*, p. 119.

[146] L.-J.-B. de Tourreil, *Religion fusionienne ou doctrine de l'universalisation réalisant le vrai catholicisme*, Paris, 1864–68, I, iii.

[147] ibid., I, 74.

[148] ibid., I, 74, n. 1.

[149] ibid., IV, 242, n. 30.

[150] Erdan, op. cit., p. 630. It will have been noticed that Erdan employs at times a highly personal phonetic spelling.

[151] ibid., p. 636.

[152] A. Guyard, *Des droits, des devoirs et des constitutions au point de vue de la doctrine fusionienne*, Paris, 1848, p. 28.

[153] 'La Femme nouvelle', *Revue encyclopédique*, Paris, 1896, no. 169 (pp. 832–40), pp. 835, 839; reprinted in *L'Eve nouvelle*, Paris, 1896, pp. 274, 314.

[154] *L'Eve nouvelle*, pp. 242f.

[155] H. Lichtenberger, *Novalis*, Paris, 1912, p. 15.

[156] Th. Gautier, *Histoire de l'art dramatique en France, depuis vingt-cinq ans*, 1858–59, I, 326.

[157] Th. Gautier, *Mademoiselle de Maupin*, Nouvelle éd., Paris, Fasquelle, 1922, p. 224.

[158] ibid., p. 398.

[159] *Contralto.*

[160] *Maupin*, p. 224.

[161] *Contralto.*

[162] ibid.

[163] J. Péladan, *Amphithéâtre des sciences mortes. Comment on devient fée. Erotique*, Paris, 1893, p. 305.

[164] J. Péladan, *Amphithéâtre des sciences mortes. La Science de l'amour*, Paris, 1911, p. 143.

[165] *Maupin*, p. 42.

[166] ibid., p. 356.

[167] ibid., p. 155.

[168] ibid., p. 399.

[169] ibid., p. 154.

[170] ibid., p. 411.

[171] ibid., pp. 403f.

[172] Mircea Eliade, *Méphistophélès et l'androgyne*, Gallimard, 1962, p. 123.

[173] A. France, *La Vie littéraire*, 3e série, III, 238.
[174] *Béatrix, Œuvres complètes de H. de Balzac*, Michel Lévy, III (1869), p. 270.
[175] Quoted by Ph. Bertault, *Balzac et la religion*, Paris, 1942, p. 178.
[176] Péladan, *Le Vice suprême. Préface de J. Barbey d'Aurevilly*. . . . Paris, 1884, p. 188.
[177] ibid., p. 202.
[178] ibid., p. 56.
[179] ibid., p. 61.
[180] ibid., p. 77.
[181] ibid., p. 73.
[182] ibid., p. 127.
[183] Péladan, *L'Androgyne*, Paris, 1891, p. 227.
[184] ibid., p. 267.
[185] A. Symons, *From Toulouse Lautrec to Rodin*, London, 1929, pp. 183f.
[186] *Vice suprême*, p. 58.
[187] ibid., p. 5.
[188] ibid., pp. 68f.
[189] ibid., p. 62.
[190] e.g., ibid., p. 23.
[191] Symons, op. cit., pp. 151f.
[192] Quoted by Mario Praz, *The Romantic Agony. Translated from the Italian by Angus Davidson*. London, 1933, p. 332.
[193] J. Lorrain, 'Mademoiselle Salamandre', in *Courrier français*, 12th December, 1886; quoted by Praz, op. cit., p. 333.
[194] Huysmans, *La Cathédrale*, p. 331, Paris, 1898.
[195] Huysmans, *A Rebours*, p. 72.
[196] *Androgyne*, p. 38.
[197] ibid., p. 261.
[198] ibid., p. 284.
[199] Cf. Halley des Fontaines, op. cit., p. 208.
[200] Huysmans, *Certains*, 1889, pp. 18f.
[201] *Vice suprême*, p. 216.
[202] Letter from Moreau to Henri Rupp, quoted by Ragnar von Holten, *L'Art fantastique de Gustave Moreau*, Paris, 1960, p. 18.
[203] Rachilde, *La Marquise de Sade*, Paris, 1887, pp. 276f.
[204] *Vice suprême*, pp. 65f.
[205] Cf. Baldick, *The Life of J.-K. Huysmans*, Oxford, 1955, p. 139.
[206] ibid., pp. 155f.
[207] Praz, op. cit., p. 337.
[208] *Vice suprême*, xi.
[209] Cf. the advice given to Léonora d'Este by her confessor: 'il est une vertu que j'exige de vous, et votre orgueil vous la rendra facile. . . . Votre tête péchera assez, helas! que votre corps du moins soit sans péché' (*Vice suprême*, p. 28).
[210] In the words of Barbey d'Aurevilly: *Vice suprême*, x.
[211] Cf. ibid., pp. 99f.
[212] ibid., pp. 99f.
[213] A. Symons, op. cit., p. 151
[214] W. Pater, *Studies in the history of the Renaissance*, London, 1873, pp. 111f.
[215] 'Epilogue' in *Leonardo da Vinci; conferenze fiorentine*, Milan, 1910, p. 308. Quoted by Praz, op. cit., p. 320.
[216] *L'Androgyne*, p. 9.
[217] ibid., p. 49.
[218] *Certains*, pp. 223f.

[219] ibid., p. 226.

[220] M. Delcourt, op. cit., pp. 10, 30, 33, 35, 81, 124, 125.

[221] ibid., p. 124n.

[222] S. de Guaita, *Essais de sciences maudites*, II, Paris, 1891, pp. 452–4.

[223] Cf. R. Jasinski, *Les années romantiques de Th. Gautier*, Paris, 1929, pp. 288ff. and Praz, op. cit., pp. 318f.

[224] Cf. Halley des Fontaines, op. cit., pp. 189–94, M. Delcourt, op. cit., pp. 84–6, 102f.

[225] *Vice suprême*, pp. 145f.

[226] Péladan, *La Gynandre*, Paris, 1891, p. 43.

[227] Halley des Fontaines, op. cit., pp. 144f.

[228] Praz, op. cit., p. 269.

[229] *Vice suprême*, xi.

[230] *Science de l'amour*, p. 113.

[231] *L'Androgyne*, p. 231.

[232] Huysmans, *A Rebours*, p. 138.

[233] See Praz for further examples of this inversion of sexes: e.g. in d'Annunzio (pp. 259, 284), Barbey d'Aurevilly (p. 313), Catulle Mendès (pp. 330f.).

[234] Novalis, *Schriften*, ed. Heilborn, I, 177.

[235] *Geistliche Lieder*, XIII, Novalis, *Schriften*, I, 343.

[236] ibid.

[237] *Schriften*, I, 123.

[238] ibid., I, 185–6.

[239] ibid., II, 391.

[240] Freud, *On the Sexual Theories of Children*, *Standard Ed.*, Vol IX, 220.

[241] *Schriften*, II, 514.

[242] ibid., I, 228f.

[243] ibid., II, 579.

[244] ibid., II, 159.

[245] Cf. E. Spenlé, *Novalis, Essai sur l'idéalisme romantique en Allemagne*, Paris, 1904, pp. 232f., 337.

[246] Lichtenberger, op. cit., p. 144.

[247] *Hymen an die Nacht*, Novalis, *Schriften*, I, 326.

[248] *Geistliche Lieder*, II, Novalis, *Schriften*, I, 330.

[249] Lichtenberger, op. cit., p. 59.

[250] ibid., p. 95.

[251] F. Hiebel, *Novalis. Der Dichter der Blauen Blume*, Bern, 1951, p. 215.

[252] ibid., p. 199.

[253] After exchanging a kiss with Mathilde, Heinrich reflects: 'Ist mir nicht zu Muthe wie in jenem Traume, beim Anblick der blauen Blume? Welcher sonderbare Zusammenhang ist zwischen Mathilden und dieser Blume? Jenes Gesicht, das aus dem Kelche sich mir entgegenneigte, es war Mathildens himmlisches Gesicht . . .' (*Schriften*, I, 107).

[254] 'Liebe Mathilde, ich möchte Euch einen köstlichen lautern Sapphir nennen.' (ibid., I, 111).

[255] *Theatrum chemicum*, vol. V, Argentorati (Strasbourg), 1622, XXX, 899; quoted by C. G. Jung, *Psychology and Alchemy*, in *Collected Works*, Routledge and Kegan Paul, vol. 12, p. 77. Cf. M. Delcourt, op. cit., p. 127: 'Né dans l'alambic ou sortant de la fleur mystique, ou encore du *saphir bleu de l'hermaphrodite*, Mercure représente excellemment l'androgyne des alchimistes.'

[256] Spenlé, op. cit., p. 58.

[257] *Science de l'amour*, p. 99

[258] *Comment on devient fée*, pp. 36, 197.

[259] ibid., p. 35.
[260] ibid., p. 145.
[261] *Science de l'amour*, p. 99.
[262] ibid., p. 95.
[263] *L'Androgyne*, p. 38.
[264] *Science de l'amour*, p. 95.
[265] ibid., p. 35.
[266] ibid., p. 119.
[267] *Comment on devient fée*, p. 306; *Science de l'amour*, pp. 62f., 86.
[268] *Science de l'amour*, p. 63.
[269] ibid., pp. 147f.
[270] *L'Androgyne*, p. 269.
[271] ibid., pp. 38f.
[272] ibid., p. 265.
[273] *Vice suprême*, p. 127.
[274] Mallarmé, *Les Noces d'Hérodiade, Mystère, publié avec une introduction par G. Davies*, Paris, 1959, p. 80.
[275] J.-P. Richard, *L'Univers imaginaire de Mallarmé*, Paris, 1961, p. 174.
[276] J. Gengoux, *Le symbolisme de Mallarmé*, Paris, 1950, p. 141.
[277] Mallarmé *Œuvres complètes*, Pléiade ed. by H. Mondor and G. Jean-Aubrey, 1951 reprint, p. 48.
[278] Gengoux, op. cit., pp. 146, 196 n. 5.
[279] *Noces, Introduction*, p. 42.
[280] *Noces*, p. 120.
[281] ibid., p. 211.
[282] ibid., p. 136.
[283] ibid., p. 115.
[284] ibid., p. 138.
[285] ibid., p. 138.
[286] ibid., p. 220.
[287] ibid., p. 79.
[288] A. R. Chisholm, *Mallarmé's Grand Œuvre*, Manchester U.P., 1962, p. 78.
[289] Mallarmé, *Œuvres*, p. 56.
[290] Chisholm, op. cit., pp. 40ff.
[291] Mallarmé, *Œuvres*, p. 37.
[292] Richard, op. cit., p. 109
[293] Mallarmé, *Œuvres*, p. 69.
[294] Gengoux, op. cit., pp. 180f, 189.
[295] A. Thibaudet, *La Poésie de Stéphane Mallarmé*, Paris, Gallimard, 2e éd., 1926, p. 390.
[296] Mallarmé, *Œuvres*, p. 47.
[297] Richard, op. cit., p. 121.
[298] For the frequency of images of the 'festin charnel' or 'amoureux', see Richard, op. cit., p. 142, who interprets the images otherwise.
[299] *A Rebours*, pp. 259f.
[300] ibid., p. 260.
[301] Mallarmé, *Propos sur la poésie*, Monaco, 1946, p. 33.
[302] P. Delior, 'La Femme et le sentiment de l'amour chez Mallarmé', *Mercure de France*, 15 juillet 1910, t. 86, pp. 193–206, p. 206.
[303] Cf. Richard, op. cit., pp. 54, 73f.
[304] ibid., pp. 98–100.
[305] C. Chassé, 'Les Thèmes de la stérilité et de la virginité chez Mallarmé', *Revue des sciences humaines*, Avril-Juin 1953, pp. 171–81, 176.

[306] M. Eliade, op. cit., p. 138.

[307] Spenlé, op. cit., pp. 256f.; cf. Novalis, *Schriften*, II, 38.

[308] H. de Latouche, *Fragoletta, nouvelle édition, Œuvres complètes de H. de Latouche*, Paris, 1867, p. 340.

[309] ibid., p. 338.

[310] ibid., p. 262: 'Auprès de vous seulement j'ai cru exister. Là, je doutais moins de ce qu'ils appellent la Providence; là, je n'accusais plus de distraction l'être capricieux qui dispense la vie'.

[311] ibid., p. 84: 'Dieu lui-même est injuste aussi, car l'existence qu'il m'a donnée porterait malheur à qui placerait en moi une espérance d'attachement'.

[312] ibid., p. 263: 'Ton Dieu, qui se joue de ses propres lois et du supplice de ses créatures?'

[313] Letter to Mme Hanska, 20–24 novembre 1833.

[314] ibid.

[315] *Conjugal Love*, §52; *Heaven and Hell*, §367.

[316] *Heaven and Hell*, §382.

[317] *Conjugal Love*, §42.

[318] *Séraphîta, Œuvres complètes de H. de. Balzac.* Michael Lévy, XXII (1870), p. 163.

[319] ibid., p. 161.

[320] ibid., p. 163.

[321] *Conjugal Love*, §71.

[322] *Apocalypse Explained*, §983.

[323] *Conjugal Love*, §48.

[324] ibid., §48.

[325] ibid., §68.

[326] *Séraphîta*, pp. 127, 218.

[327] Cf. Suzanne Lilar, *Le Couple*, Grasset, 1963, pp. 67f.

[328] Bertault, *Balzac et la religion*, Paris, 1942, pp. 174–6.

[329] F. Ancillon, *Essai sur la science et sur la foi philosophique*, Paris, 1830, pp. 269–73.

[330] ibid., p. 256.

[331] *Un Prince de la Bohème*, *Œuvres*, XI, 33.

[332] Quoted by Bertault, op. cit., p. 178.

[333] *L'Enfant maudit*, *Œuvres complètes de H. de Balzac*, Michel Lévy, XVI (1870), p. 88.

[334] *Béatrix*, *Œuvres*, Michel Lévy, III (1869), p. 270.

[335] *La Cousine Bette*, *Œuvres*, Michel Lévy, X (1869), p. 261.

[336] *Séraphîta*, p. 130.

[337] *Prince de la Bohème*, XI, 33.

[338] *Bette*, X, 261.

[339] *Séraphîta*, p. 153.

[340] ibid., p. 153, italics mine.

[341] *Heaven and Hell*, §367; cf. *Séraphîta*, p. 157.

[342] *Séraphîta*, p. 156.

[343] ibid., p. 130.

[344] ibid., p. 124.

[345] H. Evans, *Louis Lambert et la philosophie de Balzac*, Paris, 1951, pp. 205ff.

[346] *Bette*, X, 89.

[347] *Vice suprême*, pp. 77f.

[348] ibid., p. 125.

[349] ibid., p. 123.

[350] The moral ambiguity of the androgyne in Balzac's work is underlined by

the fact that, at the same time as he was writing *Séraphîta*, he was also working on the story of another androgynous person loved and desired by both a man and a woman, and that the angelic Séraphîta existed simultaneously in his mind with the perverse 'girl with the golden eyes'.

[351] A. Strindberg, *Die Gotischen Zimmer*, München u. Leipzig, 1908, p. 118.

[352] Guaita, *Essais de sciences maudites*, I, Paris, 1890, p. 71.

[353] *Préface* to Péladan's *Vice suprême*, xiii.

# THE FORTUNATE FALL AND HAWTHORNE'S *THE MARBLE FAUN*

*David Howard*

> A woman's chastitity consists, like an onion, of a series of coats. You may strip off the outer ones without doing much mischief, perhaps none at all; but you keep taking off one after another, in expectation of coming to the inner nucleus, including the whole value of the matter. It proves, however, that there is no such nucleus, and that chastity is diffused through the whole series of coats, is lessened with the removal of each, and vanishes with the final one, which you supposed would introduce you to the hidden pearl.

THAT is a fairly uncharacteristic quotation from Nathaniel Hawthorne, from his *English Notebooks* (1853)[1]—not of course from his wife's bowdlerized version. It is uncharacteristic because direct and pessimistic. More typical, still on the same subject, is this passage from *The Marble Faun* (1860), Hawthorne's last completed novel. It comes in a chapter called 'Snow-Drops and Maidenly Delights', which celebrates the virgin 'season' of Hilda, the New England heroine. Hawthorne, whose own engagement was a long one, admonishes her lover, the sculptor Kenyon, for not enjoying the condition more:

> If we knew what is best for us, or could be content with what is reasonably good, the sculptor might well have been satisfied, for a season, with this calm intimacy, which so sweetly kept him a stranger in her heart, and a ceremonious guest; and yet allowed him the free enjoyment of all but its deeper recesses. The flowers that grow outside of these minor sanctities have a wild, hasty charm, which it is well to prove; there may be sweeter ones within the

> sacred precinct, but none that will die while you are handling them, and bequeath you a delicious legacy, as these do, in the perception of their evanescence and unreality.
>
> And this may be the reason, after all, why Hilda, like so many other maidens, lingered on the hither side of passion; her finer instinct and keener sensibility made her enjoy those pale delights in a degree of which men are incapable. She hesitated to grasp a richer happiness, as possessing already such measure of it as her heart could hold, and of a quality most agreeable to her virgin tastes.[2]

Setting aside the uneasy quality of Hawthorne's imagery—elsewhere in the book Hilda is apostrophied as 'Poor sufferer for another's sin! Poor well-spring of a virgin's heart, into which a murdered corpse had casually fallen. . . .'[3]—what I want to note here is the attitude of having it both ways, the idea that Hilda can be both virgin and woman. Both passages involve the paradox that the possession of chastity brings its loss, flowers 'that will die while you are handling them'. But in the latter passage these flowers are peripheral and expendable. The enjoyment of them leads to their death indeed but also to a 'richer happiness'. All is well ordered, without a contest of choices, but with the regularities and hierarchies of garden, seasons, or sanctuary. There is not, in this slacker prose, the sense, as there is in the first passage, of the ironies and disasters of attempting to have it both ways. This sense is more often found in Melville and, on this subject particularly, in *Pierre or the Ambiguities* (1852).

F. O. Matthiessen, in his book *The American Renaissance*, accused Hilda of trying to have it both ways not in sex but in religion. In the famous chapter XXXIX 'The World's Cathedral' where Hilda, the 'daughter of the Puritans' goes to confession in St Peter's, Hawthorne and she, it is said, are attempting to enjoy both Catholicism and Protestantism. Matthiessen speaks of Hilda's 'instinctive determination to eat her cake and have it too'. Her confession is the spiritual counterpart of 'American striptease'.[4]

Now the danger of this objection is that it may be merely a moral or even doctrinal one. There is a way in which having it both ways could work very well indeed. Henry James suggests it when he counts this scene, of which he approves highly, among the examples of the 'moral picturesque'[5] in the book. What he sees in the situation is irony, the New England girl and the Catholic Church comically diminished by their confrontation.

Another less-well-known example of this kind of situation and this kind of possibility occurs earlier in the book where Hilda is rejecting her friend Miriam after witnessing her compliance in a murder. The problem, as it was in St Peter's, is what to do with the 'terrible secret':

> 'Heaven help and guide me,' answered Hilda, bursting into tears; 'for the burden of it crushes me to the earth! It seems a crime to know of such a thing, and to keep it to myself. It knocks within my heart continually, threatening, imploring, insisting to be let out! Oh, my mother!—my mother! Were she yet living, I would travel over land and sea to tell her this dark secret, as I told all the little troubles of my infancy. But I am alone—alone! Miriam, you were my dearest, only friend. Advise me what to do.'[6]

This appeal to the murderess is not intended to be picturesque in James's sense. The possibility is missed, just as it is missed in the scene in St Peter's. Hilda's right to advice and confession from what she is prepared to loathe and reject is unquestioned.

But this kind of conjunction in the earlier *Blithedale Romance* (1852) is handled with wit and detachment. And not only this—for there Hawthorne at his best is capable not only of the moral picturesque, but of using the metamorphosis of character as part of a complex vision of human diversity, of coming near in Melville's phrase 'the unfathomableness of fullness'.

These examples point to a division in Hawthorne's work. His principal theme is the American attempt to form a new society, and the tension between past and present, European experience and American optimism, which that involved. His characters too are usually caught at crises of identity, like Hilda's crisis of virginity. All of his novels, finished and unfinished, and some of his best short stories, centre on such moments of transition. All of them deal with what I would like to call a revolutionary condition, a condition where life's possibilities are freed momentarily from time and presented for human choice. The varieties of human experience parade themselves: in the New England Holiday of *The Scarlet Letter*, in the evocations of the past of *The House of the Seven Gables*, in the dance of reformers at Blithedale. And in Rome, 'the city of all time', of *The Marble Faun*.

The division occurs between the Hawthorne who attempts a synthesis at such moments, the Hawthorne in other words who attempts to have it both ways, to get the best of both old world and new; and the Hawthorne of ironies and incompatibilities. This division is most obvious in the setting of his novels. The synthesis novels—*The House of the Seven Gables* and *The Marble Faun*—are not tied to fact. They are both 'mythical' in the sense that they are crude and abstract symbolical dramas of America's use of the past. *The Scarlet Letter* and *The Blithedale Romance* particularize period and actual social scene, in the last case a period and scene personally experienced, the Brook Farm experiment. They are not of course realistic in a Jamesian sense. But they are 'romances' which take off from fact—the facts of New England in the 1630s and 1840s. And although they are pessimistic they are far more a celebration of life than the cheerfulness and hopefulness of Hawthorne's other stance.

On the one side Hawthorne presents an easy, manipulated solution, where one choice, like Hilda's flowers, is enjoyed and then conveniently dies into another; on the other side a grasp of things as they are. *The Marble Faun* is an exercise mainly in this first kind. And I want to deal with its treatment of the Fall in this light.

The loss of a comic vision is one of several disappointments in the novel compared with *The Blithedale Romance*. With it go the wit and energy of style, except in very isolated passages. The dialogue—the chapter XXXVI 'Miriam and Hilda' is a typical example—is stilted, unbelievable, and frequently absurd. I will quote one example, for the absurdity of the dialogue is a just and neglected dominant impression of the book. Kenyon intervenes to help the reconciliation of Miriam and Donatello 'two souls . . . groping for each other in the darkness of guilt and sorrow':

> 'It seems irreverent,' said he, at length; 'intrusive, if not irreverent, for a third person to thrust himself between the two solely concerned in a crisis like the present. Yet, possibly as a by-stander, though a deeply interested one, I may discern somewhat of a truth hidden from you both; nay, at least interpret or suggest some ideas which you might not so readily convey to each other.'
>
> 'Speak!' said Miriam. 'We confide in you.'
>
> 'Speak!' said Donatello. 'You are true and upright.' [7]

The book is both too long and too short; tedious and slow in development, seemingly padded out with guide-book descriptions which belong rather to *The French and Italian Notebooks.*[8] Too short in its loose ends and the congestion of the working-out of its plot. Yet there remains one of the best extended scenes in Hawthorne's fiction, the Carnival of Rome.

Many discussions of *The Marble Faun*, indeed of Hawthorne's fiction in general, centre round the idea of the fortunate fall, which is in this novel explicitly stated. 'Did Adam fall', Kenyon asks, in one of several formulations and discussions, 'that we might ultimately rise to a far loftier paradise than his?'[9] The distinction between Adam and 'us' is an interesting one and one which does not always influence this discussion sufficiently. By far the commonest version of the fortunate fall talked about—one indeed that turns up as frequently in the novel itself—is that we must sin in order to have moral and spiritual growth. Donatello, and Adam, qualify for a 'loftier paradise' by sinning.

The version I would like to emphasize is the one depending on a distinction between Adam and 'us', between sinner and those qualified to enter a 'loftier paradise'. The qualification is Adam's sin, but it does not qualify Adam. It qualifies 'us' because it gives us knowledge of sin and so destroys innocence and the original Eden. We will therefore be given a better one.

In *The House of the Seven Gables*, this version serves to distinguish the modern American couple, Phoebe and Holgrave, who only know *about* sin, from the American past, when the sins were actually committed. In *The Marble Faun* again it is the young American couple who are distinguished, this time from Europe, more specifically Italy and Rome, the 'city of all time' and also the city of art. We are presented again with Hawthorne's special involvement with the past, his sense that it must be used and discarded at the same time. And again in *The Marble Faun* as in *The House of the Seven Gables* this sense operates in a vacuum, conveyed through a personal crisis which becomes prescriptive symbolism, a myth of Europe, and Europe and America, unattached to the historical moment of its setting. Hawthorne's treatment of the fortunate fall is part of the general operation of this sense, which again is part of the book's characteristic tone of having it both ways. The fall of man, and the vast extent of the past, are merely two aspects of Europe dealt with—got the most out of—in a more general guide for Americans. They tend to predominate, in Hawthorne and in discussions of the book, which is a pity when there are passages like this (admittedly isolated) of an almost Dickensian strength:

> When we have once known Rome, and left her where she lies, like a long-decaying corpse, retaining a trace of the noble shape it was, but with accumulated dust and a fungus growth overspreading all its admirable features,—left her in utter weariness, no doubt, of her narrow, crooked, intricate streets, so uncomfortably paved with little squares of lava that to tread over them is a penitential pilgrimage, so indescribably ugly, moreover, so cold, so alley-like, into which the sun never falls, and where a chill wind forces its deadly breath into our lungs,—left her, tired of the sight of those immense seven-storied, yellow-washed hovels, or call them palaces, where all that is dreary in domestic life seems magnified and multiplied, and weary of climbing those staircases, which ascend from a ground-floor of cook-shops, cobblers' stalls, stables, and regiments of cavalry, to a middle region of princes, cardinals, and ambassadors, and an upper tier of artists, just beneath the unattainable sky,—left her, worn out with shivering at the cheerless and smoky fireside by day, and feasting with our own substance the ravenous little populace of a Roman bed at night,—left her, sick at heart of Italian trickery, which has uprooted whatever faith in man's integrity had endured till now, and sick at stomach of sour bread, sour wine, rancid butter, and bad cookery, needlessly bestowed on evil meats,—left her, disgusted with the pretence of holiness and the reality of nastiness, each equally omnipresent,—left her, half lifeless from the languid atmosphere, the vital principle of which has been used up long ago, or corrupted by myriads of slaughters,—left her, crushed down in spirit with the desolation of her ruin, and the hopelessness of her future,—left her, in short, hating her with all our might, and adding our individual curse to the infinite anathema which her old crimes have unmistakably brought down,—when we have left Rome in such mood as this, we are astonished by the discovery, by and by, that our heartstrings have mysteriously attached themselves to the Eternal City, and are drawing us thitherward again, as if it were more familiar, more intimately our home, than even the spot where we were born.[10]

Here the love-hate is very well done, the sheer intensity of the attack conveying the vitality of Rome. But this vitality, and more than that, this complete sense of attitude, this feeling for complexity, is rare in the book. Moreover, nowhere else, except in the Carnival scene, is the object, Rome, so vitally present. Notice how the paragraph runs down towards the end, how the 'astonishment' is simple and accepted, 'by and by', and how that mention of 'heartstrings' warns us that it is Hilda we are after and not Rome, and what Rome we do get will be a tourist's Rome of galleries, churches, and ruins. And it is in this Rome that Miriam, Donatello, Hilda, and Kenyon act out the fortunate fall.

My main intention is to emphasize the importance of the Americanness of Kenyon and Hilda in this matter, for what they risk and gain during the course of the book is partly their identity as Americans. They are made to undergo, especially Hilda, a series of tests and temptations, one of which is the sin-and-prosper version of the fortunate fall; that is to say Kenyon is tempted to believe this version. Throughout they are in parallel with the European couple Miriam and Donatello who act out what we might call the full or European version. They sin and provide the necessary instruction in, that is to say knowledge of, evil. Hilda and Kenyon can then retreat to their native and domestic Eden.

It is important to establish the difference between the two couples, especially between the two innocents Hilda and Donatello, because the same imagery tends to be applied to them, of a descent into darkness, forlorn wandering, and final reappearance in the light. Indeed a three-fold vision of this kind turns up in many guises in the book: for example the description of the sculptural process in terms of life, death, and resurrection,[11] or the continually emphasized account of Rome's history as consisting of three stages, Etruscan (equated with the Golden Age), Roman, and Christian.[12] Both couples in a sense do become acquainted with this three-fold vision, and do so roughly at the same times and through the same means. The possible confusion here, firmly rejected by Hilda, is expressed by Kenyon at the end of the book:

> Sin has educated Donatello, and elevated him. Is sin, then,—which we deem such a dreadful business in the universe,—is it, like sorrow, merely an element of human education, through which we struggle to a higher and purer state than we could otherwise have attained?[13]

The distinction between the couples, and between their progress, is that between sin and sorrow. Sin and guilt are the dark night of the soul through which Miriam and Donatello pass and dubiously emerge from. Sorrow at her friend's guilt, the discovery of the fact of evil, is Hilda's dark night of the soul. I want to demonstrate this distinction in the incident and detail of the book.

I want to note first one of the earliest differences established in the book, one I will develop more fully later, and that is a difference of temperament. In the first two chapters what is immediately insisted upon is the 'three-fold antiquity' of Rome, and

> a vague sense of ponderous remembrances; a perception of such weight and density in a by-gone life, of which this spot was the centre, that the present moment is pressed down or crowded out, and our individual affairs and interests are but half as real here as elsewhere.[14]

And what this sense gives rise to is a kind of 'fanciful merriment':

> When we find ourselves shading into shadows and unrealities, it seems hardly worth while to be sad, but rather to laugh as gayly as we may, and ask little reason wherefore.[15]

However it soon becomes apparent that this merriment belongs more to Miriam and Donatello than to Hilda and Kenyon. Throughout the book we are to be made aware of a New England earnestness as against a European frivolity, even with respect to the crowded and European past. 'There are sermons in stone'[16] Hilda says.

And Hawthorne does attempt in fact a re-enactment of this three-fold antiquity in his story of Donatello. This is one of the manifest weaknesses of the book, involving as it does a very crude historical myth, and combination with two other myths: the pagan myth of the Golden Age, and the Christian myth of the fall of Adam and the expulsion from Eden. It seems very much a question of 'doing' European history. However my point is that Hilda and Kenyon are involved in a rejection of all three myths, of all the aspects of Europe they involve.

These myths are introduced immediately with the statue of the faun and its resemblance to Donatello in the first chapter. The statue recalls the 'sylvan life', 'a period when man's affinity with nature was more strict, and his fellowship with every living thing more intimate and dear'.[17] This state of things is continually invoked in *The Marble Faun*, so much so that it disturbs the balance of the book, tending to make it centre on nostalgic idyll. However, in these initial scenes this accord with nature is treated as strictly pagan and is rejected by Hilda. It is important that it is a *marble* faun, apart from the discussion about art which goes on in the book which I will turn to later, because the permanence of marble raises the question of the importance and value of the 'sylvan life'. The 'flitting' quality of the faun's life is not fitted to the medium: 'I see only a corroded and discolored stone'[18] is Hilda's final reaction. Similarly when she is asked about the peculiar nature of the faun, how he seems to combine attributes of god, man, and animal, she replies, 'thoughtfully, and shrinking a little'

> 'It perplexes me, neither do I quite like to think about it.'[19]

What Hilda dislikes, as is made more clear later, is a mixture of things. God should be god as, later, good should be good and evil evil—no *felix culpa*.

Hawthorne does have immediate problems over good and evil in his Golden Age. They become obvious when it is identified with Paradise. To begin with it seems, along the lines of Hilda's disquiet, that Donatello himself contains elements that will upset things; he becomes savage and murderous at the sight of the artists' model. Yet the model is obviously the personification of evil in the book, although he is hard-pressed to keep up with the different kinds of evil that are required. When he appears from the Catacombs he is likened to a satyr 'hiding himself in sepulchral gloom, and mourning over his lost life of woods and streams'.[20] He is also taken for a pagan, i.e. a Roman spying on the Christians, and later he appears as a mad monk. In all three rôles he functions rather obscurely. Take for example his satyr-rôle: this would seem to suggest, along with what we learn of Donatello's ferocity, that the sylvan world is self-flawed. Its destruction follows inevitably from its own nature. Yet he appears in this rôle always as intruder and destroyer: I think this applies even to 'The Sylvan Dance' (Chapter X) in which he joins. Evil in the book is always exceptional whatever myth or period of history we are dealing with. The model as satyr is not really part of harmonious nature; as devil he is not really part of Eden; as mad monk he is not really part of Roman Catholicism. Always he appears as in his Roman guise, a traitor to his present world.

Now of course this makes for inadequate myth, inadequate history, and inadequate action. It really overturns Hawthorne's whole purpose, if we are to accept the pagan life, the Roman life, and the Catholic life, as essentially good. Matters are made worse by the occurrence of *general* attacks on these things, attacks in travel-book style on the crimes and battles of the past and the corruption of the church. They make it all the more apparent that Hawthorne has been unable to represent what Rome means to him. Indeed his generalizations sometimes have far more life than his action or characters as the passage about Rome quoted earlier indicates. He is able to say 'everywhere . . . a Cross—and nastiness at the foot of it'[21] but he cannot demonstrate that nastiness except in an isolated and melodramatic way. It is not only Hilda and Kenyon who are put through a process of insulation in the book, but the world and its symbolic story which threaten to contaminate them are also insulated. Miriam and Donatello after all are poor sinners, poor representatives of the mixture of good and evil. Everything is done to stress their essential innocence and misfortune, even in the actual murder. They seem almost as out of place in the Italian world as Kenyon and Hilda. Compare their 'evil' with Kenyon's vision of the wickedness of Rome after Hilda's disappearance:

> For here was a priesthood, pampered, sensual, with red and bloated cheeks, and carnal eyes. With apparently a grosser development of animal life than most men, they were placed in an unnatural relation with woman, and thereby lost the healthy, human conscience that pertains to other human beings, who own the sweet household ties connecting them with wife and daughter, And here was an indolent nobility, with no high aims or opportunities, but cultivating a vicious way of life, as if it were an art, and the only one which they cared to learn. Here was a population, high and low, that had no genuine belief in virtue; and if they recognized any act as criminal, they might throw off all care, remorse, and memory of it, by kneeling a little while at the confessional, and rising unburdened, active, elastic, and incited by fresh appetite for the next ensuing sin. Here was a soldiery who felt Rome to be their conquered city, and doubtless considered themselves the legal inheritors of the foul licence which Gaul, Goth, and Vandal have here exercised in days gone by . . .[22]

We miss rather a lot. There is some indication that Hawthorne did intend through Hilda's disappearance late in the book to introduce some of these unexplored regions of Roman life. Most of the associations above seem covered by the Palace of the Cenci, where she disappears, and there is talk of a political intrigue connected with Miriam. The fact that the Roman winter is virtually missed out—suddenly it's spring—perhaps is evidence for thinking that Hawthorne meant to substantiate some of his general remarks about the corruption of Rome, at the same time rendering Hilda's temptations and tests more exacting. But nothing comes of it except a benign aged New England jesuit and a final vision of the old masters.

But the failure really rests with the characterization of Miriam, Donatello, and the model, and the impossibility that their story should bear all the weight suggested of it, particularly the weight of the Roman past. Yet however diluted it still serves as the European contagion which the American couple must avoid. I may as well point out that to begin with there are hints that Miriam is far more wicked than she turns out. Apart from the unknown guilt from which she suffers, the episode of 'The Spectre of the Catacomb' serves as a kind of parody of the sin-and-prosper version of the fortunate fall. 'She came to me when I sought her not. She has called me forth . . .'[23] says the model; that is, Miriam does not conquer sin but sets it free, sends it abroad. But the 'bond' between them remains unexplored in this direction. And it becomes obvious that Miriam was originally innocent, although mixed up in an unpleasant enough affair, apparently a modern version of the Cenci case. The doubts about Miriam's relation to evil, whether perhaps she really is prepared to 'call it forth', dwindle into doubts about reparation for and salvation after the instinctive passionate action of one moment. It is this diminished type of the fortunate fall which we are concerned with, which causes Kenyon and Hilda so much horror, and which is maintained as doubtful throughout the book. Kenyon and Hilda are the obvious enough instruments of its suppression. There are many incidents like the song which Miriam sings at Monte Beni, which goes through the fortunate fall progression. It begins sadly recalling a 'better state' then

> when the emotion was at its profoundest depth, the voice rose out of it, yet so gradually that a gloom seemed to pervade it, far upward

> from the abyss, and *not entirely to fall away* as it ascended into a higher and purer region.[24] (my emphasis)

But I was attending to earlier parts of the myth, specifically the pre-fallen state. I have already noted Hilda's 'shrinking' from Donatello's faun-like propensities, and this American attitude is insisted upon in the first climax of the idyllic strain, which by now has taken on connotations of Eden as well as Pan, in the wild dance in the grounds of the Villa Borghese:

> Here, as it seemed, had the Golden Age come back again within the precincts of this sunny glade, thawing mankind out of their cold formalities, releasing them from irksome restraint, mingling them together in such childlike gayety that new flowers (of which the old bosom of the earth is full) sprang up beneath their footstep. The sole exception to the geniality of the moment, as we have understood, was seen in a countryman of our own, who sneered at the spectacle and declined to compromise his dignity by making a part of it.[25]

The break-up of the dance after the appearance of the model, and its comparison to a funeral-dance, makes the American's attitude more serious than at first appears.

However, the most important confrontation of the Eden pastoral comes in the middle section of the book, dealing with Monte Beni. Here in the account of the country around Donatello's villa and of 'The Pedigree of Monte Beni' there is the most extended version of the pastoral idyll. What is most important for my purposes is that it is exhibited both as a temptation and as something that is passing away; that is, to a certain extent, Kenyon is relieved from the necessity of rejecting it. This is partly due, I think, again, to the difficulties of combining the personal story with the historical scheme.

The references to the pastoral life, as Eden, Arcadia, 'the sylvan life of Etruria' etc., in this section, are too numerous to mention. What is more distinctive is the sense that everything to do with it, the towns and villages, and Donatello and the Monte Beni breed itself, is in decay. The 'delicious times' have been lost: 'mankind are getting so far beyond the childhood of their race that they scorn to be happy any longer'. They are 'all parts of a complicated scheme of progress, which commonly result in our arrival at a colder and drearier region than we were born in'.[26]

This loss of contact with nature reaches a symbolic climax when Donatello (this is after his crime, of course) attempts to call the beasts to him as he did as a child, and fails. 'All nature shrinks from me, and shudders at me!'[27] Kenyon is shown in some fairly straightforward recognitions of the limitations of this harmony with nature. He prefers New England cider to Tuscan wine. More importantly he is aware of

> the soothing and genial effects of an habitual intercourse with nature, in all ordinary cares and griefs; while, on the other hand, her mild influences fall short in their effect upon the ruder passions, and are altogether powerless in the dread fever fit or deadly chill of guilt.[28]

But it is Kenyon's involvement with the decaying process that is more fascinating. In a sense, I suppose, the decay of the pastoral life is more of a temptation to Kenyon than its ordinary existence. Its transitoriness makes it the more appealing, it exists as a kind of last chance. But the chance, I think, is a chance to see, rather than a chance to be at one with. Just like the American at the wild pagan dance, just like Hilda in St Peter's, just like the foreigners at the Carnival, Kenyon has arrived in Eden too late to be properly tempted, but not too late to pretend participation. The Eden in which Kenyon substitutes for Donatello is very much the tourist's Eden. It is a neat irony that nature may be rejecting Kenyon (hiding in the bushes) rather than Donatello in the scene mentioned above.[29]

It is Kenyon who enjoys the Eden, the substitute Eden, now; who drinks the wine 'Sunshine', mixes with the peasants, listens to the tales of the improvisatori, watches the jugglers, and dances by moonlight. 'But very seldom had they the young Count as a listener or a spectator.'[30] This is how Kenyon's enjoyment is described:

> The sculptor strayed amid its vineyards and orchards, its dells and tangled shrubberies, with somewhat the sensations of an adventurer who should find his way to the site of ancient Eden, and behold its loveliness through the transparency of that gloom which has been brooding over those haunts of innocence ever since the fall. Adam saw it in a brighter sunshine, but never knew the shade of pensive beauty which Eden won from his expulsion.[31]

That is exactly the difference between Donatello and Kenyon. Donatello's fall has left his Eden more beautiful, less dangerous, and more open to inspection. This tourist's sensation of being in paradise—the very spot where it all happened—has been expressed earlier in the book (indeed, my contention is that this kind of sensation gives the book its general tone). Hawthorne describes the gardens of the Villa Borghese:

> The final charm is bestowed by the malaria. There is a piercing, thrilling, delicious kind of regret in the idea of so much beauty thrown away, or only enjoyable at its half-development, in winter and early spring, and never to be dwelt amongst, as the home-scenery of any human being. For if you come hither in summer, and stray through these glades in the golden sunset, fever walks arm in arm with you, and death awaits you at the end of the dim vista. Thus the scene is like Eden in its loveliness; like Eden, too, in the fatal spell that removes it beyond the scope of man's actual possessions. But Donatello felt nothing of this dreamlike melancholy that haunts the spot . . .[32]

Donatello can only enjoy the straight Eden. It is Kenyon and Hilda who are in a position to enjoy the 'final charm' of the fallen paradise. They can both enjoy and reject, particularly because they are in at the death of it, and merely as bystanders. Hilda is in at the first death, the fall of man, symbolically; or in at the virtuous Roman casting the traitor from the heights; or by way of her visionary copying, in at the moment when Raphael or Guido first put brush to canvas, canvases now faded. It is very much a matter of having it both ways, indeed sometimes of having it better in one of the ways—the one you are rejecting—than the actual participants. Hilda and Kenyon appear as great advisers, as those who know the game best by watching it. As Kenyon tells Miriam and Donatello 'as a bystander, though a deeply interested one, I may discern somewhat of truth that is hidden from you both.'[33] Some things, like the great paintings in churches, are only revealed to visitors.

I have not stressed very much the element of temptation or contagion involved in these attitudes toward the Edens that appear. This is partly because there seems very little chance that, for instance, anyone will actually test the malarial charm of the villa grounds around Rome. But also because Hawthorne himself prevents it from becoming a real issue, in the attention and nostalgia he lavishes on the theme. This is having it both ways at its slackest, without the slightest danger, and perhaps more importantly, without the added relish of danger. How near can you get is far more obviously the issue in Hilda's watching of the murder, her passion for the old masters, and her involvement with the Catholic Church. When Kenyon for example imagines the perfect life he and Hilda might lead together at Monte Beni, this is treated not as a temptation of pastoral primitivism, but as one of interfering, even in imagination, with her freedom, and as such, an allowable activity in a lover.[34] What happens I suggest is that Hawthorne is thinking of the new Adam and Eve, who will be allowed to have the original Eden again. He does not really want to reject the Eden-pastoral life as much as he wants to reject the Catholic Church and European art. So that part of the distinction of couples appears to be that Kenyon and Hilda may recover the original Eden, and not merely be in at its death.

I do not want to say a great deal about the Roman aspect of Donatello's story; it seems to me that apart from the actual murder it is very skimpingly done, mainly through descriptions and discussions of Roman ruins and deeds in the chapters leading up to the murder, itself the supremely Roman act, XVI—XVIII. Here the burden of opposing views is taken by Miriam and Hilda, in, for example, the discussions of the moral to be derived from the Past,[35] of the Curtius legend,[36] and of Marcus Aurelius.[37] Miriam desires such an 'earthly king' to obey. Pat comes the observation from Hilda 'I should never look for such assistance from an earthly king.'[38] The discussions about the past and about Curtius's leap involve an opposition of stoicism and fatalism to belief in free-will and moral obligation. 'It was a foolish piece of heroism in Curtius', says Miriam.

> 'to precipitate himself there, in advance; for all Rome, you see, has been swallowed up in that gulf in spite of him. The Palace of the Caesars has gone down thither, with a hollow, rumbling sound of its fragments! All the temples have tumbled into it; and thousands of statues have been thrown after! All the armies and the triumphs have marched into the great chasm, with their martial music playing, as they stepped over the brink. All the heroes, the statesmen, and the poets! All piled upon poor Curtius, who thought to have saved them all! I am loath to smile at the self-conceit of that gallant horseman, but cannot well avoid it.'

> 'It grieves me to hear you speak thus, Miriam,' said Hilda, whose natural and cheerful piety was shocked by her friend's gloomy view of human destinies. . . 'If there be such a chasm, let us bridge it over with good thoughts and deeds, and we shall tread safely to the other side. It was the guilt of Rome, no doubt, that caused this gulf to open; and Curtius filled it up with his heroic self-sacrifice and patriotism, which was the best virtue that the old Romans knew. . .'[39]

I would note there the inadequate account of Miriam's view as 'gloomy', and also how Hilda, along lines already discussed, is able to give the Romans their due. This scene also illustrates, I think, the difficulty of combining the historical account with the story of the fall. We are far more aware—although I don't say it's a particularly interested awareness—at this stage of the book of the Romanness of things than of their embodiment of the Christian myth.

After the murder the latter emphasis is more obvious. Although the Roman comparison is kept up—Donatello has an 'heroic aspect',[40] the event 'had kindled him into a man'[41]—there are obvious echoes of Adam and Eve immediately after the fall: 'guilt has its moment of rapture too',[42] and so on. The parallels here are obvious and well known. There is the direct acquaintance with death through the body of the model-monk and the Capuchin cemetery.[43] And there is Donatello's rejection of Miriam in the Medici Gardens with its 'brown lizard with two tails'.[44] The parallel shrinking away of the American couple is also obvious: the discussion of the too easy goodness of Guido's Archangel,[45] Kenyon's refusal to see the cemetery (Hilda of course has not turned up), it being 'no place to nourish celestial hopes',[46] and Hilda's rejection of Miriam. I have already noted the peculiar tone of this last scene where Hilda continues to milk Miriam of advice, at the same time refusing her any comfort. Hilda couches her rejection in the same terms as Kenyon's refusal to see the cemetery; just as it would be morally confusing to have too close an aquaintance with death, so with the guilty Miriam:

> 'Your powerful magnetism would be too much for me. The pure, white atmosphere, in which I try to discern what things are good, and true, would be discolored.'[47]

Now this refusal to follow Miriam is also I think the author's, not merely in so far as he sides with Kenyon and Hilda—that is all too obvious—but in his arrestment of the narrative at this point. I am really making the same objection that can be made to the cosseting of Phoebe in *The House of the Seven Gables.* What happens here is far more damaging structurally I think: the scene is transferred to less dangerous territory. The idyllic middle section I have been talking about is both an idyllic evasion, a long sigh of relief after the horrors of Rome, and a leisurely and idyllic confrontation of those same horrors. It is presided over by Kenyon who of course does not know what crime has been committed. It is a fault of structure as well as one of pace and purpose, because this section, coming where it does, seems out of order, a deliberate regression to the Eden image and to a state of things where problems are more easily solved. There is no reason why there should be this return to the Eden image and at such length except Hawthorne's over-commitment to it, even or particularly as a fallen Eden, and its suitability unlike the Capuchin cemetery in Rome, as 'a place to nourish celestial hopes'. If I can put the case succinctly Monte Beni and Donatello are a sufficiently innocuous mixture of good and evil to be observed, especially through the partially ignorant eyes of the sculptor. Something like Hilda's 'spotless eyes'[48] are at work here, enabling us to get nearer evil, or rather good-evil, and extract from and deal with it safely. Hilda gets the same kind of assistance when it is a New England priest who makes the Church nearer and safer. The 'pensive beauty' of the fallen Eden is the more picturesque—unfortunately not in James's sense morally picturesque.

There is another aspect of this evasion which is reflected both in structure and pace, and that is the substitution of consideration—discussion, thought, brooding—for action. This makes short work of Donatello's Roman aspect—this is one of the places where the absurdity of conflating the fall story with the history of Rome is most obvious—and indicates a phenomenally quick onset of Christian tendencies. But more importantly the action —the murder—was a present one, however many symbolic overtones it had, and threatened to destroy the whole process and argument of the book, the whole way in which it presents its choices, which is through discussion, thought, brooding, about the past, about actions overlaid by the past, temptations and horrors at several removes like faded pictures and the corrupt Church. The book loses a momentum, a respect for action, at this point which it does not regain until the Carnival scene. Donatello and Miriam suffer a diminishment from which they never recover.

Admittedly the kind of development that is vaguely promised of them does smack of 'gothic horrors' like the Capuchin monk and cemetery, and their participation in the whole present and past brotherhood of crime.[49] It would merely be crimes at some remove instead of Eden. When the following estimation is made of Miriam, in mimicry of Macbeth, 'that she anticipated a certain solace and absolute relief in passing from one ghastly spectacle to another of long-accumulated ugliness'[50] it is unfortunately not a comic moment as a similar one would have been with Zenobia in *The Blithedale Romance*. The possibility and suppression of the comic element is something I take up later.

There is however another element which is begun and suppressed, and that is their belief and exhilaration in the efficacy of action itself, their sense of liberation after the murder. This is not, I think, merely a re-enactment of Roman triumph and the temporary hubris of Adam. The issue of the chapter 'The Faun's Transformation' is what kind of transformation. The hysterical uncontrolled tone of this chapter, like the chapter 'Governor Pyncheon' in *The House of the Seven Gables*, indicates dealing with a subject which may get out of hand, which must be forced down to size. Suggestions that Donatello has become a man, that the couple are liberated, that their relationship has a new strength, are ludicrously editorialized. The style becomes a parody of the being-fair-to-everyone attitude dominating the book elsewhere:

> They flung the past behind them, as she counselled, or else distilled from it a fiery intoxication, which sufficed to carry them triumphantly through those first moments of their doom. For, guilt has its moment of rapture too. The foremost result of a broken law is ever an ecstatic sense of freedom. And thus there exhaled upward (out of their dark sympathy, at the base of which lay a human corpse) a bliss, or an insanity, which the unhappy pair imagined to be well worth the sleepy innocence that was forever lost to them.[51]

Compare this to the indulgent treatment of other temptations, art, or the Church; when for example Hilda has her moment of rapture, equally open, one would have thought, to ironic inspection, if irony is the right word here:

> And, ah, what a relief! When the hysteric gasp, the strife between words and sobs, had subsided, what a torture had passed away from her soul! It was all gone; her bosom was as pure now as in her childhood. She was a girl, again; she was Hilda of the dove-cote; not that doubtful creature whom her own doves had hardly recognized as their mistress and playmate, by reason of the death-scent that clung to her garments![52]

Inevitably the chapter 'The Faun's Transformation' ends in terms of the manageable past:

> 'Who knows, but we may meet the high and ever-sad fraternity of Caesar's murderers, and exchange a salutation?'
>
> 'Are they our brethren, now?' asked Donatello.[53]

The next stage of the faun's story, and the next point which distinguishes the American couple from their European counterparts, is of course Christianity. I have already tried to explain the circumstances favourable to spiritual progress in the move to the country. After Kenyon has tasted the pleasures of the decaying pastoral world he is in a position to use its properties to assert his own religious feeling and to promote that of his friend. From the tower of Monte Beni Kenyon and Donatello view the Umbrian valley: 'It seemed as if all Italy lay under his eyes in that one picture'—vineyards, villas, convents, towns, villages etc.

> What made the valley look still wider was the two or three varieties of weather that were visible on its surface, all at the same instance of time. Here lay the quiet sunshine; there fell the great black patches of ominous shadow from the clouds, and behind them, like a giant of league-long strides, came hurrying the thunder-storm, which had already swept midway across the plain. In the rear of the approaching tempest, brightened forth again the sunny splendor, which its progress had darkened with so terrible a frown.
>
> All round this majestic landscape, the bald-peaked or forest-crowned mountains descended boldly upon the plain. On many of their spurs and midway declivities, and even on their summits, stood cities, some of them famous of old; for these had been the seats and nurseries of early art, where the flower of beauty sprang out of a rocky soil, and in a high, keen atmosphere, when the richest and most sheltered gardens failed to nourish it.

> 'Thank God for letting me again behold this scene!' said the sculptor, a devout man in his way, reverently taking off his hat. 'I have viewed it from many points and never without as full a sensation of gratitude as my heart seems capable of feeling. How it strengthens the poor human spirit in its reliance on His Providence, to ascend but this little way above the common level, and so attain a somewhat wider glimpse of His dealings with mankind! He doeth all things right! His will be done!'
>
> 'You discern something that is hidden from me,'observed Donatello, gloomily, yet striving with unwonted grasp to catch the analogies which so cheered his friend. 'I see sunshine in one spot, and cloud in another, and no reason for it in either case. The sun on you; the cloud on me! What comfort can I draw from this?'[54]

The point here is not merely that Kenyon is capable of a vision which Donatello cannot grasp; or that this is the safe, disinfected Italy that Kenyon and Hawthorne can deal with. As well as a vision of God's providence, it is a vision of the glory of Italy and the glory of art, 'all Italy lay under his eyes in that one picture'. And it is not only God's providence that Donatello cannot see but also these visions. Again Kenyon is being a substitute Italian getting more out of it than Donatello. Again he is being mildly tempted, as Hilda will be, 'by such grand hieroglyphics as these around us'.[55] But again the keener enjoyment is accompanied by a rejection, the sense that this visionary Italy has passed away and indeed need not be rejected: 'these *had been* the seats and nurseries of early art, where the flower of beauty sprang out of a rocky soil etc.' In the next chapter Kenyon is to prefer the 'misty cloud-region' where the hill-tops

> looked like fragments of the world, broken adrift and based on nothingness, or like portions of a sphere destined to exist, but not yet finally compacted . . . the scene represented the process of the Creator, when he held the new, imperfect earth in his hand, and modelled it.[56]

And in later chapters we take a closer look at the squalor of some of the towns and villages. The irony that Kenyon should use this false vision for the purposes of spiritual nourishment for Donatello is one, I think not, fully realized by Hawthorne. Later in the book Kenyon rejects the picturesque compensatory scheme of Providence when Hilda seems to be in the hands of the other, dangerous Italy:

> . . . the ways of Providence are utterly inscrutable . . . though [it] is infinitely good and wise,—and perhaps for that very reason,—it may be half an eternity before the great circle of its scheme shall bring us the superabundant recompense for all these sorrows![57]

The vision and scheme remain—with its obvious connection with the idea of the fortunate fall—European. I may say that in this watchfulness for Hilda, Hawthorne is neglecting even the parasitical version of the fortunate fall. The darkness and storm that come between the light in the Umbrian valley scene—that may last for half an eternity—may be either of sin or sorrow, may be the burden of either Miriam or Hilda. It may be that Kenyon, as later in the book, is yielding to the temptation to confuse the two. He does not realize that a 'special Providence' watches over Hilda. She is after all too good to be kept waiting for half an eternity.

The emphasis on New England goodness—a sheer moral capacity that demands a special Providence—is another means of distinguishing the Americans. Kenyon opposed Donatello's plan to become a monk by way of expiation with the suggestion that he go out into the world and do good deeds.

> The idea of life-long and unselfish effort was too high to be received by him with more than a momentary comprehension. An Italian, indeed, seldom dreams of being philanthropic, except in bestowing alms among the paupers, who appeal to his beneficence at every step; nor does it occur to him that there are fitter modes of propitiating Heaven than by penances, pilgrimages, and offerings at shrines.[58]

Donatello's tower is a Catholic tower, his room at the top full of emblems, like the death's-head, which come between him and God and true religion: 'do not let us burden our spirits with them, in our feeble efforts to soar upward!'[59] Hilda's tower, by comparison, is in direct contact with heaven: 'you dwell above our vanities and passions, our moral dust and mud, with the doves and the angels for your nearest neighbours',[60] Miriam tells her. And elsewhere, 'I would give all I have or hope—my life, oh how freely—for one instant of your trust in God!'[61]

Her tower has of course a Catholic shrine which she tends. Why this is there, and why Hilda is drawn to the Catholic Church I have hinted at before. While Kenyon is extracting what he can from the fallen Eden, Hilda goes through the same process with the Church—it is part of the general temptation which Rome offers her: 'Rome—mere Rome—will crowd everything else out of my heart.'[62] To begin with it is of course, like Eden, a fallen Church. Hilda's tower is 'medieval', it belongs to the period when the Catholic Church was the true Church. This contrast of periods—once again insulating the true temptation in the past—is one insisted upon both in the narrative accompanying Hilda and that accompanying Donatello's penitential wanderings. It is typical of the latter that Donatello's reconciliation with Miriam and Providence is blessed by Kenyon and a bronze statue of Pope Julius III. The churches Kenyon visits are Gothic churches, their superiority over even St Peter's symbolized by their 'pictured windows', 'true symbol of the glories of the better world'.[63] In the market square in Perugia, in the great marble fountain 'the Gothic imagination showed its overflow and gratuity of device in the manifold sculptures which it lavished as freely as the water did its shifting shapes.'[64] This we are to contrast with the grotesque Bernini fountains of Rome. There is a three-fold comparison at work here: Gothic, post-Gothic, and also the kind of naturalness and freshness, to which the Gothic is the nearest approach, symbolized by water, 'the shifting, indestructible, ever new, yet unchanging, upgush and downfall of water',[65] and also by the purity of light in contrast to stain-glassed windows; 'give me—to live and die in—the pure, white light of heaven!' says Kenyon.[66]

I do not want to follow in detail Hilda's dalliance with the Church; I have already made it obvious that I consider it another parasitical enterprise (the parasite image does occur in *The Marble Faun*—as distinct from parasitic incident and character—but without significant use: the grape-vine 'converted the sturdier tree entirely to its own selfish ends, extending its innumerable arms on every bough, and permitting hardly a leaf to sprout except its own').[67] It is more obviously absurd than Kenyon's activities:

> It was not a Catholic kneeling at an idolatrous shrine, but a child lifting its tear-stained face to seek comfort from a mother.[68]

The tone is more unpleasant also, when it appears we are not to criticize Hilda for worshipping in a Catholic fashion but rather are to praise her for worshipping herself. She tells Miriam:

> A Christian girl—even a daughter of the Puritans—may surely pay honour to the idea of divine Womanhood, without giving up the faith of her forefathers.[69]

The Catholic Church, it is suggested, would be all right 'if there were but angels to work it'[70]—Hilda is often called an angel and

> the saints above are touched by the sorrows of distressed people on earth, and yet are never made wretched by them. Not that I profess to be a saint, you know,' she added, smiling radiantly[71]

—Hilda is often compared to a saint.

The extent to which Hilda takes over the Catholic Church is extraordinary; as in her regard for the great painters

> she had a faculty (which, fortunately for themselves, pure women often have) of ignoring all moral blotches in a character that won her admiration. She purified the objects of her regard by the mere act of turning such spotless eyes upon them.[72]

This characteristic seems to be presented for approval, unlike the same thing in that 'gentle parasite' Priscilla in *The Blithedale Romance*. Indeed this taking over is presented as much better than Kenyon's straightforward antipathy toward the Church as a 'mass of unspeakable corruption'.[73] Hilda is even allowed her vision of a new Christian unity based on the best in every branch of Christianity.[74] I think Hawthorne here is involved in an irresolution similar to that over Eden: whether the Church should be enjoyed nostalgically, as a glory of the past, or whether its better part—its 'painted windows'—should be rescued and given new life. The characteristics of England, and its relations with the United States, presented the same problem to him.[75]

I am probably presenting Hilda as far more in command than she in fact is. Much—far too much—is made of her lonely and orphan quality, her apparent susceptibility. This seems to me part of the effect Hawthorne wants; not only to show an ambiguous dalliance with Europe but also innocence unconsciously pursuing such dalliance. Her use of the Church—like her use of Miriam, part of a pursuit of a mother[76]—is instinctive and uncalculated: 'She did not think; she only felt.'[77] It is also part of her unconscious pursuit of love. 'Had you been here yesterday, I would have confessed to you,'[78] she tells Kenyon. This has its gently ironic aspect—mainly at the expense of Kenyon who thinks she has become a Catholic—but it is mainly part of giving Hilda the best of everything, the best kind of development through everything. She is not being criticized for preferring the comforts of the Church to the love of Kenyon; she is being allowed to have both. In contrast the innocence of Donatello, although similarly involving him in an instinctive and uncalculated act, is led to the death's-head aspect of the Church, and the death-grip aspect of love: 'your bond is twined with such black threads that you must never look upon it as identical with the ties that unite other loving souls.'[79] The harmless quality of Hilda's innocence is made ludicrously clear in the actual circumstances of the confession. Not only is she allowed a sympathetic New England priest but it turns out that the government already know the information she gives. She is prevented from unconsciously harming her friends (I might note in passing that by means of the confessional Hilda is passing the sin back to Europe. It would not have been a good thing, after all, to have confessed to Kenyon).

I think this unconsciousness is at the heart of Hawthorne's approval of her. That she should go to confessional with the idea that what she says will be kept secret is not intended as a demonstration of her stupidity or a potentially disastrous ignorance. It is meant rather to demonstrate a naïve quality of belief and goodness the inadequacy of which demands the saving supervision of Providence. To have been better equipped would have been to be less lucky; to have been less sure would have been to be less deserving. Hilda must combine a belief in the efficacy of her righteousness with an innocence of practical result. The two necessarily go together as faith and inadequacy which deserve salvation. The right result follows not directly from the right action but as a reward; indeed the right action must look as if it would bring the wrong result. It can only be 'right' if impractical, if it is a confident humiliation before God which requires his intervention. This is what constantly happens to Hilda, a simple good action, like worrying about Miriam and going to look for her, landing her in trouble, her involvement in Miriam's guilt. She really is 'the daughter of the Puritans', who reaches the height of having it both ways, free will and fate.

The distinguishing quality of her unconsciousness is perhaps best seen when compared to its European equivalent:

> Chance and change love to deal with men's settled plans, not with their idle vagaries. If we desire unexpected and unimaginable events we should contrive an iron framework, such as we fancy may compel the future to take one inevitable shape; then comes in the unexpected, and shatters our design in fragments.[80]

This is a criticism of the planned wanderings of Kenyon and Donatello, their apparent purposelessness which is really a means to encourage the unexpected (Kenyon wants Donatello to have a chance meeting with Miriam). The unexpected can only come if there is a firm intention for it to overturn, one that must not expect the overturn. This is why Kenyon is worried by his own calculations for the chance meeting, why he 'cannot follow' Miriam in her calculation of the fortunate fall, and why, climactically, Hilda cannot allow his speculations:

> 'Oh, hush!' cried Hilda, shrinking from him with an expression of horror which wounded the poor speculative sculptor to the soul. 'This is terrible; and I could weep for you, if you indeed believe it. Do not you perceive what a mockery your creed makes, not only of all religious sentiments, but of moral law? and how it annuls and obliterates whatever precepts of Heaven are written deepest within us? You have shocked me beyond words!'[81]

Hush, you see, because if there is a fortunate fall we mustn't appear to know about it, we mustn't let on. Kenyon had in fact already been taught the lesson: his sculptures of Donatello turn out to be good only by accident.[82]

If there is one general lesson *The Marble Faun* teaches it seems to be that permanence, the permanence of art, building, thought, a way of life, inevitably involves decay. The idea of permanence is one that does not belong to the earth. It can and should only be hinted at: Hilda for instance rejects the achieved idea of the fortunate fall, but the last line of the book assures us that she 'had a hopeful soul, and saw sunlight on the mountain-tops' (it is possible that this means in context Hilda's turning away from the complexities of Miriam-Donatello). The mistake that Europe makes is to attempt permanence on earth. Hawthorne treats St Peter's as the symbol of this mistaken attempt: 'If Religion had a material home, was it not here?'[83] But it is not only materialistic religion it symbolizes. When Kenyon calls it a 'marble Eden' it takes up many of the ideas of Europe—or Italy—Hawthorne has allowed himself: the idea of permanence itself, throughout the book connected with marble, the value of art (which I have yet to comment on), and the Eden image. And also, more importantly, the circumstances of Kenyon's phrase connect these things, and the enjoyment of these things, with disease, decay, and death. There is a temptation to enjoy this supremely fallen Eden similar to the temptation to enjoy Monte Beni:

> 'The best thing I know of St Peter's,' observed he, 'is its equable temperature. We are now enjoying the coolness of last winter, which, a few months hence, will be the warmth of the present summer. It has no cure, I suspect, in all its length and breadth, for a sick soul, but it would make an admirable atmospheric hospital for sick bodies. What a delightful shelter would it be for the invalids who throng to Rome, where the sirocco steals away their strength, and the tramontana stabs them through and through, like cold steel with a poisoned point! But within these walls, the thermometer never varies. Winter and summer are married at the high altar, and dwell together in perfect harmony.'
>
> 'Yes', said Hilda; 'and I have always felt this soft, unchanging climate of St Peter's to be another manifestation of its sanctity.'
>
> 'That is not precisely my idea,' replied Kenyon. 'But what a delicious life it would be, if a colony of people with delicate lungs—or merely with delicate fancies—could take up their abode in this ever-mild and tranquil air. These architectural tombs of the popes might serve for dwellings, and each brazen sepulchral doorway would become a domestic threshold. Then the lover, if he dared, might say to his mistress, "Will you share my tomb with me?" and, winning her soft consent, he would lead her to the altar, and thence to yonder sepulchre of Pope Gregory, which should be their nuptial home. What a life would be theirs, Hilda, in their marble Eden!'
>
> 'It is not kind, nor like yourself,' said Hilda, gently, 'to throw ridicule on emotions which are genuine. I revere this glorious church for itself and its purposes; and love it, moreover, because here I have found sweet peace, after a great anguish.'
>
> 'Forgive me', answered the sculptor, 'and I will do so no more. My heart is not so irreverent as my words.'[84]

This scene is a crisis of intelligence for the book; it clearly demonstrates Hawthorne's incapacity to confront his theme. Kenyon's recognition of the ambiguities of their attitude to Italy—'Then the lover, if he dared . . .'—is diminished to ridicule and fancy. Hilda is allowed a simple and overriding 'reverence'.

I have not yet dealt with the subject of art, which occupies much of the book; this is partly because it does not seem fully worked into the narrative. In spite of his name—it would have been really overloading the plot to make Donatello go through an artistic phase—Donatello is not importantly connected with art. Miriam has to carry the burden of opposing the American couple on this matter, but this is mainly in terms of discussion of past art. Her own art is little more than a rather obvious indication of her character. Art does not figure in the enactment of the fall or Roman history. Its importance is as a temptation and European involvement for Kenyon and Hilda, and a hesitation on my own part to deal with it has much to do with it being the most tedious means of expressing the kind of involvement I have already described. Hilda's activities as a copyist, her apparent subjection to European art—'The old masters will not set me free!'[85]—and her eventual rejection of it, as lacking 'earnestness and absolute truth' and 'moral value'[86] (again, as with building, art is compared unfavourably with nature in this respect), is the most obvious example of this involvement, Kenyon goes through a very similar progression, 'the man of marble'[87] comes finally to prefer life, or love of Hilda, to art, 'Imagination and the love of art have both died out of me'.[88] This is acted out in the finding and rejecting of the marble Venus: 'I seek for Hilda, and find a marble woman!'[89]—in context this is meant for a criticism of Kenyon rather than Hilda: 'there was something dearer to him than his art; and, by the greater strength of a human affection, the divine statue seemed to fall asunder again, and become only a heap of worthless fragments'.[90]

There are differences in their stories; Hilda is devoted to art as an appreciator, Kenyon as a creator. Hawthorne is uncertain I think whether to show the inadequacy of European art or the inadequacy of art itself, although as something essentially European. Kenyon seems to reject art itself, but his art is presented as something essentially European, concerned with a false idea of permanence: 'It is especially singular that Americans should care about perpetuating themselves in this mode'.[91] But when Miriam talks about men being content with a memorial of grass,[92] the same bare opposition of art and nature seems to be supposed as with the comments on Roman fountains and the paintings in the galleries of Rome. In the chapter 'The

Emptiness of Picture Galleries' Hilda's weariness with European art leads to a straightforward nostalgia for home—American art does not figure in the contrast, she feels merely 'the exile's pain' and desires 'those days that never brought any strange event'.[93] But again elsewhere American artists who come to Rome are criticized for throwing up their chance of originality,[94] and towards the end of the book Hilda's vision of the seven-branched candlestick seems to contain promise of the superior art of the New World.[95]

Certainly both Hilda's appreciation of art and Kenyon's creation of it are shown to be distinctly American, in such scenes as the discussion of Guido's Beatrice,[96] or the difference established between Kenyon and the English sculptor who 'had foregone to be a Christian reality, and perverted himself into a Pagan idealist'.[97] What is important for my purposes is that both are shown to be taking typically parasitic roles with regard to art. Hilda's copying is too obvious an example of this; more interesting is the way in which Kenyon's art gives him an access to, which is at the same time a protection from, European or non-American experience. His art—like his love—may be described as insulating him from wild experience,[98] that is, as opposed to the experience of 'those days that never brought any strange event'. What this means in practice is shown by the scene with Miriam at his studio centring round his model of Cleopatra; this is a companion piece to the finding of the Venus at the end of the book. Here Miriam is rejected for the statue. The statue is like her—as the Venus was like Hilda—'fierce, voluptuous, passionate, tender, wicked, terrible, and full of poisonous and rapturous enchantment'.[99] Kenyon allows himself to know this woman through his art. But he rejects Miriam's plea for friendship and confidence—'you see far into womanhood; you receive it widely into your large view'[100]—when it seems that her secret may partake of the character of his Cleopatra.

The difficulty here once again is knowing whether this is about the artist and the function of art, like Holgrave and his daguerrotypes in *The House of the Seven Gables*, or whether it is about the American in Europe. There is a sense in which *The Marble Faun* is more about art than anything else. The parallel with the societies of ambiguous identity in *The Scarlet Letter* and *The Blithedale Romance* is not Rome but the artists' community. The book could be said to be a test of the artistic life in the same way that *The Blithedale Romance* is a test of the utopian socialist life. Like Blithedale this is a no-questions-asked community, free from conventional restrictions of intercourse. But the attempt to characterize this community does not go very far; the re-enactment of the fall of man takes prior place.

If the possibilities of the artists' community are dropped—possibilities perhaps of another European temptation in terms of 'brotherhood' as opposed to American isolation[101]—the opposition of the American artist's earnestness to the European's lack of such a quality isn't. This is largely how Miriam's art takes part in the argument. Her pictures are not only unhealthy—'over and over again, there was the idea of woman, acting the part of a revengeful mischief towards man'[102]—they lack real purpose:

> . . . beginning with a passionate and fiery conception of the subject in all earnestness, she had given the last touches in utter scorn, as it were, of the feelings which at first took such powerful possession of her hand.[103]

But to talk of Miriam's art is really to talk of her character, and also in a way to talk of the artistic life which Hawthorne hints at but does not really come to. The artificial model is her symbol, in terms that bring her very close to Zenobia in *The Blithedale Romance*:

> . . . a lady of exceedingly pliable disposition; now a heroine of romance, and now a rustic maid; yet all for show; being created, indeed, on purpose to wear rich shawls and other garments in a becoming fashion. This is the true end of her being, although she pretends to assume the most varied duties and perform many parts in life, while really the poor puppet has nothing on earth to do.[104]

This Miriam, who has a life of many forms without real commitment, who seems to embody a past greater and more various than that of Europe alone, 'dark eyes into which you might look as deeply as your glance would go, and still be conscious of a depth that you had not sounded, though it lay open to the day',[105] is not, as I have said, allowed much activity in the book. Her diminishment is partly a matter of making her accept all too easily the values of Hilda and Kenyon, partly a matter of carelessness over her development. It is not always easy to sense Miriam's protean quality beneath the various rôles she acts in conversations; for example it seems merely odd and awkward that she should be given the attack on nude statuary at the beginning of Chapter XIV. Obviously the protean quality must be diminished if she is to appear submissive to the earnest moral evaluations of the American couple. This diminishment can be seen in practice in the discussion she has with Kenyon about the idea of the fortunate fall. From the possibility of the idea as a conceit—Miriam is in a mood of 'fantastic, fitful gayety'—the narration shifts heavily into moral assessment:

> 'I delight to brood on the verge of this great mystery,' returned she. 'The story of the fall of man! Is it not repeated in our romance of Monte Beni? And may we follow the analogy yet further? Was that very sin,—into which Adam precipitated himself and all his race,—was it the destined means by which, over a long pathway of toil and sorrow, we are to attain a higher, brighter, and profounder happiness, than our lost birthright gave? Will not this idea account for the permitted existence of sin, as no other theory can?'
>
> 'It is too dangerous, Miriam! I cannot follow you!' repeated the sculptor. 'Mortal man has no right to tread on the ground where you now set your feet.'
>
> 'Ask Hilda what she thinks of it,' said Miriam, with a thoughtful smile.

So far you might think Miriam has been baiting Kenyon rather well. The rhythms of her talk really do seem to convey the delight of irresponsible speculation, of accounting for 'the permitted existence of sin'. But then Miriam goes on to accept her own idea and Hilda's possible judgment of it seriously:

> 'At least, she might conclude that sin—which man chose instead of good—has been so beneficently handled by omniscience and omnipotence, that, whereas our dark enemy sought to destroy us by it, it has really become an instrument most effective in the education of intellect and soul.'
>
> Miriam paused a little longer among those meditations, which the sculptor rightly felt to be so perilous . . .[106]

But it is not the diminishment of Miriam alone I am concerned with. The qualities which sometimes appear in her are also briefly predicated of the artistic life; it is a life, like that of Blithedale, of liberated possibilities without the necessity of evaluation, a kind of energetic toleration:

> . . . they sometimes find their profoundest truths side by side with the idlest jest, and utter one or the other, apparently without distinguishing which is the most valuable, or assigning any considerable value to either. . . . The world had been set afloat, as it were, for a moment, and relieved them, for just so long of all customary responsibility for what they thought and said.[107]

Hawthorne's uncertainty about this attitude is obvious—that use of 'apparently' for example—as is also the emphasis on 'value' and 'responsibility'. Even at this point, where the theme is broached, there is nothing like the sympathetic insight of Coverdale in the earlier novel.

However, if it were merely the artistic life as here hinted at which lacked full treatment, the matter would be worth little attention. But it is, I think, life in Rome, the expatriate European life, that suffers diminishment; and more than that, it is the strength of *The Scarlet Letter* and *The Blithedale Romance*, the sense of revolution which makes for their fineness, which is suppressed. Even this might not be worth saying if it were not that in the final pages of *The Marble Faun*, in the Carnival scene, this power and vision break open the ponderous fabric of the book, and a vital chaos is come again.

This is also hinted at, along with Miriam's character and that of the artists' community, in the opening pages of the book, where the weight of Rome's past, the threefold antiquity, is seen as taking away the 'reality' and seriousness of the present. And here too, in the description of the sculpture galleries, is an image of the past animating the present, filling it with a dance of old and dead forms: 'Why should not each statue grow warm with life! Antinous might lift his brow, and tell us why he is forever sad . . .'[108] etc. (I am not arguing for the quality of the prose here.) The image is perhaps more precisely caught in the allusion to a sarcophagus where

> the exquisitely carved figures might assume life, and chase one another around its verge with that wild merriment which is so strangely represented on those old burial coffers: though still with some subtile allusion to death, carefully veiled, but forever peeping forth amid emblems of mirth and riot.[109]

The image is repeated at length in the sylvan dance, which is specifically compared to the activity of figures on a sarcophagus:

> As they followed one another in a wild ring of mirth, it seemed the realization of one of those bas-reliefs where a dance of nymphs, satyrs, or bacchanals is twined around the circle of an antique vase; or it was like the sculptured scene on the front and sides of a sarcophagus, where, as often as any other device, a festive procession mocks the ashes and white bones that are treasured up within. You might take it for a marriage-pageant; but after a while, if you look at these merry-makers, following them from end to end of the marble coffin, you doubt whether their gay movement is leading them to a happy close. A youth has suddenly fallen in the dance; a chariot is overturned and broken, flinging the charioteer headlong to the ground; a maiden seems to have grown faint or weary and is drooping on the bosom of a friend. Always some tragic incident is shadowed forth or thrust sidelong into the spectacle; and when once it has caught your eye you can look no more at the festal portions of the scene, except with reference to this one slightly suggested doom and sorrow.[110]

This conjunction of death and joy is far more than the uninteresting opposition of gloom and jollity in works like *The Maypole of the Merrymount*.

However, I might appear to be merely producing more evidence for the parasitic quality of the book which I have already dealt with at length. The present, in this kind of image, is parasitic on the past, takes its death, its pastness, and its variety as the occasion and material for festival. The difference between this and the American parasiticism lies in a fundamentally comic and frenetic nature. The American couple are both more serious about Europe and less involved in it. They are more apt to see sermons in stone, to try to understand the past, to give advice; but they remain essentially bystanders as at the sylvan dance or the Carnival. They do not commit an archaic act of murder like Miriam and Donatello. And most of all perhaps, they cannot entertain more than one experience at a time: Hilda has a continual horror of 'mixture', and, one suspects, of irony. In spite of the guide-book quality of the moonlight ramble before the murder there are hints of a more vital feeding on the past, 'to ruin the very ruins';[111] 'everywhere, the remnants of old grandeur and divinity have been made available for the meanest necessities of today'.[112] The Coliseum is a characteristic image of 'mixture', 'a strange place for song and mirth':[113]

> . . . religion jostles along side by side with business and sport, after a fashion of its own, and people are accustomed to kneel down and pray, or see others praying between two fits of merriment, or between two sins.[114]

The tone in these passages is one to be found more openly in *The English Notebooks*: that the American cares more about the European past than the European.

The difference, then, is one of use of the past, one that is expressed in the contrast of Miriam's passion and gaiety with Hilda's 'reverence'. The difference becomes clear with the description of the Carnival. I might say to begin with that Miriam does not play the part in it that one might expect; she is still under the diminishing hand of the narrator. Miriam and Donatello are not made to enjoy the Carnival. Miriam should be its Queen and isn't although she is given the Queen's line:

> There may be a sacred hour, even in carnival time,[115]

which has a possible dramatic force equal to Hester Prynne's

> What we did had a consecration of its own. (*The Scarlet Letter*)

The difference is carried by the description of the Carnival itself. The Carnival is the climactic image of the decayed simplicity of Europe, and it also shows Kenyon and Hilda's (although Kenyon bears the brunt of the opposition here) final disengagement from this decay. The Carnival is given the same qualities as Monte Beni, the Church, European art; it has fallen from truth:

> It is traditionary, not actual. If decrepit and melancholy Rome smiles, and laughs broadly, indeed, at carnival time, it is not in the old simplicity of real mirth, but with a half-conscious effort, like our self-deceptive pretence of jollity at a threadbare joke.[116]

The 'old simplicity of real mirth' is like Etruria, Eden, the Gothic church, the unfaded painting or the first sketch. Like the veiled paintings in the churches it is there for the benefit of the tourists.

> The populace look on with staid composure; the nobility and priesthood take little or no part in the matter; and, but for the hordes of Anglo-Saxons who annually take up the flagging mirth, the Carnival might long ago have been swept away, with the snowdrifts of confetti that whiten all the pavement.[117]

A measure of Kenyon's disenchantment with Italy is his indifference to the Carnival now compared with his enjoyment of it the year before—to be compared, say, with his loss of interest in art.

Now if this were all it would be no better than the 'spotless' enquiry into the other properties of Italy or Europe. But the saving thing about this last section is that the alternative to this simple gaiety and the American or rather New England reverence for it is given sufficient animation, despite that diminishing hand, to make it command the book. The impression of a 'worn-out festival' is gradually replaced by an unsimple gaiety which triumphs over the new and the old simplicities. It becomes a magnificent image of a revolutionary condition, of a licence drawing on all the forms of the past, and of present society, to make a kind of dance of the dead. It includes 'hereditary forms, at which a hundred generations have laughed',[118]

> . . . festal figures in such fantastic variety that it had taken centuries to contrive them; and through the midst of the mad, merry stream of human life, rolled slowly onward a never-ending procession of all the vehicles in Rome, from the ducal carriage, with the powdered coachman high in front, and the three golden lackeys, clinging in the rear, down to the rustic cart drawn by its single donkey.[119]

It is not merely a 'sympathy of nonsense'[120] but commands the attention of the whole apparatus of church and state and real power. There seems the possibility of a revolution in earnest:

> Besides the ordinary force of gendarmes, a strong patrol of papal dragoons, in steel helmets and white cloaks, were stationed at all the street corners. Detachments of French infantry stood by their stacked muskets in the Piazza del Popolo, at one extremity of the course, and before the palace of the Austrian embassy, at the other, and by the column of Antoninus, midway between. Had that chained tiger-cat, the Roman populace, shown only so much as the tip of his claws, the sabres would have been flashing and the bullets whistling, in right earnest, among the combatants who now pelted one another with mock sugar-plums and wilted flowers.[121]

The carnival reaches out to encompass everything: 'The sport of mankind, like its deepest earnest, is a battle'.[122]

And it is as an earnestness that cannot encompass sport or violence that Kenyon pursues, and is attacked by the Carnival for pursuing, his Hilda. 'Earnest people, who try to get a reality out of human existence, are necessarily absurd in the view of the revellers and masqueraders'.[123] Hawthorne, of course, is still with Kenyon and his earnestness: 'only that we know Kenyon's errand, we could hardly forgive him for venturing into the Corso with that troubled face.'[124] But he does allow to get through the triumphant animation of his attackers, their combination of sport and battle, the grotesque extremity of their life: its violence and passion, what elsewhere is called a mask of love and death,[125] the playing of many parts, and the sudden transformation of parts. Kenyon is allowed to see this life, and rejects it, and is judged for it:

> Fantastic figures, with bulbous heads, the circumference of a bushel, grinned enormously in his face. Harlequins struck him with their wooden swords, and appeared to expect his immediate transformation into some jollier shape. A little, long-tailed, horned fiend sidled up to him, and suddenly blew at him through a tube, enveloping our poor friend in a whole harvest of winged seeds. A biped, with an ass's snout, brayed close to his ear, ending his discordant uproar with a peal of human laughter. Five strapping damsels—so, at least, their petticoats bespoke them, in spite of an awful freedom in the flourish of their legs—joined hands, and danced around him, inviting him by their gestures to perform a hornpipe in their midst. Released from these gay persecutors, a clown in motley rapped him on the back with a blown bladder, in which a handful of dried peas rattled horribly. . . .
>
> Even yet, his merry martyrdom was not half over. There came along a gigantic female figure, seven feet high, at least, and taking up a third of the street's breadth with the preposterously swelling sphere of her crinoline skirts. Singling out the sculptor, she began to make a ponderous assault upon his heart, throwing amorous glances at him out of her great goggle-eyes, offering him a vast bouquet of sunflowers and nettles, and soliciting his pity by all sorts of pathetic and passionate dumb-show. Her suit meeting no favour, the rejected Titaness made a gesture of despair and rage; then suddenly drawing a huge pistol, she took aim right at the obdurate sculptor's breast, and pulled the trigger. The shot took effect, for the abominable plaything went off by a spring, like a boy's popgun, covering Kenyon with a cloud of lime-dust, under shelter of which the revengeful damsel strode away.
>
> Hereupon, a whole host of absurd figures surrounded him pretending to sympathize in his mishap. Clowns and party-coloured

> harlequins; orang-outangs: bear-headed, bull-headed, and dog-headed individuals: faces that would have been human, but for their enormous noses; one terrific creature, with a visage right in the centre of his breast; and all other imaginable kinds of monstrosity and exaggeration. These apparitions appeared to be investigating the case, after the fashion of a coroner's jury, poking their paste-board countenances close to the sculptor's with an unchangeable grin, that gave still more ludicrous effect to the comic alarm and sorrow of their gestures. Just then, a figure came by, in a grey wig and rusty gown, with an inkhorn at his button-hole, and a pen behind his ear; he announced himself as a notary, and offered to make the last will and testament of the assassinated man. This solemn duty, however, was interrupted by a surgeon, who brand-ished a lancet, three feet long, and proposed to him to let him take blood.
>
> The affair was so like a feverish dream. . . .[126]

And when Kenyon finds Hilda she is a mock queen of the Carnival—this the final 'frolic of the Carnival'. Hawthorne's intention here I think is to make Hilda's 'delicate mirthfulness'[127] triumphant. Her throwing the rosebud at Kenyon is a deliberate echo of the original simplicity of the Carnival, a 'gentle warfare of flowers' when

> Each youth and damsel, gathering bouquets of fieldflowers or the sweetest and fairest that grew in their own gardens, all fresh and virgin blossoms, flung them, with true aim, at the one, or few, whom they regarded with a sentiment of shy partiality at least, if not with love.[128]

But Kenyon and Hilda have become so much apart from the Carnival that it is impossible for them here to have it both ways. Instead of their using the Carnival and then rejecting it, the Carnival uses them, as its victim and as its queen; includes them in *its* itinerary. We learn later that it is Miriam who arranged Hilda's appearance at the Carnival: 'the fitful and fantastic imagination of a woman—sportive because she must otherwise be desperate—had arranged this incident'.[129]

There is then a powerful if unacknowledged final ironic placing of Hilda and Kenyon. The same could be said, admitting a lesser intensity, of Kenyon's discovery of the Venus in his search for Hilda—again this seems (the details are similarly obscure) a practical joke of Miriam's.[130] They are decidely out of their depth at this point, and Hawthorne is forced to desperate evasions of that depth—like the belittling of Miriam, or Hilda's fatuous chat with the old masters—to try and keep them his moral centres. The final note of the book is one of fear, the thrusting off of that final mockery, the idea of the fortunate fall. Cries Kenyon:

> 'I never did believe it! But the mind wanders wild and wide; and, so lonely as I live and work, I have neither pole-star above nor light of cottage-windows here below, to bring me home. Were you guide, my counsellor, my inmost friend, with that white wisdom which clothes you as a celestial garment, all would go well. O Hilda, guide me home!'
>
> 'We are both lonely; both far from home!' said Hilda, her eyes filling with tears. 'I am a poor, weak girl, and have no such wisdom as you fancy in me.'[131]

There is a final recognition of the terror of the revolutionary condition, a final fear that they have not escaped uncontaminated, that they might never reach 'home', that they have become wanderers in a wasteland:

> And, now that life had so much human promise in it, they resolved to go back to their own land; because the years, after all, have a kind of emptyness, when we spend too many of them on a foreign shore. We defer the reality of life, in such cases, until a future moment, when we shall again breathe our native air; but, by and by, there are no future moments; or, if we do return, we find that the native air has lost its invigorating quality, and that life has shifted its reality to the spot where we deemed ourselves only temporary residents. . . .[132]

## NOTES

[1] Edited by Randall Stewart, London and New York, 1941, p. 52.

[2] *The Complete Works of Nathaniel Hawthorne*, Riverside Edition, ed. George Parsons Lathrop, London, 1883 (referred to hereafter as Riverside), Vol. VI, ch. XLI, p. 426.

[3] ibid., ch. XXXVI, p. 377.

[4] *American Renaissance*, New York, 1941, p. 345.

[5] *Hawthorne* (1879), in *The Shock of Recognition*, ed. Edmund Wilson, London, 1956, pp. 553–4.

[6] Riverside, Vol. VI, ch. XXIII, p. 245.

[7] *The Marble Faun*, ch. XXXV, p. 368.

[8] Riverside, Vol. X.

[9] *The Marble Faun*, ch. I, p. 519.

[10] ibid., ch. XXXVI, p. 372. Admittedly the elements here are clichés—'Italian trickery', the ascending allegory of life in the hovel-palaces, etc.—but they come together with a fine disgust.

[11] ibid., ch. XLI, p. 432.

[12] E.g. ibid., ch. I, p. 20.

[13] ibid., ch. L, p. 519.

[14] ibid., ch. I, p. 20.

[15] ibid., p. 21.

[16] ibid., ch. XVI, p. 180.

[17] ibid., ch. I, p. 25.

[18] ibid., ch. II, p. 31.

[19] ibid., p. 27.

[20] ibid., ch. IV, p. 45.

[21] ibid., ch. XII, p. 135.

[22] ibid., ch. XLV, p. 467.

[23] ibid., ch. IV, p. 46.

[24] ibid., ch. XXIX, p. 310.

[25] ibid., ch. X, p. 109.

[26] ibid., ch. XXVI, p. 276.

[27] ibid., ch. XXVII, p. 288.

[28] ibid., p. 285.

[29] ibid., p. 286.

[30] ibid., p. 278.

[31] ibid., ch. XXX, p. 318.

[32] ibid., ch. VIII, p. 92.

[33] ibid., ch. XIII, p. 245.

[34] ibid., ch. XXX, p. 318.

[35] ibid., ch. XVI, p. 179.

[36] ibid., ch. XVIII, p. 191.

[37] ibid., p. 196.

[38] ibid., p. 197.

[39] ibid., p. 192.

[40] ibid., ch. XIX, p. 206.

[41] ibid., p. 203.

[42] ibid., p. 207.

[43] ibid., chs. XX and XXI.

[44] ibid., ch. XXII, p. 230.

[45] ibid., ch. XX, p. 217.

[46] ibid., ch. XXI, p. 226.

[47] ibid., ch. XXIII, p. 243.

[48] ibid., ch. XXXVII, p. 385.

[49] ibid., ch. XIX, p. 208.

[50] ibid., ch. XXI, p. 224.

[51] ibid., ch. XIX, p. 207.

[52] Hilda's confession in ch. XXXIX, p. 407.

[53] ibid., ch. XIX, p. 207.

[54] ibid., ch. XXVIII, pp. 296–8.

[55] ibid., p. 298.

[56] ibid., ch. XXIX, p. 305.

[57] ibid., ch. XLV, p. 469.

[58] ibid., ch. XXIX, p. 309.

[59] ibid., ch. XXVIII, p. 295.

[60] ibid., ch. VI, p. 71.
[61] ibid., ch. XVIII, p. 197.
[62] ibid., ch. XII, p. 135.
[63] ibid., ch. XXXIII, p. 349.
[64] ibid., ch. XXXIV, p. 359.
[65] ibid., ch. XVI, p. 171.
[66] ibid., ch. XL, p. 417. Hawthorne had been reading Ruskin in England.
[67] ibid., ch. XXXII, p. 336.
[68] ibid., ch. XXXVI, p. 379.
[69] ibid., ch. VI, p. 71.
[70] ibid., ch. XXXVIII, p. 393.
[71] ibid., ch. XL, p. 414.
[72] ibid., ch. XXXVII, p. 385.
[73] ibid., ch. XL, p. 416.
[74] ibid., p. 422.
[75] See *The English Notebooks*, pp. 172, 351, 494 etc., etc., and the unfinished last romances.
[76] *The Marble Faun*, ch. XXXVIII, p. 396. 'She never found just the virgin mother whom she needed.'
[77] ibid., ch. XXXIX, p. 406.
[78] ibid., ch. XL, p. 418.
[79] ibid., ch. XXXV, p. 369.
[80] ibid., ch. XXXII, p. 333.
[81] ibid., ch. L, p. 320.
[82] ibid., ch. XXX, p. 315.
[83] ibid., ch. XXXVIII, p. 400.
[84] ibid., ch. XL, p. 419.
[85] ibid., ch. XXXVII, p. 380.
[86] See ch. XXXVII, 'The Emptiness of Picture Galleries'.
[87] *The Marble Faun*, ch. XLV, p. 467.
[88] ibid., ch. XLVII, p. 483.
[89] ibid., ch. XLVI, p. 479.
[90] ibid., p. 481.
[91] ibid., ch. XIII, p. 144.
[92] ibid., p. 145.
[93] ibid., ch. XXXVII, p. 390.
[94] ibid., ch. XV, pp. 158–60.
[95] ibid., ch. XL, p. 422.
[96] ibid., ch. VII.
[97] ibid., ch. XV, p. 162.
[98] ibid., ch. XXXI, p. 324.
[99] ibid., ch. XIV, p. 153.
[100] ibid., p. 154.
[101] See ibid., ch. XV, 'An Aesthetic Company', p. 158.
[102] ibid., ch. V, p. 61. She figures here as Eve, of course, as well as Gael and Judith.
[103] ibid., p. 60.
[104] ibid., p. 58.
[105] ibid., p. 65. See the same page for her Jewishness, and ch. XIII for the comparison with Cleopatra.
[106] ibid., ch. XLVII, pp. 491–2.
[107] ibid., ch. II, p. 30.
[108] ibid., p. 32.

[109] ibid., p. 32.
[110] ibid., ch. X, pp. 109–10.
[111] ibid., ch. XVIII, p. 195.
[112] ibid., ch. XVII, p. 181.
[113] ibid., p. 183.
[114] ibid., p. 184.
[115] ibid., ch. XLIX, p. 506.
[116] ibid., ch. XLVIII, p. 493.
[117] ibid., p. 494.
[118] ibid., p. 493.
[119] ibid., p. 496.
[120] ibid., p. 496.
[121] ibid., p. 498.
[122] ibid., p. 496.
[123] ibid., ch. XLIX, p. 508.
[124] ibid., p. 503.
[125] ibid., ch. XLIII, p. 451.
[126] ibid., ch. XLIX, pp. 503–5.
[127] ibid., p. 510.
[128] ibid., ch. XLVIII, p. 497.
[129] ibid., ch. L, p. 515.
[130] See ibid., ch. XLVII, pp. 483–4.
[131] ibid., ch. L, p. 520.
[132] ibid., p. 521

# THE CONSERVING MYTH OF WILLIAM BARNES

*R. A. Forsyth*

The view that a group of people hold towards their past is one of the controlling factors in their morals, religion, art, and intellectual pursuits, to say nothing of the sights, sounds, and actual feel of their daily experience.

Charles Frankel, 'Explanation and Interpretation in History', in *Theories of History*, ed. Patrick Gardiner

I need not insist upon the social, ethical, and political significance of an age's image of man, for it is patent that the view one takes of man affects profoundly one's standard of dignity and the humanly possible. And it is in the light of such a standard that we establish our laws, set our aspiration for learning, and judge the fitness of men's acts. . . . Nor is it simply a matter of public concern. For man as individual has a deep and emotional investment in his image of himself . . . [and he] has powerful and exquisite capacities for defending himself against violation of his cherished self-image.

Jerome S. Bruner, 'Freud and the Image of Man', in *Freud and the Twentieth Century*, ed. Benjamin Nelson

## I

It is a byword that the Victorians responded in many different ways to finding themselves on 'a darkling plain'. This diversity indicates not only the complexity of their situation, which resulted from the scientific and industrial revolution that transformed English life during the century, but also the characteristic vigour of their efforts to disentangle and comprehend it. Such efforts ranged from Charles Kingsley's muscular embrace to Matthew Arnold's fastidious fortification against anarchy. Other Victorians were attracted by the ritualistic fervour and traditionalism of Newman, the semi-religious enthusiasm of the Pre-Raphaelites, or the individualism of Mill; still others looked for some effective way of combining these positions.

By contrast with these earnest efforts the response of the Dorset poet, William Barnes, appears at first sight to be simply a nostalgia for the peace of the 'good old days', which it seemed had been replaced almost traumatically by the insecurity of a withered faith and a permeating materialism. Certainly Barnes looked back persistently, both in his poetry and at many other levels in his creative and personal life, to his own youth in the countryside and the rural ethos it typified. I want to suggest, however, that viewed properly within the total complex of his personality, this backward-looking habit of mind, which dictated his particularity of selection and treatment of country life and its virtues, did not result from a sentimental evasion of contemporary issues, but amounted rather to a conscious criticism unwaveringly aimed at those very issues. I think one may go even further by suggesting that Barnes's work, more especially his poetry, constituted a myth of minor though not insignificant proportions, and of a thoroughness and consistency to be measured by the graceful strength of his verse. And Barnes's achievement is enhanced in that it stands in direct opposition to the idea of progress—which became identified with technical advances and was increasingly regarded, therefore, as mechanically inevitable—an idea which more than any other characterized the popular conception of the age as it went spinning 'down the ringing grooves of change', urged on by the convition 'that the Heavenly City is at this moment having its building plots laid out on earth'.[1]

Many Victorian poets spent their inheritance of Romantic idealism in striving, for the most part unsuccessfully, to find an intellectual faith through a sort of argumentative lyricism. The source of that inheritance was, of course, the revolt of the intuitive imagination against Augustan rationalism and empiricism, the attempt to comprehend imaginatively a mechanistic and materialistic view of the universe. This led to the rediscovery of an organic relationship between man and the dynamic force of nature which took on religious overtones that were translated into poetic myth. But Barnes's myth resulted, not from an involvement in revolutionary adaptation, but from a desire to preserve; he is not a nature poet in the sense commonly applied to Wordsworth, for example. His religion is immovably Episcopalian, and he rarely philosophizes or moralizes in his poetry about the 'Spirit of Nature'. As Tennyson commented after a conversation, their only one together, about Darwinism and pantheism—near sacrilege for the good parson—'he is not accustomed to strong views theologic'.[2]

Barnes's 'myth,' to use T. S. Eliot's definition, is the 'manipulating [of] a continuous parallel between contemporaneity and antiquity . . . a way of controlling, or ordering, of giving a shape and a significance to the immense panorama of futility and anarchy which is contemporary history.'[3] His parochial isolation was not simply a regionalist limitation. It was, rather, a considered and coherent attempt to preserve an imaginative Eden—with all the emotional and religious overtones of his own youth in the vale of Blackmore—as well as the people's traditional life in 'England's green and pleasant land' from what seemed to him to be the disastrous degeneration of that ethos into the 'futility and anarchy' of the 'dark Satanic Mills' of Coketown. That Barnes's poetry is concerned largely with recording the annals of the village is clear enough. But it seems to me that his writing about this rather circumscribed topic is obliquely also a commentary on his own life, symbolizing the virtues of a rural existence in the context of the cultural revolution which Ruskin characterized as the 'storm cloud of the nineteenth century'. It is Barnes's imaginative comprehension of those virtues, his accommodation of his individual talent to an ancient tradition, which is the basis of his art and of his validity as a poet of the countryside. As Hardy observed, he held 'a unique position [as] probably the most interesting link between past and present forms of rural life that England possessed', and that position constituted the 'world of circumstance', to use Keats's formulation of the spiritual struggle of man, in which Barnes discovered his 'sense of identity'.[4] For, as Hardy continues, the uniqueness of his position resulted not only from the great span of his life—it was, for instance, 'a day almost within his remembrance when . . . a stagecoach made its first entry into Sturminster-Newton'—but also from the 'remoteness even from contemporary provincial civilization, of the pastoral recesses in which his earlier years were passed—places with whose now obsolete customs and beliefs his mind was naturally imbued'.[5]

What I am suggesting in no way denies, of course, that Barnes's excessively modest and retiring temperament found complete satisfaction in living in the countryside, nor that the creative and personal sides of his life were, as a result, aligned. As Hardy justly observed of him, 'the poetic side of his nature . . . was but faintly ruled by the practical at any time, [and] his place-attachment was strong almost to a fault' (p. lvii). But to conclude that this satisfaction was the motivating source of his poetry is both negative and tautological, leaving completely out of account, for instance, that the real significance of his many personal and creative activities lies in their knitted inter-relationship. His archaeological investigations, to take an example, led him not only to refute 'the common view that our prehistoric colonists were a pack of H. G. Wellsian savages', but also directly to evolve a 'theory of the origin of poetry and music as a trilogy of song-tune-dance . . . found . . . in Stonehenge—Chorea Giganteum, the song-dance of the giants.'[6]

Such a conclusion also leaves out of account his extended attempts to restore the language to its pristine Anglo-Saxon health, as well as, more obviously, his writing much of his best poetry in a dialect of which he said, 'It is my mother tongue, and is to my mind the only true speech of the life that I draw.'[7] The close association here between language and a particular way of life is important because it points to his continual concern with an organic wholeness of sensibility, whose image is the compactness and coherence of his conserving myth. It may be true, as Geoffrey Grigson says in the Introduction to his selection of Barnes's poetry, that,'In the narrow sense, there are not art-and-society reasons for urging that Barnes should be read' (Grigson, p. 29). I would emphasize, however, a notion expressed earlier in the same excellent essay, that Grigson 'may have suggested, wrongly . . . that Barnes was indifferent to the times, or separated from them entirely' (p. 27). Coventry Patmore too seems to me to be, even in the narrowest sense, wide of the mark when he writes, 'Mr Barnes, in his poems, is nothing but a poet. He does not there protest against anything in . . . the arrangements of society.'[8]

## II

Barnes was a countryman born and bred and, because his poetry is always about scenes and events and people he knows intimately, it has a quality of authenticity which can be derived only from first-hand experience. As Hopkins rightly pointed out, 'the use of dialect to a man like Barnes is to tie him down to the things that he or another Dorset man has said or might say, which though it narrows his field heightens his effects.'[9] It would be false, however, to think of him as an untutored yokel, for he was in fact an educated and well-informed person of wide interests. Besides being a parson and schoolmaster, he was an accomplished linguist, a somewhat eccentric philologist, a competent wood-carver; he dabbled in etymology and archaeology, invented a quadrant and an instrument for describing ellipses, played the flute, violin, and piano, sang and composed songs, and was an expert in Welsh and Persian prosody. The list could be extended; but enough has been given to establish the point and to dispel any illusion about the quality of his reclusiveness. Nor did he have, as Patmore caustically remarked, 'the advantage of being able to demand the admiration of the sympathizing public on the score that he is a chimney-sweep, or a rat-catcher, and has never learned to read' (p. 155).

It is clear that a person of such varied interests, and the exuberant participation in life that they suggest, was not one who, for instance, refused until middle-age to go to London, or to try to make his literary way, out of a sense of personal limitation. And more important is the implication, tacit in much of his prose, that the talented diversity of his activities, many of them rooted in the ancient soil of folk-lore, and all of them stressing the primacy in artistic creation of 'fitness' or harmonious proportion of form, constitutes an oblique criticism of what he regarded as the straggling and fragmentary quality of many city-dwellers' lives.

The fading rural civilization, in many of its aspects, lived richly in Barnes's imagination, particularly through boyhood memories of the prosperous market town of Sturminster-Newton, which, two miles from his home across Bagber Common, was where he received his only schooling up to the age of thirteen. For it was there, as Giles Dugdale notes, that deep into the century 'most of the articles of equipment needed in the daily lives of the country folk living many miles around . . . which, elsewhere, the Industrial Revolution was accustoming Englishmen to buy from the large towns, were still made locally by skilled craftsmen.'[10] Even the knowledge necessary for effective participation in country children's games—'We . . . braided fishing lines of white horsehair, and made floats for them, and hung them on a peeled withy wand, and made small rush baskets for our fish'—Barnes regarded as one 'level of folk-lore'.[11] The inclusive scope and intimacy of the relationship between his creative life as an artist and what could almost be called its prerequisite, the rural ethos, comes out in a letter of Sophia Williams to Barnes's son after the poet's death: 'The increase of ready-made articles and of contrivances to save trouble did not commend themselves to him. He said it destroyed invention and self-reliance in childhood, weakened the sense of responsibility in later life, and reduced things to a standard of mere money cheapness, which he thought involved cheapness of character too' (in Dugdale, p. 185).

The Rev. O. P. Cambridge, in a memorial tribute, observed of Barnes, 'His life forms a harmonious whole such as the world rarely sees.'[12] And in the opinion of Rayner Unwin, he approached 'in his activities . . . the complete man of the Renaissance'.[13] It is this quality of fulfilment which should warn us against taking too literally the poet's own statement, echoed by those not fully aware of the disciplined construction of his verse, that his poetry was a 'leisure' activity, 'simply a refreshment of mind from cares and irksomeness' (in Dugdale, p. 207). This view seems incongruous in the light of those frequent first-hand accounts in which one sees not a simple country parson, but a man profoundly involved in creation. There is, for example, his daughter's recollection of the poet's habit of sitting in his garden 'with his eyes closed and face upturned into the sunlight . . . for an hour at a time, sometimes brooding poetry through the medium of visions, sometimes thinking out a deep question of ethics or philosophy, or perhaps puzzling with a new metre' (in Dugdale, p. 180). The significant issue for us at this point is that though by far the most important of his many imaginative activities, poetry was not an exception to, but an integral part of his creative personality. And that personality gained its coherence, as inevitably as did the rural sensibility he typified, from the sense of community that crowned a country upbringing. In Barnes, microcosm and macrocosm were harmoniously integrated.

## III

Barnes's alert awareness of contemporary problems of living, and his distinctive response to them, is well illustrated by his little-known work on the emergent science of economics, entitled *Views of Labour and Gold* (1859). There his concern was 'to show the possible effect of the increase of great working-capitals and monopolies on the labourer's freedom or welfare'.[14] One could hardly describe the work as a devastating criticism of the 'dismal science', nor were his recommendations sufficiently practicable to suggest how current hard times might be alleviated. Yet the views expressed in it are so germane to the pattern of Barnes's thought and life that, despite the seemingly obsolete premises from which he reasons, one must give due weight to the earnestness of his argument and not dismiss the book as the uninformed ramblings of a crank. There is, after all, nothing more inherently sensible in the 'humanity' of Sissy Jupe, or in the pathos of Stephen Blackpool, or yet again, in Tennyson's resolution of his conflict in 'The Two Voices', than in the values of honesty and honourableness in commercial transactions which Barnes realized had been supplanted by the Utilitarianism of Bounderby and Gradgrind. And it was honesty and honourableness which he wished to see restored.

For Barnes, what was cardinal and irreplaceable was the functioning at all levels of human intercourse of Christian ethics and morality, and he seems not to have been merely timid or sentimental in holding out no great expectations that they could flourish except within the conservative guarantee of small and simply organized communites. For, as R. H. Tawney has pointed out, one of the major revolutions through which the human spirit has passed was the abdication by Christian churches in the nineteenth century of 'one whole department of life, that of social and political conduct'. As a result, they acquiesced 'in the popular assumption that the acquisition of riches was the main end of man, and confined themselves to preaching such personal virtues as did not conflict with its achievement.'[15] Barnes clearly perceived this revolution and refused to compromise his deep sense of democracy in the village community against which it offended. He clung, rather, to the 'old-fashioned' idea that labour was the measure of commercial value and repudiated the usurious exploitation of money which transformed it from a token into a self-generating commodity bearing more money. Of course, the primitive labour-barter economy he envisaged as ideal was thoroughly inadequate to the needs of an expanding industrial economy, but the following homely anecdote, which he quoted with relish, suggests his awareness of the money morality, an inherent aspect of the Manchester School, and its human implications: 'Patoo Mata Moigna, a Tonga chief, and his wife, went with an English ship to Botany Bay, where he saw people eating in a cookshop, and he thought the good house-father was sharing out food in the Tonga fashion, and went in with the claim of hunger, but was speedily kicked out with the foot of the man who had been born in the land of the Bible.'[16]

Barnes's ideal emerges as a type of Christian 'noble savage'. By formulating it in this way, one may best understand his desire to incorporate in an organic unity the virtues of Christian morality and the dignity and health, both physical and spiritual, which to his mind resulted from the varied activities and sense of community and continuity making up the rural life. Industrialism and vast urban development had made that unity difficult to attain. The moral of the anecdote about the 'noble Tongan' is that he would never have behaved in the same way as the civilized 'Christian', because his way of life was rooted in the soil and in the traditions of people who had not been corrupted by worshipping Mammon. In that idolatry, Barnes perceived, lay a moral trap into which economists such as Ricardo had fallen. It resulted from the false elevation of statistics to the status of 'Natural Law', by which industrial capitalists were able to claim as inevitable and unalterable, indeed as part 'of the nature of things', their treatment of workers under *laissez-faire*. Barnes's exposure of this moral dishonesty was as forthright as that which gave Marxism its apocalyptic force, though its impact was blunted because he did not share with Engels the advantage of being able to retaliate with the very argument of statistical analysis in terms of which the situation was being condoned and applauded. He had grasped however, the essential danger in the flux of contemporary life—the emergence of a new avarice which used the mechanical inventions of the age of steam to achieve its ends and, as it discovered the massive strength of machines, became increasingly impatient of traditional religious and ethical safeguards against economic exploitation of those who operated them.

Barnes tends, admittedly, to reduce human existence to the simplicity of an isolated and static Christian community, where 'The labour of man . . . is the making of his gear for the winning of his food' (*Views of Labour and Gold*, p. 1). But one should not be diverted from the burden of his criticism by his quaintness of orientation or expression, or the seeming obsolescence of his retaliation. For when, in the same strain of argument, he perceptively urges that 'labour is both the action of the body or mind, *and* the reaction of the work on the body or mind' (p. 31; my italics), one ought to hear as a chorus of agreement the more sophisticated complaints of later writers who inherited the culture that Barnes criticized in its early stages of growth. There is William Morris's quiet lament, implying a state of affairs that had dissolved with the advent of the division of labour and mass production: 'Time was when everyone that made anything, made a work of art besides a useful piece of goods; and it gave them pleasure to do it.'[17] And complementary to it, the frustrated outcry from D. H. Lawrence on his return home to Derbyshire in 1915, when he observed the mining people from whom he had sprung: 'These men, whom I love so much . . . they *understand* mentally so horribly: only industrialism, only wages and money and machinery. They can't *think* anything else . . . only this industrial-mechanical-wage idea.'[18] Both Morris and Lawrence would accept the implication of Barnes's statement that labour is best when it provides harmonious balance of body and mind.

Barnes's book, then, is not an academic refutation of current economic practice which had acquired scientific status through the pragmatic deductions of Adam Smith, Malthus, and Ricardo. The book really constituted a rejection of the concept of the 'economic man'. And his rejection rests on sound if somewhat neglected values, which he regarded as imperative for the health of the whole man. It is a plea against fragmenting the manifestly composite stability of rural life into meretricious divisions to be either separately catered to, or ignored, in what was for him the urban chaos. His view here, as elsewhere, is considered, and when he writes, for instance, that 'it is more healthy to rack one's mind in effectual devices to win a skilful end, than to work as a machine without a free aim or thought' (*Views of Labour and Gold*, p. 91), he is making not only a plea for the creative dignity of labour, but also very pertinent 'criticism of life'.

## IV

Geoffrey Grigson is right when he says that 'In English poetry, [Barnes's] own practice was based on the Enlightenment' (*Selected Poems*, p. 16). From another viewpoint, however, I would suggest that his poetry may be profitably regarded as reflecting both an ancient and multifarious, though uncomplex folk-culture, and the bleak age of revolution which destroyed it. This formulation points up the importance of the observation in the Preface to his *Poems of Rural Life* (1844), where, referring to himself, he writes,

> As he has not written for readers who have had their lots cast in town-occupations of a highly civilized community, and cannot sympathize with the rustic mind, he can hardly hope that they will understand either his poems or his intention; since with the not uncommon notion that every change from the plough towards the desk and from the desk towards the couch of empty-handed idleness is an onward step towards happiness and intellectual and moral excellence, they will most likely find it very hard to conceive that wisdom and goodness would be found speaking in a dialect which may seem to them a fit vehicle for the animal wants and passions of a boor' (in Dugdale, p. 113).

It is apparent from this that Barnes was aware not only of the scope and standard of his audience, but also that his function in the community was defined by the demands of the lives and langguage of its members. An observation earlier in the Preface further illuminates the issue: 'As increasing communication among the inhabitants of different parts of England, and the spread of school education among the lower ranks of the people tend to substitute book English for the provincial dialects, it is likely that after a few years many of them will linger only in the more secluded parts of the land, if they live at all' (in Dugdale, p. 112). Barnes's underlying concern here is clearly similar to that which led Wordsworth to make his famous attempt in the *Lyrical Ballads* to employ 'a selection of language really used by men'. That attempt was largely unsuccessful, but the opposite is true with regard to the impressive mass of Barnes's dialect poems. Indeed they may fairly be regarded as the practical demonstration of Wordsworth's justification of his choice of 'humble and rustic life', and his adoption of a diction purified from defects 'because such men hourly communicate with the best objects from which the best part of language is originally derived'. And language, for Barnes, was essentially speech, which he described as 'shapen of the breath-sounds of speakers, for the ear of hearers, and not from speech-tokens [letters] in books'.[19] The *beau idéal* was the speech of his youth in Blackmore Vale—a language firmly rooted in the oral tradition of the folk, and therefore untrammelled by the literary associations and importations of National English. His struggle for its continuance was life-long—'I have done some little to preserve the speech of our forefathers . . .[as it was]spoken in my youth' (in Dugdale, p. 226), was his comment on receiving a few months before his death the author's copy of his *Glossary of the Dorset Dialect*.

We read elsewhere in the Preface to his *Poems* that those members of the community he had in mind as audience were people like the ploughman and his wife. Coventry Patmore elaborates on this: Barnes's 'humble glory was to recite to delighted audiences of farmers and ploughmen and their wives and sweethearts a series of lyrics, idylls, eclogues, which, being the faultless expression of elementary feelings and perceptions, are good for all but those in whom such feelings and perceptions are extinct'.[20] Hardy suggests, in keeping with this picture of Barnes, that 'the enthusiasm which accompanied' these readings was probably 'more grateful to him than the admiration of a public he had never seen' (p. lvi). Furthermore, he published his poems in book form only relatively late, after he had for years contributed to the 'Poet's Corner' in the local newspaper. A consideration of these facts shows that his poetic function in the community was an issue consciously thought about, and one which formed an integral part of his artistic intention, as well as confirming his mode of life. This view is supported not only by the main subject of his poetry and by his use of dialect, but also by his deep and technically informed interest in old bardic poetry, many of the characteristics of which he experimented with, eventually incorporating them as basic aspects of his poetic talent. Had Barnes's interest been only historical and philological, it would have been incidental to his purpose. However, in the light of his own poetical practice, the issue takes on a central importance because of his statement in the illuminating article, 'The Old Bardic Poetry',[21] that his interest in the techniques of that poetry stems from their enabling a 'bookless and unwriting' people to remember better their lore in 'verse-locks'. For such people, 'verse is rather a need than a joy'; it is indeed their 'history'. From this central assertion, Barnes proceeds to describe the various techniques which ancient bards, and he also to a large degree, used, 'to keep together the true text, and fasten it on the learner's mind'. His knowledge was based with typical thoroughness on a study of Welsh, Irish, Anglo-Saxon, and Persian bardic writings. Many of Barnes's contributions to the 'Poet's Corner' were brief experiments resulting from his acquired knowledge, and the frequent recurrence in the body of his writings of these ancient techniques relates closely to his consciousness of the intention he expounded in his article.

The following brief examples will help to indicate the nature of 'bardic' techniques and Barnes's use of them in his poetry. First, there is 'cymmeriad . . . or the keeping of the same word through sundry verses, for the sake of oneness of time, or subject or thought', as it occurs in 'Went Hwome', where each of the three stanzas ends as follows:

As noon did smite, wi' burnén light,
The road so white, to Meldonley.

As I did goo, while skies wer blue,
Vrom view to view, to Meldonley.

Till I come down, vrom Meldon's crown
To rufs o' brown, at Meldonley.[22]

Here the repetition of 'Meldonley', effectively supported by the internal rhymes, heightens the warmth of his 'welcome hwome' by accentuating the close relationship for Barnes of domesticity and specific locality. The rhyming in these lines also derives from 'bardic' practice, for in ancient Irish poetry the rhyming of a word at the end of a line with one in the middle of the following line was known as 'union'. Then there is the Celtic 'cynghanedd' or consonant rhyme, as in 'In our abode in Arby Wood', where the repeated consonants in the two parts of the line are: u, r, b, d / u, r, b, d. Next there are the various highly complicated rhyme schemes which comprise the 'Englyn'. One of the more simple forms of this is the 'awdlau', or one-rhyme lines, as Barnes uses it in 'The Cock', after the Welsh of Siôn Powel.

> I heard the homely cock by fits to crow,
> With golden wings, ere dawn began to glow,
> And sing his cheery sounds from high to low,
> Mild in the morn, amid the glitt'ring snow.
>
> (Grigson, *Selected Poems*, p. 282)

Also to be considered among the 'verse-locks' through which the bard, with intricate security, hoped to 'fasten . . . on the learner's mind' his simple 'history,' are 'metre [which] where it is true, will forbid a word to be put in for another of less or more syllables', the conventional 'voice-rhyme, which keeps many words from displacement by any but those of like sound', and, finally, the less-well-known 'clipping-rhyme' or the rhyming of articulation, or alliteration' (*Old Bardic Poetry*, p. 306).

Aspects of Barnes's writing less specifically technical than those just listed show equally the conscious intention and scope of his association with 'bardic' practice. The persistent lack of metaphorical elaboration in his 'history' of the old civilization, for instance, might perhaps be seen as more than the result of restrained 'fitness,' in the light of his observation that 'the poet can relieve the flatness of such historical truths, as Homer did the roll of his ships, or leaders, only with a few epithets' (p. 308). Considering Welsh bardic poetry, he refers to Llywarch Hen, who had coined compound epithets such as 'greyhound-hearted', 'brushfire-hearted', which are frequently used with a similar 'instressed' precision by Barnes as in 'dark-treed night', 'peäle-twinklén stars', or 'hedge-climb'd hills'. Also, it is surprising to discover that lines such as 'or as a short-stand-quick-night-watch foreflown' and 'which at early morn with blowing-green-blithe bloom' are not discarded exercises by Hopkins, but translations from Old Friesian by Barnes (see *The Harp of Aeolus*, p. 122).

One must, then, disagree with Grigson that it is

> curious to find him down in his Dorset isolation writing that 'the measures of song . . . may themselves be measured, not only by the steps of the dramatic dance, but by the steps of a march, or by

> the strokes of oars, as in the Tonga songs of the kind called Towalo or paddle songs, which Mariner says are never accompanied with instrumental music, but which are short songs sung in canoes while paddling, the strokes of the paddles being coincident with the cadence of the tune' (*Selected Poems*, p. 16).

It is not at all curious—because Barnes's interest in this type of folk-song springs directly from his deep concern with its intimate and accepted association with the declining folk civilization he wished to preserve. Folk-songs such as those Barnes here describes are an integral part of any rural community; they are, as James Reeves observes, 'the result of oral tradition in a rural society'.[23] The English equivalents in song to dramatic dance, or the steps of a march, or the strokes of oars, were for Barnes part of the continued security of the rural way of life; and their slowly falling into disuse, or being supplanted by more lurid city-ballads, became for him a painful and continual reminder of transformation. This was so, furthermore, not only because those songs frequently accompanied some traditional craft or piece of work which might now have been displaced, but also because, as was acknowledged by Cecil Sharp (whose salvaging interest in the whole process was, by contrast, merely antiquarian) 'the folk-singer attaches far more importance to the words of his song than to its tune' (Reeves, p. 11). It is no exaggeration, therefore, to regard these songs as a vital part of the simple 'history' of country folk. H. J. Massingham even asserts of Barnes that 'His verse is the old communal folk-song made the vehicle of an individual spirit whose reinterpretation of it was an act of genius' (p. 125).

## V

Another important aspect of Barnes's presentation of his countryman's world is the relationship between his extensive description of the natural scene and his aesthetic theory. We have already noted the general absence of moralizing, philosophical speculation, or visionary insight in his treatment of nature; and his delineation of the natural world of sight and sound is a logical extension of this. While taking an intense delight in natural beauty, Barnes never submerges his personality in it. One finds in his poetry, therefore, no attempt to create luxuriant or picturesque effects. He adopts a sane countryman's attitude of objectivity and directness, and his descriptions are characterized by a sparse, fastidious selection of particular detail which precludes much metaphorical elaboration. Associated with this simplicity of line is Barnes's uncomplicated use of colour. He invariably uses, often in contrast, bright heraldic colours which stand out like symbols of his honest observation in the uncomplicated world of peace and certainty he cherished. These qualities of simplicity and colour may be seen in the following typical passage:

> I love the narrow lane's dark bows,
> When summer glows or winter blows;
> Or in the *f*all, when leaves all *f*ade,
> Yet *f*lutt'ring in the airy shade,
> And in the *sh*elter'd *sha*w the blast
> Has *sha*ken down the green-cupp'd mast,
> And time is *bl*ack'ning *bl*ue-skinn'd sloes,
> And *bl*ackberries on bramble bows,
> And *r*ipening haws are growing *r*ed.
> A*r*ound the grey-rin'd hawthorn's head,
> And hazel *br*anches, *br*okentipp'd
> And *br*own, of all their nuts are stripp'd,
> And in the leazes, *wh*iffling *wh*ite,
> The *wh*irling thistle seeds alight
> In sunshine, *st*ruck from bents' brown *st*alks
> By *st*rolling girls in Sunday walks.
>
> ('The Lane,' Barnes's italics; II, 665)

These aspects of Barnes's observation are closely related to his aesthetic theory, which is Christian in origin and application. In his 'Thoughts on Beauty and Art' (1861), he bases his definition of Beauty on the accepted deterioration of Man and Nature after the Fall. In his view, 'the beautiful in nature is the unmarred result of God's first creative or forming will' (in Dugdale, p. 276). Furthermore, because of their innate perfection, interference with any forms of Divine creation amounted to marring them; so 'if an ash-tree is polled, there grow out of its head more young runnels than would have sprouted if the work of God's first will had not been marred by the man-wielded polling-blade' (p. 277). In light of this it is no surprise to see flourishing, admittedly amidst pragmatically observed detail, the perennial yet elusive dictum, 'Nature is the best school of art' (p. 287). However, his use of 'Nature' is not as vague as its blunt statement here might lead one to fear; for through a variation of Platonism, in which the exclusive presence of uncorrupted forms associated 'Heaven' with prelapsarian Nature, he suggests that the devout may yet perceive or, construe from only partially deformed examples, the *beau idéal* of God's will, the 'seeking and interpreting' of which, 'and a working with His truth,' become the priest-like 'aim of high art' (p. 293).

Barnes's poetic practice is clearly related to his aesthetic theorizing, particularly with regard to the bare directness of the 'unmarred' objectivity of his observation. What he is, in fact, frequently attempting in his poetry is to set down pictures of those original pure forms untrammelled by any embellishment or personal interpretation. And in doing this he was not merely being pious. For in his discovery and accurate recording of the *beau idéal*, he is not only creating beauty and praising his God, but also 'preserving' from disruptive man-made forces the pristine glory of God-created rural England, where 'God's untarnished earthly good' is mainly to be found. In his view, the age had become one of 'falsehood and sham' because most of 'the beauty of God's primary work . . . [unmarred forms] in plants, animals, and man' (p. 277) was almost by definition to be found in the countryside and in the lives of the inheritors of the ancient folk civilization; and all this had been replaced by its perversion in urban existence: 'we have deal painted and veneered into an imitation of more costly wood . . . cloth shown to our neighbours for leather; paste for gems; imitations instead of nature's truth', produced by artisans radically different from 'the old workmen [who] were faithful and wrought to God, or art, or conscience, rather than to Pluto' (p. 294). He substantiates fully, in his terms, the validity of his world by criticizing the limitations of the city, which define by contrast the 'wealth' of the disintegrating rural ethos, when he observes that in the

> great towns . . . much of the beautiful in nature must be far forlorn by many of working people. Many a plain wall rises high between the workman and the glory of the passing sun, and has shut out his window-framed piece of blue sky, and the cheering whiteness of the flying cloud. Many a day of smoke has blackened the clearness of the sweet spring-tide; many a bright-leaved tree has heretofore

> given way to crowded shades of narrow rooms. Many a rood of flowery sward has become rattling streets, where, for songs of birds, they have the din of hammers. Many a cheek has been paled, and lovely piece of childhood marred, by longsome hours of over-work (p. 294).

Moreover, he extends his concept of 'beauty' to include moral actions for 'the winning of God's first given, and since forlorn good' (p. 292)—an extension exactly paralleled and illuminated by Sir Joshua Reynolds's elaboration (in the *Discourses*) of his idea of Nature to comprehend 'not only the forms which Nature produces, but also the nature and internal fabric and organization, as I may call it, of the human mind and imagination'.[24] Barnes's criticism in this context as elsewhere, then, is broadly based not in sentimental retreat from the great 'march of mind', but in a liberal and humane concern with the conditions of life most conducive to spiritual and moral health.

## VI

There is a further aspect of Barnes's aesthetic theory worth considering—the influence of the tradition of natural theology, best represented for our purposes by William Paley's *Natural Theology* (1802), which the poet probably read as a prescribed text while a 'Ten Year Man' at Cambridge in 1847. We have seen that Barnes's assumption concerning the superiority of the rural life rested on the belief that it offered the possibility of more constant contact with the greatest number of unmarred forms created by God, that the 'forms and colours of objects in a landscape [reveal] a fitness and harmony of the good of God's formative will. . . . The beautiful is also the good by reason of a fitness or harmony which it possesses' (in Dugdale, pp. 288, 278). This attitude rests on a basic assumption of Paley's *Natural Theology*: 'that in a vast plurality of instances in which contrivance is perceived, the design of the contrivance is beneficial'.[25] John Stuart Mill, however, was to suggest that if Darwin's theory of the 'survival of the fittest' proved to be correct, it would provide a radically different account of the appearances of benevolent contrivance in Nature, and 'would greatly attenuate the evidences for it'.[26] Darwinism seemed to imply that the traditional religious view of a universe contrived and regulated by divine omniscience would increasingly be replaced by new visions of a universe ordered by laws of physics or of the jungle, by human intelligence or the lawlessness of blind chance. Barnes's response to these implications is clearly one more of the elements that went into the making of his mythical world.

Natural theologians were mainly concerned to show God's beneficence towards the animate creatures of the universe by exhibiting for rational judgment evidence that inanimate creation had been adapted to their needs and gratification. And this argument for the existence and 'continuing care . . . of a ruling Providence', as Paley stated, was of necessity based on the Newtonian 'established order of nature which we must suppose to prevail, or we cannot reason at all upon the subject' (II, 190, 155). Frequently Paley's 'evidences', attempting to prove that 'Design must have had a designer. That designer must have been a person. That person is God' (II, 130), rest on a simple presupposition of the very benevolence of the Designer whose existence they are supposed to prove. At one important point, for instance, in considering the sensuous delights offered in Nature to men, he argues that this need not have been the case, for God might have made 'everything we tasted, bitter; everything we saw, loathsome; everything we touched, a sting; every smell, a stench; and every sound, a discord' (II, 150). By referring comprehensively to 'everything,' Paley tacitly ignores in his listing the actual and inconvenient presence of these qualities in many natural phenomena. It is a similar sort of 'fitness' that Barnes discovers when contemplating 'the forms and colours of objects in a landscape'. For he finds 'evidence' of 'God's formative will' in the 'green of the earth, and the blue of the sky [which] are less wearisome and destructive to the sight than would be a world of red or white, and blinds our eyes more slowly than would an earth of silvery brightness, or a lasting vision of blood' (in Dugdale, p. 288). The conclusions drawn from such characteristic statements by Barnes and those of Paley and the natural theologians generally are identical.

The retention of this established order of nature, as opposed to the emergent one propounded by Darwin, was imperative for the continuance of the world of imaginative reality Barnes created in his poetry. And it was equally important to his aesthetic, which formed a bridge between that world and the daily duties as a country parson which in Dugdale's opinion were his 'true vocation' (p. 122). For, as Paley had stated, if one laid Natural Theology as 'the foundation of everything which is religious . . . the world henceforth becomes a temple, and life itself one continued act of adoration' (II, 199). Of course, Barnes was free to choose with Disraeli the angels rather than the apes, but the point of interest here is that his choice seems to have been dictated not only by his Christian convictions, but also by his artistic realization that his myth would no longer have been viable had he chosen the latter. The evolution of a 'chance good' in a dispensation where 'God and Nature' were 'at strife' was for Barnes a degradation of that pristine and harmonious 'fitness' of 'unmarred forms' created by 'God's formative will' through which by contrast he criticized the new cosmology and its implications. In his single poem explicitly on evolutionism, 'The Happy Days When I Wer Young', where he writes on 'what's a-talked about/ By many now—that to despise/The laws o' God an' man is wise' (I, 171), Barnes feels no need to re-justify to men the ways of an inscrutable God. The usual backward-looking title of the poem heightens his sense of the immemorial sanity of rural life, thereby endorsing his belief in the justice of the natural order; and he is led to repudiate Darwinism in a significant phrase—as he did in his review of 'Patmore's Poems'[27]—as 'venom': the serpent in his Eden, in fact. It was a serpent brought 'To kill our hope an' taint our thought'. The ideas were, with an almost predatory pervasiveness, intruding on the stable perfection of his world.

## VII

As stated earlier, there is no philosophizing or moralizing about the 'Spirit of Nature' in Barnes's poetry. His prime concern is with the activities and the relationships, both amongst themselves and with their environment, of country people, and only indirectly with the natural world as such. In relating Barnes's treatment of country folk to his overall mythopoeic activity, however, one must from the outset have clearly in mind the anomaly that, although he was almost exclusively a rural poet, Barnes was never an intimate acquaintance of the local rustics; and until he achieved some renown in later life, he was scorned as an eccentric by the 'upper class'. He was no Stephen Duck or Robert Bloomfield ('literary' peasants who misguidedly tried to adopt an urbanity that ill suited their unsophisticated origins and talents). Nor can the anomaly be explained by reference to Barnes's acknowledged shyness; indeed that only complicates the issue if we place in the context of the spiritual and intellectual loneliness that must have characterized his years of greatest creativity, the observation by an ex-pupil that Barnes was 'nearly isolated' socially.[28] Furthermore, aside from scything his own grass in summer, he took no part in agricultural labour; yet the exactness of his knowledge about such matters and rural life generally (as, for instance, in his article 'Dorset Folk and Dorset'[29]), is manifest throughout his work.

These biographical details throw into illuminating relief the very obvious limitation of scope in Barnes's treatment of country people in his poetry. Rayner Unwin surely exaggerates when he writes that Barnes's poems 'depict the countryman in all the aspects of his life' (p. 158). Unlike Hardy and George Borrow, he shows no interest, for example, in the picturesque fringe of rural society composed of pedlars, tinkers, and gipsies. Also he has only a single poem, 'Culver Dell and the Squire', on a member of the gentry, all others treating of the working people. And even in that exception the squire is an ideal, if not idealized, figure. Again, except for a solitary poem, 'The Love Child', there is no suggestion of cruelty or immorality in the countryside. And this was hardly because of Barnes's ignorance of such aspects of rural life. He was probably quite aware, for instance, of the fearful and loathsome scenes of drunkenness and domestic misery which 'Rabin Hill', a contemporary dialect poet of near-by Sturminster-Newton, was later to recall as being fairly common when he and Barnes were both young (see Dugdale, p. 22). Furthermore, besides the evidence to the contrary Barnes provides in his pamphlet, *Humilis Domus: Some Thoughts on the Abodes, Life and Social Conditions of the Poor, Especially in Dorsetshire*,[30] there are his concluding remarks to the otherwise glowing account of 'Dorset Folk and Dorset': 'If I have painted a picture of Dorset life that is light, I have not given light where there is none; but I ought to say that there is among us darkness as well as light, and that you may too readily pitch on a man who is a shame to us.' For a reader of his poetry, however, there is no such man, or woman, to 'pitch on'.

It is not coincidence that the most considerable of Barnes's poems on a particular topic of social interest, 'The Common a-took in', is concerned with enclosure; for as George Sturt stated in his invaluable record of the changing village, it was this more than any other single factor that was thought to have altered the appearance of the countryside and brought about the rapid deterioration of what he called the ancient 'folk civilization'. The Enclosure Acts covered the period of rapid industrialization which transformed 'a social system of eight hundred years' duration'[31] into one which, in Hardy's words, served 'smoke and fire rather than frost and sun'.[32] The transformation resulted in what the Hammonds aptly described as 'a world in disorder' (p. 233). Yet this was ostensibly also the world presented by Barnes in his poetry. He was probably unaware, for instance, of the actual statistics showing that by 1851 in almost all the great towns the migrants outnumber the people born there,[33] or that between 1792 and 1831 Poor Law expenditure in the County of Dorset increased 214 per cent and expenses for prosecutions for crime 2,135 per cent, while the population had increased by only 40 per cent.[34] But he could hardly have been unaware of the general cultural changes which were so radically altering the world he had grown up in. E. M. Forster points to a particular instance when he observes, 'He could live through the Labourers' Revolt in 1830 without its shadows falling across his verse' (in Dugdale, p. 89). It is not only that Barnes's range in portraying the life of a world he knew intimately is restricted, but also that his presentation is limited to a particular type of observation and treatment. The result is a picture of country life that is curiously distorted, one which, if not idealized, was at least selected to illustrate and corroborate specific sentiments and beliefs about that life. The attempt to 'explain' this selectiveness (even granting fully the autonomy of the creative artist to plot his own area of imaginative activity) by saying that 'His mind was attuned to harmonies, not discords' (Cambridge, p. xx), or that he was 'a sundial recording only the shining hours' (Dugdale, p. 22) ignores the positive aspects of his achievement. It seems more accurate to state that in presenting his selective treatment of country life and its virtues, as in other fields already considered, he was motivated by a very real awareness of the contemporary cultural revolution.

## VIII

The sphere of living to which Barnes devotes most attention is the family. This is the stable axis about which spin rural activities and pastimes within the confined circle of the immediate neighbourhood, and it is a reasonable preoccupation of one born and bred in the tight isolation of a small community. His stress on warm, intimate relationships within the domestic group and among close friends is consonant with his temperatment and his artistic intention. Barnes writes consistently about such relationships, and although his dignified restraint largely forestalls sentimentality, they are invariably happy. The quiet and peace of rural domesticity he saw as a complementary commentary on the whole of rural life, whose excellence made it possible. But his attitudes here emerge not only from personal experience with his wife Julia, or from a thoughtful countryman's awareness of the family's importance in a daily routine unrelieved by much entertainment. For, on turning to the pamphlet *Humilis Domus* mentioned earlier, one finds a wider intellectual conviction based, in contrast with the conditions of the rustic poor, on the overcrowding and slums inevitable in expanding industrial cities, from which, he thought, 'there must follow a train of moral evils too loathsome for a mind brought up in moral purity to behold in imagination' (p. 4).

But Barnes was not only concerned with the home as a sanctuary for preserving 'the most lovely social Christian graces'; he also regarded it in a broader perspective as the greatest safeguard against political disruption in a revolutionary situation. He feared what in fact has subsequently happened, though not as dramatically as he had anticipated—that the family with its multiple functions would become devitalized in the more fluid social structure of large cities, especially when people lived in congested slums away from ancient rural sanctions. Joseph Ashby, a true villager, believed that in the lean years that followed on the Enclosures, the labourers in his village of Tysoe 'kept to the straight way because the village had been once a true community'.[35] And as late as 1902 Rider Haggard's exhaustive investigation into the desertion of the countryside and the decline of husbandry led him to the 'modest statement [that they] can mean nothing less than the progressive deterioration of the race'.[36] Barnes would have agreed with Hardy that 'This process, which is designated by statisticians as "the tendency of the rural population towards the large towns", is really the tendency of water to flow uphill when forced.'[37] Barnes was painfully aware that the countryman suffered irreparable loss by his migration. The point is nicely made in the following passage where he is ostensibly writing about impoverished Dorset rustics, but with the consoling implication that the *rural* slum-dweller still had the protection of a conservative social structure and the solidarity of a traditional ethos to guard him from the ravages which would undermine his urban counterpart:

> The true school for the training of good national subjects is the good father's roof: and a house training under the law of the house's head, is the only one to which we have good grounds to look for the rearing of good lawbound citizens; and the weaker may be the law of the house, the more bloody must be the law of the land; and if the social atoms of the nation are not gathered into family crystals by the house association, no monarch can afterwards form them into the strength of a sound political body (*Humilis Domus*, p. 3).

Barnes's attitude toward domesticity in country life is best observed, however, in his treatment of women, It is noteworthy, in the first place, that the vast majority of people he writes about are women and children—'The Maid o' Newton', 'Jessie Lee', 'The Motherless Child', for example, and the list could be greatly extended. Men are most frequently seen anonymously, at such work as felling trees, or else as husbands who return to the domestic hearth at sunset. Furthermore, the virtues in women which he admires most are the reliable homely ones which make for domestic stability, and his admiration is always restrained and unimpassioned. This is particularly noticeable in his love poems, which are most often not concerned with present passion, but with the expectation of happiness deferred until marriage unites the pair by the hearth of their own home, thereby establishing them as a social unit. And parallel to this, there is a considerable number of poems, such as 'A Little Lost Sister', Meäry

Wedded', 'Jenny Away from Home', based on familial relationships and the disruption of these by death, departure, or even marriage.

Clearly Barnes's treatment of women in his poetry is based on the correlation of the virtuous life and domestic happiness. These were the inseparable elements in the traditional structure of rural society. But he is concerned not only to commemorate the way of life he knew and admired, but also to deny its viability in an urban context, thereby implying that the good life crumbled with the dislocation of the rural ethos. This he frequently attempts to do by contrasting the 'accepted' excellence of the rural character with the corrupting wealth, vice, and vanity which he imputes to the urban environment. Opposed, therefore, to his estimate of unsophisticated country people, there are frequent derogatory references in the poetry to a vain, superficial, and amorphous nobility. The unreality of these personages is the measure of his elevation of the 'folk'. For no allusion is made to the local gentry as one might expect if Barnes was just being assertively democratic in an age which saw the rise of the proletariat and the establishment of the first Agricultural Labourers' Union under Joseph Arch, or fervently regionalist over the principled heroism of the Tolpuddle martyrs. Thus it is that he 'do little ho vor goold or pride,/To leäve the plain abode where love do bide' ('Knowlwood', I, 283). And Jeäne sits like some rustic Cleopatra, 'steätely as a queen o' vo'k' ('The Bwoate', I, 343); Poll the milkmaid walks, 'Wi' her white pail below her eärm/As if she wore a goolden crown' ('The Milk-maid o' the Farm', I, 80); and the poet asserts that even were he extremely wealthy, and 'as high in rank/As any duke or lord', he would remain uncorrupted in his choice of mistress though she were 'a leäser in the glen' ('My Love is Good', I, 455). Tacit criticism of the city also underlies his joy in 'Ellen Dare o' Lindenore', whose charm results directly from the rustic modesty and tranquillity of her way of life, and the beauty of her home's natural surroundings, which are the opposite of the distracting city's 'Swift bwoats, wi' water-plowén keels', its 'broad high-roads a-wore/By vurbrought trav'lers' cracklén wheels', its 'crowds a-passen to and fro,/Upon the bridge's high-sprung bow'. The mutually enhancing interaction between 'Lindenore' and 'Feair Ellen Dare' substantiates the perfection of each. Imperceptive and hurrying 'town-vo'k ha' but seldom calls/O' busines' on fair Ellen,' but Barnes, by contrast, appreciates how she epitomizes saner values, like 'Calm air do vind the rwose-bound door/Ov Ellen Dare o' Lindenore' ('Lindenore', I, 405). It is pertinent to note however that Barnes married neither 'Ellen Dare' nor milkmaid, but the daughter of the middle-class Supervisor of Excise in Dorchester.

## IX

It might be thought from the continual presence of hostility between rural and urban life in Barnes's poetry and thinking generally, that he could best be understood in terms of literary history as either a pastoralist or a regionalist. In fact neither category applies. Regionalism, as recently defined, 'establishes a comparison between the rural world, seen in terms of its richly picturesque local traits, and the complex industrial society of today, just as the old pastoral established a comparison between peasant life and the court'; it exploits, then, an historical contrast similar to that found in pastoral, 'by looking back from a present of advanced technology to the period, still not very far away, when the roads were dirt lanes, farmers walked behind horse-drawn ploughs, and the rural community depended pretty much on its own produce'.[38] But Barnes looks back neither from corrupt court nor complex city. Although he accepts in its Christian version the pastoral concept of the restoration of some Golden Age men have forfeited through sin or abusive folly, he never as a result views rural life from the vantage ground of urban sophistication on which both he and his audience live. For his perspective is governed by his faith in the exclusive value of the rural ethos, so that past and present become telescoped into the ritualistic recurrence of the seasons.

The authority of his poetry is not thereby diminished as would be the case if his method were the subtle ironies of contrast. There is no equivalent to the Forest of Arden in Barnes's presentation; his criticism is, rather, overt, in that he asserts imaginatively those very elements which give his art and personal life their mutually enhancing validity. And the historical significance of his criticism becomes clear if one realizes that it was being undertaken concurrently with the transformation of those dirt lanes into roads and the replacement of horse-drawn ploughs by such strange machines as the 'horse-drill' Donald Farfrae introduced to Casterbridge, 'where the venerable seed-lip was still used for sowing as in the days of the Heptarchy'.[39]

As might be expected, it is the apparent immutability of rural life that Barnes cherished greatly—perhaps even more than the peace and honest living he associated with the countryside. This was the source of his regret at any change that occurred, from death or decay, in the established pattern of relationships and activities.

In many of Barnes's poems, then, such as 'Hallowed Places', 'The Voices that be Gone', 'Joy Passing By', there is a nostalgic regret at the passage of time and the changes it has brought about. It is invariably associated with his strong countryman's sense of place, and it is this association which makes remarkable an otherwise common enough sentiment. Pertinent here is the Rev. Francis Kilvert's diary record of a conversation with the poet whom he visited in 1874: 'He said that some of the names of people and places mentioned in his poems are fictitious, but they all represent real places and persons. The real name of Ellen Brine of Allenburn, he said, was Mary Hames, and the poem was true to the life. In describing a scene he always had an original in his mind, but sometimes he enlarged and improved upon the original. "For instance," he explained, "sometimes I wanted a bit of water, or wood, or a hill, and then I put these in. 'Pentridge by the River', was a real place. The river was the Stour" ' (in Dugdale, p. 203). It is from such remembered localities and activities that Barnes constructs much of his rural world. For the permanance or decay of individual objects in a particular locality is not only commemorated in itself, but becomes also a symbol of the continuity or collapse of rural life as a whole. Seen in relation to past generations and the regular flow of country traditions, local objects become on the one hand touchstones of certainty and continuity in a changing world, and on the other, depressing signs of change in the structure of living. Thus it is that he frequently mourns the decay of houses (Pentridge House, for instance) which are, in their relation with domesticity, richly suggestive for him of a previously secure and beautiful life now crumbling under the weight of intrusive events. The disintegration brought about by the passage of time is to some extent, however, redeemed for Barnes by the continuity of the seasons through which he as a countryman measures it, correlating the cyclic regularity of the fugitive, recurring seasons with the activities appropriate to each being performed by the younger generation who thereby continue the established tradition. Thus even though 'My season-measur'd time's a-vled' ('Zummer Stream', I, 462), and 'we ourselves do vollow on/Our own vorelivers dead an' gone' ('Our Be'th Place', I, 275), it is nevertheless satisfying to see country life still following its ancient pattern, of a necessity which is an inherent part of its excellence:

> 'Tis good to come back to the pleäce,
> Back to the time, to goo noo mwore;
> 'Tis good to meet the younger feäce
> A-mentén others here avore.
>
> ('Zummer Stream')

Barnes, then in re-creating his own 'youth' through a presentation of remembered scenes, activities, people, and houses was not just furnishing idly with nostalgic memories an ageing man's recollection of happy bygone days, but was presenting in living terms, heightened by the productive diversity of his own life, his Christian aesthetic and the 'actuality' of his remembrances, an allegory of the new Fall of Man. This was how he viewed the Victorian cultural revolution. He immersed himself in past events, or those hallowed by ancient practice or seasonal recurrence, not simply because he was by poetic temperament a recorder and not a creator of images and symbols, but rather because by 'manipulating a continuous parallel between [the] contemporaneity' of his own long life, and the 'antiquity' of an incorruptible Eden resurrected from his innocent rural youth, he was attempting to create a stable defence amidst the 'immense panorama of futility and anarchy' of a world rapidly 'maturing' into the confusion of industrial society. And for Barnes the symbol of this confusion and spiritual desolation came to be the city because it stood 'outside' Nature, and in seeming opposition to the ancient sanctions that hallowed rural life. This was his real perception, incandescent with moral and imaginative vigour, withholding the encroaching shadows caused by a change visibly effected in the spreading towns and devitalized villages. The city was to become the image, not only of 'man's inhumanity to man';

it was also inextricably associated with the romantic turbulence of the search for individual values and a sense of identity in a world made increasingly alien, not only by materialism and rationalism, but also, and more important for Barnes, because the established incorporation of man in the ancient cosmological trinity with God and His Nature had been disrupted. Barnes's world, through which he presents his image of Man, is his defence against this 'city of dreadful night'.

That image is persuasively delineated in the quality of Barnes's serene liberty when he wrote 'My Orchard in Linden Lee', with the well-known lines:

Let other vo'k meäke money vaster
In the air o' dark-room'd towns,
I don't dread a peevish meäster;
Though noo man do heed my frowns,
I be free to goo abrode,
Or teäke ageän my hwomeward road
To where, vor me, the apple tree
Do leän down low in Linden Lea.
(I, 234)

The stanza, and the whole poem, derive from his obvious satisfaction in sitting in his orchard. But the issues raised for Barnes by this typically rural activity are rather more complex than a simple gloating would imply. For through his sitting in the orchard, unlike the less fortunate townsman who is 'fairly bound to yield to a clock-service', Barnes is able to participate in the cyclic ritual of the seasons, whose unfailing bounty is suggested by the apple tree that 'Do leän down low in Linden Lea'. And his mental and physical peace is contrasted implicitly with the restless turbulence, and 'sudden fits of crowd-moodiness [and] acts of violence' which result from the 'spiritual destitution' he associates with 'the thick herding of people in houses' in cities (*Views of Labour and Gold*, pp. 112–15). Their money-grubbing and economic slavery, their 'hirelingship' (p. 68), must lead to a spiritual subservience that is dehumanizing in contrast to the freedom of spirit he experiences. Such moments as these, amidst, and made possible by, the beneficence of 'God's untarnished earthly good', release Barnes from the enervating struggle in the cultural prison of what Lionel Trilling has called the 'opposing self'; for here he experiences that liberation of complete identity with self founded in a satisfying mode of life such as Huckleberry Finn experienced on escaping to the river from the feuding shore, discovering that 'there warn't no home like a raft, after all'.

When, in *The Mayor of Casterbridge*, Farfrae says that the new mechanical horse-drill would 'revolutionize sowing hereabout', Elizabeth-Jane comments, 'Then the romance of the sower is gone for good. . . . "He that observeth the wind shall not sow," so the Preacher said; but his words will not be to the point any more. How things change!' (ch. XXIV). In an analogous way Barnes clung to what he conceived to be an untranslatable 'language' in communicating with the deepest and most abiding sources of spiritual and moral well-being. In earlier times the presence of a beneficent order had been manifest in the appearance and regulation of the scheme of things, and was reinforced by the intricate set of correspondences between man and nature which was the rationale of the great unifying chain of being. In the emergent urban world, however, characterized to an ever-growing degree by uncertain values and a complex loneliness, the serene unity of man in God's love which had led him to 'green pastures' was dissipated in spiritual exhaustion. In attempting to justify a dispensation where God's Nature was found to be 'red in tooth and claw', and Himself, therefore, either malicious or illusory, Tennyson, for instance, at a moment of deepest despair quite naturally expressed his sense of destitution in terms of urban desolation:

> He is not here; but far away
> The noise of life begins again
> And ghastly thro' the drizzling rain
> On the bald street breaks the blank day.
>
> (*In Memoriam*, vii)

It is not, of course, just a case of facilely observing the urban 'tenor' of the image, to use I. A. Richards's term, but rather to remark the fact that in the central, and to most contemporaries, consoling poetic statement of the age, the poet frequently uses as the 'vehicle' of his imagery what Dickens referred to as 'the shame, desertion, wretchedness and exposure of the great capital'.[40] Many sensitive people found themselves living between two worlds where, from one point of view, nature was being increasingly conquered and manipulated for man's material aggrandizement; but from another, metaphysical, aspect, nature was through that process having its cosmological rôle adapted to the new man-made setting. Thus the removal of nature from the prime and immediate context of human life led men to translate optimism based on a rational dispensation into faith in progress in an industrialized environment, bringing about a radical dislocation of traditional values and standards, and replacing them, ineffectually for many, with the iron restriction of Necessity and the earth-bound aspiration of social perfectibility. This change of rôle resulted in a situation infinitely more perplexing than that implied in the simple opposition of 'God made the country, and man made the town'; it became commensurately more difficult to believe, in what seemed to Barnes and many of his contemporaries the worst of all possible worlds, that 'He prayeth best, who loveth best/All things both great and small.' The difficulty is dramatized with terrfying effect by James Thomson. In his wanderings through the 'City of Dreadful Night', whose ruin is suggested by the rubble of Love, Faith, and Hope, triple pillars that had supported a God-oriented cosmos, he meets a degenerate and forlorn man who hopes with grotesque improbability to find his way 'From this accursed night . . . to *Eden*'s innocence in *Eden*'s clime' (Sec. xviii). By contrast, the world of William Barnes embodies a way of life, an attitude of mind, rooted firmly in his efforts to conserve the 'Eden innocence' of rural Dorset—whose 'life and . . . landscape', as Hopkins expressed it, 'had taken flesh and tongue in the man' (p. 221)—from degenerating into such an 'accursed night'. Those efforts are the medium of his mythopoeic activity—his 'powerful and exquisite [capacity] for defending himself against violation of his cherished self-image'—and constitute, in fact, the very 'art-and-society reasons for urging that Barnes should be read'.

## NOTES

[1] S. E. Hyman, 'Psychoanalysis and the Climate of Tragedy', in *Freud and the Twentieth Century*, ed. Benjamin Nelson, New York, 1957, p. 170.

[2] Hallam Tennyson, *Alfred, Lord Tennyson, A Memoir*, London, 1897, I, 514.

[3] Quoted in William Van O'Connor, *Sense and Sensibility in Modern Poetry*, Chicago, 1948, p. 18.

[4] *The Letters of John Keats*, ed. M. B. Forman, Oxford, 1935, pp. 334–7.

[5] Thomas Hardy, 'The Rev. William Barnes, B.D.', reprinted in Lionel Johnson, *The Art of Thomas Hardy*, London, 1895, p. 1.

[6] H. J. Massingham, *The English Countryman*, London, 1943, p. 127.

[7] Quoted in *Selected Poems of William Barnes*, ed. Geoffrey Grigson, London, 1950, p. 10.

[8] 'William Barnes: the Dorsetshire Poet', *Macmillan's Magazine*, VI, 1862,155.

[9] *The Letters of Gerard Manley Hopkins to Robert Bridges*, ed. C. C. Abbott, Oxford, 1955, p. 88.

[10] *William Barnes of Dorset*, London, 1953, p. 21.

[11] Quoted in Dugdale, p. 20, from Barnes's 'Foresay' to Judge Udal's *Dorsetshire Folklore*.

[12] 'In Memoriam Rev. William Barnes, B.D.', *Proceedings of the Dorset Natural History and Antiquarian Field Club*, VIII, 1887, xviii.

[13] *The Rural Muse*, London, 1954, p. 152.

[14] Quoted in Geoffrey Grigson, *The Harp of Aeolus*, London, 1947, p. 121.

[15] *The Acquisitive Society*, London, 1933, pp. 231–3.

[16] *Views of Labour and Gold*, London, 1859, p. 12.

[17] Quoted in Montague Weekley, *William Morris*, London, 1934, p. 134.

[18] *The Letters of D. H. Lawrence*, ed. Aldous Huxley, London, 1932, p. 300.

[19] Quoted from Barnes's 'Foresay' to *An Outline of English Speech-craft*, in *The Harp of Aeolus*, p. 111.

[20] 'An English Classic, William Barnes', *Fortnightly Review*, XL, 1886, 664.

[21] *Macmillan's Magazine*, XVI, 1867, 306.

[22] *The Poems of William Barnes*, ed. Bernard Jones, London, 1962, I, 392. All citations of Barnes's poetry will be from this edition, unless otherwise noted.

[23] *The Idiom of the People*, London, 1958, p. 30.

[24] 'Discourse VII', 1776, quoted in H. A. Needham, *Taste and Criticism in the Eighteenth Century*, London, 1952, p. 135.

[25] *Natural Theology: Or the Evidences of the Existence and Attributes of the Deity*, London, 1802, II, 143.

[26] *Three Essays on Religion*, London, 1885, p. 174.

[27] *Fraser's Magazine*, LXVIII, 1863, 130–4.

[28] C. J. Wallis, 'Early Manhood of William Barnes', *Gentleman's Magazine*, CCLXV, 1888, 29.

[29] This article is not listed in Dugdale's bibliography (pp. 237–44). It originally appeared in *The Leisure Hour* for 1883 (which I have not been able to consult). A copy of the article in pamphlet form, presumably reprinted from *The Leisure Hour*, appears among Barnes's papers in the Dorset County Museum. It has apparently not been reprinted since.

[30] This pamphlet is among Barnes's papers in the Dorset Museum. It was probably privately printed as a pamphlet by Barnes in 1849 from the *Poole Herald*, where it first appeared.

[31] Thomas Edwards Kebbel, 'English Farmers', *Blackwood's Magazine*, CXLV, 1889, 135.

[32] Quoted in J. L. and L. B. Hammond, *The Rise of Modern Industry*, London, 1930, p. 3.

[33] J. L. and L. B. Hammond, *The Bleak Age*, New York, 1947, p. 34.

[34] G. M. Trevelyan, *English Social History*, London, 1945, pp. 475–6.

[35] Mabel Kay Ashby, *Joseph Ashby of Tysoe*, 1859–1919, Cambridge, 1961, p. 285.

[36] Quoted in Douglas Brown, *Thomas Hardy*, London, 1954, p. 38.

[37] 'The Dorsetshire Labourer', *Longman's Magazine*, II, 1883, 269.

[38] J. F. Lynen, *The Pastoral Art of Robert Frost*, New Haven, 1960, pp. 57–8.

[39] Thomas Hardy, *The Mayor of Casterbridge*, London, 1912, ch. xxiv.

[40] Quoted in Frank Kermode, *Romantic Image*, London, 1957, p. 5.

# BEDFORD PARK: AESTHETE'S ELYSIUM?

*Ian Fletcher*

IN the early 1880s, the London suburb of Bedford Park became associated rather vaguely with that vague movement, Aestheticism. An image of it as a Paradise of aesthetes has survived in memoirs, some, such as those of W. B. Yeats and G. K. Chesterton, distinguished. A second, perhaps more secure image of Bedford Park presents the first recognizable English garden-suburb. The suburb preserves also a modest place in the history of domestic architecture, for it contains buildings by Norman Shaw, E. W. Godwin and one striking house by C. A. Voysey.[1] Yet because of difficulties in the attribution of buildings, and because an account of Bedford Park involves architectural history, literary history, and even some mild sociology, little has been recorded of its early years. My concern is to recount its origins; to give some details about those who lived there: what they did, what they thought of themselves as a community.

G. K. Chesterton opens his novel *The Man Who was Thursday* with this paragraph:

> The suburb of Saffron Park lay on the sunset side of London, as red and ragged as a cloud of sunset. It was built of a bright red brick throughout; its skyline was fantastic, and even its ground plan was wild. It had been the outburst of a speculative builder, faintly tinged with art, who called its architecture sometimes Elizabethan and sometimes Queen Anne, apparently under the impression that the two sovereigns were identical. It was described with some justice as an artistic colony, though it never in any definable way produced any art. But although its pretensions to be an intellectual centre were a little vague, its pretensions to be a pleasant place were quite indisputable.[2]

Saffron Park is Bedford Park. Chesterton knew it well: he courted Frances Bloggs, his future wife, there in the 1890s. The image he elaborates in his novel and later in his *Autobiography*[3] is somewhat fantastic, somewhat inaccurate. The inaccuracy stems from Chesterton's constant quest for birds of paradox and his habit of dramatizing people in terms of their beliefs. But the point is that Bedford Park provoked images: Chesterton's was merely one of a series. It was seen as Arcadian, Aesthetic, Bohemian; as an unconscious example of a romantic Socialist Co-operative. Its physical presence alone was striking, different, isolated. In the late nineteenth century it was peopled by a close community of artists, poets, academics, journalists, actors, and cultivated members of the professional classes; self-conscious and articulate persons, very much aware of themselves as a community.

A little west and a little north of Hammersmith the grey chaos of building is clarified. Emblematically almost, the entrance to Bedford Park is marked by a level crossing over a disused railway. The noble anarchist, Sergius Stepniak, one of the few inhabitants of Bedford Park, who might himself have stepped straight out of one of Chesterton's fantasias, seemed also to have been under the impression that the line was disused. It was Stepniak's custom to walk along a small length of this railway, perhaps for the same reason as Descartes is said to have joined the Dutch Army—as a place where one could be sure of a little peace and quiet. While reading the agenda for one of his meetings of exiles, a train came down the line and Stepniak was killed. This rather brutal anecdote is told merely to show that fact in Bedford Park seems easily to touch fiction.[4]

On the farther side of the railway, one finds oneself among winding roads richly loaded with trees and houses that have been inaccurately termed 'early Oscar Wilde' in allusion to the 'aesthetic' past. In one road, Priory Gardens, we have a vista of houses with East Anglian-type gables and eighteenth-century shell-hood doorways. But the main east–west artery is the Bath Road with flowing gables and ornamental brickwork from plans prepared by Norman Shaw. The houses stand in ground that still faintly preserves the appearance of orchard land. And at the west end of the Bath Road we come to what was clearly intended to be the centre of a complex: a church; what was once a co-operative stores, and an inn. Bedford Park was planned as a self-contained village unit and to enter it, as the painter Edward Abbey observed, was like 'walking into a water colour'.

It was in 1875 that Jonathan T. Carr (1845–1915), brother of J. Comyns Carr, an art critic closely associated with the 'greenery-yallery' Grosvenor Gallery, where the painters popular in aesthetic circles exhibited, initiated the project.[5] By the 1890s Jonathan Carr had come to be regarded, according to Chesterton, not merely as

> the patriarch or the oldest inhabitant but in some sense as the founder and father of the republic. He was not really so very old; but then the republic was very new: much newer than the new republic of Mr Mallock, though filled with philosophic gossip of much the same sort, over which the patriarch benevolently beamed and brooded. At least to quote a literary phrase then much quoted, he was older than the rocks which he sat among, or the roof he sat under; and we might well have murmured another contemporary tag; a little vaguely, perhaps, from memory:
>
> Match me this marvel save where aesthetes are,
> A rose-red suburb half as old as Carr.[6]

Carr began by acquiring twenty-four acres of land adjoining Bedford House, the midmost of three eighteenth-century buildings at the entrance of the estate.[7] This property took its name from the brothers Bedford, who had owned the land up to the earlier nineteenth century, when it passed to John Lindley, Professor of Botany and Fellow of the Royal Society, who planted many trees in the area. When Bedford Park was detached from the Vestry of Old Brentford to Chiswick in 1878, it consisted of 29 acres 18 poles.

The first half-dozen houses were built in the Avenue to the designs of Coe and Robinson, and six at least by Ernest William Godwin (1833–1886), father by Ellen Terry of Gordon Craig, friend of Wilde and Whistler and, like his son, a daring theatrical designer. Godwin's corner houses are simpler than the later designs for Bedford Park: English vernacular, without Renaissance detail. Godwin had been asked to provide economical designs, after Carr had seen a vicarage designed by him, near Northampton. The early Avenue houses were ready for occupation in the autumn of 1876 and were illustrated in the *Building*

*News* for December 22nd of that year. Later, Godwin complained that his designs had been altered and it is doubtful if they can be considered among his better work.[8]

Building was carried on during 1877 to the designs of Coe and Robinson and to that year belong the semi-detached villas in the Bath Road, which strongly suggest Norman Shaw in style. Shaw designed nine types of house altogether. The Bath Road houses have large, studio-type windows, though these face south. Later designs were by Wilson, E. J. May, Shaw's assistant, and Maurice B. Adams, editor of *Building News*, who was responsible for the rather nasty eclecticism of the Parish Hall and for a number of Passmore Edwards libraries.[9] Both May and Adams became residents. We have an account of the early building from H. Fox-Bourne, editor of *The Bedford Park Gazette*:

> Continuing the old roadway known as The Terrace, leading from Turnham Green towards East Acton, the earliest road opened up was The Avenue, from which the Woodstock-Road and the Bath-Road branched out on the right-hand side . . . while this initial scheme was in process, moreover, it was being expanded by the construction of the Blenheim-Road, the Bedford-Road, and Queen Anne's-Gardens, quickly followed by Queen Anne's-grove, Newton-grove, Marlborough-Crescent, The Orchard, and the other roads and their houses now grouped in artistic variation, but in harmonious agreement with the original conception of the architect and projector.[10]

As Moncure Conway, another resident, observed in 1883, 'the pattern of streets and gardens was largely decided by Dr Lindley's trees'. Carr and a surveyor whose name is not known had laid out the roads themselves. For the *Daily News* of May 1880, the effect was rather that of a *camera obscura*. The roads are described as being designed

> with cunning carelessness to curve in such wise as never to leave the eye to stare at nothing. But one straight thoroughfare runs through the estate, and even this is bounded by the wooded hill of Acton. All the others appear closed at the end by trees and houses, and form a succession of views as if the architect had taken a hint from Nature, who, when in pleasant, lazy mood, will dispose such mighty rivers as the Rhine and Hudson to form a series of lake views.[11]

What was admired about Bedford Park was primarily the country quality, rather than the complex of buildings; not so much its sense of community expressed in its co-operative stores and clubhouse, as its insinuation into the landscape. Stories about nightingales singing in the Bedford Park gardens were current in the eighteen-eighties and nineties. Bedford Park was *rus in urbe*. The stress falls on the natural, the homely and, of course, on craft and art. *The Sporting and Dramatic News* for September 27th, 1879, stresses the homely and functional aspects of the architecture, presumably, like the *Daily News*, echoing the views of Carr and Shaw:

> We have here no unchangeable cast-iron work, but hand-wrought balustrades and palings; no great sheets of plate glass, but small panes set in frames of wood which look strong and solid, although, the windows, being large, they supply ample illumination for the spacious rooms within. There is no attempt to conceal with false fronts, or stucco ornament or unmeaning balustrades, that which is full of comfortable suggestiveness in a climate like our own—the house roof; everything is simple, honest, unpretending. Within, no clumsy imitations of one wood to conceal another, but a preserving surface of beautifully slatted paint, made handsome by judicious arrangement of colour. Mere brick is openly brick, and paint openly paint. Nothing . . . pretends to be that which it is not. Varnish is unknown. There is an old-world air about the place despite its newness, a strong touch of Dutch homeliness, with an air of English comfort and luxuriousness, but not a bit of the showy, artificial French stuffs which prevailed in our homes when Queen Anne was on the throne, when we imported our furniture from France and believed in nothing which was not French.[12]

By January 1880, 100 acres had been laid out in some 220 houses. By 1883, the number of occupied houses was 333 and later in the 1880s had risen to more than 400. The first public building, the Clubhouse, was begun in 1878 and opened on May 2nd, 1879. The original design looks like the work of E. J. May and the enlargement a few years later was certainly under May's direction.[13]

The architectural press, no less than the popular press, maintained a vivid interest in Bedford Park. *The Building News* for January 30th, 1880, describes exterior and interior of the club-house:

> The exterior is that of a plain red brick and tiled building, roofed in two divisions and decorated with a deep cove in plaster on the

> principal fronts. A porch with heavy wooden head, opens through a hall into an assembly room, 36 × 24 feet; on the right of the entrance is a small card room; on the left are a reading room, and a billiard room, each 25 × 20 feet. The walls are hung with Japanese paper of dark tone, and with choice specimens of old tapestry; some genuine old furniture, including an arm-chair carved in oak and dated 1636, is interspersed with chairs by Godwin, Morris, and Jackson, and here and there a piece of old china, sets of a cabinet or whatnot. In the assembly room there is a mantelpiece exhibited by (Aldam) Heaton in the last Paris Exhibition, the work is painted with clear, green colours and relieved by gesso-work in transparent colours and large gilded human figures, the general effect being rich and handsome, though it fits badly with the cornice and frieze of the room. At the rear of the room, a stage is being fitted up, and will be thrown into it when complete, and a ladies' billiard room is nearly finished. The oak dado and pedimented doorway to this room are from the late Church of St Dionis Backchurch ... the light is from three small windows on the east, and from glass prisms, in the ceiling, and a series of half a dozen Suggs gas burners, furnished with hoods and placed at equal distances over the table. The fireplaces have open grates set with tile-borders, by De Morgan.[14]

In his *Travels in South Kensington*, Moncure Conway gives us a further glimpse of the interior. In the Assembly or Ball-Room, were 'panels, with classical subjects wrought in gold on ebony which fill the wall space above the mantel-piece. There is a stage with a drop-scene, representing one of our streets.'[15] According to a pamphlet on the Clubhouse, dating from some time between the two world-wars, the green and gold over-mantel of the Assembly or Ball-room was part of an old organ case, presumably also from Wren's St Dionis Backchurch.[16] The gilded human figures, according to W. B. Yeats, were, in fact, Cupids.[17] *The Bedford Park Gazette* describes the bay windows as lined with broad oaken seats, with coffers under them, modelled on the antique. Flowers and ornamental shrubs, book-shelves, settees, and pieces of furniture of the dark perforated pattern made in India completed the *ensemble*. The stage itself was built with a convex inner wall. Carr was devoted to trees and this rather awkward design was to ensure that a large tree in his own garden which backed on to the Clubhouse should be saved from the axe. Consequently, it was impossible to proceed from one side of the stage to the other without being seen by the audience, though this state of affairs was later remedied.

By the close of 1879, Club membership had risen above 150 and increased steadily over the next four years. The entrance fee was three guineas and the annual subscription two. The Assembly Rooms could be hired for Balls, concerts and dramatic performances for five guineas. No betting was permitted and light 'general daily and weekly papers were taken and the chief monthly magazines'. A library was formed in 1883 and a constant flow of new books supplied by the Grosvenor Gallery library. Each member had the right to put forward the name of two ladies (members of his own family) who might use the club facilities at a cost of ten shillings and sixpence a year.

Tower House, the largest residence on the estate, was the seat of Jonathan Carr himself. Designed by Shaw, it was completed in 1879 and unfortunately demolished towards 1932. It boasted a cupola and balustrade and resembled a country-house of the Inigo Jones school. Its chimney stacks were taller than usual. The back elevation had two large projecting bays with Georgian panes which were fully glazed on the ground floor and joined by another continuous strip of glazing marked as a conservatory on the plan.

Here once again were the choice hangings; what is described as 'Early English', that is Jacobean-type furniture, dado and fireplace, this time carved out of the organ loft of St Dionis Backchurch, along with papers by Morris, and Jeffrey and Co.[11] Japanese paintings hung on the walls and the hall windows had tinted glazing. We know that Carr wished everywhere to use wood rather than stone or brick inside. Cheapness as much as aesthetic theory was the probable motive. Even so the building and decorations cost £4,000. Here Carr dispensed, as the squire of the village, liberal and continuous hospitality. A fête was held every year in the garden, generally in July, to which Ellen Terry and other notabilities often came.

In 1880, Norman Shaw's church of St Michael and All Angels was consecrated. The exterior presents a *mélange* of Perpendicular, domestic Renaissance and cottage vernacular features: a cupola, cornices, balustrade with coved gables over dormer-windows. Shaw's aim was not to overpower, but to harmonize with the surrounding buildings. The interior has a Jacobean-type screen and much woodwork. Shaw was probably influenced by the mass of dark Carolean woodwork of the Laudian church of St John, Leeds, which he had restored.

Early in January 1880, a group of members of the Architectural Association visited Turnham Green and in *The Builder* for January 31st, 1880, after an account of Shaw's church, there are some comments on the new buildings opposite:

> . . . the buildings will comprise a row or terrace of seven gables, like the old row in Holborn, and will include, beside the stores, a private house for the manager, an old-fashioned inn . . .[19]

The reference here is probably to Staple Inn, then unrestored. But here, as in Swan House, Shaw seems to have had in mind for his heavily projecting bays, Sparrowe's House at Ipswich (1670).[20] This again asserts the English vernacular theme. The old-fashioned inn was given the name of the Tabard, recalling Chaucer's pilgrims, with a sign showing a Trumpeter, painted by T. M. Rooke (who had begun as a Pre-Raphaelite and later did much topographical drawing from Ruskin). Rooke was a resident in Bedford Park.[21]

The Tabard owed its origin to the need for a licensed house 'within easy access of numerous workmen employed in the estate and', as the editor of *The Bedford Park Gazette* rather darkly continued, 'to obviate the danger and annoyance of the otherwise inevitable sale of alcoholic liquors to those workmen through other channels'.[22]

The rôle of the stores was 'to meet the demand [for] larger and more various household necessaries than was within reach of the inhabitants and to relieve them of the necessity of frequently sending to London to make purchases.' By 1883 it had ten separate establishments and one could obtain from it Groceries, Provisions, Meat, Poultry, Greengroceries, Furnishing, Fancy Goods, Coal, Wines and Spirits, China and Glass, Stationery, Drugs, Turnery, Ironmongery, House Decorations, etc.[23]

The impression gathered from the Architectural papers and from the *Gazette* is of a ye-olde-England, Ruskin and Morris medievalism. But although the exteriors of the Bedford Park houses do indeed form an architectural unity within diversity and pleasingly react against contemporary taste for stucco and Italianate Villas, the general effect remains, particularly if we take the interiors into account, of an imaginary museum, eclecticism. Both externally and internally, Bedford Park houses leave an impression of time-travelling in taste and this is typical of aestheticism; the sense in Pater's words that 'all periods, types, schools of taste are in themselves equal,'[24] a remark reflecting acute historical self-consciousness.

The impression of the artist T. Raffles Davidson, who visited Bedford Park in the later part of the year 1880 was not, however, one of eclecticism. In a description published in the *British Architect* of December 3rd, 1880, Davidson stressed the suburb's picturesqueness, its spontaneity and assymetricality, but, oddly enough, also found its general effect monotonous, mainly owing to the materials used. Instead of brown and purple tiles, green and yellow, purple and red bricks, there was, he remarked, a generally dull use of one thin red colour for bricks and tiles. He also mentions that many of the furnishings had been placed in the houses by order of the architects. Morris would certainly not have approved Davidson's prescriptions and we may be grateful to Godwin, Shaw, and May for avoiding the shrill polychromatic brickwork of a Butterfield. The vocabulary that Davidson and others apply to Bedford Park is the 'quarter', the 'village', the 'colony'. Emphatically, it was not a suburb.[25] This social distinction was to be sharply drawn by the inhabitants themselves.

According to Moncure Conway, purchasers or leasers of houses could choose their own wallpapers and colours for woodwork. The occupants were allotted a fixed amount for decorations and for the most part they chose Morris papers. Conway opined that the firm of Morris and Co. would shortly have to open a branch in Bedford Park.

The prices of houses to be leased ranged from £35 to £120. *The Builder* for April 24th, 1880, reports that a Bijou Villa in the Queen Anne style was sold at an auction for buying Freeholds for £610 and was bringing in £50 a year with a ground rent of £91.[26] The early houses, however, were reported to have inadequate drainage and this may account for the stress laid on the topic in the early advertisements, along with the marriage of utility and beauty: few houses had basements or cellars, according to the recommendations of Dr Richardson, *The Bedford Park Gazette* informs us:

> Hitherto it has been generally supposed that perfect sanitary arrangements and substantial construction are inseparable from ugliness. But it is especially claimed for Bedford Park that it is the most conspicuous effort yet made to break the dull dreariness of the ordinary suburban villa . . . an effort has been made to secure, by artistic treatment of plain bricks and tiles rather than by meretricious ornament, an effect hitherto never attempted. By placing houses varying in size and design side by side the dull monotony so often seen is avoided.[27]

But Jonathan Carr had over-reached himself. The account of his financial fall, told to Chesterton by Lucien Oldenshaw, a resident, is probably too picturesque:

> The 'patriarch' who 'benevolently beamed and brooded' over his suburb had gone bankrupt in the making of it. He lived for the rest of his life with the bailiff as his butler. He and his equally impoverished brother would spend long hours playing cards together and getting highly excited when three shillings changed hands.[28]

Fox-Bourne, the editor of *The Gazette*, is naturally more tactful:

> In order that assistance might be given to Mr Carr in further developing a project which had already assumed far larger proportions than he had contemplated, the Bedford Park Co. Ltd. was established in the Autumn of 1881. The portion of the estate then transferred to the company was valued at £265,850.[29]

Carr seems to have continued speculating. In 1884, we hear of him in connection with new building in Northumberland Avenue.

But Bedford Park was more than a speculation. It was as consciously artistic as it was conscious of any shortcomings in sanitation. The main purpose was 'to set up' a London suburb that should possess 'artistic and sanitary advantages superior to those to be found in any other surburb of London.'[30] In some ways, Bedford Park certainly anticipated Port Sunlight, Welwyn Garden City, and Hampstead Garden Suburb. Indeed, Port Sunlight is, in part, an anthology of features derived from Shaw's Bedford Park houses. But Bedford Park was related by at least one of its inhabitants, as we shall see, to the romantic Socialism of the earlier nineteenth century. John Silk Buckingham's Victoria pre-dates the Public Health Act of 1848, which stimulated a succession of model towns, projected by philanthropists and enlightened employers of labour. In *Tait's Edinburgh Magazine* for December 1848,[31] a project which would have made Ilford in Essex the first garden village was suggested. The numbers involved were to have been of the order of 5,000 to 6,000. Like the advertisements for Bedford Park, the scheme stressed air and space, wood and water, schools and churches, shrubbery and gardens, around pretty self-contained cottages, in a group not too large to deprive it of a country character, nor too small to diminish the probabilities of social intercourse. The Ilford scheme was, however, commercial and based on class selection. Like Bedford Park, it was to be a paradise for the professional class. Bromborough on the Mersey had had its paternalistic co-operative store, free school, library and sports grounds. But the nearest analogue to Bedford Park belongs also to the year 1876, when Alexander Stewart's Long Island Model Estate began. Like Bedford Park, it was for the middle-class and had no industry attached. In 1879, the first houses were built at Bourneville, rather gaunt and grim architecturally, but of reasonable density. Bedford Park, then, certainly has its place in the development of the garden-suburb. It was not Utopian like Buckingham's Victoria, nor like Saltaire or Bourneville, was it the product of enlightened paternalism. At the same time it cannot be related too rigidly to the Long Island estate. For Moncure Conway, pastor of the Ethical Church and a Bedford Park resident from 1879 to 1885, Bedford Park fulfilled in its modest, undoctrinaire way an ideal of co-operation: in his book it is related both to the medieval village and to aestheticism:

> There is not a member of the new suburb who would not be startled, if not scandalized at any suggestion that he or she belonged to a community largely socialistic. They would allege, with perfect truth, that they were not even acquainted with the majority of their neighbours, have their own circle of friends, and go on with their business as men and women of the world. Nevertheless, it is certainly true that a degree in social evolution is represented by Bedford Park and that it is in the direction of that co-operative life that animated the dreams of Père Enfantin and Saint Simon. All society indeed must steadily and normally advance in that direction.[32]

The equation is startling. One justification for Conway's claim was the presence of 'new women' in Bedford Park, but his argument is actually based on the low price range of Bedford Park houses and on the fact that owing to the large number of families who had agreed to buy or rent houses, Carr had been enabled to buy materials and labour in bulk. As a result the chief advantage of co-operation was assured. Conway cites the stores, the club with its newspapers and current literature in common, its tennis lawns, billiard rooms, conveniences, and entertainments. The success of Bedford Park as a community, Conway considered, lay precisely in its empiricism. Earlier nineteenth-century ideal communities had failed because they had started with theory and made practice conform to that. No blueprint for development had been laid down in Bedford Park, but each of the many institutions had appeared in response to a felt want. Conway is not alone in stressing the Bohemian quality of the village. 'The entire freedom of the village and of its inhabitants is unqualified by anything whatever, whether social, political or economic.' This is all too rosy to be true, but there does seem to have been some interest in co-operatives: in February 1884, a lecture was given in the Clubhouse on Leclerc's Co-operative Workshops.[33]

Bedford Park, then, provided several images. To Conway, it appeared as an example of unconscious co-operation, with a respectable Bohemianism which cut across a good deal of class structure; to others, it appeared as a commuter's pastoral[34] and to the architectural press it was a comfortable innovation. By the popular press, it tended to be seen as a Mecca of Aestheticism.

The beginnings of Bedford Park coincide in date with the rise of the Aesthetic Movement and journalists failed to distinguish between a liking for Morris papers and a philosophy of conduct. This is not the place to discuss the origins of the word 'aesthetic' or the narrower uses to which the word was put in the course of the nineteenth century. George Brimley, for example, in his essay on Tennyson in *Cambridge Essays* (1855) describes the *Lotus Eaters* as 'carrying Tennyson's tendencies to pure aestheticism to an extreme point'.[35] Brimley is polemically distinguishing a poetry that is 'picture and music, and nothing more'; a poetry which luxuriates in its evasion of moral strenuousness. A. H. Hallam had made a comparable distinction in his famous review of Tennyson's *Poems* (1830).[36] Here, Hallam defines a type of romantic poetry which is all imagery and confined to presenting dark subjective states.

As a self-conscious movement, Aestheticism gathers force in the early 1870s, is vulgarized in the 1880s and disappears by the end of that decade. It represents something of a shift from literature to the applied arts. Graham Robertson, indeed, rather naughtily suggests that the real origins of the movement are to be found in industrious old ladies in the 1850s and 1860s happily sewing away at their crooked milkmaids and lumpy flowers in the back parlours of Bayswater and Brompton.[37] The actual doctrine appears first in Swinburne's review of Baudelaire's *Fleurs du Mal* in the *Spectator* for September 6th, 1862 (reprinted in Swinburne's *Works*, Volume XIII, p. 419) and in Pater's essay on Winckelmann, which was published in the *Westminster Gazette* in 1867. Swinburne's *William Blake* (1868) gave prominence to the phrase 'art for art's sake' and five years later the phrase was embodied in the provocatively enigmatic conclusion to Pater's *Renaissance*. Through Pater and J. A. Symonds, the movement acquired also an eclectic neo-Grec quality of which Godwin's Greek-type dresses which *express* rather than constrict the body; Godwin's antiquarian Greek stage sets; the paintings of Alma-Tadema, Leighton and Poynter; Grant Allen's *Physiological Aesthetics* of 1877 and the cult of pederasty, are all symptomatic. One of the constant elements in Aestheticism was a revulsion from the ugliness and materialism of the contemporary scene and the tendency to look back to 'imaginary' 'spots of time' when the sense of beauty was normative. Historical self-awareness led to a sense of freedom in time: time-travelling might be defined as central to Aestheticism, and this sharply distinguishes it from the cult of the moment, of the 'modern', which is characteristic of 'Decadence'. The Aesthetes looked back to the eighteenth century, the Jacobean period or the Middle Ages, periods represented in Bedford Park. The movement even captured the Church through the Ritualist Movement of the 1860s[38] and the Kyrle Society gave it social emphasis, sending well-bred young women into dim homes to spread the new gospel and to suggest that the poor might forget their lot more readily by taking to water-colour painting, buying reproductions of great paintings and visiting the South Kensington Museum somewhat more often.[39] The movement coincided and became entangled with the enthusiasm for all things Japanese that became a mania in the 1880s. There was much *Japonaiserie* in the Bedford Park houses. Japan had been opened after centuries of seclusion by the Americans in 1859 and there, frozen, perfect, was a medieval feudal society.[40]

That the vulgarizing of Aestheticism had been disastrous to a genuine art-movement was widely recognized, we may gather from Graham Robertson. Indeed, he calls its beginnings, those of the only genuine art-movement that England had ever known.[41] The patriarch of Bedford Park, Jonathan Carr himself, gave a lecture at the Clubhouse on January 27th, 1883, with the title: 'The harm Aestheticism has done to the spread of Art.'[42]

Aestheticism was all too easy to ridicule. Indeed, by providing an easy rôle for poseurs of all types, it parodied itself. The early years of Bedford Park witnessed both alarmed and amused Philistine satire of the movement. From 1880 on, George du Maurier elaborated his gallery of Aesthetes in *Punch*: Basil Giorgione (a symbiosis, it seems, of Pater and Wilde, whose rôle as half-caricaturing, half proselytizing entrepreneur of Aestheticism in the earlier 1880s brought much discredit on the movement); Leonora della Robbia de Tudor, one of those young women, amateurs of the Beautiful, who pursue art—without ever quite catching it; Westpond Tumpkyns, shining light of the Dullialilytanty Society, Cimabue Brown, Prigsby, the critic, Maudle, the painter, and Jellaby Posthelthwaite, the aesthetic poet. Literary satire kept pace with du Maurier. Pater had been satirized as Mr Rose in Mallock's *New Republic* of 1877, with its atmosphere of leisured Socratic conversation in a country-house setting. Besant and Rice's *Monks of Thelema* of 1878 also has a country-house setting, satirizes Pater and contains an aesthetic young woman who is dressed in 'neutral tints', parts her hair on the side and corrects her neighbours in a low voice when they commit barbarities on art: 'she was not pretty, but she was full of soul'. And the most famous of such satires, still within these early days of Bedford Park, was Gilbert's *Patience* of 1881.[43]

That there were several Aestheticisms in a social no less than a doctrinal sense, was recognized by Henry James in his *Tragic Muse*, which first appeared in serial form in 1889, with its rather awkwardly half-satirical, half-sympathetic portrait of Gabriel Nash, whose doctrine is Paterian but whose defensive paradoxes are Wilde's. James distinguished the 'worldly semi-smart' Aesthetes, associated perhaps with Lady Archibald Campbell and such fashionable painters as Mrs Jopling Rowe, from the 'frumpy, sickly lot who wore dirty drapery' in 'some dusky dimly-imagined suburb of culture, peopled by phrasemongers . . . who had no human use but to be held up in the comic press, which was probably restrained by decorum from touching upon the worst of their aberrations.'

It was in 1882 that the new suburb was decisively linked with Wilde and the Aesthetes by Walter Hamilton in his *Aesthetic Movement in England*, where a culminating chapter of twelve pages is devoted to Bedford Park. Here, the Aesthete's programme—of applying the spirit of art to every detail of modern life—has transcended the single object of furniture, the perfectly designed book, the perfect exterior and interior design of a single house; the single artistic personality and its expression through dress and manner—for Dandyism, turning oneself into the impassibility of a statue, where the suffering that constitutes the condition of art is charmed away—was naturally part of the programme. Even the artistic group has been transcended. All is united in an ideal community: the most elaborate synthesis of the arts possible, where art has triumphed over ugliness and modernity in every detail.

Hamilton writes as an apologist, and lyrically insists on the English rather than the Japanese element in Bedford Park:

> The sunlight wavers and flickers on the red brick fronts of the houses; many of the doors are open, and the neat halls are visible with clean cool Indian matting, square old-fashioned brass lamps; comfort and cleanliness everywhere, lightness and grace abound. Even the names on the doorposts have a touch of poetry and quaintness about them. Pleasaunce, Elm Dene, Kirk Lees, Ye Denne.[44]

Hamilton notes the reaction against High Victorian (and perhaps Regency) metalwork:

> Nearly every house has a balcony, not the ordinary kind of iron abomination jutting like a huge wart on the face of the house.[45]

These wooden balconies *Punch* used for a drawing reproduced in the issue of August 25th 1883:

> Scene: Aesthetic Neighbourhood. (The background represents a gabled Bedford Park-type house.) Two figures are walking thoughtfully away.
>
> Converted Betting Man (Plays Concertina in Salvation Army):

'Pooty 'ouses they builds in these subu'bs, Mr Swagget.' Mr S. (Reformed Burglar and Banner-Bearer in the same): 'Ah! and how 'andy them little bal-co-nies would a' been in former . . .' A warning flourish on the concertina and Mr S. drops the subject.[46]

Three birds at a swim: Aestheticism, Philanthropy, and the Working Class. The joke refers to Canon J. W. Horsley, a resident, who devoted himself to the reclamation of criminals and used to ask them to stay with him at his Bedford Park house.

But how Aesthetic was Bedford Park? Shaw somewhat incongrously decorated four of his early houses in the Avenue with sunflowers and the sunflower like the lily and the poppy was much prized by the Aesthetes as an emblem.[47] Hamilton found Aestheticism on a visit to the School of Art.

One young Lady was just putting the finishing touches to a very life-size representation of that aesthetic favourite, that bright emblem of constancy, the brilliant sunflower. I noticed, too, that in many instances the young ladies were decidedly of the aesthetic type, both as to the mode of dress, and to the fashion of arranging the hair.[48]

The Chiswick School of Art had been built in 1880–1881 to the design of Maurice B. Adams.[49] There were two directors, E. S. Burchett, from the South Kensington Department of Science and Art, and F. Hamilton Jackson, from the Slade School, who was also a resident. The committee included Adams, Jonathan Carr and several artists, who, like Jackson, were resident on the estate. In spite of the inclusion of severer studies such as Anatomy, Drawing from Life and the Antique, the emphasis in the teaching fell very much on the decorative arts that were so prominent in Aestheticism.[50]

Moncure Conway's description of Bedford Park, like Hamilton's, comes at the climax of a volume devoted to arts and crafts. Though he described it as Thelema, an ideal village, a Utopia in brick and paint, Conway was aware that it was in danger of becoming too self-consciously isolated a community. 'Now and then the fair riders of Hyde Park extend afternoon exercise to enjoy a look at the new suburb.'[51] John Bright and Renan visited and admired. Conway's chapter on Bedford Park appeared in *Harper's Magazine* and transmitted its image to an American audience.[52]

Satire, good-humoured and less good-humoured, of Bedford Park was frequent, particularly in the early 1880s. Hamilton quotes two ballads *Ye Haunted House* and the more amusing *Ballad of Bedford Park* which had appeared in the *St James's Gazette* of December 17th, 1881. Some of the verses bear quotation:

> In London town there lived a man
>   a gentleman was he
> Whose name was Jonathan T. Carr
>   (as has been told to me).
>
> 'This London is a foggy town'
>   (thus to himself said he),
> 'Where bricks are black, and trees are brown
>   and faces are dirtee.'
>
> 'I will seek out a brighter spot,'
>   continued Mr Carr.
> 'Not too near London, and yet not
>   what might be called too far.
>
> ' 'Tis there a village I'll erect
>   with Norman Shaw's assistance
> Where men may lead a chaste correct
>   aesthetical existence.'
>
> With that a passing 'bus he hailed
>   (so gallant to be seen)
> Upon whose knife-board he did ride
>   as far as Turnham Green . . .
>
> 'Tis here my Norman tried and true
>   our houses we'll erect;
> I'll be the landlord bold and you
>   shall be the architect.
>
> 'Here trees are green and bricks are red
>   and clean the face of man;
> 'We'll build our houses here,' he said,
>   in style of good Queen Anne.'
>
> And Norman Shaw looked up and saw,
>   smiled a cheerful smile.
> 'This thing I'll do,' said he, 'while you
>   the denizens beguile.'

To work then went these worthy men,
  so philanthropic both;
And none who sees the bricks and trees
  to sign the lease is loth.

'Let's have a stores,' said Jonathan;
  said Norman, 'So we will,
For nought can soothe the soul of man
  Like a reasonable bill.'

'A Church likewise,' J.T. replies—
  Says Shaw, 'I'll build a Church,
Yet sore, I fear, the aesthetes here
  will leave it in the lurch.'

'Religion,' pious Carr rejoined,
  'in Moncure Conway's view,
Is not devoid of interest
  although it be not true.

'Then let us make a house for her,
  wherein she may abide,
And those who choose may visit her,
  the rest may stay outside;

'But lest the latter should repine
  a tennis ground we'll make
Where they on Sunday afternoons
  may recreation take.'

Then each at t'other winked his eye
  and next they did prepare
A noble Clubhouse to supply
  with decorations fair.

With red and blue and sagest green
  were walls and dados dyed,
friezes of Morris there were seen
  and oaken wainscote wide.

Thus was a village builded
  for all who are aesthete
Whose precious souls it fill did
  with utter joy complete.

For floors were stained and polished
  and every hearth was tiled

And Philistines abolished
  by Culture's gracious child.

And Jonathan and Norman
  found so much work to do.
They sold out to a company
  to put the business through.

Now he who loves aesthetic cheer
  and does not mind the damp
May come and read Rossetti here
  by a Japanesy lamp.

While 'Arry' shouts to 'Hemmua':
  'say, 'ere's a bloomin' lark,
Them's the biled Lobster 'ouses
  as folks call "Bedford Park." '[53]

That sounds like a malicious insider: dubious drains, Aestheticism, agnosticism, speculative building, are all present. The ballad seems to have been, perhaps for its medieval associations, the chosen vehicle for verse-satire on Bedford Park. In the Supplement to the Special Number of the *Lady's Pictorial* for June 24th, 1882, Horace Lennard tells how a young couple were able to marry by discovering Bedford Park. The young lady was an Aesthete and

Said she, I have for Art a zeal,
Most high and grand is my ideal,
And a very little way, now-a-day, you know,
Five hundred pounds will go, go, go.

No modern house for me will do,
All sham and plaster, damp and new;
I won't have stucco and varnished paint,
But something old and quaint, quaint, quaint.

A journey by District Railway leads them to Turnham Green:

They left the station and turned to the right,
When a picture strange arose in sight:
'O look!' cried the youth to the maiden 'Quick!
Houses of red brick, brick, brick, brick!'

A pretty porch soon came in view,
The house looked old, although 'twas new,

A lady artist there did dwell,
So the youth gave a ring at the bell, bell, bell.

And in reply to his remark
They said this place is Bedford Park,
And all these houses erected are
By Mr Jonathan Carr, Carr, Carr. . . .'

The Tabard, the Stores and the Church are all featured:

A tavern o'er the way they spied,
Where marvels more they met inside,
For nut-brown ale and sack within
Were sold at the Tabard Inn, Inn, Inn.

And just next door there stood a store,
Which an Early English aspect bore,
Where each artistic serving-man
Wore a costume of Japan-pan-pan.

The Bedford Parkites are so good
They have propped up with post of wood
Their red-brick Church, because you see,
It must supported be, be, be.

In *Youth* for 6th April, 1883, a certain pseudonymous 'Madge' records that:

> We . . . met some people who live at Bedford Park . . . I have never seen the place except from the vantage point of the window of a railway carriage, whence it appears rather a glare of red brick, which makes the eye long for trees, many and large. We were, therefore, much surprised to hear these ladies talk of the place in a curiously exalted strain. I really thought for a few moments they were conversing about Paradise, and wondered at the exactness of detail that seemed to characterize their information. Flowers always blooming, and skies always bright, sun always shining, existence idyllic, etc., etc.; these were a few of the phrases. Consequently it was quite a shock when the elder lady, including me in the conversation, remarked, 'And then our drainage is so perfect!' I was really disconcerted for a moment. She added 'and our club is so charming!' . . . I then . . . enquired 'Where is this delightful place?' Maud and I were regarded as outer barbarians because we not only had never been to Bedford Park, but actually knew no one who lived there. It appeared incredible to our new acquaintances: and when the elder lady said 'And have you not seen our newspaper?'

and I replied, humbly, 'No, I didn't know you had one,' she seemed quite compassionate over so much ignorance. From her air of incredulous surprise one would have thought I had said I had never heard of *The Times*. . . . I had heard of this aesthetic colony, of course, and found that I had been by no means wrong in imagining that Tennyson must have had them prophetically in his mind's eye when he wrote the line—

> They think the cackle of their burg the
> murmur of the world.[54]

The identification of Bedford Park with Aestheticism is also stressed in an article contributed to *The Whitehall Review*, based, according to Fox-Bourne on material distorted from *The Bedford Park Gazette*, which had devoted part of its first issue to an account of the origins of the suburb, along with some contemporary comment.[55]

*The Bedford Park Gazette*[56] first appeared in July, 1883, and the editor's image of the Bedford Park comunity stressed Bohemianism and respectability.

> In no other suburb of London is so much individuality combined with so much hearty co-operation for the benefit of all.

He pointed out that the residents included:

> busy merchants . . . a far larger proportion of officers retired from military service than are to be found in any other district of so limited a space, here meet on common ground with artists, authors, men of science, and members of professions, whether the profession be that of the Bar, or that of the Stage. And in spite of these differences and divergences—or is it not rather in consequence of them? —it happens that during these few years of our lifetime as a 'village or community' we have established so many local institutions that we now find it necessary to have a Gazette of our own in which to chronicle their doings.[57]

The status of the actor, we may note, though not yet secure, has certainly risen, perhaps owing to the prestige of the Bancrofts and Irving. In rebutting the image of Bedford Park as an aesthetic colony, is Fox-Bourne accurate?

Out of about five hundred persons listed in the *Gazette* as resident in the month of August 1885, it is possible to identify Generals (3), Colonels (4), Majors (2), Commanders, R.N. (1)

and six Captains, whether military or naval is not stated. These were probably attracted to Bedford Park after the *démarche* of 1881 and by cheap prices rather than wallpapers, or the chance of a game of billiards with a poet. None of the service persons (with the exception of the actor, Captain Percival Keene, who was manager of the Club from 1879 to 1881) took any part in the social and intellectual activities of the suburb. Of declared artists, only twenty are to be found in the *Gazette* or in the *Year's Work in Art* for the year 1884, which I take to be Bedford Park's apogee. There were in addition at least six architects, one sculptor, and fifteen authors and journalists.

Among such a close group tensions were certain. A contributor to the *Gazette*, admitting some Aestheticism in the early years of Bedford Park, found that by 1883 it had become a place fit for Major-Generals. But, adopting a tone of friendly criticism, he observed:

> On rare occasions I have noticed costumes, male and female, which would be more noticeable in some other suburbs of London than they are in Bedford Park, where everybody seems to be tolerably free to wear and do and be what he or she likes best. . . .[58]
>
> Your Club is, I suppose, a fair index of your whole colony. Doesn't a zealous and devout clergyman of the Established Church often play billiards there, with a short pipe in his mouth? and doesn't the wife of another zealous and devout clergyman act gracefully in farces and comedies at the amateur theatricals . . . there performed?[59]
>
> Your Bedford Park Committee appears to exist for the sole purpose of starting new institutions. Out of your population of 2,000 or 3,000, only a few take an active part in the society mania. The same names occur again and again in this committee, and on that; and I fancy your 'leading spirits' must always be in a fever of excitement between amateur theatricals and amateur concerts, lawn tennis matches and playing at firemen's duties. Can they stand the excitement for long?[60]

The answer was they couldn't. A crisis rose among the governing body of the Art School. Maurice B. Adams was criticized by implication in the *Gazette* and retorted angrily and elaborately in *The Richmond and Twickenham Times*, and the next issue of the *Gazette* was the last. It had survived for a year only. A breach in the community had been made.

The number of painters or of literary persons living in Bedford Park in the first six or seven years of its existence may not have been large. The names, however, add another perspective: A. W. Pinero, John Butler Yeats, and his two sons, W. B. and Jack Yeats, John Todhunter, poet and dramatist, Mark Perugini, historian of the theatre and the ballet, George Manville Fenn, prolific novelist, James Sime, Richard Bowdler Sharp, ornithologist, Frederick York Powell, Icelandic scholar and poet, Sergius Stepniak, 'Man of the Steppes', author of *Underground Russia*, Julian Hawthorne, son of the great American novelist, Moncure Conway, and H. R. Fox-Bourne, editor of *The Gazette*, who is remembered for his two-volume history of English newspapers. In later years, Bedford Park was to attract Professor Oliver Elton, Sydney Cockerell, St John Hankin, the dramatist, the publisher Elkin Mathews, the novelist Edgar Jepson and others. The stage was represented by William Terriss, Harry Nichols, Dora Burton, and in later years C. B. Cochran. Painters included H. M. Paget, Birket Forster, Starr Wood, Charles Pears, W. B. Wollen and T. M. Rooke.[61]

Bohemianism in Bedford Park most readily proclaimed itself in dress. Terriss and York Powell seem to have left most impression, York Powell, in particular, booming round corners with his menacing and misleading eyebrows, immense beard, and yachting-cap. But not only dress was Bohemian; Bedford Park not merely contained eccentrics who might have figured in some Chestertonian extravaganza, but the whole village itself partook of an 'attractive unreality':

> More especially . . . about nightfall, when the extravagant roofs were dark against the afterglow and the whole insane village seemed as separate as a drifting cloud. This again was more strongly true of the many nights of local festivity, when the little gardens were often illuminated, and the big Chinese lanterns glowed in the dwarfish trees like some fierce and monstrous fruit.[62]

So Chesterton, and not unhistorically. Such festivities were indeed frequent in Bedford Park: costume conversazione or *tableaux vivantes* or fancy dress balls, they seem to have spent half their time dressing-up, like some of the early inhabitants of Welwyn Garden City. Of these tableaux, a contemporary poet, George Barlow, gives us a hostile glimpse:

> 'twas at that
> Delightful Fancy Fair at Bedford Park,
> When, you remember (did I tell you, dear?
> Oh this is my first letter: so it is)
> That Mr Barnes, the great tall clumsy man,
> Dressed as a bearded woman: it wasn't nice.'[63]

Moncure Conway is naturally more enthusiastic:

> There is . . . a rumour in the adjacent town of London that the people of Bedford Park move about in fancy dress every day. And so far as the ladies are concerned it is true that many of their costumes, open-air as well as other, might some years ago have been regarded as fancy dress, and would still cause a sensation in some Philistine quarters. At our last fancy dress ball, some young men, having danced until five o'clock, when it was bright daylight, concluded not to go to bed at all, but went out to take a game of tennis. At eight they were still playing, but though they were in fancy costumes they did not attract much attention. The tradesmen and others moving about at that hour no doubt supposed it was only some new Bedford Park fashion. There seems to be a superstition on the Continent that fancy-dress balls must only take place in the winter . . . it does not prevail here. It was on one of the softest nights in June that we had our last ball of that character. The grounds [i.e. of Tower House] . . . were overhung with Chinese lanterns, and the sward and bushes were lit up, as it were, with many-tinted giant glow-worms. The fête-champêtre and the mirth of the ballroom went on side by side, with only a balcony and its luxurious cushions between them. Comparatively few of the ladies sought to represent any particular 'character'; there were about two hundred present, and fancy costumes for both sexes were *de rigueur*, yet among all these there were few conventionally historical or allegorical characters . . . The ladies had indulged their own tastes. in design and colour, largely assisted, no doubt, by the many artists which Bedford Park can boast. . . . There is hardly an evening of the spring and summer when Bedford Park does not show unpurposed *tableaux*.[64]

Though *The Gazette* hardly underwrites Conway's hectic account, there can be no doubt that costume soirées were frequent and popular. *The Richmond and Twickenham Times* carries a report of a ball given at the School of Art on the 3rd June, 1884.[65] Dancing lasted until four in the morning. The lights were subdued by rose and amber tinted paper, and F. Hamilton Jackson, one of Bedford Park's artists, provided 'sumptuous special decorations, and three choice tapestry hangings.' Costume, on this occasion, was partly historical: the painter, Hargitt, was robed as William Shakespeare; Dr Gordon Hogg, the Bedford Park Medical Officer of Health, appeared as Claudian; his wife as Edith Plantagenet; Moncure Conway, as a friar. Mrs Edward Wyman, wife of the President of the Sette of Odde Volumes, appeared as 'Night' in a dress of 'cut steel crescent moon, with stars to match, long black tulle veil with spangles, dress black lace and satin; trimmed with stars and spangles and silver lace, black spangled shoes, black gloves.' Miss Violet Wyman, as 'Mistress Mary', sported a primrose muslin kerchief 'festooned with crossed silver rake and hoe, pale blue floral polonaize over delicate primrose quilted satin petticoat, trimmed with diagonal wreaths of silver bells, cockle shells, chatelaine of silver garden tools, white gloves.' George Haité, another Bedford Park painter, appeared in the Court Costume of George IV, wearing the orders of St Estable and the Sette of Odde Volumes, with hair dressed and powdered in the fashion of the period. Miss Dawson was dressed in 'flowering robes and veil of Esther, jewelled crown and cincture'. Three of the costumes were Japanese and there were several examples of costume explicitly following contemporary paintings: Mrs T. Field Fisher's 'Roman Princess', we are told, faithfully copied the draperies in Alma Tadema's 'Colisseum', while Mrs Moncure Conway appeared as 'a lady after Rossetti'. Barlow in his poem had related the 'fancy-fair' at Bedford Park with costume-drama at the Lyceum. Particularly with non-historical costume, however, this passion for dressing-up was not so much antiquarian as self-expressive. These Bedford Park revellers were time-travellers, escaping from the present, breaking down the limits between art and life.

Treating life in the spirit of art extended to other activities. In the 1890s, the bicycle fever shook Bedford Park and Cecil Aldin in his autobiography describes how

> this little oasis was crowded with fat and thin, short and long, men and women, boys and girls learning, or becoming expert at the art of taking exercise on the new low bicycles. Nightly the talk in the houses and the club was about the latest gears or ball-bearings, the newest type of handle-bars, lamps or pneumatic seats. The bicycle cult became a mania. Everyone caught it, from children just able to walk, to grandmothers.

In the evening there were torch-light rides round the 'confines of our own little colony'. These parades were organized at the club, a notice being put up stating the time and day. Large and small Chinese lanterns were fixed at every available spot on the bicycles, some attaching long bamboo poles to the handle-bars and hanging the lanterns from these. The first 'meet' was a fiasco. The lanterns were lit; the bicyclists began their ballet on wheels in formation of three; the night was fractured by crashes and only ten out of fifty or sixty starters managed to ride out the *mêlée.*[66]

Of the many Bedford Park Societies, the Musical Society, the Conversazione Club founded in 1883, and the Bedford Park Reunion dating from 1882, and others, the most interesting and historically significant was the Amateur Dramatic Club.[67]

This began with informal entertainments in 1879, but was formally inaugurated in 1881: subscription: half a guinea a year, with half a guinea entrance fee. On July 15th, 1880, George Macdonald, poet, novelist, and mystic, along with his family, gave a dramatized version of *Pilgrim's Progress*. For about eight or nine years, the Society offered on the average either three or four plays a year, mostly farces and melodramas, with *tableaux vivantes*, readings, pantomimes. In 1884, a local resident, Alexander Hatchard, wrote a one-act play which was acted at the Clubhouse. *The Bedford Park Gazette* found its dialogue 'witty and refined' and one or two of the London papers were favourable. There are two other instances at least of Bedford Park residents writing plays for the suburb's dramatic company: Oliphant Downs, author of a one-act play 'The Maker of Dreams', who was killed in the first world war, and John Todhunter.[68]

Todhunter's *A Sicilian Idyll* was produced over four days in the week of May 5th, 1890. All the Bedford Park productions had the advantage of Bedford Park artists to design scenery and costumes. With the *Sicilian Idyll* we have the spectacle of a Bedford Park dramatist, supported by Bedford Park artists, with a cast that included a majority of residents, playing before an audience that brought in artists, men of letters, and the aristocracy from the metropolis.[69]

Among the audience was the young William Butler Yeats, who had persuaded Todhunter to write the *Idyll* in the first place. In Yeats's mind was the notion that Todhunter's play should inaugurate a yearly festival, a kind of Dionysia at Bedford Park.

The Clubhouse, Bedford Park

No. 3 Blenheim Road: home of the Yeats family. 1877

John Todhunter. Posthumous oil painting by H. M. Paget taken from a photograph by Elliott Fry. National Portrait Gallery

*Overleaf* The Church, Bedford Park. From a lithograph by T. Hamilton Jackson

Sketches of a later performance of the *Sicilian Idyll* at St. George's Hall

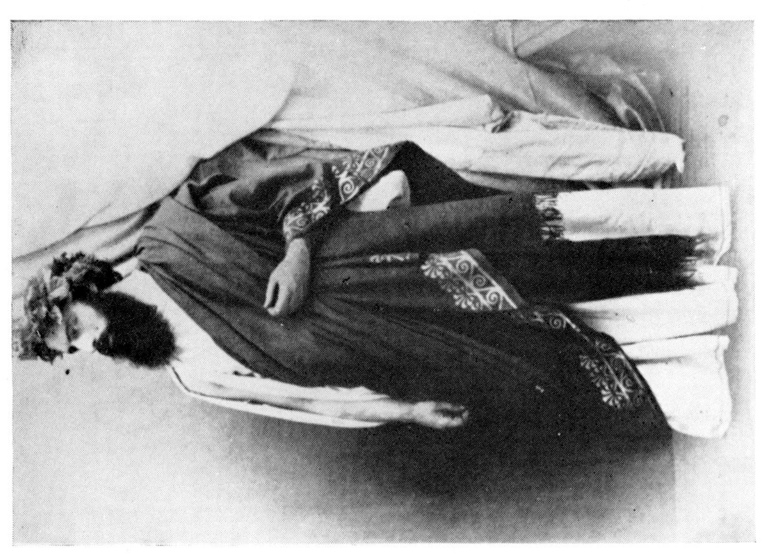

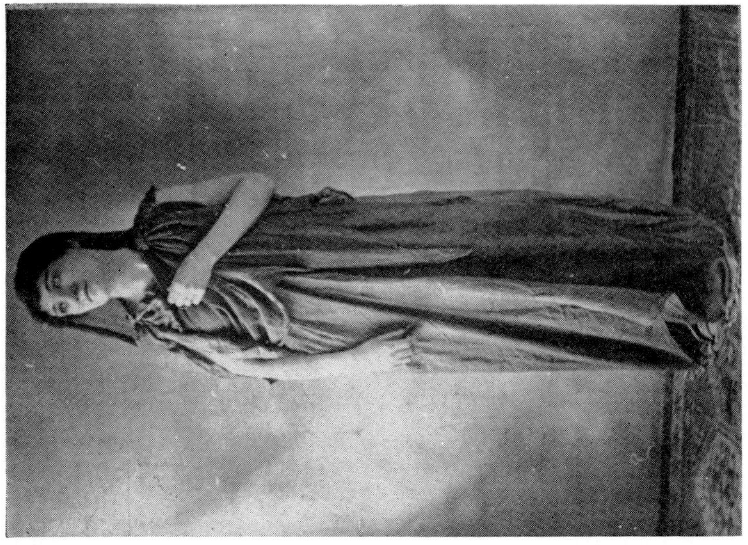

The 1890 production of the *Sicilian Idyll*
*Left* Florence Farr
*Right* Edward Heron-Allen

The 1890 production of the *Sicilian Idyll*
*Left* Florence Farr and Edward Heron-Allen
*Right* A group of performers

Florence Farr: 'Do I inspire thee?'

The subject of the play, a pastoral based on Theocritus, was peculiarly appropriate to Bedford Park itself. The *Idyll* was a poetic play, depending more on words than on naturalistic scenery. Yeats saw it as the beginning of an attempt to bring back poetry to a theatre now dominated by naturalism for a small, defined 'aristocratic' audience. It was the first step in freeing the theatre from commercialism.

Yeats had been excited by the Macdonald family's presentation of *Pilgrim's Progress*, which had been played

> before hangings of rough calico embroidered in crewel work, [I] thought that some like method might keep the scenery from realism.[70]

An unpublished letter of John Butler Yeats written in April 1885 records his son's admiration for Todhunter as poetic dramatist:

> Willie . . . watches with an almost breathless interest your career as dramatic poet—and has been doing so for a long time—he has read everything you have written most carefully.
> —he finished when at Howth your Rienzi at a single sitting—'the' sitting ending at 2 o'clock in the morning.[71]

Todhunter's *Helena in Troas* was given the following year at Hengler's Circus, Great Pulteney Street (chosen for its suitability for Greek settings). Every detail, whether of acting or setting, was controlled by E. W. Godwin who, in this play, as in his production of W. G. Wills's *Claudian* of 1883, carried archaeological realism to its extreme. The distance between the patient detail of Godwin's production and the non-naturalistic décor of Yeats's ideal was not as remote as might appear. Godwin, before Oscar Wilde, was concerned to use costume dramatically: the 'truth of masks', dandyism applied in the theatre (and indeed Wilde's article of that name is little more than a tesselation of Godwin's ideas: its documentation is most uncharacteristic of Wilde). The terms in which Godwin's productions were discussed show how it was possible for Godwin's scholarly recreations to be modulated into quasi-symbolist theatre. Speaking of *Claudian*, for example, Wilde refers to Godwin as exhibiting the life of Byzantium 'not by a dreary lecture and a set of grimy casts, not by a novel which requires a glossary to explain it, but by the visible presentation before us of all the glory of that great town.'[72] Costumes were 'subordinate' to the unity of artistic effect . . . the artist has converted an antiquarian motive to a theme for melodies of time.'[73] Godwin himself had written: 'As speaking involves poetry and music, as architecture involves painting and sculpture, so dressing involves in principle all these.'[74] And Lady Archibald Campbell (for whose Coombe Players, Godwin had provided open-air productions of Shakespeare's and John Fletcher's pastoral plays), with special attention to blending costumes with natural scenery, found that in *Helena in Troas*

> line and colour [took] the place of language, the play ultimately reverted to that plastic ideal which lies at the basis of all Greek art.[75]

Yeats did not see Godwin's production, but at the time when *A Sicilian Idyll* was being mounted he wrote of its

> solemn staging, its rhythmical chorus and its ascending incense [which moved] the audience powerfully. . . . Many people have said to me that the surroundings of *Helena* made them feel religious. Once get your audience in that mood, and you can do anything with it.[76]

And *Helena in Troas*, Yeats recognized, had drawn not merely the cultivated public who cared for verse-drama, but filled the theatre with the ordinary run of theatre-goers. Here we have all the prescriptions for the Abbey Theatre and Yeats's Noh Drama: 'the seeming natural expression of the image', the drama communicating, in a way that is strictly analogous to Mallarmé's ideal theatre, to the laity no less than the clerisy;[77] the use of myth and of stylized painted back-drops.

But Todhunter and Bedford Park were to prove a disappointment. After the limited success of *A Sicilian Idyll* (it was played at other small theatres over the following years), Todhunter attempted to conquer the London commercial stage on its own terms, not with poetry but with Ibsenite, or more accurately, Pinero-like 'problem' plays. He failed. And the Bedford Park Amateur Dramatic Company lapsed into comedy and melodrama once again.

The principal part in *A Sicilian Idyll* was taken by Florence Farr. Miss Farr, or Mrs Emery (she was separated from her husband) lived at Brook Green, but was often at her brother-in-law's at Bedford Park. She had studied embroidery with May Morris and in that resembled a number of the Bedford Park ladies. She was also not dissimilar to the Bedford Park 'new women', though she pushed her feminism far beyond theirs.[78] It was said that she was prepared to commit adultery on principle, as a protest against the double standard of morality. A photograph of her, taken at the time the *Idyll* was mounted, shows her lolling somewhat voluptuously in a hammock. She sent the photograph to the highly respectable Todhunter (Bernard Shaw describes him as bearded like a picture of God in an illustrated family bible). On the back of the photograph Miss Farr mischievously wrote: 'Do I inspire thee?' History does not record whether this was a suggestion that she was to act as Todhunter's muse, or one of another kind.

Miss Farr's part in the *Idyll* was much praised and Yeats remembered the beauty of her verse-speaking for the rest of his life. It had the self-forgetting passion that he demanded.[79] Miss Farr was to have some success on the London stage, but, according to Shaw, her early life had been too easy; she was always too much the dilettante. In the early years of the present century she collaborated with Yeats in reading poetry to the zither, 'cantillation', dabbled in occultism, and in journalism for *The New Age*, retaining charm and courage to the end of her life. A young man, who met her when she was just short of fifty, described her as: 'a wonderful Egyptian-looking person, habited in purples and ambers and scarlets and great hats and veils . . . glamorous and vivid.'[80]

That the 'Queen Anne' style was in the middle 1880s still *di moda* and sympathetic to the publicist of a new aesthetic millenium, we may gather from a lecture given at the Bijou Theatre, St Leonards, by Oscar Wilde on 'The House Beautiful' and reported in *The Artist and Journal of Home Culture* (5, 22–23 of 1884). 'Queen Anne suggested . . . possibilities for the introduction of a balcony here, or a gabled window there, which the strictness of the pure classical school rendered impossible; and it is evident that the lecturer's sympathies are more with Fitz-Johns Avenue and Bedford Park than the Quadrant.' Genial satire persists in, for example, H. Francis Lester's *Under Two Fig Trees* of 1886 where there are allusions to Queen Anne houses, damp, the cultivation of sunflowers and the Clubhouse.

Yet in 1888, in Wilde's *Woman's World*, a Miss M. Nicolle, discussing Japanese art-ware, was to write:

> . . . when five or six years ago, Bedford Park was supposed to be the Mecca of Aestheticism, a Philistine poet addressed a sarcastic invitation to the faithful to
>
> 'come and read Rossetti there by a Japanese lamp.'
>
> Much has happened since then. Bedford Park is no longer aesthetic (if indeed it ever was so) and the appreciation of Japanese art-wares has long ceased to be confined within its narrow bounds.[81]

By 1888, indeed, Bedford Park was distinctly old hat. The late 1880s saw some rather mean terrace-housing in Blandford Road and one or two monotonous new roads were added to the estate on the south side of Bath Road. But its hour was not over. In the 1890s, the Calumet Talking Club, designed to encourage improvisation and style in that art, could still bring together J. B. Yeats, York Powell, James Sime and Stepniak.[82] And in 1893 the Irish Literary Society—parent of the Irish Literary Theatre and the Abbey Theatre—was founded from the Yeats house at 3 Blandford Road.[83] Camille Pisarro visited his son Lucien, a resident from 1897 to 1901. Lucien had been led there by Charles Ricketts, who described Bedford Park as the home 'of the elect of the art world'.[84] Bedford Park appears five times in Camille's *œuvre*. And in 1891, the most remarkable of Bedford Park's houses was built, to the design of C. A. Voysey: 14, South Parade. It is white, deliberately contrasting with the surrounding red brick, with a green roof, whose horizontality is remarkable in a period which generally shows as much roof as possible. The fenestration of the front is delightfully piquant, and is only matched in the side elevation of some houses by Shaw, May, and Adams.[85]

The Amateur Dramatic Club continued with its three plays a year, Children's Ballet, and Pantomime, in which young and old would take part. And in May 1914, the last production before the first world war, Ronald Coleman, who was living near by at Ealing, took part in a production of *Hindle Wakes*. But at some time round the turn of the century, the overall subscription to the Club was discontinued and it split into separate institutions. This, more than any other factor, broke the sense of community. Some of the original residents, such as H. M. Paget, Rooke, and Adams, lived on into the 1920s and 1930s, but after about 1905

Bedford Park ceased to attract artists and men of letters. The Fancy Dress Balls were dropped after the first world war and the Amateur Dramatic Society was discontinued just before the second. The Club and its contents were sold to C.A.V. Engineering Works, and is still being used for its original social purpose.

For the period round the turn of the century, Chesterton is the liveliest authority. To Chesterton, Bedford Park was a microcosm of heresy: Imperialist, because it was Agnostic, and man must have faith; mildly Aesthetic, sometimes Occultist, and because of its heresies, pessimistic. Like Yeats, in his autobiographical fantasias, Chesterton tended to see personality as an epiphany; something issuing dramatically as gesture, or stylized into pose. For him the typical Bedford Park resident of the turn of the century was St John Hankin, the dramatist. Hankin was something more atheistic than an atheist; 'a fundamental sceptic, that is a man without fundamentals . . . he despised democracy even more than devotion.' Hankin, who wrote for *Punch*, was, indeed, deeply melancholy like many comic writers, and committed suicide. He wore formal dress, unlike 'the artistic garments affected by Bedford Park as a whole' and, in Chesterton's view, was typical of the era; not eccentric, but centric. 'He had a low opinion of the world, but he was a man of the world.'[86] That is one version of the decline of Bedford Park. Chesterton gives another in a ballad:

Dear Olga, it was Long Ago,
If life may be accounted long,
When by the windows (often bow)
Or on the stairways (seldom strong)
Summoned (perhaps) by copper gong
Fixed up by Craftsmen pure and stark,
We met in that amazing throng
People we met in Bedford Park.

There was a velvet long-haired beau
I could have murdered (which is wrong),
There was a lady trailing slow
Enormous draperies along.
And there was Yeats; not here belong
Sneers at the stir that made us mark
That heathen but heroic song
People we met in Bedford Park. . . .

Princess, we both have come to know
What might have been a happier Ark
For Hankin and for Yeats and Co.
People we knew in Bedford Park.[87]

Roman Catholicism may have been a happier ark than occultism or agnosticism or aestheticism, but no one suggested it was prevalent in Bedford Park.

If Bedford Park had any common ethos, that ethos was genteelly Bohemian. Bedford Park was not co-operative: it was only self-supporting in the arts. Otherwise it depended on the District Railway that took its time-travellers back to the highly time-conscious City of London. Yet it will always provoke an image of Elysian Aestheticism. And if, as Graham Robertson suggested, Aestheticism came with dear old ladies in Brompton, Mr John Betjeman has also suggested that it went with dear old ladies in Bedford Park:

> Here until just before the second world war gentle craftsfolk survived making Celtic jewellery in their studios or weaving on hand-looms among the faded sunflowers of a now forgotten cult.[88]

## NOTES

[1] For the architecture of Bedford Park, see H. Mathesius, *Das Englische Haus*, Berlin, 1904, *passim*; R. Blomfield, *Norman Shaw*, London, 1940, pp. 35–8. W. B. Yeats describes his reaction to Bedford Park in *Autobiographies*, 1926, pp. 52–6, pp. 139–41 and *passim*. The Yeats family were resident between 1876 and 1880 and again from 1888 until J. B. Yeats left for Dublin in 1901. G. K. Chesterton has a chapter on Bedford Park in his *Autobiography*, London, 1937, 'The Fantastic Suburb', 12th impression, pp. 133–53. Miss Phyllis Austin records memories of the 1880s and 1890s in 'The Enchanted Circle', *Architectural Review*, 133 (1963), pp. 205–7.

[2] *The Man Who was Thursday*, 5th ed., London, 1944, p. 5.

[3] For Chesterton, Bedford Park was an enclave of Imperialism (Materialism), Agnosticism, Pessimism, and Occultism.

[4] The inquest proceedings, however, tell a somewhat different story.

[5] For Carr, see the obituary in *Chiswick Times*, XX, 1032, February 5th, 1915, p. 6, c. 2. He was educated at Bruce Castle School, Tottenham, and King's College, London. William Terriss, the actor, a fellow-resident at Bedford Park, and F. C. Selous, the explorer, were among his contemporaries at school. Carr married Agnes Fulton, daughter of a civil engineer, who lived at Bedford House, one of three eighteenth-century houses on the site of Bedford Park. An enthusiastic Radical, he acted as political secretary to John Stuart Mill when Mill stood for Westminster in 1865, though this reads somewhat oddly as Mill is reported neither to have canvassed for himself nor to have allowed anyone to canvass for him. Carr had a wide variety of interests, many friends, a tenacious memory. By temperament he was genial and optimistic, which probably accounts for his

continuous and in general unsuccessful speculations in property. See *Bedford Park Gazette*, II, May 1884, p. 140, c. 2. and *Pall Mall Gazette*, March 11th, 1884. There is a brief description of him in an undated pamphlet *The Bedford Park Club*, p. 2: 'hurrying along intent on business, top hat rather at the back of the head, low-cut, turn-down collar below the short beard, and almost always a cheerful red tie'.

[6] *Autobiography*, London, 1937, p. 140. The two lines quoted parody the famous couplet in J. W. Burgon's prize-poem *Petra* (1845), p. 14.

Match me such marvel, save in Eastern clime,—
A rose-red city—half as old as Time!

[7] The three houses were Bedford House, Melbourne House, and Sidney House. Sidney House was demolished in the 1890s, to make way for a block of flats between the Avenue and Woodstock Road. See 'Changing Chiswick and its Neighbourhood', MS. MP 3303, Chiswick Public Library, for Bedford Park before 1876. See also W. H. Draper, *Chiswick*, London, 1923, *passim*.

[8] For Godwin and Bedford Park, see D. Harbron, *The Conscious Stone*, London, 1949, pp. 113, 151, and 157. This, the only book on Godwin, is not altogether satisfactory as an account of the total artist. See *The Building News*, 33, November 9th, 1877, pp. 451–2, for a description of the early houses. This mentions that the plots for the Avenue were 75 feet in depth by 50 feet of frontage. Buildings were set back by 15 or 20 feet from the pavements. Godwin's houses provoked much criticism, particularly of the interiors. Rents were £95 per annum. Coe and Robinson's houses were illustrated in *The Building News*, 32, p. 192. The rental of these houses was £55 per annum. Shaw's houses were illustrated in *The Buildings News*, 33, p. 614.

[9] Blomfield, op. cit., pp. 133–8, states that Shaw was helped in designing Bedford Park by Adams, 'a well-known draughtsman, though not a very good one'. This is corroborated by the account in *The Building News*, January 30th, 1880. Maurice Bingham Adams published *Artistic Conservatories*, London, 1880, *Everyday Life and Domestic Art*, London, 1882, *Artists' Houses*, London, 1883, *Examples of Old English Houses*, London, 1888, and *Modern Cottage Architecture*, 2nd ed., revised and enlarged, London, 1912, *Cottage Housing*, London, 1914. His buildings include New Rectory House, Merton; Belle Vue, Dublin Bay; J. C. Dollman's houses at 12 and 14 Newton Grove, Bedford Park, an inventive work with attractively irregular fenestration on the side elevations; Queen's Mead Cottage, Windsor, and a house and studio on the Queen's Mead Estate. See also R.I.B.A., 72,036, pam. 150, for sketches for cottages by Shaw and Adams.

[10] *Bedford Park Gazette*, 1, July 1883, p. 2., c. 1.

[11] As quoted in *Bedford Park Gazette*, 1, July 1883, p. 2., c. 1. The frequent extracts from newspaper accounts of Bedford Park in the *Gazette* is remarkable. The present account mentions that in 1880 houses were being built at the rate of five a week and stressed that they were neither mansions nor mews. It refers also to 'lofty poplars, adding infinitely to the poetry of the landscape' against which is marked the 'quaint outline of the many-gabled houses'. Poplars are prominent in a set of water-colours of the suburb by Bedford Park artists, which was reproduced in chromo-lithography and was popular in the early 1880s. Miss Phyllis Austin speaks of 'None of your London sooty planes here. Lilacs, laburnum, may (pink, red, and white), mountain ash, copper beech, limes and acacias lined every pavement. To walk in the roads on a spring evening was an Arcadian adventure.' *Architectural Review*, 133, p. 205. *The Building News*, 33, p. 451, c. 1. mentions that The Avenue was planted with limes.

[12] *Bedford Park Gazette*, 3, March 1883.

[13] *Bedford Park Gazette*, 1, July 1883, p. 2., c. 1. unequivocally ascribes the Clubhouse to Shaw; similarly, the editor attributes the whole of Bedford Park to Shaw alone, but there was a feud between Adams and the editor, H. Fox-Bourne.

[14] *The Building News*, 38, p. 124, c. 3 and p. 125, c. 1. (January 30th, 1880).

[15] *Travels in South Kensington*, London, 1882, p. 228.

[16] *The Bedford Park Club*, n.d. (4)

[17] *Letters to the New Island*, by W. B. Yeats, ed. H. Reynolds, Cambridge, 1934, p. 114. The interior was altered first in the Edwardian period and later in 1964.

[18] Wallpaper was also supplied by W. Woollams and Company; see letter to *The Builder*, XXXVIII, 1931 (February 7th, 1880), p. 169. These were of 'Queen Anne' patterns, though in many cases worked in colours specially suggested by Aldam Heaton for the estate.

[19] *The Builder*, XXXVIII, 1930, p. 140 (January 31st, 1880), p. 139, c. 3.

[20] See N. Pevsner, 'Norman Shaw' in *Victorian Architecture*, ed. P. Ferriday, London, 1963, pp. 240–1.

[21] For the 'Tabard', William de Morgan had provided tiles in the hall, which was panelled with cedar from St Dionis Backchurch. Insistence on the medieval robust Englishness was rather curiously diffused in the 1880s. Even the apparently French-influenced Rhymers Club in the early 1890s used Dr Johnson's 'Cheshire Cheese' for its meetings, drank beer from tankards and smoked churchwarden pipes. Their programme included a reaction against so-called English Parnassianism, with its cult of old French forms. See W. B. Yeats, *Letters to the New Island, Cambridge*, pp. 142f. for the Rhymers' programme and James K. Robinson, 'A Neglected Phase of the Aesthetic Movement, English Parnassianism', *Publications of the Modern Language Association*, 68, II, 1953, pp. 733–54. For T. M. Rooke, see 'Extracts from T. M. Rooke's letters to Sir Sydney Cockerell', *The Old Water-Colour Society's Club, Twenty-first Annual Volume*, ed. R. Davies, London, 1943, pp. 16–25. Plans of the Tabard, St Michael, the Stores, and Tower House, are in the Victorian and Albert Museum, 1705–1725, Press Mark DD 11.

[22] *Bedford Park Gazette*, 1, July 1883, p. 2, c. 3.

[23] A leaflet dated 1886 is among the Bedford Park archives in the Acton Central Library (Acc. No. ME 5195). The heading is 'The most Liberal Stores in the World.' Items not listed above as sold include Artist's Colours (Winsor and Newton's), Patent Medicines, Perfumery, Wines, Cigars, Cigarettes and Tobaccos. 'Livery. Every description of work, at the lowest prices. Carriages well turned out, with experienced coachmen.'

[24] *The Renaissance: Studies in Art and Poetry*, 2nd, rev. ed., London, 1877 (x).

[25] 'A Visit to Turnham Green', *British Architect*, XIV, p. 240, c. 2. Moncure Conway and the popular journalists tend to use the word 'suburb' more freely.

[26] *The Builder*, XXXVIII, 1942, p. 520.

[27] *Bedford Park Gazette*, 1, July 1883, p. 15, cc. 1–2.

[28] M. Ward, *Return to Chesterton*, London, 1952, p. 25.

[29] *Bedford Park Gazette*, 1, July 1883, p. 3, c. 1.

[30] From the *Daily News* of May 1880, as quoted in *Bedford Park Gazette*, 1, July 1883, p. 2, c. 3.

[31] 'London Lanes and the Village Association' in *Tait's Edinburgh Magazine*, XV, 845–52. The scheme stressed sanitation, and an ideal plan of the village shows steeply gabled houses in gardens. The density was low and there were some small public open spaces. For another early ideal city, see James Silk Buckingham, *National Evils and Practical Remedies, with the Plan of a Model Town*, London, 1849.

[32] op. cit., p. 232.

[33] *Bedford Park Gazette*, 10, April, 1884, p. 116, c. 4.

[34] A poem called 'The New Arcadia' was published in the *Bedford Park Gazette*, 5th November 1883, p. 54, c. 1. The tone is whimsical. The poem features an Aesthetic shepherdess sketching in her garden.

[35] *Essays*, 3rd ed., London, 1868, p. 24. G. M. Young suggests that the origins of Aestheticism owe much to the lectures of James Garbett (1802–1879), Professor of Poetry at Oxford from 1842 to 1852. Its manifestations are various and include word-painting and sonnets for works of art, in literature; formalism and 'The Truth of Masks', poetic archaeology in the theatre.

[36] This essay was in part re-published in the *Remains in Verse and Prose*, London, 1862, pp. 294–305. For the full text see *The Poems of A. H. Hallam, together with his Essay on Alfred Tennyson*, ed. R. le Gallienne, London, 1893, pp. 87–139. It had a strong influence on the early W. B. Yeats and the Rhymers' Club in general.

[37] *Time Was*, London, 1931, p. 36.

[38] A good source for the Ritualist connection with the Guild Movement and its capture by Christian Socialism is A. W. Crickmay's *A Layman's Thoughts on Some Questions of the Day*, London, 1896.

[39] The Kyrle Society was founded in 1876 by Octavia Hill and Miranda Hill, for the purpose of 'Diffusion of Beauty'. Its activities included collecting flowers for decorating the houses of the poor, planting small gardens in crowded urban areas, providing entertainments and oratories for poor parishes and providing a choir for singing in such parishes. Its members painted panels; they illuminated texts and carved brackets and decorated blank walls in club-houses and parish-halls. The Society was deeply involved also in the provision of open spaces and this branch of their work was taken over by the National Trust. Octavia Hill was a close friend of Charles Loch, Secretary of the Charity Organization, poet and a resident of Bedford Park. Miss Hill built and managed cottages. Her attitude, like Loch's, was strictly practical and paternalistic. The Kyrle Society's published pamphlets include some on the appreciation of paintings. The Society was continuously satirized in *Punch*.

[40] For the reception of Japanese Art in the 1850s and after, see, particularly, J. A. Michener, *The Floating World*, London, 1955; Hugh Honour, *Chinoiserie: The Vision of Cathay*, London, 1959 and Elizabeth Aslin, 'E. W. Godwin and the Japanese Taste' in *Apollo*, 1962, pp. 779–84. Oriental art seems to have been known to some Parisian artists in the middle 1850s. The periodical *Once a Week* started to publish an account of Japan in July 1860, and this article was illustrated by prints, while Sherard Osborn's *Japanese Fragments*, London, 1861, also contained reproductions of prints. In 1854 an exhibition of Japanese applied art had been held in London in the gallery of the Old English Water Colour Society in Pall Mall, though the impact of the applied arts was, in England, to be felt somewhat later than that of the prints. Japanese Lacquer, bronze and porcelain were shown in London at the 1862 Exhibition. In the earlier 1860s, Whistler and Rossetti were enthusiasts in the collection of Oriental china. When the Victoria and Albert Museum of Practical Art at South Kensington was founded in 1882, two thirds of the exhibits were Japanese, though these were not of high quality. W. Burges in an article on the International Exhibition, *Gentleman's Magazine*, CCXIII, 10, July 1862, had associated Japanese art with Gothic. Burges stressed the assymetricality of Japanese art and Godwin's designs for wallpapers are noticeably assymetrical, e.g. as Miss Aslin has pointed out, the sparrow and the bamboo design of 1872. We may relate, perhaps not too fancifully, the asymmetricality of the Bedford Park Houses with the Bohemianism

of its inhabitants. Porcelains, screens, and prints had been available from the 1860s at Farmer and Rogers' Oriental Warehouses in Regent's Street; Liberty's was founded in 1875 at the height of the Japanese mania.

[41] Graham Robertson, *Time Was*, London, 3rd printing, 1931, p. 36.

[42] *Bedford Park Gazette*, 1, July 1883, p. 9. c. 1. Other relevant topics of Club lectures include: 'Dress Reform' and 'The Responsibility of Women to the State'. John Todhunter, another prominent Bedford Park resident, had satirized Aestheticism somewhat affectionately in a sonnet 'An Utter Person Uttered Utterly' in *Kottabos*, 1882, and reprinted in Hamilton, op. cit., p. 31.

[43] See also F. C. Burnand's 'The Colonel', which was produced in February 1881 at the Prince of Wales Theatre. Here Lambert Streyke, the principal Aesthete, is distantly modelled on Wilde, though as Dudley Harbron observed, he more nearly resembles Charles Augustus Howell. The play is amusingly described in *Punch*, LXXXIX, 'The Colonel in a Nut Shell', pp. 81–2, and in F. C. Burnand's *Records and Reminiscences* 4th Revised edition, London, 1905, pp. 358–69. Godwin enjoyed the play, but found the 'Aesthetic Room' rather inadequate and suggested how it should have been decorated, see D. Harbron op. cit., p. 153. N. H. Kennard's *There's Rue for You*, 2 vv., London, 1880, has an aesthetic villain-hero and some evocative descriptions.

[44] *The Aesthetic Movement in England*, London, 1882, p. 117. Hamilton tells us that his attention was directed to Bedford Park by a friend 'whose interest in the Aesthetic Movement was intense'.

[45] op. cit., pp. 117–18.

[46] *Punch*, LXXXIV, p. 87. See also R. Blomfield, op. cit., pp. 37–8.

[47] Sunflowers were certainly much cultivated in Bedford Park. 'Do you remember how they used to mock at me because years ago, when we were here before, I said I would have a forest of sunflowers and an underwood of love-lies-bleeding and there were only three sunflowers after all? Well, I am having my revenge. I planted the forest and am trying to get the love-lies-bleeding. . . .' *The Letters of W. B. Yeats*, ed. A. Wade, London, 1954, pp. 68–9. *The Bedford Park Gazette* refers to the local painter G. Haité's 'excessive reverence for the sunflower', but Haité assured the editor that he 'deprecates the false worship of the flower by the aesthetes.' Aston Webb declared: 'We have now certain well-known aesthetic villages not far from town, where people live in "cots" and fill their gardens with sunflowers, where ladies dress to suit the houses,' in obvious reference to Bedford Park.

[48] op. cit., pp. 121–2.

[49] This is one of Adams' better buildings and, as the coloured pen-sketch at the Chiswick Public Library shows, its flowing roof-line modulates in very attractively with the gabled houses on either side. However, a letter from Shaw to Lethaby now at the R.I.B.A. makes it clear that Lethaby worked with Shaw's sketch (also in the R.I.B.A. library V. 11/123) for the front. Shaw inserted the large central dormer. The building was bombed during the Second World War and has been rebuilt.

[50] *Bedford Park Gazette*, 1, July 1883, p. 14, cc. 1–2.

[51] op. cit., p. 232.

[52] *Harper's Magazine*, LCII, CCCLXX, March 1881, pp. 481–90. There is a brief, anonymous description of Bedford Park in *Chambers's Journal*, Fourth Series, December 31st, 1881, pp. 839–40. This stresses asymmetricality in the housing, the variety of size, from family mansion to 'cosy little dwelling which brings the idea of "love in a cottage" from the realms of fancy'.

[53] *Bedford Park Gazette*, 1, July 1883, pp. 12–13, cc. 2 and 1 quotes twelve verses and R. Blomfield, op. cit., pp. 34–6.

[54] Indignantly quoted in *Bedford Park Gazette*, 10, April 1884, p. 125, c. 2 and p. 126, c. 1.

[55] Quoted in *Bedford Park Gazette*, 5, November 1883, p. 52, c. 1.

[56] The unique file of the *Gazette* is held in the Chiswick Public Library. It appeared first at 2*d*. and the price was increased to 3*d*. in January 1884.

[57] *Bedford Park Gazette*, 1, July 1883, p. 3, c. 2.

[58] *Bedford Park Gazette*, 3, September 1883, p. 30, c. 1.

[59] *Bedford Park Gazette*, 5, November 1883, p. 51, c. 1.

[60] *Bedford Park Gazette*, 3, September 1883, p. 30, c. 1. The article estimates that there are 400 houses in Bedford Park with a total population of between 2,000 and 3,000.

[61] In 1882, Bedford Park artists not mentioned in my text included T. G. du Val; Dover Wilson; F. Hamilton Jackson (1848–1923), illustrator of many travel books and the author of *True Stories of the Condottieri*, London 1904 and *Intarsia and Marquetry* London, 1903; E. Blair Leighton (1853–1922), a costume and anecdotal artist who was particularly attracted to illustrating Tennyson. For Blair Leighton, see A. Yocking in *The Art Journal*, 1913; Mrs. Turner, figure painter and draughtsman; Charles Pears, illustrator; Edward Hargitt, painter in water-colour; Sutton Palmer; Joseph Nash; W. B. Wollen (1857–1936), who later became a War Artist in the South African War; J. G. J. Penderel-Brodhurst (1859–1944); L. A. Calvert; Miss M. Barry; Miss A. S. Fenn, daughter of Manville Fenn; C. G. Hindley; A. W. Strutt; H. M. Paget and his brother, Walter; J. C. Dollman (1851–1939), chiefly known as an illustrator. The work of five or six of these artists appeared regularly in Grosvenor Gallery exhibitions.

[62] *The Man Who Was Thursday*, 5th ed., London, 1944, p. 6.

[63] *An Actor's Reminiscences and other Poems*, London, 1883, pp. 67–8. This extract along with a few more lines was reprinted in *The Bedford Park Gazette*. The poem itself is dated June 1882. Robert Owen's model co-operative colonies were to have included fancy-dress balls, with the ladies attending in bloomers. The 1880s witnessed the sudden appearance of a number of books on Balls. A. Holt's *Fancy Dress* in its second edition, London, 1881, keeps topical with an Aesthetic Pierrot modelled on Gilbert's Bunthorne.

[64] op. cit., pp. 228–9.

[65] June 7th, 1884, p. 3, c. 6.

[66] *Time I Was Dead*, London, 1934, pp. 69–71.

[67] The Reunion met on the last Saturday of the month.

[68] For Todhunter's verse, see the article contributed by W. B. Yeats, to *The Magazine of Art* (Buffalo) in 1889 and reprinted in W. B. Yeats's *Letters to Katharine Tynan*, ed. R. McHugh, Dublin and London, 1953, pp. 152–4, and *Letters to the New Island*, Cambridge, Mass, pp. 174–92, for Yeats's review of *The Banshee and Other Poems*, London, 1888. In the early 1900s, Todhunter was to write on the non-naturalistic drama in 'Blank-verse on the Stage', *Fortnightly Review*, LXXI, n.s. (1902), pp. 346–60.

[69] Yeats mentions, as present on the third night, theatre personages such as Alma Murray, Winifred Emery, Cyril Maude, and William Terriss; Lady Archibald Campbell; Mrs. Jopling Rowe, the painter; the poet, Mathilde Blind, Theodore Watts-Dunton and May Morris. *The Sicilian Idyll* was reviewed favourably in *The Theatre*, 15, June 1st, 1890, p. 330. Costumes were designed by A. Baldry, a pupil of Albert Moore's.

[70] *Letters to the New Island*. This may refer to a later visit by the Macdonald family, since Yeats places the event a few months prior to the production of the *Idyll*.

[71] Unpublished letter in the library of the University of Reading.

[72] *Intentions*, London, 1891, p. 233.

[73] ibid., p. 234.

[74] *Dress and its relation to Health and Climate*, London, 1884, p. 2.

[75] 'The Woodland Gods', *Woman's World*, 1888, p. 3, c. i. *As You Like It* had been produced at Coombe in July 1884 and was attended by the Prince and Princess of Wales. *The Faithful Shepherdess* was given seven performances in the summer of 1885 and the Prince and Princess were again present, as they were at the pastoral scenes of Tennyson's *Becket*, produced under the title of *Fair Rosamund* in July 1886. Godwin freely cut and added to his texts. Lady Archibald's leanings were away from archaeological realism. She believed in amateur acting because of its 'freedom of mood'. She makes an explicit comparison between Godwin and Wagner and invariably describes the Coombe productions in terms of music. Godwin, she noted, however, was opposed to cantillation, believing in 'concord-in-discord' where verse-speaking was concerned. The Enthoven Collection at the Victoria and Albert Museum contains much material about Godwin's productions. The extreme of naturalistic presentation at this moment was reached in the work of another total-artist, Sir Hubert Herkomer (1849–1914). His private theatre was in a deconsecrated chapel in the grounds of his house at Bushey. Herkomer was producer, actor, composer of words and music (which he orchestrated), and stage-designer. His first ambitious production 'An Idyl' was produced in June 1890. Particularly admired were his atmospheric effects achieved by entirely calculated means—a sheet of fine gauze stretched at a certain angle in front of a great canvas on the rear wall on which was painted a graduated blue sky.

[76] *Letters to the New Island*, p. 134. Yeats did not actually witness Godwin's production, but report of it seems to have inflamed his imagination. The play was certainly much discussed and illustrated in contemporary magazines, e.g. *The Era*, May 22nd, 1886; *The Lady*, May 23rd, 1886 (by Mrs. Oscar Wilde); *The Dramatic Review*, III, 6973, May 22nd, 1886 (by Wilde himself). H. M. Paget, a Bedford Park artist and friend of J. B. Yeats, furnished *The Graphic* with an illustration which shows the chorus and the principal actors. The original water-colour is in the collection of the University of Reading. Lady Archibald Campbell's description closely parallels that of Yeats: 'when, like figures on a marble frieze, the band of white-robed maidens wound through the twilight past the altar of Dionysus, and one by one in slow procession climbed the steps, and passed away, the audience were absolutely stilled in their excitement. All minds were held in strong emotion as by the voice of some God which "when ceased men still stood fixed to hear." The pure keynote of beauty was again struck.' Loc. cit., p. 3, c. 1.

[77] See Mallarmé's prose, *passim*.

[78] *The Whitehall Review* article had taken particular exception to the Ladies' Discussion Club: 'the female tongue has been publicly unloosed'.

[79] *Autobiographies*, London, 1926, pp. 149–51.

[80] The Letters of W. Dixon Scott, ed. M. McCrossan, London, 1932, pp. 69–70. For Miss Farr, see also Yeats's *Autobiographies*, *passim*; *Florence Farr, Bernard Shaw, W. B. Yeats*, ed. C. Bax, London, 1947; *The Letters of W. B. Yeats*, ed. A. Wade, London, 1954, *passim*. Miss Farr wrote two occultist plays with Olivia Shakespear, which were privately printed: *The Beloved of Hathor* and *The Shrine of the Golden Hawk*. Her *Dancing Faun*, London, 1894, was published in Lane's 'Keynotes Series' and had a cover-design by Beardsley. Her *Music of Speech* appeared in 1909. She was a member of the Rosicrucian Society of the Golden Dawn, published a volume on *Esoteric Egyptology* and translated Tamil poetry. A 'Mrs. Emery' was living in Bedford Park in the early 1880s, but it is by no means likely that this was Florence Farr.

[81] *Woman's World*, 1888, p. 94. Other elegaic references to Bedford Park can be found in *The Artist and Journal of Home Culture*, e.g. XI, December 1st, 1890, p. 369: 'Is art deserting Bedford Park and are suburban schools of art becoming impossible owing to the increased facilities of train and "tram" between the outlying districts of the metropolis? We hear that the Bedford Park School of Art is closed, and that artists cannot be induced to open it.'

[82] It consisted of twelve members who 'met in their respective houses every second Sunday at nine, and often did not disperse until three in the morning'. John Butler Yeats favoured the Club because it was 'without fixed forms or fixed quarters, where all things were discussed in a free spirit'. See John Butler Yeats: *Letters to his son W. B. Yeats and Others*, ed. J. Hone, London, 1944, p. 86. Other members included: Moncure Conway, Todhunter, Dr. Gordon Hogg, F. H. Orpen, F. York Powell, Fox-Bourne and inevitably Jonathan T. Carr. In Lady Gregory's draft autobiography, now in the Berg Collection of the New York Public Library, there is an account of a visit paid in 1897 to the Yeats house at 3 Blenheim Road. Lady Gregory describes Edward Martyn sitting to Yeats senior, while Susan Mitchell sang to divert the painter.

[83] W. P. Ryan, *The Irish Literary Revival*, London, 1894, pp. 51–5.

[84] W. S. Meadmore, *Lucien Pisarro*, London, 1962, p. 82, and Nos. 1005–1009 in C. S. Pisarro and L. Venturi, *Camille Pisarro, Son Art et son Œuvre*, Paris, 1939. Vol. 2., Plate 202 shows a Bedford Park scene.

[85] The most recent article is by J. Brandon-Jones in *Victorian Architecture*, ed. P. Ferriday, London, 1963, pp. 269–87. This includes a bibliographical note. Mr. Brandon-Jones refers to an earlier design of 1888 for a house on this site, now in the R.I.B.A. This looks like a more conventional suburban house with a 45-degree tiled roof, rough cast and ground floor red-brick exterior. See, for the later design, *The British Architect* for September 1891. 14 South Parade seems faintly to look back to Godwin's White House of 1878–1879.

[86] *Autobiography*, London, p. 146. Chesterton would probably have been in one sense delighted had he known that between 1911 and 1914, Francis Herbert Bacon, consecrated Titular Bishop of Durham by Arnold Harris Mathew, frequently administered conditional baptism, confirmation, and re-ordination to Anglican clergymen, 'usually in his domestic oratory at 33 Esmond Road, Bedford Park'. Mathew had obtained his orders from the Old Catholic Archbishop of Utrecht in 1908 and they were therefore valid. See, P. Anson, *Bishops at Large; Some Autocephalous Churches of the Past Hundred Years and their Founders*, London, 1964, p. 85. Bacon eventually resubmitted to the Anglican Church and became Vicar of St. Gabriel's, South Bromley, in the East End of London, where there was a nest of these autocephalous figures.

[87] M. Ward, *Return to Chesterton*, London, 1952, pp. 27–8.

[88] *Daily Telegraph*, August 22nd, 1960, p. 11.

# PIERROT AND FIN DE SIÈCLE

*A. G. Lehmann*

Au clair de la lune
Mon ami Pierrot
Prête-moi ta plume
Pour écrire un mot.
Ma chandelle est morte
Je n'ai plus de feu,
Ouvre-moi ta porte
Pour l'amour de Dieu.

Au clair de la lune,
Mon ami Pierrot,
Filons, en costume,
Présider là-haut!
Ma cervelle est morte.
Que le Christ l'emporte!
Béons à la Lune,
La bouche en zéro!

Laforgue

## PRE-HISTORY

PIERROT, an essentially French interpolation into the repertory of the *commedia*, has in early days a strictly limited range of context and significance. Molière, who gave him his name in *Dom Juan*, makes of him a zany peasant; his Charlotte, dazzled by the seducer, is brutal and frank about his defining characteristic:

PIERROT
—Tu ne m'aimes point.
CHARLOTTE
—Ah! Ah! n'est-ce que ça?
—Oui, ce n'est que ça, et c'est bien assez!
—Mon Dieu, Pierrot, tu me viens toujours dire la même chose.
—Je te dis toujours la même chose parce que c'est toujours la même chose; et si ce n'était pas toujours la même chose, je ne te dirais pas toujours la même chose.
—Mais qu'est-ce qu'il te faut? Que veux-tu?
—Jerniquenne! Je veux que tu m'aimes!

The eternal situation in half a dozen lines. But in other respects the character is vague and incomplete. For Molière, who knew his *commedia dell'arte*, arrived at Pierrot with an even longer familiarity with the world of French farce; in which Gilles le Niais has something of his Italian cousin Pedrolino or Gian-Farina and half a dozen similar products of the open-air stage. Molière's earliest known comedy, *La Jalousie du barbouillé*, revolves indeed around such a figure, who bequeaths to Pierrot —though not in *Dom Juan*—his flour-daubed round face and unprepossessing paunch, as well as his inability to compel affection. When the Italian players in Paris seized on this addition to the gallery of masks and assigned him a place in the brisk affairs of their stage, the figure remained subaltern to the more positive roles of Pantaloon, the Doctor, Brighello, Pulcinella.

There is some evidence indeed that the Italian comedian Domenico, who first introduced him, did so largely because Harlequin had evolved in France in the direction of wit, cunning, resourcefulness; a new figure was needed for the lumpish valet, and Pierrot was the name he received. In Gherardi's repertory he appears invariably as a valet, the butt and messenger of whoever happens to be on-stage; a rustic, good-for-nothing dullard, credulous and sceptical by turns, and always at the wrong time, or frankly imbecile or feigning imbecility to avoid the stick.

Harlequin eclipses him at every conceivable turn; among strongly drawn silhouettes his is the only one whose 'character' it is to be without a forcible intention. The plasticity of the rôle is —potentially—without limit: on a white ground all shades can be reflected; but it is to be feared that the white peasant's blouse and floury countenance, old images of innocence, denote in the surviving comedies nothing better than stupidity. And even the mournful symbol from which today Pierrot is hardly to be separated—the moon—appears only in a context which shows how totally unaware Gilles-Pierrot is of its connection with blighted love. In *L'Empereur dans la lune*, where his master the Doctor is obsessed with a telescope and fashionable Cyrano-like speculations, his stupidity amounts almost to blasphemy:

> Et vous voulez me faire accroire que la lune est un monde comme le nôtre! La lune! Par le jerenibleu! J'enrage! Je ne serai pas assez sot pour convenir que la lune soit un monde; la lune, la lune, morbleu, qui n'est pas plus grande qu'une omelette de huit œufs!

Nothing here of the pathetic moon-struck outcast. Pierrot is always and ever the rustic; his impulses are fitful but positive, and have to do with food as well as pretty maids:

> Pierrot, qui n'a rien d'un Clitandre,
> Vide un flacon sans plus attendre,
> Et, pratique, entame un pâté.

And so he remains, on the return of the Italian comedians to Paris (1716) after their temporary banishment—an ignominious but also undistinguished *comparse* of the versatile troupe. The blows that rain on his back leave no more trace in the spectator's mind than those that fell to the lot of Gilles le Niais or Molière's *barbouillé*. If, after reading Gherardi's collection of Italian comedies we turn again to Watteau's Gilles, we see at once, beneath the exquisite treatment of the costume, the true sense of the pose. The haunting melancholy of the figure arises from the lot of the actor, and in no way from the nature of his rôle: the Goncourt brothers are inventing a prettified past when they claim that 'c'est le duo de Gilles et de Colombine qui est la musique et la chanson de la comédie de Watteau'. 1789 swept away many attractive frivolities; in fact the Italian *commedia* had fallen out of favour ten years earlier, the troupe had lost its royal patronage and been suppressed in 1780, and the scene of its long career is today commemorated only by the name of the Boulevard des Italiens. The name and nature of Pierrot, however, were kept alive in another context. For whatever happened to the subsidized theatre companies of Paris, the fairground show and boulevard trestle survived very much without change, as Callot had depicted them two centuries before or as Rowlandson recorded them in the English provinces, with acrobats, tight-rope walkers, performing dogs, pantomimes. The Paris boulevards had their share of popular shows, as the Pont-Neuf had had in 1600; and it was to be expected that, with or without influential patronage, they should make their way in the popular quarters of the city. The history of these entertainers is hard to assemble and probably not worth writing; but we are fairly well documented on the only one which concerns our present purposes, namely the *Théâtre des Funambules*. In the no longer very savoury Boulevard du Temple, one Madame Saqi ran a promising line in performing dogs, supported by acrobats and farcical mimes (she was not permitted speaking parts, by virtue of police regulations on the theatres of Restoration France). Her establishment was in a very full sense of the word a flea-pit; if it paid its way, it paid its employees the barest living wage. But among these employees was a general props and odd-job man of great physique and endless patience, Gaspard Debureau, who some time between 1826 and 1829 achieved the right to put on pantomime *intermezzi* which helped to draw a good house. He was not much more than literate; but his gifts as a mime were uncanny; and as the months went on he spared time from the performing dogs to develop his *intermezzi*. For a reason which none of his biographers has fathomed he elected to explore the role of Pierrot, sometimes in traditional costume, more commonly not, but always retaining the unmistakable floury mask. Starting with sketches suited to his physique —the despised scene-shifter toppling into pails, the tramp, the buffoon enduring all his partners' jokes—he added, by purely intuitive stages, a completely new range of exploits. Pierrot appears as old-clothes man, jeweller's apprentice, cobbler, grocer, orang-outang, photographer, gardener, hermaphrodite or devil; setting fire to wigs with studied malevolence, chasing the tailor with a sabre, capering around his Colombine with a candle; sometimes fooled by Harlequin but once—at last!—eliminating him by sawing him in half with a gigantic saw. Pierrot, transformed from cringing zany, delights the crowds by surrendering to every mad or ignoble impulse—as well as displaying the most touching pathos on occasion. The fame of these performances reached the notice of Charles Nodier, who in 1828 'discovered' them for the literary world; in 1832 they became an institution, or even something more, on the publication by Jules Janin, the smart theatre critic, of a small book on Debureau. . . .

All this is familiar ground. What may be less familiar is the special slant given by Janin to Debureau's transformations of Pierrot. For though attention has been given to the inaccuracies of the little book, to the romantic vamping-up of Debureau's life to suit a romantic *persona*, less has been paid to the sense underlying Janin's interpretations. The following passages are central.

> 'Gilles c'est le peuple. Gilles tour à tour joyeux, triste, malade, bien portant, battant, battu, musicien, poète, mais, toujours pauvre comme est le peuple; c'est le peuple que Debureau représente dans tous ses drames; il a surtout le sentiment peuple [. . .].

> 'Il soutient que les soubrettes n'existent plus, que les types comiques sont effacés, que le financier, le politique, le poète se ressemblent tous, qu'ils ont la même figure et le même habit; d'où il conclut que la comédie d'autrefois n'est pas possible dans cette société nivelée [. . .] Le théâtre ignoble est le seul possible aujourd'hui. Ne me parlez pas des autres: ils sont morts [. . .]
>
> 'Pierrot, exposé à toute la malice d'Arlequin et de Colombine, savez-vous ce que c'est que Pierrot? C'est le misanthrope de Molière. Alceste s'indigne dans le grand monde, dont il combat les travers; le Pierrot des Funambules s'indigne dans le peuple, dont il brave l'attaque brutale.'

The picture is not quite coherent; but it tells us much about the reactions of Janin, Victor Hugo, Théophile Gautier, or George Sand to the latent possibilities of mime. In an age when *Lucrèce Borgia* and *Angelo, tyran de Padoue* are 'dramas' dedicated to the People's cause, when Michelet has already begun his monumental researches into the People, when repression and governmental violence excite the democratic imagination of a Philipon and a Daumier, this authentic and 'ignoble' mime stood out by virtue of a licence, a humanity, which the blasé theatre-goer might envy. Debureau a grotesque?—but what else had Victor Hugo declared to be central to modern aesthetic? A grotesque then, as true and wholesome in heart as Quasimodo. The point was not lost on Théophile Gautier. And Molière, whom Rousseau never forgave for making a fool of Alceste, Molière at last was seen in a meaningful light: had he only realized what his instinct was leading him to discover in the highest creation of his *œuvre*!

Reflections of this kind passed clean over Gaspard Debureau's head. He had had a hard existence, bore something of a grudge to the world, and remained a moneyless fleapit mime. It is likely that the bloodthirsty and unbridled variations of the Funambules Pierrot echo the new taste for popular melodrama aroused by Robert Macaire and the industry of Frédéric Lemaître and Lacenaire; but Debureau never paid much attention to the fuss made of him by educated critics. To be sure, his celebrity among them came in useful a couple of years later when, walking in the park at Belleville, he was provoked by some jeering urchins, laid about them with a heavy stick, and found himself in court next day on a murder charge. Thanks largely to his notoriety he was acquitted; but the incident served to underline the darker, more misanthropic side of his performances which the public found increasingly hard to distinguish from his private life (and there was trouble too with Debureau's Colombine who played true to form in the Quartier du Temple). There were deep passions and a susceptible streak in the modern Pierrot. Still, the People, by and large, can do no wrong; and Jules Jamin's panegyric was certainly not a thing of the past when Daumier created his magnificent *tête de Pierrot*, to modern eyes so unexpectedly powerful a treatment. Though not a likeness of Debureau there is no question but that this study is meant to convey the Rembrandtesque force of a man of the people who has known suffering, looked on evil in many forms, and achieved self-respect only despite—or perhaps through—the humiliations of his rôle.

Debureau's son, who followed in his father's footsteps in the Théâtre des Funambules, was it would appear a very different figure. Drained of the brutal vitality of Gaspard, Charles was in life, as well as on stage, a nervous, slender, sickly figure; through him the romantic identification of life and art was consummated in an intense and neurotic profile, dogged by nightmare, suicidal gestures, endless protest and threats of revenge against the careless malice of the world. The invariable white linen costume, black skull-cap, the elegance of movement have been recaptured by Barrault in *Les Enfants du Paradis*; it is Charles, not Gaspard, that Maurice Sand chose to copy for the Pierrot of his *Masques et bouffons* (1847). Does the black skull-cap suggest some affinity with Hamlet? Nothing more likely; moreover, the suspect simplicity of the smile in a drawn white face is overlaid by a degree of abstraction—even intellectualization—of costume which takes us far from the rudeness of the father. The nonchalance of the pose catches the eye: despite its insolence, Maurice Sand's Pierrot is not at ease. Gaspard may have embodied the suffering People, but Charles is certainly aware of being the artist, the precarious outcast.

He acted for some years opposite his father, and they were not the only great Pierrots of the mid-century. The genre caught on; there was Guyon; there was an ex-pupil, Paul Legrand, who followed Gaspard (in 1846) before moving over to a rival entertainment. Legrand was a victim of his rôle in a somewhat more trivial sense,—that is to say he sacrificed its formal authority to the promptings of public taste. His costume sufficiently illustrates the decline: sentimentalized, his mime was enriched with a patter of remarks about poverty and neglect, admissions of idleness, sobs and laughter. The last traces disappear of the *commedia* with its tautness, its reliance on a formal pattern of movement. Understandably, Legrand is the ancestor of a long line of decadent and trivial Pierrots—the hero of Michel Carré's highly successful *L'enfant prodigue* (in which M. *and Mme* Pierrot wring their hands to music over a wayward son), or the music-hall figure whose costume is a hybrid of clown and traditional Pierrot motif; the agile Hanlon Lee brothers; or—last popular avatar—the Co-optimists. From Charles and the *cercle des Funambules* founded in 1887 by Larcher, P. Margueritte, Najac and Beirrier, descends a stricter conception of the art of mime.

Leaving aside the posterity, we remark simply that around 1850 Paris appeared to an onlooker like Gavarni to be alive with Pierrots. If we turn to his *École des Pierrots*, we might believe that the Quartier du Temple is all but exclusively populated by the tribe. Inevitably, at this point Pierrot escapes from the ban of silent mime and becomes literary property.[1] Théodore de Banville, before setting to work on the *Odes funambulesques*, writes both his *Pauvres saltimbanques* and an *Histoire des petits théâtres de Paris*—less exuberant than Janin's effusion, but more influential. Théophile Gautier, *le bon Théo*, is no mime; but to amuse his friends and celebrate his birthday in 1862 he writes and performs a mediocre verse sketch *Pierrot posthume* (with décor by Puvis de Chavannes) in which Pierrot appears—echoes of Debureau père et fils—as 'l'être passif et déshérité qui assiste, morne et sournois, aux orgies et folies de ses maîtres'. In fact, Maurice Sand's *Masques et bouffons* offers the now idle and crestfallen poets of a police-state Empire a repertory of images from which—not by coincidence—Pierrot stands out as the figure most akin to themselves. He slips easily into the climate of 'decadent' literature; and Jean Richepin, the truculent leader of early decadence, *le César des gueux*, put on at the Trocadéro a *Pierrot assassin* in which Sarah Bernhardt played the title role—a role in keeping with the mood of Richepin's *névrosés*. Paul Margueritte's *Pierrot* is seen returning from Colombine's funeral, haunted by the sight of the *croque-morts* and the horrid suspicion that it is he who did her to death. Huysmans' *Pierrot sceptique*, written jointly with Léon Hennique, is, significantly, dressed all in black—he has taken a diabolical turn. In the literary group which took its name from the café *Le chat noir*, a prominent artist member, Adolphe Willette, drew Pierrots and moons obsessively, presently founded his own review *Pierrot*, and developed a species of Pierrot-album made up of sloppy texts, strip-cartoons (the first, *Mon rosier est mort*, appeared originally in *Le Chat Noir*), and *histoires sans paroles*. His memoirs, *Feu Pierrot*, are little more than a trivial account of their early days. In his hands Pierrot totters towards the kind of album kept on the drawing-room piano, but has at least the grace to be saturated with 'modern' pessimism; this figure 'n'est plus la facétieuse canaille de la tradition funambulesque; il est devenu artiste, c'est-à-dire un poète "honni par les gens sérieux";' he reads Schopenhauer, takes the moon to be a gleaming skull. A decisive turn, as it happens; but we can forget the sentimental rose-tree and eau-de-Cologne Pierrots of Willette's friends.

## SYMBOL

Two major poets in France resist the sentimental or clownish embroidery of Pierrot, and instead take the image to the limit beyond which the name and associations of the traditional part are on the point of disappearing: Laforgue and Verlaine. The former in a manner which is clearly a continuation of Richepin and the *Chat Noir* group; the latter to a stage of decomposition for which neither precedent can be found nor sequel imagined.

Laforgue, almost as much as Adolphe Willette, considered that he *lived* the part of Pierrot. From Bourget and Richepin he picked up in his early years the new 'decadent' view of poets as pariahs. A virtuous and respectable education, and later his post at the Prussian Court as reader to the Empress Augusta, developed his leaning towards Baudelairian dandyism. An evident reticence in relations with the opposite sex is matched by a peculiar sympathy towards those legends and images in which purity or indecision—or both—acquire a special pathos or significance: Lohengrin, Hamlet, Pierrot. And in his soundings of philosophy and modern astronomy, evolution, the unconscious according to Hartmann, the *scientisme* (as the French call it) which is part of his ironically detached pessimism, he developed his own form of obsession with the Moon, which played with such devastating effects upon the unconscious levels of human behaviour, a coquettish patroness of all aberrations in the universal Maya. Plainly, Laforgue's Pierrot was not to be a precisely simple being, if he reflected his author's pre-occupations in full. And if, in addition, the presentation of Pierrot is to conform to Laforgue's ideal of distorting and cramping the movements of his unconscious as little as possible, by a species of allusive fragmentation or *pointillisme* (he learnt the idea from Impressionism which as a *peintre manqué* he pursued with the closest interest in the years when he was also busy with Pierrot) then it is clear that the coherence of the image will be tested to destruction.

Laforgue's *Complaintes* have been shown by Pierre Reboul to be more directly autobiographical than their detached tone would encourage one to suppose. Even without these demonstrations it is easy to see in the tenuous verse a thread of uneasy flirtation (Laforgue's word), a so to speak *inverted* Pierrot posture. Colombine—Woman—is, to him, a relentless machine working out the Laws of the Unconscious; Pierrot the fascinated but entirely lucid victim, attempts both to participate and to stand outside; to remain alive, 'a dupe', and to stand outside, 'a dilettante'.

The first Pierrot poems, in the *Complaintes*, form part of a continuous dialogue or 'flirtation' carried on in different lights, at various stages, in a constructed sequence. The *Complainte de Lord Pierrot* presents, unexpectedly, a philosophizing dandy ('Inconscient, descendez en nous par réflexes') with a heart 'chaste et doux', proposing first sadistic revels, though not in the most convincing tone ('—Tout cela vous honore, Lord Pierrot, mais encore?') and then a stream of cosmological perplexities ('Oh! de moins en moins drôle; Pierrot sait mal son rôle?'). In the second, *Autre Complainte*, Pierrot is involved still in a *galant* dialogue against the machine of the Unconscious—

> Et si ce cri lui part: 'Dieu de Dieu! que je t'aime!'
> 'Dieu reconnaîtra les siens . . .'

He holds his own with these retorts; and the close even anticipates lucidly a final twitch of the unconscious:

> Enfin, si, par un soir, elle meurt dans mes livres,
> Douce; feignant de n'en pas croire encor mes yeux,
> J'aurai un: 'Ah ça, mais, nous avions
> De Quoi vivre!
> 'C'était donc sérieux?'

Here and in the *Complainte des Noces de Pierrot* it is possible to sense the presence of the Observer of the dialogue, the Pierrot-voyeur whose aim, *en définitive*, is not dupery but dilettantism, the artistic control of senseless Maya; and in the *Imitation de Notre Dame la Lune*, where a whole series of Pierrot poems is really the centre-piece, Pierrot—dandy, dilettante, artist—proceeds to develop his Schopenhauer pessimism, unobtrusively, into a veritable aesthetic. These 'éclairs d'identité entre le sujet et l'objet' are on the one hand privileged instants of identity with the Unconscious; on the other hand the search for them, a tortuous and delicate, oblique search, is rewarded by a problematical freedom from the unbending laws of the physical and psychological universe. On this view, any arbitrary lineaments for a Pierrot figure become the signs of a disastrous failure in the quest; Pierrot-Laforgue remains therefore a fluid, formless subject, determined only by the individuality of the poet, an *absence* from the object world which he observes (Professor Reboul has excellently analysed this absence) to the precise extent that world is rendered in terms of lunar beauty. Pierrot is dissolved; the world instead takes on the significances of his costume, pallid face, hesitancy, hopelessness.

Once again Pierrot turns to his partner; their dialogue is framed in scenes whose character, *antisolaire*, is the opposite of comforting. He belongs to a tribe essentially the same as Mallarmé's *mendieurs d'azur*, if less single-minded:

> Ils vont, se sustentant d'azur,
> Et parfois aussi de légumes,
> De riz plus blanc que leur costume,
> De mandarines et d'œufs durs. . . .

But at least he has gone beyond the phase of Prufrock—like hesitations over Colombine. At several points the themes of the *Complaintes* recur ('Tu sais si la femme est cramponne . . .') but only to be dismissed: Colombine is so vague that she can be turned at will into almost any generic partner—des félines Ophéliés/Orphelines en folie. Pierrot-Hamlet is free from his *duperie*,

> Lune, consomme mon baptême,
> Lave mes yeux de ton linceul;
> Qu'aux hommes, je sois ton filleul;

Et pour nos compagnes, le seul
Qui les délivre d'elles-mêmes

knowing that 'la lune est stérile', that her true worship is Art ('Tu fournis la matière brute, je me charge de l'œuvre d'art'), and that —as Schopenhauer has taught—the worship of Art is a liberation from the Will, a voluntary sterility. The sequence of *Pierrots* and *Locutions de Pierrot* ends in a frozen landscape, a *nuit blanche*, a pathetic and total disillusion, a shrug of the shoulders:

Je ne suis qu'un viveur lunaire
Qui fait des ronds dans les bassins,
Et cela, sans autre dessein
Que devenir un légendaire. . . .

The tone and the personal attitude are, by the end of the *Imitation*, firm; the dilettante has overcome humiliation by a form of humorous detachment which it would be misleading to call simply ironic, though in its way it is as uncompromising as the detachment of Thomas à Kempis who lent part of the title.

Pierrot is the complete philosopher of Intuition, which he calls the Unconscious: his stylized rôle in the *commedia* is quite dissolved away and in its place Laforgue has set a stylized pose of total, deathlike, amused passivity. The wind blowing through the vacuous lunar scene—

Importun
Vent qui rage!
Les défunts?
Ça voyage—

flaps up his arms, twists *les manches en saule*, flings him 'tumultuously' *en figures blanches*; the epigraphs from Hamlet sprinkled through the *Imitation* and the *Derniers Vers* remind us insistently that behind the mask the comedian has ceased to suffer.

Encore un de mes pierrots mort;
Mort d'un chronique orphelinisme;
C'était un cœur plein de dandysme
Lunaire, en un drôle de corps.

There is some incongruity in the thought that at the time Laforgue was writing the *Complaintes* he had also in train a very different composition, *Pierrot fumiste*. This violent and scabrous farce is in a way the *rêve de compensation* to go with Prufrock: Pierrot ('en habit blanc et cravate noir, monocle incrusté dans l'arcade sourcillière,' supreme dandy and impotent poet) misbehaves at his wedding, reads the *Pornographe illustré* during the cortège, flouts bourgeois platitude and feminine cunning, scandalously neglects his Colombine; when respectability, impatient with the never-consummated marriage, pronounces legal separation against the impossible bridegroom, he violates her savagely and dances off to Cairo. The sketchy scenario, however incongruous, is nevertheless also in the line that leads from the *Complaintes* to the *Imitation*—Pierrot is a *fumiste* because the wind of *ennui* can at an instant become the wind of death and puff him like smoke into nothingness; knowing this, his outrages are no more significant than Colombine's sighs; and art is the alibi. Which perhaps explains why after *Pierrot fumiste* Laforgue was not moved to develop the legend more coherently. All the *Moralités légendaires* are linked to the Pierrot theme, though it appears nowhere in them—poor well-meaning Hamlet murdering his Ophelia, old Pan baulked of Syrinx but finding Art; a case can be made out for seeing Laforgue's *Lohengrin* as merely the loftiest of the poet's variations. This is no more than saying that Laforgue has by 1885 reached a position in which his own rendering of any scene, any legend, all experience, is in the rôle of Pierrot; the *Derniers Vers* and the *Fleurs de bonne volonté*, no less than the *Moralités*, are part of the legend of himself. It is unimportant that the *name* is missing from these remarkable *Derniers vers*: the manner is by now so complete that we recognize the *persona* soliloquizing.... None of Laforgue's numerous imitators reached this level of transcendental sophistication. And it is uncertain how he himself could ever have moved beyond it, for that matter; but *le vent de l'ennui*, changing, treated this Pierrot as he had disposed of his fictions, and so saved him the trouble.

Verlaine's approach to Pierrot, it has been suggested above, is not quite that of the *décadents*, despite his aggressive association with several groups who laid claim to that title; not perhaps so worked out as in the case of the metaphysical Laforgue, the results are, in their own way, equally original and subtle. Verlaine's real starting-point, if one can speak of anything so precise, is in the intuition that by comparison with Harlequin, the primitive Pierrot is infinitely plastic, barely a character for all his greed, lechery, or foolishness: he is weak, *disgracieux*. Yet white and innocent, no doubt, too, a *grotesque* in the negative sense. And therefore vague, assimilable to other cognate images—to Baudelaire's *vieillards* as well as Richepin's *gueux*. Mallarmé's long poem, *Le Guignon*, would seem to have haunted him (as well it might: first published in 1862, it was reprinted in *Lutèce*, 1883; by Verlaine himself in his *Poètes maudits*, 1884, in *Le Décadent* in 1886, and in *La Revue rose* in 1887); it is an elaborate and disconcerting treatment of the theme of exile, the *mendieur d'azur* whipped by a cold wind, repelled by the world, hunted to self-destruction by *le guignon*. Verlaine's later *nostalgie de la boue*, his tramping the northern plain with Rimbaud, is prefigured in an important early poem or '*eau-forte*', *Grotesques*: here the decadent theme of artist-vagabond-outcast, much more narrowly treated than it had been by Mallarmé, takes on a peculiar and troubling light:

C'est que, sur leurs aigres guitares
Crispant la main des libertés,
Ils nasillent des chants bizarres,
Nostalgiques et révoltés!

C'est enfin que dans leurs prunelles
Rit et pleure—fastidieux—
L'amour des choses éternelles
Des vieux morts et des anciens dieux!

These disturbing figures, gypsies, poets, twitching 'la main des libertés', and (like the *mendieurs d'azur*) mocked by the *filles*, meet an end very much in key with that of Villon's Hung Men:

Tout vous repousse et tout vous navre,
Et quand la mort viendra pour vous,
Maigre et froide, votre cadavre
Sera dédaigné par les loups!

So far, the looseness and imprecision of the image can be explained by eclecticism in the putting together of disparate echoes. But in the mature writing of *Jadis et Naguère* the Grotesque suddenly acquires an unmistakable Verlaine quality; the image ceases to be eclectic, crystallizes in a hair-raising vision of—Pierrot.

Ce n'est plus le rêveur lunaire du vieil air
Qui riait aux aïeux dans les dessus de porte;

Sa gaîté, comme sa chandelle, hélas! est morte,
Et son spectre aujourd'hui nous hante, mince et clair.

Et voici que parmi l'effroi d'un long éclair
Sa pâle blouse a l'air, au vent froid qui l'emporte,
D'un linceul, et sa bouche est béante de sorte
Qu'il semble hurler sous les morsures du ver.

Avec le bruit d'un vol d'oiseaux de nuit qui passe,
Ses manches blanches font vaguement par l'espace
Des signes fous auxquels personne ne répond.

Ses yeux sont deux grands trous où rampe du phosphore,
Et la farine rend plus effroyable encore
Sa face exsangue au nez pointu de moribond.

This vision—scarecrow? ghost? corpse?—has taken plasticity to the point of decomposition. Only Verlaine, no doubt, would have dared to call the result Pierrot; only Verlaine in his *nouveau système* could so fuse helplessness, the white fright of shroud-blouse and floury death-pallor caught in a flash of lightning, the blank and windy limbo, the macabre and hideous transfiguration of the zany. We are in a world in which the effort of *Sagesse* to put a shape to living has been lost, in which the further artifice of mask and costume are discarded; what remains in a timeless, meaningless jumble of fears and regrets, is the deeper terror of the poet's sense of drift. A limiting case again? No doubt; and after *Pierrot*, Verlaine's *Pierrot gamin* (from the collection *Parallèlement*) is positively arch in its return to street corners and libidinousness, to the social entity which a tattered and ageing Verlaine saw himself as able to remain—with the 'subtil génie/De sa malice infinie/ De poète grimacier':

Va frère, va camarade,
Fais le diable, bats l'estrade
Dans ton rêve et dans Paris
Et par le monde, et sois l'âme
Vile, haute, noble, infâme,
De nos innocents esprits!

Grandis, car c'est la coutume,
Cube ta riche amertume,
Exagère ta gaieté,
Caricature, auréole,
La grimace et le symbole
De notre simplicité!

We may not be ready to give much for Verlaine's *simplicité*; but in this last avatar of the white flapping blouse and flour-daubed face it is curious to see how Pierrot's innocence remains symbolic for him—symbolic of the detachment, the total irresponsibility, of the poet: each licentious gesture establishing the innocence more fully, indeed, and emphasizing the wayward integrity. Verlaine's *canaille* inflexions, no less than Laforgue's broken moonlight, bear witness to the only style of heroism recognized by the *fin de siècle*: the heroism in this case of Sancho Panza twisted by the dreams of Don Quixote.

## NOTE

[1] A curious novel, by Henri Rivière (1860), is worth a note as one of the more naïve testimonies to the Funambules vogue: the central figure, Pierre, a neurotic retired sea-captain, sets up in show-business and, after imitating Gaspard Debureau's career fairly closely, concludes it with a brutal and hysterical murder of his Alexandrine's admirer, on-stage.

# ART AS SECOND NATURE

*Michael Hamburger*

## *The Figures of the Actor and the Dancer in the works of Hugo von Hofmannsthal*

### I

HOFMANNSTHAL'S evolution—from the 'pure' lyrical poet of the eighteen-nineties to the dramatist, writer of dance scenarios and librettist of later years—still puzzles a good many critics, though few now dare to deplore the 'disjecti membra poetae', as many did in his lifetime. Hofmannsthal's need for 'lyrical drama' or melodrama in the strictest sense, that is for a medium in which words are fused with music, is closely connected with the 'word-scepticism' expounded by the fictitious Lord Chandos of his justly famous *Letter*.[1] That the so-called Chandos crisis was not confined to any one period of Hofmannsthal's life, but anticipated even in the works of that early poetic phase which it is often said to have terminated, was suggested in my Introduction to Hofmannsthal's *Poems and Verse Plays*.[2]

Hofmannsthal's experience of the inadequacy of words—already hinted at in his first verse play of 1891—involved a whole complex of related matters. Above all, it was inseparable from his awareness of living in a civilization lacking in style, cohesion, and continuity. One of his very first prose pieces, published at the age of seventeen, contains this observation: 'We have no generally valid tone in conversation, because we have no society and no conversation, just as we have no style and no culture.' Hofmannsthal's concern with total art grew out of this dissatisfaction. Art, in this early phase, was the means of creating dreams and illusions powerful enough to banish the barbarous realities of the age.

Like much Symbolist doctrine, Hofmannsthal's was based on a stark dualism. Only a fusion of all the arts, and their reduction to a common core of expression that was not self-expression alone, but gesture, ritual, and myth, could resist the fragmentation of culture.

In his early essay on Paul Bourget, also published when he was seventeen, Hofmannsthal wrote that in an age of individualism 'no understanding is possible between two persons, no conversation, no connection between today and yesterday' (the theme of his first verse play *Gestern*, written in the same year); 'words lie, feelings lie, even our self-awareness lies'. The essay shows the rather Nietzschean addiction at this time to strong sensations, the desire 'to feel rushing, living blood: *à sentir sentir*'; but when Hofmannsthal writes, 'if we can die of the body, we also owe to the body, to the senses, the foundation of all poetry', he is stating a belief which he was to modify, but never wholly renounce. The unity of body and mind is explicitly or implicitly upheld in all the works of his maturity; there are formulations of it in his novel *Andreas* and in his late play *The Tower*. This belief was one basis for Hofmannsthal's aesthetic of gesture. Indeed, the early essay opens up the whole complex of Hofmannsthal's most characteristic preoccupations; from his 'word-scepticism'—clearly expressed here ten years before the Chandos *Letter*—to the questions of individuality and tradition.

Hofmannsthal's interest in the actor and dancer goes back to the same early period. Both the actor and the dancer could transcend words, circumstance, and personal identity. Hofmannsthal put it like this in an early tribute to Eleonora Duse, the first of two such tributes written in 1892: 'We do not know where the limits of her art might be. Not in individuality, since she has none, or any whatever.' In a letter of the same year Hofmannsthal tells his friend that it makes no difference whether he knows Italian well, since Duse 'acts the sense, not the words'.

It is significant, too, that the so-called 'Chandos crisis' should have been most clearly anticipated in another tribute to an actor, Hofmannsthal's review, in 1895, of a book on Friedrich Mitterwurzer. Here Hofmannsthal remarks:

> For people are tired of listening to talk. They feel a deep disgust with words. For words have pushed themselves in front of things. Hearsay has swallowed the world. . . . We are in the grip of a

> horrible process in which thought is utterly stifled by concepts. Hardly anyone now is capable of being sure in his own mind about what he understands, what he does not understand, of saying what he feels and what he does not feel. This has awakened a desperate love for all those arts which are executed without speech: for music, for the dance, and all the skills of acrobats and jugglers.

Akin to these last is the clown who plays such an important, though concealed, part in Hofmannsthal's much later comedy *The Difficult Man.* One more link with the Chandos *Letter* occurs here. When Hofmannsthal goes on to say that 'usually words are not in the power of men, but men are in the power of words', he is paraphrasing a remark by Francis Bacon in the *Novum Organum*; and it has only recently been recognized that the Lord Bacon who is the recipient of Hofmannsthal's imaginary letter owes much more than his name to the historical personage.[3] The borrowed passage, however, leads to another suggestive of that 'word-mysticism' which Hofmannsthal described as the reverse side of his own 'word-scepticism': 'Whenever we open our mouths, ten thousand of the dead speak through us.'

The actor, like the poet, is a *persona* in the original sense of the word—a mask or mouthpiece through which the dead speak. That is why Hofmannsthal was able to allow him an ideal and archetypal function which most of his predecessors and contemporaries reserved for the dancer; and that is why he could write in his late collection of aphorisms, *Buch der Freunde*: 'There is only a slight and seeming difference between the ephemeral, modest fame which an actor wins and the "lasting fame" of the poet.' The full force of that casual remark comes home to one if one imagines how it would have been received by Stefan George, by one of his idolatrous followers, or even by one of Rilke's more devout lady admirers. (Rilke himself could have understood it, and understood that it was aimed not at poetry, but at the cult of personalities.) Hofmannsthal's poems on the deaths of actors are especially revealing in this connection. The earliest was written for the same actor Mitterwurzer after his death in 1897; and it is the question of identity that makes these occasional poems relevant to Hofmannsthal's deepest and most constant concerns:

> . . . He fell: then all the puppets collapsed with him  
> Into whose veins he'd poured his own life-blood.  
> Now speechlessly they died; and where he lay

There also stretched out a heap of corpses
In wreck and ruin: knee of a drunkard
Pressed into a king's eye; Don Philip
With Caliban a nightmare round his neck,
All of them dead.

Then we knew whom death had taken from us:
The sorcerer, the great great conjurer.
And we came from our houses, gathered round,
And so began to talk of what he was.
Who was he though, and who else was he not?

He crept out of one mask into another,
Sprang from the father's into the son's body
And changed his shape as though it were his clothes.[4]

Much the same question is posed in the poem *On the Death of the Actor Hermann Müller* of 1899, though here Hofmannsthal dwelt more poignantly on the dualism of real and assumed identity, of the dream projected on the stage and the reality from which even actors were not exempt:

Yet when the play was fading, and the curtain
Came down in silence like a painted eyelid
Over the magic cavern emptied now of life
And he stepped out, a stage appeared before him
Like a wide, sleepless eye for ever open
On which no curtain mercifully falls,
The terrifying stage, reality.
Then all the arts of transformation dropped
From him, and his poor soul walked quite unclothed
And gazed from a child's eyes . . .

True, this dualism did not detract from the actor's exemplary function, since it was one that Hofmannsthal himself experienced and rendered in all his earlier works. Yet the Symbolist notion of 'the stage as dream image'—the title of an essay by Hofmannsthal published in 1903—had to be reconciled with reality in some way, much as the ideal of impersonality had to be reconciled with what was valid in personality. The change is apparent in Hofmannsthal's later tributes to actors and in his later writings on the theatre. Hofmannsthal's own dramatic works of the transitional period bridge the gulf in several different ways. The essay on 'the stage as dream image' recommends De Quincey, Poe and Baudelaire as favourite authors of the perfect designer of stage décors; but Hofmannsthal jotted down the draft of a crucial passage of the essay on the back fly-leaf of a volume containing Shakespeare's *Macbeth*, *Hamlet*, and *King Lear*. Hofmannsthal's modification of the Symbolist aesthetic owes a great deal to his study of Shakespeare, of the Greek dramatists whose works he adapted at this time, as well as Calderon, Molière and the whole repertory of classical, medieval, and modern drama. It was in his lecture on Shakespeare of 1905 that Hofmannsthal remarked on the 'mystically living space between characters' which became such an important element in his own art; indeed he was to coin a new word, 'allomatic', to describe the mysterious relationship.

Hofmannsthal began by celebrating the 'truth of masks' and of that dream image which the stage opposes to the 'terrifying stage, reality'. So in this Prologue to the *Antigone of Sophocles* (1899):

> You have no need to let my mask perturb you:
> even the dearest beings that you know,
> they only let you see the masks they wear:
> the eye of man cannot bear that which is real.[5]

The masked Spirit of Antigone in this Prologue asserts that only on the stage is there truth,

> all other things
> are parables and playings in a mirror.

But in 1903 Hofmannsthal began to write his *Everyman*, the first of his plays derived from medieval and Baroque dramatic conventions that make the theatre an allegory of life. A passage in his *Prologue to a Puppet Play* (1906) marks the significance of the change: 'From this dream I rise and step over into that other dream which is called human world and human life.' In 1902 Hofmannsthal had also begun that adaptation of Calderon's *Life is a Dream* which was to occupy him for the rest of his life, gradually turning into his own most personally committed play, *The Tower*. The dualism of dream and reality had become far less drastic and far more complex. If life was not as real as it had once seemed, the stage did not need to be as dream-like as Hofmannsthal had believed; and if personality was not as individual as it had seemed, Hofmannsthal could now draw closer to the current realistic and social drama. Even psychological comedy, he was to discover soon, could include the wordless gesture, the mystery, and the myth.

In a third article on Eleonora Duse, written in 1903, Hofmannsthal found it necessary to modify his earlier tributes to her. Duse had now become greater than the parts she played; she had 'suffered the afflictions of our age like no one else, and in a magnificent way'; she had acquired wisdom and become 'the embodiment of an unnameable tragic force'. Here Hofmannsthal's personal acquaintance with the actress—she was to play the title rôle in his *Electra*, and Jocasta in his *Oedipus and the Sphinx*—may seem to have involved him in a contradiction; but a diary entry of 1904 points to an inherent paradox that bears on the question of individuality, and Hofmannsthal's changing attitude to it. '*Paradox of the Actor*: Duse today can impersonate only herself, i.e. in every rôle she acts the mature woman grown wonderful through love and suffering, i.e. she now raises every rôle to the universal plane.' Personality, Hofmannsthal implies here and elsewhere in his later work becomes a positive value as soon as it embraces more than the merely individual and circumstantial.

Professor Frank Kermode touches on the same paradox in his essay *Poet and Dancer before Diaghilev*[6] when he suggests that there is no absolute contradiction between T. S. Eliot's doctrine of impersonality in art and Wallace Stevens's claim for 'the presence of the determining personality'. Since I shall be unable here to draw all the necessary parallels between Hofmannsthal's attitudes and those of other Symbolist and post-Symbolist writers, all my remarks should be set in the context of Professor Kermode's admirable and more comprehensive study. The paradox in question is only one of many crucial matters which his essay illuminates.

The same change and the same paradox are evident in the last of Hofmannsthal's poems in memory of actors, that written on the death of the great actor Josef Kainz, whom Hofmannsthal had also known personally and who had acted in two of his plays. The manuscript of the poem in the Vienna Nationalbibliothek is dated October 2nd, 1910. Like the later Duse, and unlike the two other actors commemorated in poems by Hofmannsthal,

Kainz is seen not only as the vehicle of transformations, but as a personality equal to, or greater than, the parts enacted; as

> One untransformed in many transformations,
> A great enchanter never himself enchanted,
> A man unmoved who moved us, one
> Who when we thought him near was far from us . . .
> Messenger to us of a nameless lord.

The allusion to an unexplained mission indicates a kind of personality that is more than individuality. Kainz, in the same poem, becomes the 'actor without a mask', and another passage dwells on an aspect of this kind of personality that Hofmannsthal also emphasized in other later writings:

> O how life clutched at him, and never yet
> Could quite ensnare him in the mystery of
> Voluptuous transformation! How he *stayed*!
> How royally he stood fast!

Hofmannsthal's cult of the actor had its roots in his early intuition that the very word self is 'little more than a metaphor', and that 'we and the world are not different things'. This intuition was the source of much of Hofmannsthal's early lyrical poetry and early lyrical drama, though even in these works Hofmannsthal was looking for an ethical principle that would prevent this metaphorical self from simply evaporating, and govern its relationship to the here and now. Though the individual could never be autonomous or clearly circumscribed, true personality demanded a commitment not only to the flux of being—'to have genius is to participate in the unreason of the cosmos', Hofmannsthal noted towards the end of his life—but to some fixed point outside the self. This is the constancy or loyalty attributed to Kainz in the poem, though the actual commitment is not explained.

What Hofmannsthal attempted everywhere, in his life and works, was to combine both these commitments—to be loyal to certain conventions and institutions, yet to remain open to the mystery and the flux. As he wrote in his prologue of 1926 to Brecht's first play *Baal*, 'we move within forms and conventions without sacrificing the mystery of life to them', contrasting this attitude with that of the younger generation. In Brecht's play and its 'crude inarticulate language' Hofmannsthal saw 'the end of individualism . . ., that child of the seventeenth century which the nineteenth fattened up'; he both censured and welcomed them as an expression of an amorphous energy, a chaos that might engender a new age.

I do not wish to suggest that Hofmannsthal ever finally unravelled this complex of problems and paradoxes. 'The shaped work settles the problem', he wrote, and the verb implies that problems are only 'solved' in the abstract. Comparing the mime and the dancer with the actor in his essay *On Pantomime*, Hofmannsthal had written that the former must be 'lacking in individuality, which cannot be conveyed in any medium other than language'; yet a diary entry of 1921 reads as follows: 'The individual is inexpressible. Whatever is expressed, immediately takes on a general aspect and ceases to be individual in any strict sense. Language and individuality are mutually exclusive.' We are left with the paradox and the mystery with which Hofmannsthal had been at grips for thirty years, and the inference that the individual is inexpressible in any medium whatever. This points to the core of Hofmannsthal's own art—an art of 'I-suppression', Hermann Broch called it—and comes as close as I wish to come to an explanation of Hofmannsthal's cult of the actor, his renunciation of lyrical poetry, and his resort to various mixed media. In the same late prologue to Brecht's play the actor is characterized once more as 'the amoeba among living creatures, the indeterminate archetypal creature that lets the situation prescribe whether it is to be animal or vegetable'; and 'that is why he is the symbolic man'.

## II

The tension between Hofmannsthal's 'word-scepticism' and his 'word-mysticism' is apparent in all his writings on actors and dancers. The actor's medium, like the poet's, is words, and both actor and poet are subject to the limitations and responsibilities imposed by that medium; yet both also transcend them—the poet by his capacity to render the timeless moment and transform circumstance into myth, the actor by his capacity to render not the words, but the sense, in pure gesture. It is this latter aspect of the actor that accounts for Hofmannsthal's tendency to speak of actors and dancers as though their function were one and the same.

Hofmannsthal's dance libretti are less well known than his opera libretti, but he wrote quite a number of them, for the traditional ballet, for Diaghilev, and for the solo dancer Grete Wiesenthal, a close personal friend. Dance forms an important part of several of Hofmannsthal's dramatic works, beginning with the climax of his *Electra*, that 'nameless dance' of the heroine that is pure ecstasy and ends with her collapse. The first work that Hofmannsthal offered to Richard Strauss, in 1900, and well before Strauss's composition of *Electra*, was a ballet libretto, *The Triumph of Time.*[7] This was the first of a long succession of dance libretti and 'pantomimes' no less various in setting and style than Hofmannsthal's plays and opera libretti; the last, *Achilles in Skyros*, was written in 1925.

'Dance', Frank Kermode has written, 'is the most primitive, non-discursive art, offering a pre-scientific image of life, an intuitive truth. Thus it is the emblem of the Romantic image. Dance belongs to a period before the self and the world were divided, and so achieves naturally that 'original unity' which modern poetry can produce only by a great and exhausting effort of fusion'[8] Hofmannsthal's earliest references to dance belong to the brief phase in which he combined a Nietzschean vitalism and primitivism with a taste for the latest refinements of 'decadent' art. His second essay on Duse of 1892 speaks of artists as 'raising the unconscious to an awareness in words that die away, in fugitive gestures, and immersing it in dionysian beauty.' In the same year he praised Swinburne's poems as vessels filled with 'darkly glowing, potent wine of life, pressed from grapes from which dionysian ecstasy and anguish and dance and madness well mysteriously blended.' This tribute draws on the international vocabulary of contemporary aestheticism; but even in later years dance retained its associations for Hofmannsthal with orgiastic ecstasy, anguish, and madness. Where he tried to render these in another medium—as in a whole succession of mythical dramas of which *Pentheus*, *Leda and the Swan* and *Semiramis* are outstanding—he produced only drafts and fragments. Only 'fugitive gestures', wordless and 'nameless', could convey them.

Yet Hofmannsthal's essays and his dialogue *Fear*—a work closely akin to Paul Valéry's *L'Ame et la Danse*, but written some fifteen years earlier—at least evoke such moments in words, in a rhythmic and vivid prose peculiar to his visions of primitive mysteries. So in his *Dialogue on Poems* of 1903, mainly a tribute to Stefan George's works, which contains this passage on the ancient wine-press:

> Those who press the grapes feel like gods. They feel as though Bacchus were right in their midst while they work by night. As though he were stamping beside them, his long robe gathered up to above the knee, in the red juice whose very vapour intoxicates. They are at once bathers and dancers: and it is the drunkenness of their dancing that makes their bath rise higher and higher. The new wine gushes from the press in streams; like little ships the wooden cups sway on the purple flood. . . . In the vapoury darkness, amid screams, amid swaying torchlight, and the splashing of the blood of the grape, suddenly Aphrodite is born from the purple foam: Bacchus rose from the wine-press, wild as a leaping wave, and drenched a garment, so that it flowed down like a shining nakedness, and out of a girl he created the goddess around whose body desire and rapture flow.

*Fear* (1907) is a dialogue between two Greek dancing girls, Laidion and Hymnis.[9] Its theme is Hofmannsthal's constant concern with the trammels of individuality and the casting off of those trammels in art. Laidion suggests to Hymnis that all their impersonations and transformations in the dance are incomplete, because they can never wholly escape from personal desire, from hope, and its concomitant fear. Laidion is obsessed by the thought of a barbarian island community whose dancing is impersonal, because it is an annual rite, not a professional skill. Its women are 'virgins and have forgotten it, they are to become women and mothers and have forgotten it: to them everything is ineffable. And then they dance.'

At this point in the dialogue words fail Laidion—'She begins to sway from the hips. Somehow one feels that she is not alone, that many of her kind are around her and that all are dancing at once under the eyes of their gods. They dance and circle as dusk falls: shadows detach themselves from the trees and sink down into the crowd of dancers, and out of the treetops rise great birds housing the departed spirits, and join the circle and beneath them all the island vibrates like a boat filled with drunken people . . .'

Laidion has only heard about the island from a sailor; and the element of doubt as to whether there really is, or ever has been, a place where women could be 'happy without hope', that is wholly divested of their personal desires and fears, is an ironic reflection on the literary cult of the dancer in Hofmannsthal's time. Yet clearly the dancer was less subject to those complications and paradoxes which beset Hofmannsthal's cult of the actor as 'symbolic man'. Hofmannsthal's essay on Oscar Wilde of 1905, itself the celebration of a myth[10] concludes with a quotation from the Persian that sums up the peculiar mystery which Hofmannsthal attributed to the dance; 'He who knows the power of the dance of life fears not death. For he knows that love kills.' Hofmannsthal's *Electra* alludes to the same mystery.

At the same period, in 1906, Hofmannsthal wrote a tribute to Ruth St Denis, who became a personal friend and visited him at Rodaun the following year. Hofmannsthal's letters of these years confirm the deep impression made on him by 'the incomparable dancer', as the title of the essay calls her. After discussing the influence of the East on Ruth St Denis's art and on contemporary Europe generally—but with the reservation that 'a whole youth, immersed in the dream of the East, or the intuition of a second, the glimpse of a single temple dancer, a single image, may have condensed into these unforgettable gestures, these dances'—Hofmannsthal continues:

> Yet I shall hardly attempt to describe her dancing. Whatever one could describe in a dance would never be more than the incidentals: the costume, the sentiment, the allegory. Here nothing is sentimental, nothing allegorical, and even the costume, that glittering drapery which amid the enchantment of rhythmic, gradually intensifying movements suddenly yields to sudden nudity, the vision of which is rendered mysterious by the strange colouring of the light, and grave, severe as the vision of an undraped sacred statue in the enclosed space of a temple—this costume embroidered with gold (or whatever else she might wear on other occasions) is of incomparably small importance.

Hofmannsthal dwells on the dancer's smile, comparing it to that enigmatic smile which fascinated generations of writers after Pater, and which Hofmannsthal had already invoked in his early verse play *Death and the Fool*—

> a mysterious smile always present in her motionless eyes: the smile of a Buddha statue. A smile not of this world. An absolutely unfeminine smile. A smile somehow related to the impenetrable smile

> in pictures by Leonardo. A smile that attracts the souls of uncommon persons and, from the first moment, but lastingly, alienates the hearts of women and the sensual curiosity of very many men.—And now the dance begins. It consists of movements. It consists of movements that merge with the next in an unceasing rhythmic flow. It is the same as what one saw the little Javanese girls dance in Paris in 1889, and this year the dancers of the King of Cambodia. Naturally it is the same thing to which all oriental dancers aspire: to the dance itself, the essential dance, the silent music of the human body. A rhythmic flow of incessant and, as Rodin says, of right movements.

Hofmannsthal then praises 'the incredible immediacy of what she does, that severe, almost rebuffing immediacy' which makes Isidora Duncan seem like a 'professor of archaeology' in comparison with 'this Lydian dancer who has stepped down from the relief.' Yeats and Valéry would have seen the point of this tribute; it is in the tradition which Frank Kermode has recorded in *Romantic Image* and in his postscript to it, the essay quoted above.

A shorter appreciation of Nijinsky's performance in *L'Après-Midi d'un Faune*—the poem which Stefan George had copied in his hand from Mallarmé's manuscript and presented to Hofmannsthal—was published in 1912. Like Duse and Kainz, Nijinsky fitted into no scheme; he was no simple dancer, but 'something between the producer, the performer, and the inventor, uniting all three functions in one person'. Hofmannsthal's remark that both the poem and the music are in a sense subordinated to Nijinsky's original creation, and his stress on the concentration, economy, and 'density of texture' that distinguish Nijinsky's art, are tributes to the dancer's active and positive personality; but Hofmannsthal's choice of the word 'pantomime' to describe this dance, and his comparison of it once more with classical sculpture, relate even this exceptional phenomenon to the idea of a total art that renders the inexpressible.

The Austrian dancer Grete Wiesenthal was trained for the ballet. Mainly under the impact of seeing Isidora Duncan dance in Vienna, and with the help of the painters Rudolf Huber and Erwin Lang, she developed her own kind of 'expressive' solo or group dancing—the latter together with her sisters. Her autobiography, *Die Ersten Schritte*, touches on her association with Hofmannsthal, of which she writes in a letter:

Grete Wiesenthal in Hofmannsthal's *Das Fremde Mädchen*

> Hugo von Hofmannsthal was truly interested in, and receptive to, the art of dance—and so, beside Gustav Mahler and Alfred Roller, he was one of the first to recognize my kind of dancing and give it his support. It was just at the time when my sisters and I turned away from the so-called classical ballet, which had become rigid and lifeless, and we were allowed to infuse the dance with new life and vigour. And that is how the pantomime *Das Fremde Mädchen*, a work by Hugo von Hofmannsthal which he wrote for me, came to be performed; the same pantomime was later filmed as well.

Hofmannsthal had written another dance libretto, *Amor and Psyche*, for Grete Wiesenthal, in 1911, and he published the two works in a separate volume, together with his dialogue *Fear*, his essay *On Pantomime* and related writings by Goethe and Chuang-Tsu. The later libretto, *Das Fremde Mädchen*, is remarkable for its realistic setting and the fascination for a rich young man of a squalid, criminal underworld—a theme that had preoccupied Hofmannsthal ever since his first story of 1894, *The Tale of the 672nd Night*, and his poems and verse plays of the same early period.

Hofmannsthal's essay *On Pantomime* (1911) is the most comprehensive and illuminating of all his writings on the actor and the dancer, not least because it subsumes both figures and reduces both arts to their common element of gesture. 'A pure gesture is like a pure thought that has been stripped even of the momentarily witty, the restrictedly individual, the grotesquely characteristic,' Hofmannsthal writes, and goes on to distinguish all these accretions from true personality. In a letter to Carl Burckhardt of 1928 Hofmannsthal outlined the plan of a comedy never completed in which one character, a notorious liar, decides to become a dancer and 'says he has chosen this profession because he adores the truth, and dancing is the only profession in which there is *nothing but* truth'. This is the truth rendered in gesture, and only in gesture or in pre-articulate thought. The essay continues:

> In pure thought, personality appears by virtue of its nobility and strength, though not in a way perceptible at once to everyone. So too in pure gestures the true personality comes to light, and the renunciation of individuality is more than amply compensated. We see a human body that moves in a rhythmic flow, in response to infinite modulations prescribed by an inner genius. It is a man like ourselves who moves before us, but more freely than we ever

> move, and yet the purity and freedom of his gestures conveys exactly what we want to convey when, inhibited and spasmodically, we discharge our inner plenitude. But is it only the freedom of the body that delights us here? Does not the soul reveal itself here in a special way? Does it not discharge its inner plenitude as in music, but more immediately still, with greater concentration? Words arouse a sharper sympathy, but it is vicarious, as it were, intellectualized, generalized; music, a more intense sympathy, but it is vague, longingly digressing; that evoked by gesture is clear and all-embracing, vividly present, joy-giving. The language of words is seemingly individual, but in truth generic, that of the body is seemingly general, but in truth highly personal. Nor is it body that speaks to body, but the human whole that speaks to the whole.

The essay refers to Ruth St Denis, Nijinsky, and Sada Yakko, but also to Eleonora Duse; and in a letter to Strauss of 1912 Hofmannsthal calls Nijinsky 'the greatest genius of mime on the stage today (next to Duse, but superior to her as a mime)'. A letter of the same year to Eberhard von Bodenhausen also connects the two arts: 'The sight last night of the aged Sarah Bernhardt applauding the genius Nijinsky moved me deeply despite all *cabotinage*. . . . Mysterious mysteries—how generation is linked to generation and the torch is handed on.'

## III

The painter, the sculptor, the architect, the composer, the juggler, and the clown—these are a few of the figures who would have to be related to those of the actor and the dancer to make this survey complete. Hofmannsthal's concern with style extended to crafts and pastimes, to furniture and utensils, to gardens—in which he saw a symbol of all art—and to the minutiae of social convention. His writings on the visual arts, including architecture, are as perceptive as those on literature, the theatre, and the dance, and as rich in those moments of vision which make his essays an essential part of his imaginative work.[11]

It would also be necessary to show how gesture supports, or takes over from, words in Hofmannsthal's own plays and opera libretti; and how Hofmannsthal's 'word-scepticism' pervades their motivation and dialogue. One instance is the Casanova-like figure

Florindo in his comedy *Cristina's Homecoming*, of whom one could say that he makes love to women out of an extreme reluctance to talk to them. 'Words are good,' he says, 'but there's something better.' (*He seizes her hand*) 'I don't want to turn this thing into talk.' The Captain, Florindo's opposite in other respects, shares the conviction that 'with us all that is finest and most beautiful lies between words.' And there is a gloss on this comedy in Hofmannsthal's prose piece *Ways and Encounters* (1907), where he writes: 'Not the embrace, it seems to me, but the encounter is the truly decisive erotic pantomime', because 'the encounter promises more than the embrace can keep', and 'at no moment is sensuality so soulful, or soulfulness so sensual as in the encounter.' This is Hofmannsthal's philosophy of gesture on another plane. The gesture celebrates a moment—and more than a whole lifetime can contain; it is fugitive and timeless. Such moments and gestures recur throughout his plays and libretti; and everywhere they are dialectically contrasted with that sense of continuity, that loyalty to a single moment of commitment which Florindo lacks, and the Captain possesses despite his adventurous past. Florindo is merely a 'word-sceptic'; the Captain is a 'word-mystic' as well.

The reference to music in the essay *On Pantomime* suggests that Hofmannsthal thought less well of, and had thought less deeply about, this art than about acting, dancing, or the visual arts; and it is true that Hofmannsthal was primarily what the Germans call an *Augenmensch*, a man more receptive to visual than to auditive impressions. In an early postcard to Marie Herzfeld,[12] accepting an invitation to listen to piano music in her house, Hofmannsthal added: 'But I know nothing at all about music, and don't like people who talk about it cleverly—evidently because I can't do so myself.' Since Hofmannsthal could talk very cleverly about literature and the visual arts even in his adolescence, the admission is of some interest. 'Although I am really unmusical . . .', he admitted to Strauss as late as 1923; but the correspondence itself and scattered references to music and composers elsewhere show that his taste and interest in music developed in later years.

The sympathy aroused by music, Hofmannsthal writes in the essay, is 'vague, longingly digressing'; though he may have had Romantic music in mind here—and it was the heavily Romantic tendencies in Strauss's music of which he least approved—the remark is generally valid in that music is a progressive art, dependent on duration in time. What Hofmannsthal feared in his collaboration with Strauss is that the moment and the gesture might be lost in a continuum of sound (if not in a continuum of noise, such as the Wagnerian 'erotic screaming' which Hofmannsthal found brutish and revolting). Nothing is more telling in this regard than Hofmannsthal's letter to Strauss of 1911 about the staging of *Ariadne auf Naxos*, the most delicately lyrical of all his libretti:

> Even if I think . . . only of the two groups, Ariadne-Bacchus, Zerbinetta and the four men—even then I must tell myself that they need a mysterious power higher than music alone in order to reveal their ultimate significance at all. The subtly conceived exiguity of this play, these two groups acting beside each other in the narrowest space, this most careful calculation of each gesture, each step, the whole like a concert and at the same time like a ballet—it will be lost, meaningless, a tattered rag, in incompetent hands; only in Reinhardt's, yours and mine can it grow into a singing flower, the incarnation of dance. *Love* is what it needs, enthusiasm, improvisation. . . .

The operative words here are gesture, concert, ballet, singing flower, incarnation of dance, love, and improvisation. Music, to Hofmannsthal, was one means of making up for the lyrical poetry he had renounced because it was at once too personal in origin and too difficult to reconcile with the social, conventional functions of language; but music was one means only, and not the most effective at that. It had one obvious advantage over the spoken word, even when combined with it in opera: 'Song is marvellous because it tames what otherwise is nothing but the organ of our self-seeking, the human voice.'[13] But total, concerted art aimed at the realization of the timeless moment and the pure gesture; and their paradigm was the dance.

In an address of 1902 Hofmannsthal had described art as 'second nature',[14] saying that 'in colours it is the totality of nature which seeks to reveal itself to the human eye'. Whether opera or ballet, spoken play or mime, the perfectly realized stage work could revert to nature if it was as seemingly effortless, generic, and spontaneous as a flower; seemingly, because even a flower is the product of a complex and highly differentiated process of which we are not necessarily aware. The more complex the artifice employed, the closer a work of art would be to organic nature, and the more simple and inevitable it must seem to the audience; yet in the end the different media of art mattered no more than the individual artist and the conventions he had inherited, borrowed or adapted. What mattered to Hofmannsthal was that all three should become transparent vehicles of the mystery.

## NOTES

[1] English version in Hugo von Hofmannsthal, *Selected Prose*, London, 1952, pp. 129–41. See also Donald Davie's comment on the *Letter* in *Articulate Energy*, London, 1955, pp. 1–5.

[2] Hofmannsthal, *Poems and Verse Plays*, London, 1961, pp. xx and xxxii.

[3] See H. Stefan Schultz: 'Hofmannsthal and Bacon' in *Comparative Literature*, Oregon, vol. XIII, No. 1, 1961.

[4] Translated by Stephen Spender. In H. v. Hofmannsthal, *Poems and Verse Plays*, London, 1961, p. 67.

[5] Translated by Christopher Middleton, *Poems and Verse Plays*, London, 1961, p. 545.

[6] In *Puzzles and Epiphanies*, London, 1962, pp. 27–8.

[7] Though Strauss rejected it, it was eventually performed with music by Alexander von Zemlinsky.

[8] F. Kermode, op. cit., p. 4.

[9] English version in Hofmannsthal: *Selected Prose*, London, 1953, pp. 155–64.

[10] English version in *Selected Prose*, London, 1953, pp. 301–5.

[11] The important letter on *Colours* is included in *Selected Prose*, London, 1953, pp. 142–54. The sequence of five letters to which it belongs, *Die Briefe des Zurückgekehrten*, is one of many prose works by Hofmannsthal that can be read as essays or as fiction.

[12] Unpublished; in the British Museum, Egerton MSS. 3150. The card is undated, but the blurred postmark points to March 3rd, 1893.

[13] Hofmannsthal, *Aufzeichnungen*, Frankfurt, 1959, p. 28.

[14] A conception probably borrowed by way of Goethe from Lord Shaftesbury.

# 'AUBREY BEARDSLEY, MAN OF LETTERS'

*Annette Lavers*

---

Of the man who had in 1896 edited the *Savoy* with him, Arthur Symons wrote this memorable sentence, the only one perhaps which can be accepted without reservation in an essay which too often 'n'est que littérature': '*Anima naturaliter pagana*, Aubrey Beardsley ended a long career, at the age of twenty-six in the arms of the Church'.[1] Five years had been enough for an artist who had sprung fully-armed from childhood, to advance the art of drawing more than anyone else had done since Dürer, according to some critics, and in the process to become so representative of his time that Max Beerbohm, who was born in the same week, could maintain all his life what he had said in 1895 as a joke, that he 'belonged to the Beardsley period'. *Punch* also duly registered this phenomenon by a caricature of 'Britannia à la Beardsley'[2] in whom one recognizes, in a scandalous dress and surrounded by exaggeratedly diabolical attributes, the famous *Beardsley woman*, whose smile bodes nobody good.

Beardsley, however, would have wished to be known instead as a writer; he had long tried his hand at several genres, had insisted once on describing himself as 'Aubrey Beardsley, man of letters' on a library admission form, and, devoting to literature a sizable part of his precious time, disobeyed the rule which he had set himself and which he used often to repeat: 'I have not much time to live, and therefore it must be: work, work, work.'

The little that survives of this great ambition—three poems (*The Three Musicians*, *The Ballad of a Barber* and a translation of Catullus, *Carmen CI*), and an unfinished 'romantic novel', first conceived as a *Story of Venus and Tannhäuser*, then published in fragments in the *Savoy* with the title *Under the Hill*[3]—has nonetheless imposed an image of Beardsley as the epitome of 'decadence' in literature as well as art.

Beardsley had begun his career as a child-prodigy, as a pianist, and the versatility of his gifts was a disservice when it came to his proper recognition as a writer. His literary works, as a result, have never received the thematic analysis they deserve. In his own time and over the first third of the present century, the tone of critics no less than journalists towards Beardsley has been oddly patronizing. Their consensus has been that Beardsley's literary work betrayed an amateur's hand, almost, it seems, as though his pretensions (tremulous enough indeed) were resented. 'He was ambitious of literary success, but any aspirations were wisely discouraged by his admirers', Robert Ross observed, and Ross rarely lacked lucidity or sympathy.[4] Beardsley, however, seems not to have been discouraged and persisted in literary projects to the end.

Beardsley laid considerable stress on the flavour of isolated words and phrases, on the rhythm of sentences. He also felt it essential to describe with absolute fidelity certain quite definite conceptions and effects of sensibility. He was not prepared to rely on felicities which arise from technique alone. It was precisely this somewhat Flaubertian behaviour which led Symons to deduce that Beardsley lacked the literary temperament and made desperate attempts to force nature. Yet sufficient evidence exists of Beardsley's literary facility; in his letters, his small humorous poems, in that pleasure in the pure act of writing itself that induced him to undertake, with his friend Rothenstein, a dialogue (which regrettably seems to have disappeared). But, whether Beardsley realized it or not, literature for him was more than a gratuitous game.

His youth, his humour, his reserve had also led Beardsley to adopt the always too successful disguise of the butterfly. As a consequence his sincerity, both as man and as artist, came to be buried under a mass of anecdotes as trivial as those who spread them. Yet, pure artist as he virtually was, Beardsley was not well equipped to defend his writings on a purely intellectual level. He preferred to allow meanings shape and body in his work and in his life. To Jacques-Emile Blanche,* who painted his portrait at Dieppe while he was writing *Venus and Tannhäuser*, Beardsley's personality was an enigma, which only Symons's later article could, to some extent, resolve. That solution was nevertheless reached only by means of a particularly limited atomism, to be explained no doubt by the absence of any fundamental sympathy between the two editors of the *Savoy* (as may be gathered, indeed, from Beardsley's letters to his publisher, Leonard Smithers).

Symons's attitude seems in particular to have prevailed completely on *Under the Hill* (and we may confidently suppose that he took the same view of *Venus and Tannhäuser*): 'Taken literally, this fragment is hardly more than a piece of nonsense, and was hardly meant to be more than that.' Even Burdett, who excellently shows how, in view of the true decadence in taste and morals during the Victorian era, the so-called decadence of the Beardsley period was in fact an inevitable and healthy reaction, writes apropos of *Under the Hill* (he obviously had not read the unexpurgated version) that Beardsley 'is an instance of an author who is all technique and no humanity'.[5] Yet, in more perceptive fashion, Symons had written that 'it could never have been finished for it had never been really begun'. Is this not a suitable description of so many first works, where the future writer clumsily attempts to embrace the whole of his world and where the tentative character of his actual life is reflected?

How, then, are we to interpret this *Fête Galante* in which a puerile Venus and Tannhäuser settle on a Babylonian terrace to a supper as epic as that of Trimalchio, followed by a bacchanalia and a ballet worthy of the French *Régence* to the strains of a music which strongly reminds one of the *Prélude à l'Après-Midi d'un Faune*[6]—this work in which all influences are amalgamated; in which all the contrasts, beloved by this period, between decadence and barbarism are resolved, thanks to the brisk pace of a tale as gay and as irreverent as if it had been written by a Voltaire or a Crébillon fils?[7]

Let us first note that misunderstandings about its meaning are only too easily explained by the fragmentary state of the 'novel'. Such fragmentation has several causes.

First, the extreme outspokenness of the tale which made publication in its entirety impossible except for private circulation. Secondly, the difficulties met by Beardsley in his dealings with various publishers. What he used to call 'his own little variations on the Tannhäuser theme' was first to be published by Henry and Co., and later was announced by John Lane (a drawing meant to illustrate the text existing in both cases). Beardsley had only been the artistic editor of the *Yellow Book*, which was published by Lane, for a few months, when the trials and condemnation of Oscar Wilde occurred, to be followed by a wave of puritanism. Lane yielded to pressure exerted by *bien-pensant* circles which insisted on Beardsley's dismissal, partly because Beardsley's name was associated with Wilde's in the public mind since he had illustrated *Salome*, but chiefly because the representative quality of his art made him an obvious candidate for the part of scapegoat. Beardsley was naturally much depressed by this unexpected blow. Moreover, he was now compelled to change the title of his work and the names of his characters so that he could offer the book to another publisher without laying himself open to the risk of being sued. He did so, according to Symons, 'not quite willingly', and it is easy to see why. As one of his early drawings shows, the Tannhäuser-theme had long fascinated Beardsley. With the names altered the immediate significance of the parody was certain to be lost. The choice of Helen to replace Venus is by no means bad, probably indeed the only one possible, although it has the drawback of calling immediately to mind images of Paris and Faust.[8] But by whom could Tannhäuser himself be replaced? The manuscript, indeed, proves that no substitution was possible: the protagonist was nearly called the abbé Aubrey! The choice of the 'abbé', 'cet être indéfinissable qui n'est ni Ecclésiastique ni séculier' according to Voltaire, shows Beardsley's literary sensitivity to French literature: as Paul Léautaud, for example, has shown, this character is for many people the actual symbol of the eighteenth century. The final choice of name, Fanfreluche, was unfortunate, for, taken with the inevitable cuts in the text, the image remains of a futile character who reminds one all too readily of the most minor of *fin de siècle* productions. The new name also destroyed the original satirical tension, since the hero's name and his behaviour no longer contrast with one another, but remain simply pleonastic. And what can be said about the transformation of the necessary Priapusa into a contingent Mrs Marsuple?

Why did Beardsley discontinue his novel? After a year, the *Savoy* itself stopped appearing for lack of financial support. Then there were the difficulties naturally surrounding publication of a work which had been in part published already, and of which the greater part was certainly unpublishable. There was failing health.

But a deeper reason than any of those may be found in Beardsley's psychological evolution, which, as I hope to show, made him bring his story to a conclusion in his own life:[9] indeed most of his work can be viewed as an attempt to reach a satisfactory synthesis of his various tendencies.

It is interesting to notice that expurgation brings new devices: a way, for instance, of presenting events elliptically and with *non sequiturs*, which has analogues in the design and stylization of the drawings. Some of the censored material is introduced as seemingly erudite footnotes, a device Beardsley had probably come upon in that seventeenth- and eighteenth-century fiction he so relished. Interesting in themselves, such devices nonetheless merely increase the impression of mere artificiality left by *Under the Hill* and altogether break the brisk pace of the original version.

Someone who had been struck by the extraordinary images which people Beardsley's drawings once asked him whether he had fantastic visions. He allowed himself, Beardsley answered, only to have them on paper. But several things seem directly to contradict this. Each scene in *Venus and Tannhäuser* is first described with the fantastic precision which is Beardsley's hallmark; the tableaux then become animated and the story resumes its momentarily interrupted course. Settings and characters first come to the author as if they were petrified by a magic wand, and it is this first state which is illustrated. But all the details appearing in the drawings play a part in the story, which is a perfect literary equivalent. There exists, therefore, a vision which could be expressed as a story, as a drawing, or as both of these. The story is conceived as a string of scenes (chapters, in *Venus and Tannhäuser*), but conversely the drawings have a literary background. Beardsley had even the bold idea (as only someone so diversely gifted could have) of a chapter entirely consisting of drawings, as is shown by one of his letters to Smithers. There are some drawings illustrating scenes which were never written. At other times Beardsley announces drawings of which the literary transcription alone exists, such as the description of the game of *petits-chevaux* at the Dieppe casino, which Beardsley particularly liked and where he wrote the greatest part of his novel, or the description in *The Three Musicians* of the famous pianist (suggested by Liszt) day-dreaming in the fields, and of which there was a drawing, since, as Blanche records, destroyed.

This, and not only his artistic excellence, probably explains Beardsley's feeling of independence and his constant desire not to be considered a mere illustrator. He hoped an ingenious use of vocabulary might help him to escape such a limiting judgment: thus *Le Morte D'Arthur* is 'embellished'; *Salome* is 'pictured' and *The Rape of the Lock* 'embroidered' by his drawings. Beardsley's work had also been characterized from the outset by a curious distance between text and illustrations, which particularly exasperated the critics and the *bourgeoisie*. Beardsley and Henry Harland, the two editors of the *Yellow Book*, even thought of making this a principle and distinctive feature of their review, as is reported by Henry James in the account he gave of the call they paid on him in order to secure his contribution to the new publication.[10] But this distance does not occur when Beardsley illustrates his own works.

Forced to spend most of his time at home because of his health and artistic commitments, Beardsley wrote numerous letters of which the most interesting have been published in two collections. These are addressed respectively to André Raffalovich, the poet and novelist who converted him to Catholicism, and to Leonard Smithers, publisher of the *Savoy*, of *Venus and Tannhäuser* and of the last drawings.[11] On the cover of the first collection a cross; on the fly-leaf of the second, the sardonically smiling Beardsley woman: the contrast is almost too obvious. A knowledge of these letters is essential for a proper understanding of the Beardsley personality.

Smithers, an 'unfrocked' solicitor, addicted to drink and drugs, and well acquainted with most excesses, had, nonetheless, taste, business-sense, and courage.[12] At a moment when no one dared pronounce the name Wilde, it was Smithers who published the *Ballad of Reading Gaol*. When Lane summarily dismissed Beardsley, it was Smithers who offered Beardsley a regular income for life in exchange for anything he might produce (Wilde calls him 'Smithers, the publisher and owner of Aubrey'). Smithers always tried to fulfil this engagement, so far as the irregularity of his finances allowed. He was eventually to specialize in luxury editions and erotica and was thus quite prepared to accept what other publishers might have rejected outright. Several witnesses (Rothenstein in particular) testify that it was probably thanks to Smithers that projects which would have remained quite unrealized became for Beardsley a reality, and that Smithers opened to him certain fields of life and art which fascinated because they seemed to hold out to Beardsley not the pleasure merely but the secret of being. In a letter that Beardsley wrote to Smithers at a time when living in London was already out of the question because of his health, Beardsley describes the various symptoms which have delayed his work, and particularly a tooth which had been extracted. Having playfully drawn it in order to show its size, and Smithers having made a joke which can be guessed, Beardsley answered, anticipating the Freudian hyperbole: 'Yes, *everything* is phallic-shaped.'[13]

Raffalovich, whom Beardsley met at about the same time, also opened up a new field to him, and one with which he was certainly less familiar. Raffalovich was in many ways ideally suited to the role of Beardsley's mentor (his help was material, no less than spiritual and psychological, for, along with Smithers, he provided Beardsley with financial support. As Wilde put it, he 'financed B. to any extent'). Then Raffalovich was French-speaking and had been educated in France, a man of letters himself, a converted Jew, and a friend of John Gray (1866–1934), whose *Silverpoints* of 1893 had contained some of the first translations into English of French *symboliste* verse.[14] Finally, Raffalovich seems to have possessed a combination of broad-mindedness and moral preoccupations that Beardsley much needed at that particular moment. Beardsley's letters to Raffalovich are first addressed as a joke to 'my dear Mentor' and signed 'Télémaque', and contain answers to exhortations which cannot be read at present (if they have survived). One can to a certain extent guess at their content from the readings which Beardsley was advised to make and which he punctually carried out: histories of the Church and of various Orders, lives of saints and books by them. The charm and the energy of a St Teresa obviously impressed Beardsley, as well as the patience and solicitude of his mentor. But he felt prayer to be uncongenial to him, and described himself as 'a sorry beadsman'. In a letter to Raffalovich, he evokes the coming of Christmas with emotion; but writes to Smithers about the Christmas card of the Virgin and Child which he had drawn for the *Savoy*, as 'a silly pseudo thing' which could only be enhanced by a faulty reproduction.

Beardsley, after being wronged by life had been granted what he craved: on one hand money and glory; on the other a spiritual nourishment which he had not been able to find in hedonism. The first impression of the two sets of letters—a living example of the 'parallelism' dear to Verlaine and here experienced with less insight, is of a certain amusement felt by Beardsley in seeing himself as the possible prize of competing mentors (though Smithers was exempt from any proselytism). Having illustrated the *Lysistrata* with a series suitable only for private circulation and which he was to implore Smithers to destroy in that famous last letter, but which he himself could only see as 'in a way the best thing I have ever done', Beardsley first announced the fact to Raffalovich, and then informed Smithers of his having done so. He then awaited reactions. Reading Cazotte, Beardsley was struck with the notion of a tale, *The Celestial Lovers*; and teased Raffalovich, who had alluded to a sermon on guardian angels he had heard preached. It was, Beardsley wrote, 'a strangely suggestive subject'.

At first, it is with Smithers that one feels him to be most at ease. That cynical gaiety, the keynote of their relationship, better suited his current fascination with the French eighteenth century. When Beardsley writes to Raffalovich at this time, he believes himself, so it seems, obliged to adopt a more sober, pensive tone. His very vocabulary changes and other, earlier letters of his (no less than certain stylistic devices in the *Venus and Tannhäuser*) show that the new vocabulary harks back to that which he had used as a child. A mechanism of defence, and one that is not unusual with the Decadents (from Walter Pater on). Slowly this state of things alters, but it is only through many hesitations that we can distinguish a psychological progression. The devotion of his friend wrests from Beardsley, a month before being received into the Church, this exclamation of thankfulness: 'Do not think, my dear XXX, that your kind words fall on such barren ground. However I am not a very fruitful soil; I only melt to harden again.' He dares confess to him this state of mind: 'I am quite paralysed with fear. I have told no one of it'—the fear being less of death itself than of not being given the chance of realizing all his potentialities.

And, when finally converted, his was the very movement of Tannhäuser fleeing from all sorrows and vicissitudes of earthly life, first under the mountain, at last into repentance:

> I feel now, dear XXX, like someone who has been standing waiting on the doorstep of a house upon a cold day, and who cannot make up his mind to knock for a long time. At last the door is thrown open and all the warmth of kind hospitality makes glad the frozen traveller. . . . I gave myself up entirely, utterly to feelings of happiness.

Some people have shown surprise at the broadmindedness of this mentor. Raffalovich helped his catechumen to explore the literature of the eighteenth century, introducing him, for example, to the work of Restif de la Bretonne. Reacting enthusiastically to the *Liaisons Dangereuses*, which he began to illustrate, Beardsley wished to know something of Laclos. Of his own accord, Raffalovich copied and sent to him an article out of the *Biographie Universelle*. Beardsley freely discussed with his mentor the *Thousand and One Nights*, and Casanova's *Memoirs*—'that great and appalling work'. The aspect of religion to which Beardsley was introduced was, therefore, the broadly humanistic tradition associated with the Jesuits. And, in fact, most of his religious acquaintances in England first, and later in France, were Jesuits.

It is all the more striking to recognize his undoubted Jansenist leanings; religion to him could only mean repentance and mutilation. He knew the history of Racine, whose portrait was constantly in front of him in the room at Mentone where he died. Even at the height of his incredulity, when he was writing his novel at Dieppe and when his conversation left Symons and Blanche speechless, Blanche recounts that Beardsley recited the choruses out of *Esther* and *Athalie* like prayers. He read Sainte-Beuve's *Port-Royal* and 'a Port-Royalist version of St. Augustine's *Confessions*', probably that by Arnauld d'Andilly. About this, he declares himself 'quite astonished at what [St Augustine] says about beauty and the use of the eyes'.

To his correspondent who told him about a Jesuit who enjoyed some reputation as a painter, he answered with this significant sentence: 'But what a stumbling block such pious men must find in the practice of their art.' And finally, just before he was received into the Church in February 1897, he wrote what seems to be his spiritual testament:

> Heine certainly cuts a poor figure beside Pascal. If Heine is the great warning, Pascal is the great example to all artists and thinkers. He understood that to become a Christian the man of letters must sacrifice his gifts, just as Magdalen must sacrifice her beauty.

Such opinions suggest a deeper explanation of Beardsley's conversion, which is generally explained simply by a fear of death. There was in him an undoubted masochistic streak, which is conspicuous in his attitude towards his illness and the certainty of an early and possibly sudden death. Symons has commented on his 'astonishing tranquillity of nerves' in spite of constant ill-health, a tranquillity which is not entirely accounted for by his very real courage and humour, but is a typical feature of masochism: while suffering occurs, guilt is assuaged. This can be felt in many of the descriptions Beardsley gives of his state of health in his letters, but naturally alternates with states of depression. Thus, if religion appealed to him, it is to a large extent because his own interpretation of it guaranteed that it brought him psychological security.

He also appears obsessed at this time with the theme of the unworthy sinner and with that of penitence. After having read the *Confessions*, he asked whether there existed a good biography of Mary Magdalen or a good study on her, and read those by Lacordaire and by the Père Valmy. One finds among his early drawings one on *La Faute de l'Abbé Mouret*, another on Tannhäuser, a *Litanie de Marie-Madeleine*. All these characters were to be treated later in quite another manner with the title *The Repentance of Mrs XXX*. His taste for *La Dame aux Camélias* intrigued Symons, who nevertheless took him to Puys to visit Dumas fils. According to Symons, the unlikely character of the theme did not escape Beardsley; but what is *La Dame aux Camélias* if not an occasion to dream about total sacrifice, not only that of happiness, but that of dignity also? The psychological and social objections to such a work would have been irrelevant for Beardsley's purpose, since he obviously kept only the echoes which could be integrated to his world. Similarly, the story of Tannhäuser is essentially that of a sinner whose crimes are so great that the Pope thought himself bound to refuse absolution, and who might be saved only as an example of divine mercy. The irony in *Venus and Tannhäuser* is doubtless an indication that Beardsley wished to make fun of an all too popular theme; but unquestionably he also felt that he was much more suited to be the hero of the story than many of those who had chosen it before him. It can thus be seen how deep in fact were the roots of this supposedly meaningless tale.

The attraction of the Tannhäuser theme is due to its two facets. Among those who had been drawn to it, let us mention only Wagner, probably the immediate source of Beardsley's inspiration, who knew his music intimately as well as his prose works; Baudelaire whose article cheered the composer after the failure of his opera in Paris (1861); Swinburne, to whom Baudelaire had dedicated his article and who had written on the same subject his poem *Laus Veneris*.

The story as it appears in Wagner's opera runs in this way: Tannhäuser who had sought refuge in the Venusberg from the sorrows of life tires one day of an existence entirely devoted to pleasure and goes back to the court of the Landgrave of the Wartburg, the company of the other Minnesingers and the love of Elizabeth. A singing contest is announced; everyone hopes that Tannhäuser will triumph as of old and obtain the hand of the girl whose heart he has already conquered. The theme is announced: what is Love? By what signs does one recognize it? Listening then to Wolfram von Eschenbach glorifying pure love,—the emanation of the heavens, the fountain that one does not dare to sully,—then to Walther, then to Biterolf who can only see damnation in 'cheap delights', Tannhäuser, who has everything to lose in revealing his secret, cannot help making an impassioned profession of faith: none of those present really understands what love is; its sign is pleasure. Let them go under the mountain, to the school of Venus! In this way he fulfils the promise of always remaining her champion, which had been his sole answer to the imprecations of the forsaken goddess. This is also the only time when an attempt is made to give a complete view of love and to explain how it was that Elizabeth herself had previously chosen Tannhäuser from among all others because she had sensed in him something more genuine. But at the sight of the murderous indignation of the knights and of Elizabeth's sorrow, Tannhäuser does not dare to maintain this attitude and finds himself forced into the artificial and in fact perverted alternative of angelism and bestiality, the alternative that can be observed in Beardsley himself. Tannhäuser's despairing return to the mountain in the medieval legend, and his eternal ignorance of the miracle of the flowering stick are transformed by Wagner into what amounts to the final defeat of the Venusberg.

What was to be the meaning of the completed *Venus and*

*Tannhäuser*? A long sub-title imitated from those of the seventeenth and eighteenth centuries gives the synopsis of the story:

> The story of *Venus and Tannhäuser*, in which is set forth an exact Account of the Manner of State held by madam Venus, Goddess and Meretrix, under the famous Horselberg, and containing the Adventures of Tannhäuser in that place, his journeying to Rome, and return to the loving mountain.

Was it to have been a parody where nothing would have differed from the original except in a very *fin de siècle* irony? That would have been in keeping with the historicism typical of the nineteenth century, with its gothic railway stations and its *Moralités Légendaires*. Beardsley, according to Blanche, did not know the *Moralités*. It is interesting to note that among several other Wagnerian themes Laforgue did not choose that of Tannhäuser. And it is difficult to believe that Beardsley could have been ignorant of the writer who employed the Pierrot theme so relentlessly, and specialized in the mischievous tone by which the Decadents expressed their ambivalent feelings towards the writers of previous ages, those who could afford to write without their tongue in their cheek.

Beardsley had also thought for a long time of writing a parody of *Rhinegold*, which he called in *Under the Hill* 'Wagner's brilliant comedy'. There is, in any case, in *Venus and Tannhäuser* a triple desecration: religious, medieval, and Wagnerian, a desecration of all that he once revered, although whether this is genuine or whether it expresses a liberation is difficult to say. Beardsley's title has no mention of Elizabeth, no mention either of the final absolution. Does this indicate a return to the medieval ending, or an ironical twist in the tail, the return to the Venusberg being welcomed by Tannhäuser? A curious episode which concerns one of Beardsley's drawings may perhaps help us here. When Beardsley's first publisher, J. M. Dent, gave the artist permission to reprint some of his early drawings, Beardsley thanked Dent by sending him one made for the part of the tale which was never written: *The Return of Tannhäuser to the Venusberg*—a new version of an old drawing. One can see the hero, the living image of repentance, torn by the thorns which separate him from the mountain and holding towards it pathetically lean hands. Dent, very touched by this new and unexpected atitude, and not having read the title well, thought this was Tannhäuser returning not *to* but *from* the Venusberg, and advised Beardsley to make use of his recent experience of suffering to illustrate *Pilgrim's Progress*. This evoked mixed feelings in his sarcastic correspondent.

Before going to Paris, and then on to Mentone in search of the sun, Beardsley stopped at Dieppe for a while in 1897. He wrote to Raffalovich that memories from 1895 kept him company. These memories were of two kinds: 'Do you want any erotic drawings?' he wrote to Smithers. But he asked Raffalovich for Wagner's prose works as well as for a study on Wolfram von Eschenbach (which perhaps indicates that the treatment given by Wagner to the Tannhäuser theme did not seem satisfactory to him in point of motivations). As often happens, it seems that in Beardsley's case self-dramatization acted as a catalyst to bring forth a different but no less real personality: in the same way as he pictured himself in various period costumes, he saw himself now as Tannhäuser, now as Eschenbach, the author of *Parsifal*.

Quite apart from psychological considerations, given the dual nature of inspiration for Beardsley, it is evident that an examination of technique is of first importance in order to determine the true significance of the themes and of his work as a whole.

However short, Beardsley's career was nevertheless divided into several distinct phases which reflected transient interests; as Ross said in an excellent phrase: 'Critical appreciation under his pen meant creation.' It was at first the imitation of Burne-Jones which took on a new zest after Beardsley's meeting with the painter himself (July 1891), and left in all his work the Pre-Raphaelite pout, and an emphasis on design.[15] Then, the illustrations for *Le Morte D'Arthur* (1892), a commissioned work for which Beardsley assimilated overnight an idiom which for the most part remained foreign to him (though less, it seems, than is commonly stated). In doing so, he beat Morris and his disciples at their own game, but he had not the strength to finish the work in spite of his contract. By then he was already wholly absorbed in the next phase, which flowered in the illustrations to *Salome* (1894). It was mainly from Japanese prints (the influence crept into one at least of the *Morte D'Arthur* illustrations) and Greek Vase paintings that inspiration now came. Such influence was combined with recent technical acquisitions and a new interest in contemporary life in the next phase, that of the *Yellow Book*

(1894–1895), the Bible of the Decadence. What followed was a passion for the eighteenth century and the illustrations for the *Rape of the Lock* and of his own *Under the Hill* in the *Savoy* (1896), although, as we shall note, there is an important distinction between the two. Three months before his death, Beardsley felt in full possession of his art, and was more vibrant than ever with creative energy. He decided to illustrate *Volpone* (he often changed interests and plans in those last months) and wrote to Smithers: 'It will be an *important* book . . . I have definitely left behind all my former methods.' New indeed, this latest manner seemed to break with the most pronounced characteristic of all his earlier manners: stylization; it was founded on a fresh and serious study of reality. Beardsley at Mentone asked for books on perspective and anatomy, and announced a list of drawings for *Volpone*. Of these he was able to finish only ten or so, which suggest at least something of this new orientation.

It is essential, therefore, to realize that the typical rhythm in Beardsley is to become totally engrossed in a particular atmosphere, expressed in a definite technique, and then to abandon it completely. It would be rash indeed to attempt to confine Beardsley, as some have done, within a single phase and its supposed implications. Yet one must insist that *Venus and Tannhäuser* was written at the height of Beardsley's fad for the eighteenth century, and the French eighteenth century in particular, with all its refinements and vanities, its art of enjoyment, its gay corruptions, its passion for opera and ballet. The keynote of text and illustration is profusion. The most typical feature, frequent enumerations in the text (of decorations, shoes, masks, names, and habits, etc.), reflects an attempt to grasp reality by the means of saturation and excess. The illustrations of the *Rape of the Lock* had contrived to give an impression of spaciousness, derived mainly from variation in thickness of line, equivalent to musical *pianissimo* and *fortissimo*. In *Under the Hill*, Beardsley goes knowingly too far: the monstrous proliferation of rococo detail devours space, stifles the characters, rapturously exists for its own sake. There remain none now of the empty spaces which so mysteriously acquired colour and texture by juxtaposition; characters and planes are now only distinguished by a close weave of hatching and stipple. In the opposition, so charmed for Beardsley, between the beautiful and the grotesque, it is the latter which triumphs here, characterized as always by inexhaustible licence, where only surprise and ingenuity are the law, and where more than in any other realm of art the sole rule is to please, and success establishes *a posteriori* the canon. It is Carnival, where everything is allowed.

The *Ancien Régime* and its myth seem specially designed to slake this transient thirst for pure decoration, even at the expense of meaning. It is the age of senseless survivals, of pompous spellings, of sumptuous names, and complicated etiquette. There is a ceremonial under the hill, where Venus is a queen even more than a goddess. In the nostalgic dedication to an imaginary cardinal which opens the book, Beardsley, typically in half-earnest, assumes the subservient part of the artist of those days, very different from the priestly prestige which had been acquired since the days of Romanticism. This dedication, moreover, reminds us that there had been an aesthetic conversion to catholicism before a religious one. It is easy to see what in that religion attracted Decadents, and Beardsley in his present state of mind more than anyone else. It is the religion of rites and traditions, of fossils and relics, of symbols as powerful as realities. Like an aristocracy, it has its order of precedence and does not neglect the prestigious aspect of exoticism, when a halo of titles *in partibus* enhances the glory of real titles. It welcomes all extremes, and knows how to reconcile effusion and hierarchy like gold and pastel shades in an Italian primitive painting. Abounding in subtle exegeses, it does not however despise absurd hagiographic episodes like that of St Wilgeforte's beard which is worn by one of the heroines of the bacchanalia in *Venus and Tannhäuser*. (It is noticeable incidentally, that *Venus and Tannhäuser* is much more anti-clerical than *Under the Hill.*)

One has to take all this into account when one examines certain permanent themes in Beardsley's work. For it contains a real 'comédie humaine' (a repertoire of which can be seen, for instance, in the drawing entitled 'The Toilet of Helen'), and it is precisely Beardsley's fidelity to certain types, in spite of their unsuitability for some commissioned work, which could expose him to the charge of perversity.[16] The most striking are two, whose physical interpretation can vary slightly but whose significance remains the same.

After the first phase in which his masters were Burne-Jones,

Mantegna, and Botticelli, Beardsley did not try any longer to represent Beauty. Even to that point, it had not been pure beauty, but a beauty permeated with history, literature, and feeling. The ideal he painted, so difficult to express without mawkishness, is, grace, 'loveliness', 'irritating' because it 'can never be entirely comprehended or ever enjoyed to the utmost'. It can be seen in Venus, in the singer in *The Three Musicians*, in the princess of the *Ballad of the Barber* 'as lyrical and sweet as one of Schubert's melodies'. In front of this image of purity we find the entirely corrupt characters, often at the same time inhibited and full of sadistic obsessions. To render their psychological complexity, Beardsley's art, which consists essentially of lyrical lines, endeavours to reach the particular: stippling, a veritable uniform, attempts to indicate on their faces blemishes and wrinkles. They are the Barber, Priapusa, or that curious personage in the drawing significantly chosen by the artist for his own book plate (and later adopted by Herbert Pollitt), laden with books, who does not dare to look directly at a buxom naked lady. This latter type must not be confused with what could be called Beardsley's *roués*, his Laclos, his Messalina, his Valmont, his Herodias, august monsters who carry their heads high and whom the author has endowed with a robust dignity.

One image seems to have held a perpetual attraction for Beardsley. It is that of the 'toilette' scenes, which he has interpreted in all his successive manners. These are nearly always characterized by the contrast between the pure and the corrupt, which gives them their well-known aspect of a Black Mass. Here, for instance, is Venus sitting at a dressing-table on which are piled candles, flowers, perfumes, and fashionable books. (It will be remembered that candles exerted a fascination on Beardsley; he had intentionally achieved among gossip writers the reputation of being able to work only by their light:[17] thus imagery associates, safest of guides where artists are concerned, work and pleasure!) By an assimilation which recalls eighteenth-century erotic vocabulary, the dressing-table becomes an altar on which is accomplished a strange ceremony. Beauty, the equivocal substitute of the ultimate good, passively appears as a victim on whom the desires of all converge and who offers a strong contrast with the motley crowd which surrounds her. She abandons herself to the care of the officiant, one of the corrupt, but whose experience gives an impression of security because it suggests a bottomless and properly maternal indulgence. Both live together in a symbiotic relationship which seems obscurely to express the fundamental ambiguity of life; which is at the same time experience (and therefore corruption or qualified morals at least) and ideal, faceless depth and brilliant surface.

After the angelism of the first drawings, and perhaps in reaction to the hard labour of the *Morte D'Arthur*, sadistic fantasies seem briefly to have fascinated Beardsley.

Reading Wilde's *Salome* (from which he soon felt remote enough to begin scattering his illustrations of that work with caricatures of its author),[18] Beardsley was first moved by the climax of the drama, entirely of Wilde's invention, where Salome proudly claims all responsibility for her behaviour and, seizing Iokanaan's head triumphantly, cries out 'J'ai baisé ta bouche, Iokanaan, j'ai baisé ta bouche.' Of his own accord, Beardsley illustrated this scene with a drawing which appeared in the *Studio* (April 1893) and brought him the commission for the whole work.

Sadistic also is the poem of the *Barber*, which Beardsley illustrated with a 'toilette' scene and which shows very well that for him sadism was not sought out for its own sake as the extreme form of sensation, but on the contrary adopted when for some reason normal reactions were impossible.[19] Sadism is significantly absent from *Venus and Tannhäuser*, where the whole point is to suppress all such taboos. Beardsley sent his ballad to Smithers for publication in the *Savoy*, but Symons, the literary editor, seems to have criticized it. Beardsley then, with a characteristic sense of insecurity as man of letters, begged Smithers to publish the ballad under a pseudonym (and in that case, he facetiously asked, what about 'Symons'?). But in a postscript which he felt compelled to write he declared that he reserved his opinion, and that after all his ballad seemed to him 'rather interesting'. Another letter tells us that the poem did not stop there, and that there was a spirited post-mortem of the Princess, but this sounds rather like one of the outrageous jokes which found their way into *Venus and Tannhäuser*.

Other works represent the triumph of mental equilibrium. It is that of happiness normally obtained in the poem of *The Three Musicians*; but it is significantly obtained as a defiance of the moralists personified by the prudish English tourist, who 'sent up a prayer for France'. For this takes place in France, the only country according to Beardsley which knew how to achieve happiness. Many French words in *Venus and Tannhäuser* show to what an extent his sensibility had been fashioned by his readings in French literature which ranged widely.[20] The equilibrium is more scabrous in the novel—a free interpretation of Rabelais's *Abbaye de Thélème*—where the spiritual place still is France, of the Regency period, and in which the question is to integrate all the sexual deviations (with a completeness in cataloguing which cannot always be carried out with an entirely straight face). The two extremes, therefore, can be seen to tend towards each other and meet half way, with, if necessary, a little hypocrisy, so as to try and dissolve a painful opposition into blissful identity. The pure become less childlike than childish. Beardsley's Tannhäuser is not a dandy but a fop, whose nostalgia of the earth gives way to a hundred trivial preoccupations. His Venus is a universal prostitute without being divested of the radiant sovereignty which characterizes her in the drawing *Venus between Terminal Gods*. She is the type of 'toilette' heroine, who knows all about corruption but lends to it her smiling complicity. Conversely, the main feature of corruption here is its reassuring aspect, due to its limitless experience. For the real divinity of the Venusberg is not Venus; it is Priapus, or, rather, a significantly feminine Priapusa. A tutelary personage, at the same time mother and procuress, she intrudes in all the lovers' activities, rejoicing in these incarnations without which she cannot really exist. And vice, thus tamed, becomes as venerable as Erda or the Mothers in the second *Faust*. This character as well as the drawings made to illustrate the first unexpurgated translation of *Lysistrata* (and, in another mood, the illustration of *Ave Atque Vale*) show that through the French 'libertine' tradition it is in fact the spirit of Paganism that Beardsley was trying to achieve both in his art and in his life. MacColl very rightly calls *Venus and Tannhäuser* 'a Lucian-like extravaganza'.[21]

Finally, the 'voyeur' tourist is also present implicitly: this is what the reader is forced to become, since he is constantly needled by the challenges of the author to follow him if he dares. For this is not a novel, it is a tale where the teller ceaselessly watches the reaction of the hearer. Recognition of this fact allows us to avoid certain pitfalls of interpretation. We read for instance in Holbrook Jackson's book[22] that 'there are passages which read like romanticized excerpts from the *Psychopathia Sexualis* of Krafft-Ebing', and Mario Praz, the only commentator who bothered to give a brief thematic analysis of one of Beardsley's literary works (the *Barber*) but who had not read *Venus and Tannhäuser*, quoted this sentence which he probably thought highly representative of the work as a whole.[23] That is true enough, if we recall the undoubted interest Beardsley found in eroticism and his obvious desire to be exhaustive, but we must be careful to notice that *Venus and Tannhäuser* gives not the least impression of fantasies thrown indiscriminately on paper. The *libertinage* is there, but held in a hand of iron. There is reason to think that it is precisely such control that Beardsley admired so much about the *Liaisons Dangereuses*, as is shown by the interview he gave to the *Idler*,[24] in which he says that the illustrations he was preparing for the book would be 'not at all *galant* but severe and full of restraint'. Detachment, humour, and a Voltairean irony (he greatly enjoyed Voltaire's *La Pucelle*) play a great part in his book, as well as changes in tone like those found in Laforgue, and without their manic vulgarity. And there can be felt through such changes the mixture of admiration and compassion at the sight of the infinite variety of human desires which is also found in a Brantôme, a Restif, or a Sade. But a phrase of modern psychology, although inelegant, can probably best account for the work; it describes the child as a 'polymorphous pervert', and indeed the impression one derives from *Venus and Tannhäuser* is that love is a marvellous game, full of infinite possibilities, and suited to adults as well as to children. Since, however, a return to childhood can only be unsatisfactory and hypocritical, a malaise is sometimes felt in the novel where everything is not idealized. Unspeakable laughter, jokes, and gestures represent an absolute evil, a Manichaeanism which no synthesis can assimilate and which makes the author impotently wonder. That insistent question of the precise satirical scope of Beardsley's work requires a positive, if qualified answer.

*Venus and Tannhäuser* is then a tale told by a voice, suave, singing, and with analogies even to the line in Beardsley's drawings. To declare, as does Symons, that 'every sentence' is 'meditated over, written for its own sake, and left to find its way in its own paragraph', atomized, amounts merely to parading one's own lack of ear. Like the drawings, the novel is full of hidden ironies and curious *double-entendres*, and like them derives most of its charms from a double contrast: that between the stylization and a selective and sensitive realism which reaches the essence of the thing depicted, and that between the abundance of the details and the precision of the pattern, as in those cadenzas by which the virtuoso demonstrates not only his ingenuity but also his control. Already in 1891, Beardsley was writing to A. W. King, his former headmaster:

> I should like to write something somewhere on the question of *line* and line drawing. How badly the importance of outline is understood, even by some of the best *painters*! It is this sense of the harmony of *lines* which makes the superiority of the old masters over the moderns, who seem to believe that harmony in colours is the only thing which matters.

One can only suppose that those who, like Blanche (fascinated by the contemporary fashion which Beardsley so consciously opposed) refuse Beardsley's right to be a complete artist because he did not use colour, see Chopin, according to the same reasoning, not as a composer, but as a pianist.

The technique of *Venus and Tannhäuser* has a triple function. It helps to charm, to divert the reader; but, on the other hand, it helps also, like Nessus' shirt, to torment him at leisure. More profoundly, it allows the author to unify what must seem the ill-assorted elements of the work; to marry, in Baudelarian terms, the 'spleen' to the 'ideal'. And this ideal is a world of fantasy and evasion, with the specific 'decadent' nostalgia for the morning and virginal things. It is yet another version of pastoral: dream of innocence, of the Golden Age; lost paradise, vast enough, though, to contain all aberrations; but, strangely, giving an impression of artless simplicity, which is expressed, so Beardsley says, by 'a perfect fifth'. That it should exert such a powerful influence is surely an indication that the attempted synthesis was unsuccessful. These pastoral landscapes, drenched in light, are to be found nowhere, like those, drowned in elemental gold, of Claude, whom Beardsley admired so much; or at most, as in the *Three Musicians*, in a France conceived as inaccessible Arcadia. It is only by keeping reality at arms length that Beardsley can surrender to lyricism. Beerbohm had felt this, since he wrote in a perceptive obituary article (in the *Idler*, May 1898) that Beardsley 'enjoyed life but was never wholly of it'. For this is how we must interpret an otherwise apparently quite gratuitous episode, that of the refined and mythological unicorn, Adolphe, Venus' favourite. This is the only character in the novel whose behaviour expresses feelings and not the physiological whim of the minute; but his animal form forbids him any direct contact with his divine mistress, by whom he daily fears to be abandoned. It is in Adolphe, rather than in the paltry Tannhäuser, that we find the symbol of the artist. The significance of this episode is confirmed by the allusion to St Rose of Lima's legend in *Under the Hill*, she, who had taken a vow of chastity and to whom on her wedding day the Virgin (significantly coming out of a painting, art in this manner rescuing the dreamer when reality becomes too pressing) came to assume her into heaven. According to his own testimony, Beardsley found some particular charm in the drawing (quite one of his best) which he made to illustrate this episode. He seems to have been fascinated by the pattern of seclusion from the world for the sake of a divine partner (the pattern already of the Tannhäuser legend) and it is understandable why he should be so struck by Pascal's history and by the *Confessions* of St Augustine with their intensly personal, 'I and Thou' relationship with God.

This flight before life is actually conspicuous in the tale in a sense more profound than that expressed by the ostensible flight 'under the hill' (granting all the Freudian implications of that) and reveals itself by a continual game of hide-and-seek, a movement to and fro between life on the one hand, and on the other art, artifice, books, civilizations. Just this laid Beardsley open to the charge of decadence; recent studies allow us as easily to term it 'Baroque'.[25] We find the quality evident enough in drawings, in the illustrations to *Salome*, for example, the way Beardsley has of ignoring perspective to a marked degree, more so than it is ignored in, say, Far Eastern art; of cancelling the distinction between drawing and frame, leading the imagination astray by prolonging hair in the flame of a candle, scattering all over some realistic shape motifs of pure decoration. Elsewhere, this ambiguity occurs in the subject: a lady plays the piano in a meadow, another sits on a rearing horse in front of a theatre curtain. In the Venusberg, where all-powerful Priapusa is a *fardeuse*, smart people have their adornments painted on their skins and play with fans made of live moths. One finds there a sort of Balzacian 'concurrence à l'état-civil' to the second power, in the matter of names, showing that the experience of life is constantly born from the experience of books: the plants there are 'unknown to Mentzelius', Venus is 'not at all like the lady in Lemprière'. One is at first surprised to hear that Beardsley did not like *A Rebours*. This is doubtless because of the coldness emanating from Huysmans' learned lists, for his book has something deliberate about it, while Beardsley's is the catalogue of all he so passionately relished.

There is in the tale yet another episode whose meaning is not at first very discernible but which becomes clear in view of our previous arguments. It has the beauty and the typical features of Rimbaud's *Illuminations*, and its mysterious character shows the profoundly phantasmagoric origin of much of *Venus and Tannhäuser*. It is reprinted in *Under the Hill* with the title *The Woods of Auffray* (Auffay, not Auffray, is situated near Dieppe) and tells about 'a still argent lake—a reticent, romantic water that must have held the subtlest fish that ever were' and of 'its unruffled calm, its deathly reserve', and ends with this astonishing sentence: 'Perhaps the lake was only painted, after all. He had seen things like it at the theatre.'[26] What was elsewhere the pleasant charm of reverie becomes here the narcotic attraction of nirvâna. The fascinating and ever changing waters of the pond which so attract and frighten Tannhäuser at the same time, while undoubtedly having a sexual significance, symbolize an exile still more radical than Tannhäuser's flight to the Venusberg, and betray a taste for nothingness.

And indeed death was soon to bring a solution to this *difficulté d'être*. Symbolically it was preceded by the letter asking for the destruction of the *Lysistrata* drawings which had, not so long before, seemed to Beardsley the best things he had done. This jansenist recantation—identical with that of Tannhäuser in Wagner's opera—has been interpreted as a rejection of Decadence by a Decadent. This is untenable, for it is the obscenity that Beardsley regretted; and the epithet would have been better applied to *Venus and Tannhäuser*. But that decadent aspect of Beardsley's work had not been chosen from any superficial perversity: it corresponded to very deep exigencies. Applied to the Tannhäuser theme, it strikes a singularly deep note and makes us see, in this apparently disjointed work, the proof of a prolonged reflection on man, the plaything of pleasure, 'divertissement' and death.

## NOTES

[1] *Aubrey Beardsley*, London, 1898.

[2] It is reprinted in *Some Unknown Drawings of Aubrey Beardsley*, collected and annotated by R. A. Walker, London, 1923.

[3] In this article, *Under the Hill* refers to the work published in the *Savoy*, then in volume form by Lane in 1904; *Venus and Tannhäuser* to the volume published in 1907 by Smithers for private circulation. A few minor works must be added: a short story, 'The Story of a Confession Album', printed in *Tit-Bits*, XVII, No. 429, Jan. 4th, 1890, and an article on 'The Art of the Hoarding' written for *The New Review*, XI, July, 1894, and reprinted in A. E. Gallatin, *Aubrey Beardsley, Catalogue of Drawings and Bibliography*, New York, the Grolier Club, 1949, as well as in *A Beardsley Miscellany, selected and edited by* R. A. Walker, London, 1949. The latter also contains an unfinished poem, 'The Ivory Piece', a slightly different version of 'The Ballad of A Barber', and a prospectus for *Volpone*, written for the Smithers edition. The *Catalogue* of The *Gallatin Beardsley Collection in the Princeton University Library*, compiled by A. E. Gallatin and A. D. Wainwright, Princeton, New Jersey, 1952, mentions three pages of notes for a short story which was not written, 'The Celestial Lover', also alluded to in the letters to Raffalovich (see below). Gallatin in his *Bibliography* also states that 'a poem written at the age of 13, entitled "The Valiant" appeared in *Past and Present*, his school magazine', and that he wrote plays which he performed with his sister. Beardsley also wrote a farce, *A Brown Study*, which was performed at the Royal Pavilion, Brighton, in aid of some charity. He then started a comedy, *A Race for Wealth*, 'but got no further than writing the first act'. He also planned essays on Rousseau, George Sand, and others. In the letters he wrote, there are numerous references to literary plans, and to a translation of Juvenal's Sixth Satire, which he illustrated. Robert Ross (op. cit., p. 20) states that Beardsley began to write a play 'in collaboration with Mr. Brandon Thomas'. Osbert Burdett in *The Beardsley Period*, London, 1925, p. 195, mentions a poem, and William Rothenstein in *Men and Memories*, London, 1932, a dialogue, which he and Beardsley began to write. Mention must also be made of the short poetic text appended to the drawing 'The Death of Pierrot'.

[4] *Aubrey Beardsley*, London, 1909.

* *Propos de peintre. De David à Degas*, Paris, 1919. See also the Introduction to *Sous la Colline*, Paris, Floury, 1908 (a translation of *Under the Hill*).

[5] op. cit., p. 195.

[6] First performed in Paris on December 23rd, 1894. The date of the ballet starring Nijinsky is 1912. The influence of Beardsley on Art Nouveau has often been discussed, but that which his work, chiefly *Venus and Tannhäuser* (text and illustrations) and the drawings of the *Savoy* period, had on the first *Ballets Russes* seems to have gone largely unrecognized—except by their main creators, Diaghilev and Alexandre Benois. Yet, if one remembers the immensely stimulating effect these ballets had on Western art, it is well worth mentioning. Diaghilev, who had been keen to meet Beardsley at Dieppe in 1895 (see for instance *The Letters of Oscar Wilde*, London, 1962, pp. 733–4), organized in 1897 an exhibition of contemporary British art at St Petersburg, and requested from D. S. MacColl, in September 1898, an article on Beardsley for his recently-founded periodical *Mir Iskusstva* (*The World of Art*). The article appeared in Russian in 1900, in Nos 7 and 8 (an English translation was printed by R. A. Walker in *A Beardsley Miscellany*). Diaghilev shared with Beardsley a taste for a contrast between refinement and barbarity, for luxury, and, among musical and artistic works, for those expressive of a lyrical sensuality. He had also a particular liking

for Conder's work. As for Benois [speaking about his friends and himself], he wrote that 'the drawings of Beardsley and T. T. Heine . . . were . . . to have an important influence on our artistic creativeness' (*Reminiscences of the Russian Ballet*, London, 1941, p. 174. See also on this A. Haskell, *Diaghileff*, London, 1935, pp. 98–9 and 117, and Serge Lifar, *Serge de Diaghilev*, Editions du Rocher, Monaco, 1954, pp. 73, 75, 81). Benois's self-confessed infatuation with 'the elaborate splendour of the Court Festivals of the Rococo period' (op. cit., p. 350) is identical with that shown by Beardsley in his novel, and André Gide describes Benois's sets for *Le Pavillon d'Armide* (1909) in his article 'Les Représentations russes au Châtelet' (in *Nouveaux Prétextes*, Paris, Mercure de France, 1911, p. 316) as a 'décor d'un Louis XIV à peine retouché par Aubrey Beardsley'. But the spirit of Beardsley's work matters more here than narrowly technical influences, and could be absorbed all the more readily since Benois makes it clear that the *Mir Iskusstva* group were drawn to the ballet by the Wagnerian ideal of the *Gesamtkunstwerk*: 'It was no accident that what was afterwards known as the *Ballets Russes* was originally conceived not by the professionals of the dance, but by a circle of artists, linked together by the idea of Art as an entity. Everything followed from the common desire of several painters and musicians to see the fulfilment of the theatrical dreams which haunted them; but I emphasise again that there was nothing *specific* or *professional* in their dreams. On the contrary there was a burning craving for Art in general.' (op. cit., p. 371). If one remembers the place held by spectacles in Beardsley's novel, and his inexhaustible invention in the matter of costumes, one can say that, had he lived, he might have had a fruitful career as a designer and writer of libretti.

[7] This syncretism is typical of Beardsley, and of the period and another instance of it can be found in Salome's library. In the first version, it includes Zola's *La Terre*, Ibsen, *Les Fleurs du Mal*; in the second, Zola's *Nana* and *Les Fêtes Galantes*, the Marquis de Sade, *Manon Lescaut* and *The Golden Ass*.

[8] The new title, *Under the Hill*, was borrowed from the name of his friend More Adey's family home in Gloucestershire (cf. *The Letters of Oscar Wilde*, p. 533). The combination of a descent underground and of an eighteenth-century atmosphere of revels and sacrilege calls to mind the famous Hell-Fire Club, the members of which met 'under the hill' near the Dashwood mansion at High Wycombe, but there seems to be no evidence that Beardsley knew of this.

[9] Two attempts have been made to complete *Venus and Tannhäuser*. The *Catalogue* of the Princeton Gallatin Collection (op. cit., p. 33) mentions '*Venus und Tannhäuser. Eine romantische novelle von Aubrey Beardsley*. Hannover, Paul Steegemann Verlag (1920). Translated by Prokop Templin. Chapter 1 to 10 by Beardsley; 11 to 18 and epilogue by Franz Blei.' In an edition published by the Olympia Press, Paris, 1959, and called *Under the Hill*, the text of the latter work is combined with that of *Venus and Tannhäuser*, and completed by John Glassco. In the latter book, the contrast between the genuine psychological motivations apparent in the first part (Beardsley's) and the mechanical devices in the continuation admirably shows the difference between an erotic novel and a pornographic one.

[10] See *The Lesson of the Master, and Other Stories*, by Henry James, with the author's preface, The Chiltern Library, London, 1948.

[11] *Last Letters* of Aubrey Beardsley with an introductory note by the Reverend John Gray, London, 1904. One or two letters are addressed to Gray, who also played some part in Beardsley's conversion. MSS. of some of these letters are in the collection of the University of Reading. *Letters from Aubrey Beardsley to Leonard Smithers*, ed. with introduction and notes by R. A. Walker, London, London, 1937. Among letters reprinted *in toto* or in fragments, one should also

consult those written to King, a former Headmaster of Beardsley's in Arthur W. King, *An Aubrey Beardsley Lecture, with an Introduction and Notes by R. A. Walker and Some Unpublished Letters and Drawings*, London, 1924; those written to Ross, some fragments of which are quoted in various books; those written to Rothenstein, quoted in the latter's *Men and Memories*, and above all those to Beardsley's sister Mabel, with whom he showed complete frankness. Some of these are printed in the *Princeton University Library Chronicle*, XVI, No. 3, 1955.

[12] For Smithers, see *The Early Life and Vicissitudes of Jack Smithers*, London, 1939.

[13] Let us mention in this connection the drawing entitled 'A Footnote'—a psychological comment by way of a pun—which shows Beardsley as an artist (holding a brush), in fancy dress but with an invalid's slippers, and fatefully tied to the statue of a faun.

[14] On Gray and Raffalovich see Brocard Sewell, *Two Friends: John Gray and André Raffalovich*, Aylesford, Kent, 1963.

[15] Rothenstein tells the following anecdote: Burne-Jones's reputation being attacked by some young painters, Beardsley leaped to Burne-Jones's defence on the ground that, in the realm of design at least, the master was inimitable. Whereupon Rothenstein interjected: 'Imitable, Aubrey, surely, imitable!', delighting Beardsley. An influence on Beardsley which may not have been sufficiently emphasized is that of Puvis de Chavannes, whom Beardsley was eager to meet while on holiday in Paris in 1892. Puvis's painting *L'espérance*, now at the Louvre Réserve, has some similarities to Beardsley's *Mysterious Rose Garden*, sometimes referred to as *The Annunciation*.

[16] It is obvious that Beardsley himself thought of his work as a unity, and could use its fragments in various ways. A facsimile published in *A Beardsley Miscellany* shows that *The Ballad of a Barber* was to be Chapter IX of *Under the Hill*. The drawing 'L'Education sentimentale' was later cut in two, and the left-hand character renamed 'Mrs Marsuple'. Many characters can be recognized in several drawings, sometimes through several periods and some of them are described in his literary works.

[17] This unlikely story is disproved by Rothenstein, who gives one of the sanest accounts of Beardsley.

[18] The relations between Beardsley and Wilde, whom he had met at Burne-Jones's in 1891, rapidly deteriorated, the cause being unknown (there probably were several). Ricketts writes that 'there was from the first a covert antagonism between the two men' (*Oscar Wilde*, Recollections by Jean-Paul Raymond [an imaginary author] and Charles Ricketts, London, 1932, p. 52). Beardsley seems to have resented Wilde's patronage, and is the object of one of his rare cruel remarks: 'Dear Aubrey, he knows France so well! He has been to Dieppe, once.' As for Wilde, he had intensely disliked Beardsley's illustrations for *Salome* and told Ricketts: 'My Salome is a mystic . . . and dear Aubrey's designs are like the naughty scribbles a precocious schoolboy makes on the margin of his copy books.' What he could have thought of the caricatures of himself, we do not know.

One therefore understands Beardsley's bitterness over the unfair episode of the *Yellow Book* (a publication despised by Wilde, incidentally); his much publicized letter to Smithers (December 19th, 1897) about a new magazine to be called *The Peacock* to which Wilde was on no account to be allowed to contribute, is doubtless to be interpreted only in the light of the fear caused by his former dismissal, for he was said by Smithers to have been much struck by the *Ballad of Reading Gaol*, and there was talk of his having dinner with Wilde at Dieppe in 1897. This fear was not without foundation: Ricketts states (p. 38) that his own illustrations of Wilde's *Sphinx* suffered because they '[shared] in the disapproval with which most of the author's books had been received', and Beardsley could not afford to fall out of favour with the public, since the problem of a suitable means of publishing his work, once the *Savoy* had ceased appearing, was urgent (this is well shown by Haldane Macfall's otherwise prejudiced study *Aubrey Beardsley, The Man and His Work*, London, 1928).

There had been, on the other hand, a long-standing hostility between Wilde and Raffalovich for literary and personal reasons (see for instance *The Letters of Oscar Wilde*, pp. 173–5, about a difference of opinion concerning one of Raffalovich's books published in 1885), and Raffalovich did not shrink from attacking Wilde, even while the latter was in prison, for his influence and, according to him, bogus personality in his *Uranisme et unisexualité* (Paris, Masson, and Lyon, Storck, 1896)—Raffalovich was a sublimated homosexual. In a footnote on p. 249, for instance, he writes that 'M. Aubrey Beardsley, un jeune artiste du plus grand talent, a eu la malencontreuse chance d'illustrer cette *Salomé* médiocre de douze dessins que je déplore en les admirant—mais il n'a pas été dupe de cette publication'.

Mention may be made here of Robert Merle's *Oscar Wilde, ou la 'destinée' de l'homosexuel* (Paris, 1955) in which the author, in the middle of a subtle textual analysis of Wilde's works, gives in three astonishing pages (pp. 145–7) a 'psychoanalysis' of Beardsley which shows a complete ignorance of every aspect of his life, work, and character. Beardsley, mentioned for the first time in the book, is here taken as the type of the homosexual converted to catholicism, unable to adjust his life and his faith and taking refuge in 'an inexplicable illness' and death. After Beardsley's conversion, it is alleged, 'sa vie devient une lutte atroce où la folie, à chaque pas, semble le guêter [*sic*]'.

'En juin 97, deux mois après sa conversion, il se rend à Dieppe, *où il sait que Wilde se trouve* [author's italics], et, de là, il écrit à un ami qu'il se tient prêt à quitter la ville à tout moment, "*car il y a ici des gens assez déplaisants. . . . Et, si je reste, j'ai peur que des complications regrettables surgissent.*" Effectivement il rencontre Wilde plusieurs fois dans la rue et, à chaque fois, il s'enfuit "en courant". . . . Cette conduite est évidemment anormale. Si Aubrey Beardsley voulaits à ce point éviter Wilde, il pouvait l'éviter partout ailleurs qu'à Dieppe. . . . Rien, en fait, n'attachait Beardsley à Dieppe, même pas son art, puisque, depuis sa conversion, il ne peut plus dessiner. . . . Il trouve enfin le courage de s'enfuir pour de bon. Il s'établit a Menton.' On the question of the *Peacock*: 'Cela est fou, évidemment. Quel danger peut faire courir à son âme un article anonyme de Wilde dans une revue où il publie lui-même un dessin? En dépit des apparences, c'est évidemment lui-même et non pas Wilde, que le malheureux poursuit de cette persécution. Trois mois plus tard, il meurt enfin, à vingt-cinq ans, d'une maladie de poitrine.' The fact that Beardsley's illness was nothing new, that Wilde was not the only Englishman who liked Dieppe and spent some time there (indeed, it is to avoid people he knew while not being too far away that he chose to stay in near-by Berneval), that Beardsley (as has just been said) had many reasons for avoiding a public association with him and did not have to tear himself away, that, furthermore, he was writing to Raffalovich, Wilde's enemy, that Dieppe meant a lot to him, and that he never intended to spend more than a short time there on his way to Paris, that he went to Menton for his health, that he went on drawing to within a few days of his death, that Wilde could not write an anonymous article without immediately giving himself away by his style (the experiment was tried by other friends), that Beardsley would not have been an occasional contributor to the *Peacock*, but the editor: all this invalidates Merle's interpretation.

As for Beardsley being homosexual, it is on the contrary very striking that, although he lived among many writers and artists who were, it was never seriously maintained about him. What may have given rise to such speculations is that angelism and homosexuality have common psychological roots; these are evident, for instance, in Beardsley's drawing 'A Snare of Vintage', about a significant episode of Lucian's *True History*, which he chose to illustrate. Beardsley's attitude towards co-education on the other hand, is highly sensible (see his comment on the education of children in England in his letters to Raffalovich, February 1897).

[19] This character who

> . . . cut and coiffed, and shaved so well
> That all the world was at his feet
> . . . could with ease
> Curl wit into the dullest face.

and

> Yet with no pride his heart was moved;
> He was so modest in his ways!
> His daily task was all he loved,
> And now and then a little praise.

is entirely of Beardsley's invention. One recognizes in the poem a dramatization of his personality, tastes, and inhibitions.

[20] One may mention here that the mysterious quotation on the drawing 'Portrait of Himself' (*Yellow Book*, Vol. III) is the opening sentence of Cyrano de Bergerac's comedy *Le Pédant Joué* (1654). 'Bergerac' is also a character in *Venus and Tannhäuser*.

[21] The theme of the tenacity of the life-force is a major one in Art Nouveau, and can even become an interest less in nature than in 'biological prehistory', as in the numerous drawings by Beardsley which make use of the foetus-motif (see on this Robert Schmutzler, *Art Nouveau*, London, 1964).

[22] *The Eighteen-Nineties*, London, 1922.

[23] *The Romantic Agony*, London, 1933.

[24] The interview, given about Christmas 1896, appeared in March 1897.

[25] See, for instance, Jean Rousset, *La Litterature de l'âge baroque en France*, Corti, 1947.

[26] The complete passage is as follows: 'The landscape grew rather mysterious. The park, no longer troubled and adorned with figures, was full of grey echoes and mysterious sounds; the leaves whispered a little sadly, and there was a grotto that murmured like a voice haunting the silence of a deserted oracle. Tannhäuser became a little *triste*. In the distance, through the trees, gleamed a still argent lake—a reticent, romantic water that must have held the subtlest fish that ever were. Around its *marge* the trees and flags and fleurs de luce were unbreakably asleep. The Chevalier fell into a strange mood, as he looked at the lake. It seemed to him that the thing would speak, reveal some curious secret, say some beautiful word, if he should dare wrinkle its pale face with a pebble.

'"I should be frightened to do that, though," he said to himself. Then he wondered what might be upon the other side; other gardens, other gods? A thousand drowsy fancies passed through his brain. Sometimes the lake took fantastic shapes, or grew to twenty times its size, or shrunk into a miniature of itself, without ever once losing its unruffled calm, its deathly reserve. When the water increased, the Chevalier was very frightened, for he thought how huge the frogs must have become. He thought of their big eyes and monstrous wet feet, but when the water lessened, he laughed to himself, whilst thinking how tiny the frogs must have grown. He thought of their legs that must look thinner than spiders', and of their dwindled croaking that never could be heard. Perhaps the lake was only painted, after all. He had seen things like it at the theatre. Anyway, it was a wonderful lake, a beautiful lake, and he would love to bathe in it, but he was sure he would be drowned if he did.'

A tentative interpretation of these 'drowsy fancies' may be suggested: the waters being the symbol of sexuality—conceived here as a fountainhead not of pleasure but of meaning—, and Tannhäuser's desire to throw a pebble expressing a desire to establish communication, albeit by a hostile gesture. The size of the lake, now huge and full of frightening and repelling frogs, now puny and comical, can be explained both anatomically and as a representation of Beardsley's fluctuating attitude to a problem which loomed large in his mind. The following sentence suggests that the whole question may not have any reality except in Tannhäuser's imagination and fears, and is rather encouraging; but the episode ends with a statement of Tannhäuser's certainty of being drowned if he bathed in the lake. The presence of this lake in the Venusberg, as well as the situation of the episode near the end of the manuscript, as it stands, is a further indication that Beardsley had not resolved all his anxieties. The fact that this passage was enlarged and rewritten several times in MS. is a proof of the importance Beardsley attached to it (my thanks are due to Mr. Brian Reade, who enabled me to consult the MS. in the Department of Prints and Drawings of the Victoria and Albert Museum during the recent exhibition).

# WAGNER AND FORSTER: *PARSIFAL* AND *A ROOM WITH A VIEW*

*W. J. Lucas*

## I

YOU can't read very far in Forster's work without realizing the potency of music's hold over him. Not only does he employ it in various of his novels as something integral to his thematic concerns, he also writes about it with a particular affection: composers, he is never tired of suggesting, tell the truth in a manner and with a purity impossible to the literary or graphic artist; music, he says, 'seems to be more "real" than anything, and to survive when the rest of civilization decays'. If he were ever to establish a hierarchy of the arts, music undoubtedly would take pride of place.

His greatest love is reserved for Beethoven, and when Forster speaks of music it is to him that he most readily turns. But Beethoven is one among several composers, of whom none is more important than Wagner. Wagner, indeed, is a passion that begins with Forster's youth and continues at the very least until 1939 and the famous essay, *What I Believe*, in which he writes:

> The strong are so stupid. Consider their conduct for a moment in the Niebelung's Ring. The giants there have the guns, or in other words the gold; but they do nothing with it, they do not realize that they are all-powerful, with the result that the catastrophe is delayed and the castle of Walhalla, insecure but glorious, fronts the storms. Fafnir, coiled round his hoard, grumbles and grunts; we can hear him under Europe today; the leaves of the wood already tremble, and the Bird calls its warnings uselessly. Fafnir will destroy us, but by a blessed dispensation he is stupid and slow,

> and creation goes on just outside the poisonous blast of his breath. The Nietzschean would hurry the monster up, the mystic would say he did not exist, but Wotan, wiser than either, hastens to create warriors before doom declares itself. The Valkyries are symbols not only of courage but of intelligence; they represent the human spirit snatching its opportunity while the going is good, and one of them even finds time to love. Brünnhilde's last song hymns the recurrence of love, and since it is the privilege of art to exaggerate, she goes even further and proclaims the love which is eternally triumphant and feeds upon freedom, and lives.

Of course, since that *was* written in 1939 one's immediate reaction is to suspect that Forster is cheering himself up. Perhaps he is—a little. But there's also a confidence about the passage which suggests that he isn't merely spinning metaphors and refusing to face the reality of the catastrophe (there is, after all, a modest good sense in the championing of Wotan who 'hastens to create warriors before doom declares itself'). Just before the words I've quoted Forster has been saying that all society rests upon force, and this choice of *The Neibelung's Ring* to prove the validity of his contention he regards not as fanciful but unavoidable: music is 'real' because it embodies the essential truth of so vastly complex a situation as that existing in the Europe of 1939; the threat Hitler represents is part of a reality that art, and especially music, fully contains. Art tells the truth, and we can see in Forster's use of the Wagnerian myth a habit of mind that looks to discover in art the enduring elements of any situation which may come to exist in the temporal world.

Now Forster is prepared to admit that not all music yields such explicit meanings: its truths may resist any attempt at a discursive revelation; they may be too allusive, too deep, too purely themselves. But however that may be with some composers, it isn't the case with Wagner. In an essay called *Not Listening to Music*, which he also wrote in 1939, Forster wryly confesses that his delight in Wagner springs from the fact that his music *is* explicit.

> I used to be very fond of music that reminded me of something, and especially fond of Wagner. With Wagner I always knew where I was; he never let the fancy roam; he ordained that one phrase should recall the ring, another the sword, another the blameless fool and so on; he was as precise in his indications as an oriental dancer.[1]

*Not Listening to Music* is, in fact, concerned largely with distinguishing between music 'that reminds me of something' and 'music itself', and Forster goes to some pains to confess his readiness in earlier years to put Beethoven in the former category—under Wagner's influence. And although he doesn't in fact mention it, almost certainly he has in mind *Howard's End*, and the use that's there made of Beethoven's fifth symphony.

It's in the famous description of the concert at the Queen's Hall that Forster, for the first time in the novel, uses music to remind us of something.

> . . . the music started with a goblin walking quietly over the universe, from end to end. Others followed him. They were not aggressive creatures; it was that that made them so terrible to Helen. They merely observed in passing that there was no such thing as splendour or heroism in the world. After the interlude of elephants dancing, they returned and made the observation for the second time. Helen could not contradict them, for, once at all events, she had felt the same, and had seen the reliable walls of youth collapse. Panic and emptiness! Panic and emptiness! The goblins were right.

Forster's tactic with Helen Schlegel in the scene calls for some comment. For her, Beethoven's music provides an explanation of her own personal experiences, its truths validate the significance that, dimly enough, she had felt lay beneath the mess of her abortive engagement to Paul Wilcox. And there's nothing in the passage to suggest that Forster thinks she's wrong; indeed the point is that, for him, the music's right, and she's his way of focusing its truths and of making them available to the reader. Now what Forster is offering in *Howard's End* is an account of English society that's intendedly comprehensive;[2] and although he has more recently described the novel in deprecating terms as a 'hunt for a home', there's no doubt that it has an apocalyptic note to it. So 'panic and emptiness' is necessary, because it helps to sustain that note, it is what the Wilcox 'outer world' of 'telegrams and anger' finally comes to. And that is why Helen is made to recognize it in Beethoven's fifth symphony; for the music is truthfully apocalyptic.

Actually Forster's confidence that the music *is* telling this kind of truth leads him to introduce the identical phrases taken from the experience of the music into episodes essential to the central themes of *Howard's End*: of past and present, the rural against the urban, personal relationships and the business world. And one begins to develop a resistance to the phrases simply because they're so obtrusively fed in—we're too insistently prodded in the right direction. In fact this method, because it arises out of an apparently uncritical contentment with the 'truths' of art, is responsible for most of what's unsatisfactory in the novel; potentially intricate and troubling situations are too neatly slotted into the overall pattern: 'truth' produces a crop of improbabilities. It's difficult to take seriously, for instance, the *dénouement* of Henry Wilcox's liaison with Jackie Bast, or of Helen's with Leonard Bast because—and this is to Forster's credit—they are well enough realized as individuals to make the formal requirements of their being coupled seem damagingly intrusive. In fact it's legitimate to wonder whether this type of novel can ever deal adequately with the sort of theme that *Howard's End*, for all Forster's subsequent disclaimers, aspires to. Can an artist expect of another art-work that it should perform the platonic function of revealing the coherence subsisting in his own work's deliberately chosen confusions? Surely it's asking too much; and what I think survives as finest in Forster's novel isn't the pattern of connection but the confusions themselves, which have a vitality and integrity that's merely stifled by the constricting demands of 'only connect'.

Yet if this is true of *Howard's End*, what's to be said for *A Room With a View*, the first novel at which Forster had tried his hand? For in this novel music is of the utmost importance. We learn a great deal about the heroine, Lucy Honeychurch, through the music she plays; for example we are meant to take her transition from Beethoven through Schumann to Mozart as pre-figuring her decline into a probable future of middle-class sterility. And since so much is made out of these three names it's unfortunate that the truths their music carries should seem suspiciously to reflect particular limits to Edwardian taste; Lucy, we learn, 'tinkles' a Mozart sonata: it's all either of them is good for. But having entered this *caveat* I must add that I think the employment of music in *A Room With a View* is far more successful than in *Howard's End*. For one thing, though we may disagree about Forster's implied estimate of the composers he uses, we have to acknowledge that he employs them with considerable tact to solve what is, after all, a difficult technical problem: how to get Lucy to reveal the truth about herself which she won't consciously admit.

For another, the central truths are borne, not by Beethoven, but Wagner. Not that Beethoven is to be blamed for the failures of *Howard's End*; but *A Room With a View* is on a much more modest scale than the later novel, so that Wagner's music-drama has a mythic completeness sufficient at least for the meaning of the novel to find itself in. Forster's novel offers, as it were, a version of Wagner's complex truth, and on the whole it does so without seriously distorting character or situation.

Now the Wagnerian myths—the dramatic material out of which his music-dramas were in part fashioned—can be taken as formidably inclusive embodiments of even the most complex situations, whether psychological, social, or political. And as we've already seen, Forster makes *The Niebelung's Ring* yield up the truth about Europe in 1939. Of course, this sort of application may seem impermissibly loose; and anyway how can an essay which begins with a disavowal of religious belief go on to talk of 'blessed dispensations'? Still, in fairness to Forster it ought to be said that such objection would almost certainly strike him as unreal. And that, because he grew up during the last decade of the nineteenth century, when, as I'll suggest, to doubt the answerable truths of Wagner's myths would be difficult if not impossible.

What *The Niebelung's Ring* did for the world of 1939, *Parsifal* did for the world of 1908. It made sense, of certain features at least, of the contemporary situation, and *A Room With a View* takes its own meaning from the truths embodied in Wagner's music drama. How it does so I'll try to show, but first I need to indicate the fact of Wagner's compulsive appeal at the time of Forster's youth and early manhood, and to suggest how the *Parsifal* myth might be apposite to his concerns.

## II

In the essay which I've already mentioned, *Not Listening to Music*, Forster has admitted that he used to be 'especially fond of Wagner'. No doubt his stay in Germany—he was there at the beginning of this century—gave him the chance to experience Wagner-worship at first hand; and this may have had something to do with the considerable affection he came to feel for the country itself. But whatever additional point might have been given to his awareness of Wagner by that stay, the years in Germany couldn't have created it. For Forster was born in 1879 and grew up in the last years of the nineteenth century; and this was the very time at which Wagner's reputation became, quite simply, gigantic. So any literate person then coming to maturity would inevitably be caught up in some reaction to the man and his art; you couldn't ignore either him or his popularity.

There's no great need to labour this point, it's well enough known already. But there may be some use in suggesting that claims to ignorance quickly reveal themselves as poses; it strengthens the feeling of Wagner's ubiquitous reputation. As late as 1902, for example, Shaw was playing this particular game.[3] In that year his *The Perfect Wagnerite* went into its second edition, and Shaw contributed a preface for it in which he said that:

> The preparation of a Second Edition of this booklet is quite the most unexpected literary task that has ever been set me. When it first appeared I was ungrateful enough to remonstrate with its publisher for printing, as I thought, more copies than the most sanguine Wagnerite could ever hope to sell. But the result proved that exactly one person buys a copy on every day in the year, including Sundays; and so, in the process of the suns, a reprint has become necessary.

Amusingly enough, Shaw has to accept here that the image of himself as sponsor of failed causes won't extend to Wagner; not even *he* can make the master unpopular. And one has only to turn to Beardsley's *Venus and Tannhäuser* to see that Shaw's discovery was several years overdue. It's true that at first sight Beardsley's use of the myth may serve merely to suggest that Wagner enjoyed a vogue with *fin de siècle* artists, and was therefore unpopular—a word which, for them, had the useful ambiguity of meaning either little known or widely disliked. But a closer look confirms that Beardsley is, in fact, reacting in predictable sort to Wagner's popularity. The fey impropriety of his *Venus and Tannhäuser* is merely a way of spitting on the altar.

It may also be useful to delimit fairly roughly the period of Wagner's unquestioned supremacy, in order to show how closely it coincided with Forster's own early years. Thus it can be said that the reputation hadn't by any means won its way before 1880. In 1878, for example, the year before Forster was born, Edmund

Gurney published an article in the July number of *The Nineteenth Century* in which he makes this criticism of Wagner.

> In his theory and much of his practice Wagner has missed this fact, that true aesthetic correspondence is due to the subtle and harmonious blending of emotional appeals *severally expressive and beautiful in their kind*; so that not only in professing to unite the 'symphony' with the drama does he ignore the structural differences between high organic development in music and in poetry, but in detail after detail, and probably owing to an unconscious want of melodic fertility, he has cut off the very chance of a vital union. The mere garment of one art thrown over another will do little if their two essences are not interfused. Wagner, in exact opposition to Beethoven, confessedly sits down to evolve music out of long strings of external conceptions, with the result that his music, however brilliantly coloured, tends to sink into arbitrary symbolism.

I quote that, not so much for the details of Gurney's objections, as to draw attention to his tone. The points are made with a show of decent argument, and there's nothing in his unforced assumption that Wagner's work is legitimate material for criticism to indicate that Gurney regards himself as a voice crying in the wilderness. But the fact is that such a tone could hardly have survived the next ten years. Samuel Butler, for example, recorded his opposition to Wagner in these terms.

> I went to the Bach choir concert and heard Mozart's *Requiem*. I did not rise warmly to it. Then I heard an extract from *Parsifal* which I disliked very much. If Bach wriggles, Wagner writhes. Yet next morning in *The Times* I saw this able, heartless failure, compact of gnosis as much as any one pleases but without one spark of either true pathos or true humour, called 'the crowning achievement of dramatic music'.

The difference in tone from Gurney isn't simply to be accounted for by the fact that Butler is confiding his thoughts to a notebook. It's rather that his anger is called out by the assumption of *The Times* reviewer that, in finding *Parsifal* 'the crowning achievement of dramatic music', he was offering a critical commonplace —which he was.

Now that entry couldn't have been made before 1882, since *Parsifal* was first performed in that year, and in its feeling of familiarity with the work it's likely to belong at earliest to the middle years of the 1880s; and it could, of course, belong to any time up to 1902. Which makes the point about Wagner's reputation neatly enough. For from the middle 1880s it grew with enormous rapidity to colossal proportions, and in this it was no doubt aided by the considerable efforts of the English branch of the Wagner Society which, in its quarterly magazine—called, inevitably, *The Meister*—was busy making available in English all Wagner's works. And a quick glance at Shaw's three-volume *Music in London: 1890–94* confirms the degree to which Wagner dominated the concert hall.

Yet in spite of the vast appeal of his music, it would be wrong to assume that interest in Wagner began and ended there. By the end of the century, indeed, he held a position second to none, less as a composer than as *the* type of the great artist. Nor is this very surprising. In an age which had increasingly found it necessary to reinforce or replace religious truths by the truths of art, artists could expect to be turned into sages. Real love for Wagner entailed a pilgrimage to Bayreuth; and quite probably the worshippers who in the 'eighties and 'nineties made the trip to the small German town were driven by the same hopes that had spurred an earlier generation up Rydal Mount.

It was with this fervent admiration for Wagner all around him that Forster grew up. He would have known of the importance of Bayreuth and with it of *Parsifal*, and also of the near-religious awe in which the master was held. And these three features of Wagner's reputation are intimately linked, as Butler's fury has suggested, and as I now want to make clear.

## III

In March 1891, Shaw wrote in his music column a reply to a letter which he'd seen in one of the daily papers.[4]

> For the life of me I cannot see why the recent suggestion that the score of *Parsifal* may find a place on Signor Mancinelli's desk at Covent Garden should be scouted as 'profane'. I leave out of the question the old-fashioned objection, founded on the theory that all play-houses and singing-halls are abodes of sin. But when a gentleman writes to the papers to declare that 'a performance of Parsifal, apart from the really religious surroundings of Bayreuth

> Theatre, would almost amount to a profanity,' and, again, that 'in the artificial glare of an English opera-house it would be a blasphemous mockery,' I must take the liberty of describing to him the 'really religious surroundings,' since he admits that he has never seen them for himself. In front of the Bayreuth Theatre, then, on the right, there is a restaurant. On the left there is a still larger restaurant and a sweet-stuff stall. At the back, a little way up the hill, there is a café. Between the café and the theatre is a shed in which 'artificial glare' is manufactured for the inside of the theatre; and the sound of that great steam-engine throbs all over the Fichtelgebirge on still nights.

The terms of the letter from which Shaw quotes indicate clearly how *Parsifal* and Bayreuth were typically regarded at this time. The work was a sacred drama and performance of it required consecrated ground. And for all the aseptic common-sense that he shows in answering the letter, not even Shaw disputes the fact of *Parsifal*'s truly 'religious' nature. So, in discussing Mendelssohn's *Elijah*, he remarks:

> it is not really religious music at all. The best of it is seraphic music, like the best of Gounod's; but you have only to think of Parsifal, of the Ninth Symphony, of . . . the inspired moments of Handel and Bach, to see the great gulf that lies between the truly religious sentiment and our delight in Mendelssohn's prettiness.

Taken together, these two quotations show how, for the late nineteenth century at all events, *Parsifal* occupied a particular place in Wagner's *œuvre*: it isn't religious simply because of its subject-matter—for Mendelssohn's subject is, if anything, more religious; and we can assume that although the gentleman whose letter Shaw savages might feel that the ninth symphony expressed 'the truly religious sentiment', he wouldn't scout as profane the suggestion that it should be performed elsewhere than at Vienna. In other words, it isn't any single factor that explains *Parsifal*'s unique appeal; several combine to give it it's aura. And, however briefly, these need enumerating.

In the first place it's not difficult to regard *Parsifal* as occupying a position very similar to that of *The Tempest*. Since both were taken to be last works each could be interpreted as the last message of the dying master. Indeed it's an aspect of the desire to turn artists into sages that, in the 1890s, this view of Shakespeare's play gained particular currency. And with rather more justification *Parsifal* can also be turned into a final testament, for Wagner himself saw it as the last work he would ever write for the theatre, and his immediate circle knew of this resolution. Besides, resolutions often become prophecies, and it was no secret that Wagner was in abysmally poor health, nor that he might die at any moment. According to his biographer, Ernest Newman, the task of Wagner's closest relatives and friends was to keep him alive until he could finish his work.

> On Cosima fell the major burden of these last distressful years. Richard could afford to indulge himself in fits of peevishness and the dark discouragements arising from his heavy work and his broken health. But for Cosima there was no relief possible even of this sorry kind: she had to endure infinitely in patient silence, sustained by one thought alone, that of keeping him alive for the completion of his mission.

The mission referred to was, in fact, *Parsifal*, and that Newman should light on such a word instructs us how to regard the attitude of Wagner and others to this last great enterprise.

Several other factors contributed to the aura which from the outset surrounded the stage-dedication-play. Although Wagner seems to have begun the actual composition in 1878 his poor health retarded progress, and the scheduled performance dates had repeatedly to be postponed—a fact certain to increase speculation and concern. Moreover, Newman stated that Wagner was especially fearful of any production, dreading the disparity between his dream and the stage actuality; and we are told that during rehearsals he suffered torments over the inadequacies in the presentation of certain scenes. And it's not overmuch to sense that embedded in this anguish was an accompanying fear—that *Parsifal*, of which so much had come to be expected, would disappoint its audience. The fear is surely present in Wagner's desire that *Parsifal* should be given at Bayreuth alone, and that it should be performed for an audience of patrons. Newman says that the composer's most agonizing problem lay in preventing commercial companies handling the work, and he adds:

> We can hardly doubt that had he been unable to solve this problem in any other way he would have gone to the extreme length of withholding the work even from Bayreuth, for a production there

> would mean that the Munich Intendanz would at once exercise its legal rights, and after that the descent of *Parsifal* to the German theatres *en masse* would have been practically certain.

In this frame of mind Wagner, in September 1880, wrote to his patron, the 'mad' Ludwig of Bavaria:

> how, indeed, can a drama in which the sublimest mysteries of the Christian faith are shown upon the stage be produced in theatres such as ours, before audiences such as ours, as part of an operatic repertory such as ours? I could have no ground of complaint against our Church authorities if they were to protest, as they would be fully entitled to do, against a stage presentation of the holiest mysteries complacently sandwiched between the frivolity of yesterday and the frivolity of tomorrow, before a public attracted to it solely by frivolity. It was in the full consciousness of this that I gave *Parsifal* the description of a 'stage-*dedication*-play'. I must have for it therefore a dedicated stage, and this can only be my theatre in Bayreuth. There alone should *Parsifal* be performed. Never must it be put before the public in any other theatre whatever as an amusement; and my whole means are devoted to finding out by what means I can secure this destiny for it.

It would have taken a man several times more obtuse than King Ludwig to miss the point of such a letter. Accordingly, he annulled all previous contracts for the play; and in a private letter, he told Wagner:

> I am wholly in agreement with you that *Parsifal*, your solemn stage-dedication-play, shall be given only in Bayreuth, and never be desecrated by contact with any profane stage.

There is no reason to suppose the King had his tongue in his cheek when he wrote that letter, and the significance of his terms hardly needs insisting on: they look forward to the letter Shaw ridiculed, and show that for its contemporary audience *Parsifal*'s over-riding importance lay in its being no mere work of art. For it was the master's last work, its subject was sacred, it could be seen only by the initiated, and they had to make a pilgrimage to see it. Small wonder, then, that it should come to occupy so special a place, or that it should seem to reveal truths beyond the reach of ordinary art.

In very general terms, *Parsifal* presents the opposition between Christian and Pagan forces. For Wagner's work is a version of the grail legend, and it relies for most of its details on the thirteenth-century *Parsifal* by Wolfram von Eschenbach. Very briefly, this is the situation with which the music-drama opens. Titurel, the former grail king, is now in his grave but not dead. Mysteriously, he is kept alive by being always in sight of the holy grail which, with the spear, it is his and his knights' duty to guard. The principal threat to this duty comes from Klingsor, a magician who time and again has lured grail knights into his garden and then turned them against their former master. In this he has been assisted by Kundry, a beautiful and seductive woman who, for having laughed at Christ on the Cross, has been forced to wander through the world laughing ceaselessly. Now Klingsor has gained power over her against her will, indeed she longs to repent; but in spite of this she always turns against the bringer of repentance. And it's she who has lured into the garden Titurel's son, Amfortas.

The new king had wanted to begin his reign by killing Klingsor, but once he'd got into the magic garden the sight of Kundry made him forget his mission, and her beauty caused him to drop the holy spear, which was then captured by Klingsor, who wounded him with it. At the beginning of *Parsifal*, then, Amfortas lies mortally wounded but unable to die. He can only be healed if the spear is re-captured from Klingsor and laid on the wound, and only someone totally innocent can manage this—a holy fool. And this, of course, is Parsifal himself, who, as a total outsider—he comes from the forest—brings health to the diseased, and who in the course of the drama not only recovers the spear and heals Amfortas but also rescues Kundry from Klingsor and baptizes her.

Now in most details of the fairly complicated plot, Wagner stays so close to von Eschenbach's version that his divergences can fairly be regarded as minor. But one is considerably more than that. In his *Parsifal* Klingsor retains control of Kundry by deliberately unsexing himself, and this detail seems to have been his own invention; it isn't in von Eschenbach nor, so far as I've been able to discover, in any version of the legend prior to his own. As we shall see this detail is very important for *A Room With a View*; and indeed it's time to turn back to Forster, and suggest some of the reasons for his coming to see in *Parsifal* a theme that could validate the discoveries his own art was making about contemporary society.

## IV

The English Institute Essays for 1959, *Edwardians and Late Victorians*, contains a very interesting essay by Richard Ellmann, called *Two Faces of Edward.* Ellmann is struck by the fact that Edwardian literature is thoroughly secular, 'yet so earnest that secularism does not describe it'. And he both illustrates and tries to account for this fact.

> Almost to a man, Edwardian writers rejected Christianity, and having done so, they feel free to *use* it, for while they did not need religion, they did need religious metaphor.

And:

> The Edwardians were looking for ways to express their conviction that we can be religious about life itself, and they naturally adopted metaphors offered by the religion they knew best.

And again:

> The Edwardian writer granted that the world was secular, but saw no reason to add that it was irrational or meaningless. A kind of inner belief pervades their writings, that the transcendent is immanent in the earthy, that to go down far enough is to come up. They felt free to introduce startling coincidences quite flagrantly, as in *A Room With a View* and *The Ambassadors*, to hint that life is much more than it appears to be, although none of them would have offered that admission openly. While Biblical miracles aroused their incredulity, they were singularly credulous of miracles of their own. . . . The central miracle for the Edwardians is the sudden alteration of the self; around it much of their literature pivots.

This is well said, and I suppose that, to an extent, Ellmann's generalizations hold true for Forster. All the same it's difficult to be satisfied with the implied suggestion of his credulity in *A Room With a View*, because this isn't, I should have thought, at all the sort of controlling response we're likely to have to the novel. Lucy Honeychurch's conversion has about it a feeling of seriousness whose rightness it's as difficult to avoid acknowledging as it may be to account for. However we may want to regard the miracle—if that's the right word—we're unlikely to see in it the work of a 'singularly credulous' man.

Still, Ellmann's awareness that the Edwardian novelist wanted to 'be religious about life itself' can certainly be applied to Forster, and so can his noting the Edwardian's use of religious metaphor. Indeed *A Room With a View* centres its concern on the two words 'Love' and 'Truth', and these take on a peremptory authority from the religious metaphors which so frequently provide their immediate context.

Superficially, the novel is a slight enough comedy. It's about a young girl's education in the ways of sexual and social snobbishness, which on the one hand she's educated to accept and on the other to reject. But this subserves a far more radical theme, expressed through a paradox whose present familiarity shouldn't obscure the force it would have had in 1908. Briefly it's this: that the appointed guardians of middle-class values, governesses and clerics, are the dedicated representatives of a class-consciousness which, for all its apparent decency and tolerance, kills off all hope of a free individual life; and that they are opposed by individuals who are, therefore, social outcasts: of necessity because they are iconoclasts of conventional morality and religion; by choice because they won't conform to demands that thwart a full life. In other words, those who apparently protect society are killers, and those who apparently threaten it, have the vitality which is 'life itself'. Still, to set the paradox down like this is to make the novel seem windily portentous. Can so apparently slight a comedy bear this heavy load? If Forster were the 'singularly credulous' man that Ellmann suggests, then not. But, for reasons that I'll try to show, it both can and does.

*A Room With a View* opens in Florence at the Pension Bertolini, where Lucy Honeychurch, a young girl of conventional middle-class background, and her chaperone, Charlotte Bartlett, are sharing rooms without a view. Staying at the same Pension are two working-class men, George Emerson and his father. Their rooms do have views and they offer them to the ladies. After much argument and soul-searching Miss Bartlett ungraciously accepts their offer. Another guest at the Pension needs to be noted. That first evening, when the Emersons are being so obtusely importunate about exchanging rooms, the ladies discover that Mr Beebe, a clergyman whom they had both previously known, is staying at the Bertolini, and that when he returns to England it will be to take up the living in Summer Street, the Surrey town where Lucy lives.

Now during her stay in Florence Lucy begins to suspect possibilities in life at which she hadn't previously guessed; she is profiting, we are told, from 'the eternal league of Italy with youth', and her progress towards the education of self-discovery reaches its first climax when, on a general outing, George kisses her. But she is 'saved' by Miss Bartlett, intent on offering Lucy a different education, and whisked off to Rome.

The second half of the novel takes place in Summer Street. Here, Lucy becomes engaged to a man she doesn't love. His name is Cecil Vyse, and he is clever, rich, and well connected. But Lucy's conformist plans of entertaining the grand-children of famous men—plans which cause her a good deal of half-recognized inner distress—are disrupted. Cecil, who in all ways is a social snob, meets for the first time the Emersons in the National Gallery, where they are mispronouncing Botticelli's name. He invites them to become tenants of a small and hideous cottage in Summer Street, and they accept his offer. So Lucy and George meet again; and again he kisses her. But 'Lucy had developed since the spring', and she's been so well educated by Miss Bartlett that she's able to repulse George, and won't admit to loving him.

For all that, however, the kiss does produce some direct results. Lucy breaks off her engagement to Cecil. Then she plans to go to Greece with the Miss Alans, two old spinsters she'd met at the Pension in Florence. Miss Bartlett and Mr Beebe approve the plan and plot together to block Mrs Honeychurch's objections. But at the last moment old Mr Emerson saves Lucy. Quite by chance she encounters him in Mr Beebe's vicarage, and he forces her to confess the truth: that she has been deceiving herself all along in pretending she doesn't love George. This is her conversion. And the novel ends with the two young people back at the Pension in Florence, sharing their room with a view.

Even this bare outline of the plot makes clear how committed Forster is to probing at weaknesses in the Edwardian social fabric; *A Room With a View* finds him very much the critic of society. And the outline should also be sufficient to show that with Forster, as Trilling noticed, correct political attitudes get raised to the level of moral perceptions. It's for this reason that the values by which the Emersons live are seen as morally superior to those which constrain Lucy; their acceptance of the equality of women goes with their concern for integrity in personal relations—

'Truth' and 'Love'. Conversely, incorrect political attitudes are proof of moral impercipience. Inevitably, therefore, Cecil is to be judged by his attitude to the Emersons and Lucy. The men he judges by extrinsic matters of taste, clothes, and speech. And in his courtship of Lucy it's soon apparent that he can't conceive of any relation other than 'the feudal', that he's incapable of understanding 'the comradeship after which the girl's soul yearned'. So, when he tries to tell her he believes in democracy—as a smart young man would— she snaps back, 'you don't know what the word means'. Her reply convinces him only of the fact that her rebelliousness is best remedied by removing her from her family circle into one of polite London society; and of such a remedy we're informed:

> A rebel she was, but not of the kind he understood—a rebel who desired not a wider dwelling room, but equality beside the man she loved.

The comedy of Cecil's impercipience reaches its peak in his readiness to see Lucy as a work of art. When she does lose her temper with him, he feels in an aggrieved way that 'she had failed to be Leonardesque . . . her face was inartistic.'

Now so far there's nothing in Forster's treatment of Cecil which takes him beyond the range of social comedy. The judgments made against him are typical, but that's part of the mode: sins of class self-sufficiency, of snobbishness in ideas and taste, male complacency—all these are present in the type Cecil represents: he's very much the product of his society. Yet it seems to me that Cecil is also typical in another, more radical, sense. And this comes out in the following description of him.

> He was medieval. Like a gothic statue. Tall and refined, with shoulders that seemed braced by an effort of the will, and a head that was tilted a little higher than the usual level of vision, he resembled those fastidious saints who guard the portals of a French Cathedral. Well educated, well endowed, and not deficient physically, he remained in the grip of a certain devil whom the modern world knows as self-consciousness, and whom the medieval, with dimmer vision, worshipped as ascetism.

Cecil's sterility is here being emphasized in terms that can't easily be related to the sort of typicality he's so far been given.

And nor can George's condemnation of him. 'You cannot live with Vyse', he tells Lucy:

> 'He's only for acquaintance. He is for society and cultivated talk. He should know no one intimately, least of all a woman. . . . He is the sort who are all right so long as they keep to things—books, pictures—but kill when they come to people.'

It's very important we note that Forster isn't discovering the cause of Cecil's sterility by enquiring into the sort of person he uniquely is. There's no effort, that is, to uncover it through psychological insight, feeling for the way an individual psyche is acted on by, and reacts to, social factors, though this would seem to be the way for the social critic. Instead, however, Forster's terms are highly allusive. Judgement isn't restricted to Cecil's social typicality; it works centrifugally—'He was medieval'—with the result that he becomes typical in a more absolute sense.

And once you notice Forster's tendency to carry typicality beyond boundaries imposed by social considerations, it can be seen to apply to all the novel's key protagonists. For example when Lucy sees George in Florence:

> She watched the singular creature pace up and down the chapel. For a young man his face was rugged and—until the shadows fell upon it—hard. Enshadowed it sprang into tenderness. She saw him once again in Rome, on the ceiling of the Sistine chapel, carrying a burden of acorns.

George, that is, is the opposite of Cecil; his virility matches the other man's sterility. It allows for social comment, of course: the man beyond society's constricting claims attains to a fullness denied to those subdued by them: damn braces, bless relaxes. But by bringing in Michaelangelo's nude youths—symbols of the body's perfection, of fruition—Forster gives George a larger significance. And for all the blatant symbolism of the Sistine Chapel it would be difficult to condemn him of empty portentousness, because by and large he so unobtrusively makes this idea of fruition grow out of the social comedy. For example, clothes are used in *A Room With a View* as extrinsic marks by which class self-consciousness is mistaken for real value. And so when Lucy accidentally comes on George during his swim with her brother and Mr Beebe, and in his nakedness he forces her to bow to him, she reflects:

> She had bowed—but to whom? To Gods, to heroes, to the nonsense of schoolgirls. She had bowed across the rubbish that cumbers the world.

The rubbish is the heap of men's clothes, and the last sentence there demonstrates how sure Forster's narrative grip is, how little he seems to betray the slackness of singular credulity. For it *can* be a continuation of Lucy's thought—she recognizes the clothes as rubbish that cumbers the world; or it *can* be Forster telling you what she'd in fact done, whether she recognized it or not. And the very indirectness of the sentence allows with admirable tact for the indirect processes of Lucy's mind, the difficulties she has in coming to perceive the truth that's borne in on her. She approaches it when, trying to defend Cecil's rudeness to her mother, she acknowledges that 'Good and bad taste were only catchwords, garments of diverse cut.' It's the tact, then, implicit in Forster's employment of clothes and the body's nakedness that lets him carry George's significance beyond the social terms the novel may seem to be settling for. And it's because of this that he can justly view with such seriousness Lucy's half-glimpse of a truth George embodies, so that her turning away from it rightly calls out his severest judgment. When she breaks off her engagement to Cecil, yet denies to George that she loves him, Forster notes:

> It did not do to think, nor, for the matter of that, to feel. She gave up trying to understand herself, and joined the vast armies of the benighted, who follow neither the heart nor the brain, and march to their destiny by catch-words. The armies are full of pleasant and pious folk. But they have yielded to the only enemy that matters—the enemy within. They have sinned against passion and truth, and vain will be their strife after virtue. As the years pass, they are censured. Their pleasantry and their piety show cracks, their wit becomes cynicism, their unselfishness hypocrisy; they feel and produce discomfort wherever they go. They have sinned against Eros and Pallas Athene, and not by any heavenly intervention, but by the ordinary course of nature, those allied deities will be avenged.

Not the least of the strengths of that fine passage is the feeling of revulsion that's engaged for what might appear relatively trivial social sins: cynicism and hypocrisy become deep hurts against human worth. It's a shame, of course, about the donnish interpolation of Eros and Pallas Athene, especially since failure to think and feel will be avenged 'by the ordinary course of nature'. Why bring the Gods in at all? But you don't have to look hard for the answer. Forster needs to compensate for the Christian overtones released by his sentence about 'passion and truth', and 'strife after virtue'. It's in such phrases that we recognize the truth in Ellmann's perception: that the Edwardians wanted to use religious metaphor to express their conviction 'that we can be religious about life itself'. The trouble about using such a phrase of *A Room With a View* is that Forster's tact makes it seem clumsy; and yet the truth is that he *is* prepared to be deeply serious about life itself, as the passage above shows and as does this following one, in which Miss Bartlett works to bring Mr Beebe over to confirming Lucy in her sin.

> Mr Beebe considered.
>
> 'It is absolutely necessary,' she continued, lowering her veil, and whispering through it with a passion, and intensity, that surprised him. 'I know—I know.' The darkness was coming on, and he felt that this odd woman really did know . . .
>
> 'Yes, I will help her,' said the clergyman, setting his jaw firm. 'Come, let us go back now, and settle the whole thing up.'
>
> Miss Bartlett burst into florid gratitude. The tavern sign—a beehive trimmed evenly with bees—creaked in the wind outside as she thanked him. Mr Beebe did not quite understand the situation; but then, he did not desire to understand it, nor jump to the conclusion of 'another man' that would have attracted a grosser mind. He only knew that Miss Bartlett knew of some vague influence from which the girl desired to be delivered, and which might well be clothed in the fleshly form. Its very vagueness spurred him into knight-errantry. His belief in celibacy, so reticent, so carefully concealed beneath his tolerance and culture, now came to the surface and expanded like some delicate flower. 'They that marry do well, but they that refrain do better.' So ran his belief, and he never heard that an engagement was broken off but with a slight feeling of pleasure. In the case of Lucy, the feeling was intensified through dislike of Cecil; and he was willing to go further—to place her out of danger until she could confirm her resolution of virginity.

That owes some of its feeling of an encroaching horror to the packed symbolism—the 'beehive evenly trimmed with bees' for example. Yet to draw attention to the symbolism too exclusively is to coarsen the very fine poise of intention the passage has, its tact; it leads into the use of those large, general terms that don't sufficiently define the quality of Forster's writing. Evil, darkness, horror: the words are too strident. Yet it's difficult to see how to avoid them, and the feeling for them is there. The poise, though, checks us, because it's by means of *that* that we see how deeply Forster buries his seriousness in the social terms the passage retains. It isn't that he's hiding his intentions under the mask of social manners, but that they fully emerge only in and through the rendering of his comedy. That's why, for example, the sentence 'Miss Bartlett burst into florid gratitude' has a power and subtlety that are uniquely Forsterian. 'Florid', of course, because that's how a spinster governess would react to the clergyman's offer; the word defines with a beautiful precision her social unease. Yet 'florid' also means highly-coloured; and as we take up that meaning our minds reach back to the scene where, coming on Lucy and George kissing, Miss Bartlett had stood 'brown against the view'. Mr Beebe's promise of help produces an unnatural, heightened gaiety that's totally at odds with her former deadly sombreness.[5] The word places Miss Bartlett socially, but it also directs us towards a far more sinister significance.

A scene such as this one suggests with great force how she and Mr Beebe attain mythic status. For the values they come to represent do have a feeling of absoluteness about them, and they give the governess and cleric a typicality beyond whatever they possess as types in Forster's social comedy. And this is equally true of George and Cecil and Lucy. Yet with all of them the deeper significances are so firmly grounded in their social typicality that they have to be approached through it. Forster, that is, operates in *A Room With a View* as a social critic yet through such criticism is able to get at deeper, more permanent, truths—about 'life itself'. And those are the truths of *Parsifal*.

## V

As I've already suggested, Forster's use of music is tactically important in his novel. It's in Lucy's playing that the truths about herself that she won't openly acknowledge emerge. For example, in Mrs Vyse's 'well-appointed flat' she plays Schumann.

> The melody rose, unprofitably magical; it was resumed broken, not marching once from the cradle to the grave. The sadness of the

> incomplete—the sadness that is often Life, but should never be Art—throbbed in its disjected phrases. . . .

J. B. Beer, in *The Achievement of E. M. Forster*, has noticed how important Lucy's piano-playing is, but without doing it full justice; and he seems not to recognize just how carefully Forster works. For example, Beer quotes the song Lucy plays just before her final meeting with Mr Emerson, and refers to it as 'a song which Cecil has given her'. Which is true but less important than the fact that it's Lucy Ashton's song from *The Bride of Lammermoor*. But he's further out in his account of the most crucial scene of the novel. This is the Sunday afternoon when George kisses Lucy for the second time and she breaks off her engagement. Before he arrives Lucy is asked to play the piano. She chooses the music of the magic garden from Gluck's *Armido*. According to Beer:

> Cecil asks her to follow this with the garden music of *Parsifal*, but she refuses, and then turns to see that George has entered without interrupting. Again, the playing of Gluck and the refusal of the *Parsifal* music are significant.

But neither at this point nor at any other does Beer say *why* this is significant, and on his terms I don't think he can really explain why it should be. Here is what I take to be the most important section of the scene; it starts where Beer's quotation stops.

> Such music [*Armide's*] is not for the piano, and her audience began to get restive, and Cecil, sharing the general discontent, called out: 'Now play us the other garden—the one in "Parsifal".'
>
> She closed the instrument.
>
> 'Not very dutiful,' said her mother's voice.
>
> Fearing that she had offended Cecil, she turned quickly round. There George was. He had crept in without interrupting her.
>
> 'Oh, I had no idea!' she exclaimed, getting very red; and then, without a word of greeting, she reopened the piano. Cecil should have the 'Parsifal', and anything else that he liked.
>
> 'Our performer has changed her mind,' said Miss Bartlett, perhaps implying, 'she will play the music to Mr Emerson.' Lucy did not know what to do, nor even what she wanted to do. She played a few bars of the Flower Maidens' song very badly, and then she stopped.[6]

In other words, although she refuses to play the music, she *does* attempt it. And the real significance is both in the refusal *and* the bad playing. Lucy's refusal to play the music is instinctive, indeed she fears 'that she had offended Cecil'; deftly Forster implies how split are her conscious and unconscious desires. And it shows climactically in her wanting to play *Parsifal* for Cecil yet being unable to do so: 'She played a few bars . . . very badly, and then stopped.' The fact is that, though consciously she may not recognize it, the truth of her situation is borne in *Parsifal*; and George's presence serves to make it the more insistent. It's not for nothing that the chapter in which this scene occurs should be called 'The Disaster Within'.

*A Room With a View* works by presenting a basic opposition of pagan and Christian as holy and devilish; being on the side of life is being religious about it. *Parsifal* works by presenting a basic opposition of pagan and Christian as devilish and holy; again, though, being on the side of life is being religious about it. Forster's 'good' people have the same motives as Wagner's—to defend 'life itself'; and though there isn't a point-by-point correspondence—Forster isn't writing a prose version of *Parsifal*—the novel's protagonists owe their mythic status to their author's availing himself of the structure of oppositions in Wagner's work.[7]

In the first place it's clear that the Emersons are strikingly similar to Titurel and Amfortas. They cherish certain values which we've seen are to be taken as sustaining and quickening: 'Love is of the body', old Mr Emerson tells Lucy; and keeping that truth in sight keeps him alive, though his age and frailty are stressed. In addition, we're informed that he has been educating his son to inherit his own concerns and values: 'All my teaching of George has come down to this: beware of muddle.'

Yet again, George is wounded in his attempt to defeat the enemy. Like Amfortas he breaks into the magic garden, but is dispossessed of his weapon.

> From her feet the ground sloped sharply into view, and violets ran down in rivulets and streams and cataracts, irrigating the hillside with blue, eddying round the tree stems, collecting into pools in the hollows, covering the grass with spots of azure foam. But never again were they in such profusion; this terrace was the well-head, the primal source whence beauty gushed out to water the earth.
>
> Standing at its brink, like a swimmer who prepares, was the good man . . .

> George had turned at the sound of her arrival. For a moment he contemplated her, as one who had fallen out of heaven. He saw radiant joy in her face, he saw the flowers beat against her dress in blue waves. The bushes above them closed. He stepped quickly forward and kissed her.
>
> Before she could speak, almost before she could feel, a voice called, 'Lucy! Lucy! Lucy!' The silence of life was broken by Miss Bartlett, who stood brown against the view.

George's love is snatched from him by the almost magical appearance of Miss Bartlett, who turns it against him. The wound of love: it could be cliché, but it isn't, again because of the way the myth is contained in the social terms. Governesses exist to protect their charges against that sort of assault, to educate them into belief in 'a cheerless, loveless world'. And there's nothing incredible about George's suffering; only it *is* a sort of death-in-life melancholia, like Amfortas's inability to die. 'He has gone under,' his father tells Lucy. 'He will live; but he will not think it worth while to live. He will never think anything worth while.' Naturally he can only be healed when his love is returned—when the spear is laid on the wound.

Of course, Lucy makes frail attempts to return George's love. And there are moments when, however unwittingly, she is brought near an acknowledgment of the meaning of their relationship, of what she has done to him. Chief among these is the playing of the *Parsifal* music: the badness of her playing there points her complicity; and her inability to make up her mind as to which side she's on is Kundry-like in its helpless vacillation. She refuses to play for Cecil, sees George, resolves that she *will* play for Cecil, but 'did not know what to do, nor even what she wanted to do'. And though she tries to escape Miss Bartlett's clutches she's little enough able to do it. In Florence the Reverend Cuthbert Eager hints that Mr Emerson was responsible for his wife's death.

> 'Perhaps,' said Miss Bartlett, 'it is something that we had better not hear.'
>
> 'To speak plainly,' said Mr Eager, 'it is. I will say no more.' For the first time Lucy's rebellious thoughts swept out in words—for the very first time in her life.
>
> 'You have said very little.'
>
> 'It was my intention to say very little,' was his frigid reply.

> He gazed indignantly at the girl, who met him with equal indignation . . . 'I suppose it is only their personal charms that make you defend them.'
>
> 'I'm not defending them,' said Lucy, losing her courage, and relapsing into the old chaotic methods. 'They're nothing to me.'

Miss Bartlett and Mr Beebe together compose a formidable opposition to the Emersons; and in so anti-clerical a novel it's not surprising that even Mr Eager connects Lucy's interests in the Emersons with 'their personal charms'. It's the claims of the body that all three fear. And in this they're joined by Cecil. But Miss Bartlett and Mr Beebe are the main threat; and their league is not only suggested in the scene where Mr Beebe promises help, but in Miss Bartlett's dressing for church 'in the very height of fashion'. It's another aspect of the brown/florid opposition.

Like Klingsor, Miss Bartlett deploys Lucy to hurt the enemy whom she identifies from the outset: when she takes over George's room in Florence she sees his mark of interrogation pinned over the wash-stand; for him it stands for an open questioning of life, for her: 'Meaningless at first, it gradually became menacing, obnoxious, portentous with evil.' Like Klingsor, too, Mr Beebe's strength is in his sexlessness: 'his belief in celibacy . . . came to the surface and expanded like some delicate flower.'

Lucy, I've said, isn't capable of saving herself. So she can only be saved by the holy fool. And he has also to manage the return of George's love. Now in *Parsifal* these two elements—the healing of Amfortas and baptizing of Kundry—are separate, but Forster manages to bring them together because, in returning George his love, the fool saves Lucy; he snatches her from the clutches of Miss Bartlett and Mr Beebe. But to do this he has to get into the enemy's stronghold as Parsifal had to get into Klingsor's castle. And so it's in Mr Beebe's vicarage that Mr Emerson has his final meeting with Lucy. Now I realize that it might seem far-fetched to make the old man both Titurel *and* Parsifal figures, but that's what Forster does. For like Parsifal he is a social outsider, and the particular quality of his innocence is insisted on throughout the novel—it's a not very acceptable saintliness. In fact Mr Emerson seems to me the least satisfactory person in the novel because he's too simply a mythic creation, and too little realized in social terms. But however that may be there's no denying his ultimate significance, as the scene in the vicarage makes clear. For he saves

George by getting Lucy to admit that she loves his son, and she is 'converted' by her admission: confession is also baptism, as the terms of the scene insist.

> [Lucy] could not understand him: the words were indeed remote. Yet as he spoke the darkness was withdrawn, veil after veil, and she saw to the bottom of her soul.

And though Mr Beebe comes in unexpectedly, Mr Emerson doesn't let him regain the girl. He tells the vicar that Lucy has loved George all along.

> She turned to Mr Emerson in despair. But his face revived her. It was the face of a saint who understood.
>
> 'Now all is dark. Now Beauty and Passion seem never to have existed. But remember the mountains over Florence and the view. Ah, dear, if I were George, and gave you one kiss, it would make you brave. You have to go cold into a battle that needs warmth, out into the muddle that you have made yourself; and your mother and all your friends will despise you, oh my darling, and rightly, if it is ever right to despise. George still dark, all the tussle and the misery without a word from him. Am I justified?' Into his own eyes tears came. 'Yes, for we fight for more than Love or Pleasure: there is Truth. Truth counts, Truth does count.'
>
> 'You kiss me,' said the girl. 'You kiss me. I will try.'
>
> He gave her a sense of deities reconciled, a feeling that, in gaining the man she loved, she would gain something for the whole world. Throughout the squalor of her homeward drive . . . his salutation remained. He had robbed the body of its taint, the world's taunts of their sting; he had shown her the holiness of direct desire. She 'never exactly understood,' she would say in after years, 'how he managed to strengthen her. It was as if he had made her see the whole of everything at once.'

A frequent objection against this scene is that its terms are too vague, that moral uplift has been too easily bought. On the contrary, though, it seems to me that it's most artfully composed: in it Forster sets up a series of echoes, of tremors of associations with earlier scenes, phrases, words. The novel's pattern is here finally realized: 'Deities reconciled'—Eros and Pallas Athene; 'dark'—the vast armies of the benighted; 'muddle'—beware of muddle; 'he had made her see the whole of everything at once'—the room with a view in Florence, given Lucy by Mr Emerson.

And *those* terms have provided focal points for a structure that itself echoes and sets up tremors of associations with the *Parsifal* myth. Which gives point to Lucy's feeling that 'in gaining the man she loved, she would gain something for the whole world'. The generalization takes its validity from the scene's significance, the metaphoric relatedness we feel it to have to a truth about the human situation implicit in Parsifal's healing powers.

One last objection may remain. That my account suggests a hardness of attitude on Forster's part which doesn't allow for the fact that Miss Bartlett and Cecil are, at least partly, saved. But I can't feel this as a serious objection, because Forster's touching on the *Parsifal* myth at so many points leaves him free to find his version in social terms; and Kundry's repentance may present itself as of general relevance to that. On the other hand, it's as well in the face of so much recent criticism to affirm how tough Forster's hostility is to whatever opposes 'life itself'. Anyway that's nearer the truth of the matter than accounts that come within distance of talking about his 'gentle humanist philosophy'.

## NOTES

[1] It may appear from this that Forster is concerned less with music that holds the truth of a situation than with music that reflects its more superficial aspects—that is, programme music. But this isn't actually so. Because, to take one example, the ring of which we are reminded by a musical phrase, itself reminds us of a further something, this time far more complex.

[2] Chapter Six begins: 'We are not concerned with the very poor. They are unthinkable, and only to be approached by the statistician or the poet. This story deals with gentlefolk, or with those who are obliged to pretend that they are gentlefolk.' Which, whatever one thinks of the irony, is a way of saying that the novel is concerned with those who together *do* form a comprehensive picture of English society.

[3] Actually Shaw's preface is dated 1901, but the edition didn't come out until the following year.

[4] This and a following quotation are drawn from Shaw because, as a regular music-critic and an exceptionally intelligent man, he was in a unique position to register Wagner's importance in England during the 1890's.

[5] Forster's use of brown as a colour associated with horror and death is traditional enough. All the same I suspect he was relying on a passage from *Modern Painters* (he knew Ruskin's work pretty well), Vol. III, part IV, in which Ruskin says that for the medieval artist 'grey and brown, were . . . hues of distress, despair, and mortification, hence adopted always for the dress of monks; only the words "brown" bore, in their colour vocabulary, a still gloomier sense than it does with us.' Ruskin then gives some examples of Dante's use of 'brown', and says 'Now, clearly in all these cases, no *warmth* is meant to be mingled in the

colour.' How closely these terms apply to Miss Bartlett doesn't, I imagine, need underlining.

[6] When Forster was writing *A Room With a View* the only performance of *Parsifal* given outside Bayreuth had been a piratical one at the Metropolitan Opera House, New York, in 1903. And the music was only generally available through a piano-score which was, of course, much sought after. Again, this suggests how sure Forster's touch is for social nuances of taste.

[7] And, of course, it's here that the true significance of *Armide* lies. For Gluck's opera is also about this opposition, in which a Christian knight, Rinaldo, falls in love with a pagan woman, Armide, but is eventually recalled to his Christian duties.